AN EERDMANS HANDBOOK
CHRISTIANITY IN TODAY'S WORLD

Organizing editor
ROBIN KEELEY

Consulting editors
DR ROBERT BANKS
Theologian, Canberra, Australia

JOHN BRIGGS
Senior Lecturer, Department of History, Keele University, England

THE REV. J. ANDREW KIRK
Associate Director, London Institute for Contemporary Christianity;
Theologian Missionary, Church Missionary Society, London, England

DR RICHARD MOUW
Professor of Christian Philosophy and Ethics,
Fuller Theological Seminary, Pasadena, California, USA

DR C. RENE PADILLA
General Secretary, Latin American Theological Fraternity

PROFESSOR KLAAS RUNIA
Professor of Practical Theology, Theological Seminary
of the Reformed Churches, Kampen, Netherlands

THE REV. VINAY SAMUEL
Executive Secretary, Partnership in Mission, Asia

DR TITE TIENOU
Assistant Professor of Theology and Missiology,
Nyack College, New York, USA

AN EERDMANS HANDBOOK
CHRISTIANITY IN TODAY'S WORLD

WM. B. EERDMANS
PUBLISHING CO.
Grand Rapids, Michigan

ACKNOWLEDGMENTS

This book was the brainchild of John Briggs, who was responsible for the original idea and the basic outline.

We are indebted to the following for additional material:
Dr Denis R. Alexander, Dr Richard Bauckham, The Rev. Jonathan Chao, Patricia Gundry, Dr Jorge E. Maldonado, The Rev. Michael Nazir-Ali, The Rev. Dr Theodore Stylianopoulos, The Rev. Dr Benjamin Wentsel.

Extra research was done by Helen Schooley.

Some of the facts and figures were drawn from Dr David B. Barrett's *World Christian Encyclopedia,* Oxford.

The charts, maps and diagrams are by Tony Cantale Graphics.

Photographs are by ZEFA, except the following: Andes Press Agency/Carlos Reyes 40, 42-43, 227, 237, 282; Australian Religious Films 188, 192, 193; G Bedford/On Being Magazine 81; Bildhuset AB 295; Martin Blogg 128; John Callister 199; Camerapix/Hutchison 16-17, 20, 173, 218, 229, 240, 246, 248, 254, 298, 336, 339, 345, 376; Christian Aid 14, 340; Church Missionary Society 88, 153, 163, 378; John Cleare Mountain Camera 268-69; Peter Cousins 70; Gerry Cranham 96; Paul Craven 73, 78, 108; James Davis Worldwide Travel Library 50; Tony Deane 160; Julio Etchart 65 (right); Fritz Fankhauser 38. 52, 59, 62, 67, 100, 165, 212-13, 306, 353, 360; Peter French/Kaina-O-Kai 305; Terry Gough 310; Sonia Halliday Photographs/Sister Daniel 117/Jane Taylor 174; Michael Harper 133; Alan Howard 127; Ikyrkans Internationella Av-Tjanst 285, 315; Peter Jennings 169, 204; Lion Publishing/David Alexander 32, 190-91, 217/Jennie Karrach 34/Philippa Smart 316; Methodist Missionary Society 74 (above), 76; Moravian Church House 65 (left); Marion and Tony Morrison/South American Pictures 125, 239; Open Doors 156, 215; Brian Osborne/Lime Tree Studio 119, 126; Christine Osborne/Middle East Pictures 140, 147, 184, 195; Overseas Missionary Fellowship 304, 370; Caroline Penn 47; Popperfoto 29, 253, 292, 344, 358, 365, 366; David Pytches 230-31; Jean-Luc Ray 99, 107, 138, 148, 149, 166, 172, 224, 233, 235, 296, 301, 312, 318, 322; Jon Reynolds 90; Mick Rock 68, 329; Salvation Army 65 (top left); Oystein Sandsdalen 55; Science Photolibrary 251, 289; Doug Sewell 71, 74 (below), 82, 93, 102, 114, 116, 122, 180, 187, 252, 261; Clifford Shirley TEMA-Mission '83, 110-11, 359; Topham 34, 35; David Townsend 12, 374; Peter Trainer/London City Mission 323; Harold W. Turner 35, 105, 141; Neil Wigley/Centre for Black and White Christian Partnership 363; Olav Wikse 205, 266; Woodmansterne 87; World Council of Churches 61, 129, 130, 145, 146, 150, 178; World Vision 167, 220, 294, 300, 321

Published, under the title
Christianity: a World Faith by
Lion Publishing plc
Icknield Way, Tring, Herts, England

This American edition published 1985 by
William B. Eerdmans Publishing Company
255 Jefferson S.E., Grand Rapids, Mich. 49503

Library of Congress Cataloging in Publication Data
Main entry under title:
Christianity in today's world.
1. Christianity — 20th century — Handbooks, manuals, etc.
BR481.E37   1985   270.8'28   85-6905
ISBN 0-8028-3618-6

Printed in Italy by
New Interlitho SPA, Milan

Preface

Soon we will be in the third Christian millennium. How does the faith of Jesus look two thousand years on? For all its struggles, and despite areas of decline, it is remarkably lively.

This Handbook is a portrait of the world-wide followers of Jesus Christ in the last quarter of the twentieth century. It is an up-to-date picture, looking back only enough to understand the present context. And it is a portrait rather than a survey: concentrating on ideas, trends and movements rather than statistics.

How does the picture differ from one that would have been painted a generation ago? Chiefly in global balance. For centuries Christians have longed and prayed for a genuinely international family of faith. Now at last it has come. During the 1980s Christians in the southern hemisphere are overtaking northern Christians in numbers. And in many ways Africa, Asia and Latin America are the centres of vitality and action, more than counterbalancing the decline in Western Europe.

Of course the sky is not blue all over. Christians face real struggles. They do not always win (any more than their founder did). Yet with the wide-ranging scope of this book an overall view can emerge. It is a view which is full of hope, with a great variety of people and movements working out the meaning of Jesus' message in a new world – not least in Eastern Europe and in China.

The chapters look at the many-sided Christian community from several angles. In the first part, *Christians in Today's World*, the focus is on the great confessions and some major modern movements. Part Two, *In Every Place*, moves round the six continents, seeing the very different situation in each region. And the third part charts the way Christians are at work in *Faith, Thought and Action* to understand and apply their beliefs today.

The sixty-three contributors are drawn from seventeen countries and six continents. If we add others who have helped (some of whose names are on the facing page), the international spread is wider still. They write from within the movements and confessions they describe, so ensuring an authentic insider's feel, but preserving a healthily critical spirit.

Christianity is truly a world faith – the most fully international of all the faiths. And so no one can properly appreciate its impact without knowing something of the world-wide picture. It is hoped that this Handbook will prove to be an indispensable introduction, and serve to open up for an international readership the appeal of a living faith in action.

Contributors

Dr Miriam Adeney, Adjunct Professor of Missions, Regent College, Vancouver, Canada.

Dr Mortimer Arias, Bishop Emeritus Iglesia Evangelica Metodista en Bolivia, Visiting Professor Evangelization and Hispanic Studies, School of Theology, Claremont, California, USA.

Dr Robert Banks, Theologian, Canberra, Australia.

The Rev. Dr George Beasley-Murray, Senior Professor of New Testament Interpretation, Southern Baptist Theological Seminary, Louisville, Kentucky, USA.

The Rev. Dr Kwame Bediako, Minister of the Presbyterian Church of Ghana.

Dr Robert Bos, Co-ordinator, Wontulp-Bi-Buya College, Townsville, Queensland, Australia

John Briggs, Senior Lecturer in History, Keele University, England.

Dr Joseph Burgess, Executive Director of Theological Studies, Lutheran Council in the United States.

The Rev. Canon George Carey, Principal of Trinity Theological College, Bristol, England.

Michael Cassidy, Founder and Southern Africa Team Leader, African Enterprise.

John M. Clark, Regional Secretary for Middle East and Pakistan, Church Missionary Society, London.

Lord Coggan, formerly Archbishop of Canterbury.

The Rev. Roger Cowley, Lecturer, Oak Hill College, Southgate, London.

The Rev. Dr Paul Ellingworth, Translation Consultant, United Bible Societies, United Kingdom.

Prof. Samuel Escobar, Associate General Secretary, International Fellowship of Evangelical Students in Latin America; Professor at Evangelical Seminary, Lima, Peru.

Dr Gabriel Fackre, Abbot Professor of Christian Theology, Andover Newton Theological School, Massachusetts, USA.

Dr Raymond Fung, Secretary for Evangelism, Commission on World Mission and Evangelism, World Council of Churches, Geneva.

The Rev. Dr Rex Gardner, Senior Consultant Obstetrician and Gynaecologist, Sunderland District General Hospital, England.

The Rev. Dr Roger S. Greenway, Associate Professor of Missions, Westminster Theological Seminary, Philadelphia, USA.

Dr Paulos Mar Gregorios, Metropolitan of Delhi and the North, India.

Dr Michael Griffiths, Principal of London Bible College, England.

Prabhu S. Guptara, Freelance writer and broadcaster, Ethnic Arts Adviser to the Greater London Council, England.

Keith Harder, Pastor, Fellowship of Hope, Elkhart, Indiana, USA.

The Rev. Canon Michael Harper, Executive Director, Sharing of Ministries Abroad.

The Rev. Peter Harris, seconded to the A Rocha project, Portugal.

Dr Walter R. Hearn, Adjunct Professor of Sciences at New College, Berkeley, California, USA and the Editor of a Newsletter of American Scientific Evaluation.

Dr James M. Houston, Professor of Spirituality and Chancellor, Regent College, Vancouver, Canada.

The Rev. Cecil Kerr, Director, Christian Renewal Centre, Rostrevor, Northern Ireland.

The Rev. J. Andrew Kirk, Associate Director, London Institute of Contemporary Christianity; Theologian Missioner, Church Missionary Society, London, England.

The Rev. Dr Charles Kraft, Professor of Anthropology and Intercultural Communication, School of World Misson, Fuller Theological Seminary, Pasadena, California, USA.

Dr Peter Kuzmic, Director, Biblical Theological Institute, Zagreb, Yugoslavia.

Tony Lane, Lecturer in Historical Theology, London Bible College, England.

Dr David Lyon, Senior Lecturer in Socio-analysis, Bradford and Ilkley College, England.

Bishop Morris Maddocks, Archbishops' Adviser for the Ministry of Health and Healing, England.

The Rev. Dr Wayan Mastra, Chairman, Christian

Protestant Church of Bali, Indonesia.

John Mitchell, Director, World Development Movement, London, England.

The Rev. John Morison, Bardsley Missioner, Church Army, England.

Dr Richard Mouw, Professor of Christian Philosophy and Ethics, Fuller Theological Seminary, Pasadena, California, USA.

Bishop Lesslie Newbigin, formerly Church of South India; now a United Reformed minister, Birmingham, England.

Dr Rene C Padilla, General Secretary, Latin American Theological Fraternity.

The Rev. Dr Pablo E. Perez, Organizing Pastor, Casa Linda Presbyterian Church, Dallas, Texas, USA.

Dr Roger Pooley, Lecturer in English, Keele University, England.

Professor Klaas Runia, Professor of Practical Theology, Reformed Seminary, Kampen, Netherlands.

The Rev. Vinay Samuel, Executive Secretary, Partnership in Mission, India.

J. Norberto Saracco, Emmanuel Centre for the Preparation of Christian Leaders, Buenos Aires, Argentina.

Letha Dawson Scanzoni, professional writer and speaker, Greensboro, North Carolina, USA.

Dr Quentin Schultze, Lecturer in Department of Communications, Calvin College, Grand Rapids, Michigan, USA.

Waldron Scott, President, American Leprosy Mission.

The Rev. Dr David A. Shank, Group for Religious and Biblical Studies, Abidjan, Ivory Coast.

Dr Lewis Smedes, Professor of Theology and the Philosophy of Religion, Fuller Theological Seminary, Pasadena, California, USA.

Dr Howard A. Snyder, Author and Pastor, Irving Park Free Methodist Church, Chicago, USA.

The Rev. Professor Douglas C. Spanner, Professor Emeritus of Plant Biophysics, University of London, England.

The Rev. Dr Russel P. Spittler, Associate Professor of New Testament and Associate Dean for Academic Systems, Fuller Theological Seminary, Pasadena, California, USA.

Jim Stebbins, Part-time Pastor of a Baptist Church, Australia.

Brian C. Stiller, Executive Director, Evangelical Fellowship of Canada.

Tom Stransky, Mount Paul Novitiate, New Jersey, USA.

The Rev. Chris Sugden, Registrar, Oxford Centre for Mission Studies, England.

The Rev. Dr Anthony Thiselton, Senior Lecturer in Biblical Studies, University of Sheffield, England.

Dr Tite Tienou, Assistant Professor of Theology and Missiology, Nyack College, New York, USA.

John C. Tigwell, State Director, Scripture Union, New South Wales, Australia.

Alexander Tomsky, Head of East European Studies, Keston College, England.

The Rev. Dr Geoffrey Wainwright, Professor of Systematic Theology, The Divinity School, Duke University, USA.

Dr Roger Williamson, Executive Secretary, Peace and Human Rights, British Council of Churches.

The Rev. Dr N.T. Wright, Assistant Professor, Faculty of Religious Studies, McGill University, Montreal, Canada.

CONTENTS

PART ONE
Christians in Today's World

1.1 THE CONTEMPORARY SCENE

The Global Village
JOHN BRIGGS

In 1903, the same year as the first powered flight, a German thinker, Erich Marcks, described the world of his time as 'more than ever before, one great unit in which everything interacts and affects everything else, but in which also everything collides and clashes'. Since then these two key aspects of modern life – our closeness to each other in the way of communications, and yet our distance from each other in international understanding and co-operation – have become more and more apparent.

That first conquest of the air by the Wright brothers has led on to a revolution which has shrunk the dimensions of the globe; the scattered nations of the different continents have become one world in a new and more vital way. The efficiency of the Whittle jet engine applied to civil aviation in the 1950s was followed by the development of the jumbo jet with its vast payload in the early 1970s. The heavens were further penetrated when the first rocket-launched space satellite, Sputnik 1, was sent up in 1957. This was followed four years later by the the first men in space, a Russian in April 1961 and an American a month later. In 1969 the first men landed on the moon and by the end of that decade almost 5,000 artificial satellites were orbiting in space, not only providing instant television communication across the world but also adding yet another frightening dimension to the scope of military conflicts.

Part of the same process of shrinking the world to manageable dimensions has been the development of the telegraph and telephone, the typewriter and camera, radio and television. But the uses of the technology remain ambiguous: the possibilities of mass culture also bring the potential for that manipulation of minds intrinsic to modern propaganda. If the press played a crucial part in the rise of European nationalism, radio and television have both played their part in nurturing the nationalism of the Third World.

Vigilance becomes more and more critical. The broadcast, which can be heard by the illiterate and uncritical, can

Christianity was born in a world where most people lived in small towns or in the countryside. Even such a city as Jerusalem had quite a small population. How has the faith adapted to life in today's vast cities, with their wholly man-made environments?

easily project the all-too-persuasive message of demagogues. Broadcasts can give more power to the authorities than the printing press – they cannot be heckled, and the right of reply can easily be withheld.

GOVERNMENT AND THE INDIVIDUAL

Writing in 1930, the Spanish philosopher, Ortega y Gasset, diagnosed the most important fact of that epoch as the rise of the 'masses'. The word itself is significant: the mass-production processes of modern industry made their political impact as a vast, impersonal, mass society came into being, quite different from the elite-dominated liberalism of the previous periods.

Such a society – with its urgent urban and industrial problems and its mass electorate – made new demands on the agencies of government, calling for an administrative apparatus far beyond what had been needed a generation before. Everywhere the tendency has been towards 'big government', and even such lusty advocates of private initiative as Ronald Reagan and Margaret Thatcher in the early eighties have only been able to curb the extension of government activity at the margins. And yet, because of the complexities of modern life, these same big governments are often unable to achieve the tasks they set themselves. This combination of high claims and under-performance has been recognized as a threat to political stability.

In the mid-1980s, however, our fears are not chiefly of ineffective government. We are more conscious of totalitarian regimes, as well as increasingly bureaucratic and party-dominated democracies taking too little regard of the rights of the individual. Forms of government are needed that combine effectiveness with proper participation – not only from individuals but also from a wide diversity of groups representing many different minority interests, ethnic, religious, regional. This is not easy but it remains crucial.

Lord Acton properly identified oppression by a majority as worse than that by a minority, since minority government must be inherently unstable but from the acts of a tyrannous majority there is 'no appeal, no redemption, no refuge but treason'. But party rule, the embodiment of the idea of majority government, is unavoidable in the mass societies of the late twentieth century.

Throughout the contemporary world, highly organized parties occupy a central place in the political structure. This is true in the East and West, in the post-colonial world as much as in the world of long-established political procedures. In mass societies the party is the only means by which the mass of the people can find a political voice. But how can it be ensured that the party sets people free to share in politics and government, rather than stifling them into a frustrating passivity? This is a major political issue of our day.

This tea-picker on a small farm in Limuru, Kenya, is an expert who can pick fifty kilos a day. Her life is vastly different from that of a city-dweller in an industrial country.

TECHNOLOGY AND THE FUTURE

The world has experienced enough industrial revolutions to be wary of those scaremongers who greet new inventions with pessimistic foreboding, especially in the world of work. The vacuum cleaner, the washing machine and the central heating system all conspired towards the demise of the domestic servant, but they did not create mass unemployment. This, it is argued, is because new technology also creates new demands, and new possibilities for humane employment.

The computer and the microchip – as much as jet-propulsion and internal combustion, or even the steam power of early industrialization – need to be assessed in terms of their expansionary possibilities. They give modern industry the opportunity of maximizing efficiency, controlling waste, improving on optimum precision, synthesizing information to inform the modern workman so that he can work more proficiently than his predecessors in any previous generation. Things impossible yesterday become possible today through the harnessing of this technology, as when life is saved because a scanner offers early diagnosis of cancer. The old dictum 'necessity is the mother of invention' is stood on its head. 'For the first time in history,' claims Tom Stonier, 'the rate at which we solve problems will exceed the rate at which they appear.'

But we need to tread with caution here. The new

technology presents dangers as well as promise, especially when it is set within a global context and when social cost is set beside economic gain. And modern men and women are increasingly succumbing to the temptation to deify the new technology into an idol that enslaves the spirit.

The quest for technological advance can easily snowball without ever facing the critical question as to whether it is either necessary or desirable. There is a snobbery about keeping up with the latest technology which is as seductive in the developed as in the developing world.

Heart-replacements and similar achievements of modern surgery hit the headlines and bring relief to a small number of patients, but even in wealthy nations they divert scarce and costly resources from a much larger number of suffering people. This

The technologies and industries of the late twentieth century need vast supplies of power to fuel them. The increased cost of oil during the 1970s made an already difficult economic situation much worse – especially for the poorer nations of the world.

That second industrial revolution 'multiplies man's brainpower with the same force that the first industrial revolution multiplied man's muscle power.'
V. Sydney Webb

temptation is similar to that of some Third World countries, which are seduced into buying prestige technology which is quite out of tune with the needs of their economies and labour markets.

MORE PEOPLE, BIGGER CITIES

See Stewards of Creation; Bread for the World

The world's population now doubles every thirty years: a quarter of all the people throughout history who have survived their first year of life are alive today. But feeding the world's millions, themselves a product of increased availability of food, continues to be problematical.

Why should this be so, when science and mechanization have apparently so vastly improved agriculture? Partly because floods and droughts still devastate, and refined strains of crops have sometimes proved more vulnerable to disease than the varied strains of earlier ages. Moreover, applying insecticides (such as DDT, first used in 1939) and chemical fertilizers has sometimes backfired on the omniscient agriculturalist, and factory farming too has encountered the difficulties of concentrated production of livestock. The use of fertilizers has also made agriculture more dependent on international trade.

One of the greatest tragedies of the late twentieth century remains the lack of political will to apply the developed world's surpluses to the needs of the developing nations' starving millions. Accordingly, the old

Malthusian spectre of population expansion running ahead of resources still haunts us today. We face a more-or-less-apparent ecological crisis: fossil fuels exhausted, the seas polluted, the land overcropped, the deserts getting larger, forests and rivers devastated by acid rain. But most of us do not let ourselves get too worried about tomorrow's problems, nor indeed do the politicians, their vision ever limited by short-term electoral mandates.

At the present moment the impact of science on a population acts in two directions: it extends life expectancy by bringing some illnesses under control, yet at the same time it produces a technologically-developed society which tends to

In the developing world a rapidly increasing proportion of the population are children. (It is quite otherwise in the West, where the larger proportion are elderly.) What kind of world will these children make as they grow up? And what spiritual values will they inherit?

spawn new illnesses. In the Western world, birth control and legalized abortion have radically limited population growth, whilst the medical prolongation of life has quite radically increased the proportion of people living beyond retirement age. The result is that a declining working generation has to support the ever-expanding post-employment years of most citizens.

This expanding population will increasingly be an urban population. By the year 2000, we are told, a third of the world's population will be living in cities of over 10,000 inhabitants in size – in a man-made environment, dependent on imported food, with the cities' waste presumably borne away on ever-increasing supplies of water through ever-

more-complicated sewerage systems.

It remains to be seen whether that City of Mankind will be more civilized than what has gone before, or whether mass culture for mass man will lead to a new barbarization. Certainly, in the late twentieth century, conflicts between different groups remain, the difference between rich and poor has become greater, not less, while the racialism of the downtown ghetto casts its shadow over the life of the whole city. With the emergence of the new, man-made environment, the old moral landmarks seem to have disappeared, and a society, less conscious of both its roots and its direction, pluralist in its culture, is moving from toleration to permissiveness in many areas of life.

But ironically, this permissiveness of a wide range of divergent patterns of individual behaviour manages to coexist with a degree of public intolerance. Racial conflict still exists, religious and political dogmatists continue to get an audience, opinion is narrowly prescribed and rational discussion all too easily lapses into violence.

'The dream has grown of a city as a place fully adequate to man's dignity, from its skyscrapers to its subways...Even simple people nowadays regard science as magic and salvation, creating the good life of the City of Man.'
David Edwards

THE REVOLT AGAINST THE WEST

Between 1945 and 1960 no less than forty countries, with a total population of 800 million forming more than a quarter of the world's inhabitants, revolted against colonial rule and secured their political independence.

Freeing themselves from the economic influence of the transnational corporations was, however, proving a more difficult task, reflecting the increasing importance of the strategic raw materials of these territories on the world's markets.

The movement for independence very often constituted not only a revolt against an alien imperialism but also a rejection of the traditional order – a revolt not only against the West but against the past as well. That is why Nehru confessed that his commitment to independence arose only partly 'because the nationalist in me cannot tolerate alien domination... even more because for me it is the inevitable step to economic and social change'. These emerging elites to be effective had to secure mass support, and they did so with the use of all the paraphernalia of party propaganda in the West.

Yet not all revolts against the West have involved rejecting the past. Take, for example, the overthrow in 1979 of the Shah, Persia's autocratic ruler, rich on his nation's oil revenues and strong, it was supposed, because of the patronage of American might. This has all the hallmarks of a traditional revolt, under the leadership of conservative holy men, against the modernization of the state. The Western historian may be confident about the inevitability of the process of secularization; nonetheless he still has to learn how to spell 'Ayatollah' and to realize that Islamic revivalism can put in jeopardy basic human rights as

much as state Marxism.

So then, in the post-imperial world there has been a dramatic shift of emphasis from Europe and America to the continents of Africa and Asia. In Europe the population began to contract, but everywhere else it grew, especially as European health-care was exported globally. Predictions speak of the twenty-first century as the era of the Pacific. And if one compares the westward development of the United States and the Russian movement into Siberia together with the industrialization of Japan, the theme seems worthy of careful consideration.

The balance of modern international relations has changed quite dramatically since the days of World War II, as the equilibrium now centres on the two extra-European superpowers of the United States and the Soviet Union. Such was the power constellation – becoming clear in fact from 1900 onwards – which lay behind the emerging cold war conflict fifty years later between capitalism and Communism. Despite the growth of neutralism and the uncertainty of the relationship between Russia and China, this conflict was to dominate international affairs for the next half-century, for all the periodic searches for detente. These two patrons of global power politics sought to extend their influence by buying the allegiance of Third World countries with programmes of economic and military aid, and by direct intervention when all else failed.

In Asia, competition between

'Of what elevation to man is a method of broadcasting when you have only drivel to send out? What mark of civilization is it to be able to produce a 128-page newspaper in one night, when most of it is either banal or vicious and not two columns worth preserving?' Mahatma Gandhi

A SHRINKING WORLD

66 Modern communications have made our world smaller. We know more facts about each other in the different hemispheres than ever before, and we hear news of distant peoples far more quickly.

But although news is transmitted so fast, do different people really understand each other better than they used to? It is a smaller world technically, but are its inhabitants closer emotionally? **99**

67 DAYS
was the fastest the famous clipper ship Cutty Sark did the journey from Australia to the English Channel. That was in 1869. There was no faster method for news to travel.

FRACTIONS OF A SECOND
is all it takes for a radio message, beamed by satellite, to travel from New York to the South Pacific. And in French Polynesia in 1979 there were 507 radio sets per 1,000 inhabitants.

The republican guard in Africa's Gabon: millions of people whose parents were under colonial rule now live in independent nations (see chart overleaf). This represents one of the most significant new facts in the modern world.

communist and non-communist forces led to tragic conflicts in Korea, Vietnam and Cambodia. In Africa, the retreat of the old colonialism allowed for ideological imperialism to compete for the allegiance of the new Africa. In some of the newly-independent countries there was civil war – either old tribal or new ideological. The range of political allegiances which emerged stretched from the apartheid of Boer nationalism to the Cuban-supported Communism of Ethiopia and the revolutionary unpredictability of Gaddafi's Libya, potentially the most dangerous because the most unstable element in the jigsaw of the world's post-nuclear

search for security. In Latin America inequality, the oppression of the poor, increasing trampling on human rights, tough ideological struggle and guerilla movements perpetuate the instability of regimes that cannot be policed into secure neighbours for the United States. The Soviet move to install nuclear weapons in Castro's Cuba at the end of 1961 indicated just how fragile is the 'pax ballistica'. The most powerful nation in the world seems slow to realize that injustice and the denial of human rights are the seedbeds of revolutionary forces potentially more powerful than any the CIA can bring under control.

Within the framework of superpower politics and their associated satellite activities, smaller nations have sought to group together to protect their independence and to promote their joint interests. Such groupings, weak or strong, may exist for primarily political or economic or defence purposes, but all in some small way question the continuance of the sovereignty of the nation state. Examples of supra-national organizations in the modern world are easily given: the Organization of African Unity, the Organization of American States, the European Economic Community, the North Atlantic Treaty Organization, the South-East Asian Treaty Organization offer but a random sample.

Very often, as with the European Economic Community, there is a mixture of political idealism and economic realism behind the complexities of such groupings. The difficulties that these organizations face in action should not obscure the need they demonstrate to think beyond national terms in the world of the late twentieth century. This is further seen as many transnational corporations exercise an authority far greater than that of many nation states. The existence of these powerful corporations, taken with the vast debts owed by many developing countries to the bankers of the developed world, illustrate the general maldistribution of power between the rich North and the poor South – the theme of the Brandt Report, *North South: a Programme for Survival,* 1980.

CHANGES IN MARXIST STATES

While the old imperial powers had to adjust to the discovery of what role they should play in a post-imperialist world, the newer imperialism of Soviet influence has not been without its difficulties – Tito's Yugoslavia early leaving the Warsaw Pact; in 1953 an uprising in the German Democratic Republic, ruthlessly suppressed by Soviet military action; June 1956, an uprising which saw the reinstatement of Gomulka in Poland. Then in October 1956, the Budapest revolution witnessed the attempt of Imre Nagy to embrace multi-party government and a neutralist policy in Hungary, but in the context of the Suez crisis Soviet intervention was swift. In the event it has been fascinating to see how Janos Kadar, seen in the West in 1956 as the betrayer of Hungary's freedom, has in the thirty years following been able to develop in Hungary a more open and relaxed society; this has not appeared to threaten Moscow, whose leaders know that the Eastern bloc desperately needs the exchange currency that Hungary's freer economy is able to purchase. Twelve years later Alexander Dubjek, in seeking to liberalize the Czechoslovakian state, did not present such a reassuring image, so the Russian tanks rolled in. By contrast, Ceausesco's Romania has been able to wed orthodox Marxism at home to independence in foreign affairs, without apparent reprisal.

More recently, in the summer of 1980, Poland – already enjoying greater freedom than most Soviet satellites – witnessed the growth of the free trades union movement 'Solidarity' under the leadership of Lech Walesa. In a deteriorating economic situation and supported by the popular piety of Polish Catholicism, that movement grew, and as it grew so its political demands became bolder until in December 1981 it was made illegal, and martial law declared. The strength of the movement was such that it continued an underground existence producing a stalemate in Poland yet to be resolved.

Across the other side of the world the Sino-Russian rift became open from 1960, and this has continued to be an important factor in the world balance. Domestically Mao Tse-tung lost the presidency of the People's Republic of China in 1958 following the 'Great Leap Forward'. From 1965 onwards he was seeking to use the Red

THE NEWLY-INDEPENDENT NATIONS

66 The list of nations that have become self-governing during the period 1942-84 contains representatives from each of the six continents. This period has almost, but not quite, seen the end of old-fashioned colonial rule. The people involved are a considerable proportion of the world's population. 99

1942
Ethiopia

1943
Lebanon

1946
Jordan
Syria

1947
India
Pakistan

1948
Burma
Ceylon (now
  Sri Lanka)
Israel

1949
Indonesia

1951
Libya

1953
Laos

1954
Cambodia (now
  Kampuchea)
Egypt
North Vietnam,
  South Vietnam,
  (now the
  People's Republic
  of Vietnam)

1956
Morocco
Sudan
Tunisia

1957
Ghana
Malaya (now
  Western Malaysia)

1958
Guinea
Iraq
Kuwait

1960
Benin
Cameroon
Central African
  Republic
Chad
Gabon
Ivory Coast
Madagascar
Mali
Mauritania
Niger
Nigeria
Senegal
Somalia
Togo
Upper Volta (now
  Burkina Faso)
Zaire

1961
Sierra Leone
Tanganyika (now
  Tanzania)

1962
Algeria
Burundi
Jamaica
Rwanda
Trinidad and Tobago
Uganda
Western Samoa
Yemen Arab
  Republic

1963
Eastern Malaysia
Kenya
Zanzibar (now
  Tanzania)

1964
Malawi
Malta
Zambia

1965
Gambia
Maldive Islands
Singapore

1966
Barbados
Botswana
Guyana
Lesotho

1967
Anguilla
South Yemen

1968
Mauritius
Nauru
Rio Muni (now
  Equatorial Guinea)
Swaziland

1970
Fiji
Tonga

1971
Bahrain
Qatar
United Arab
  Emirates

Guards to sweep away bureaucratic conservatism and thereby to hasten China's economic and cultural development, a process which became increasingly authoritarian as the army was called in to restore order. The Cultural Revolution had come to an end before Mao's death in 1976. Relationships with the West, which had already begun to reopen, have subsequently been cautiously developed and the management of the domestic economy has been moderated very considerably. China has once again entered cultural contact with the outside world.

THE UNSTABLE PEACE AND THE NUCLEAR THREAT

It has to be confessed that the twentieth century has been one of war and conflict. Global or local, hot or cold, its dimensions strike terror throughout the world. The casualties of the

See Ferment in Poland; War and Peace

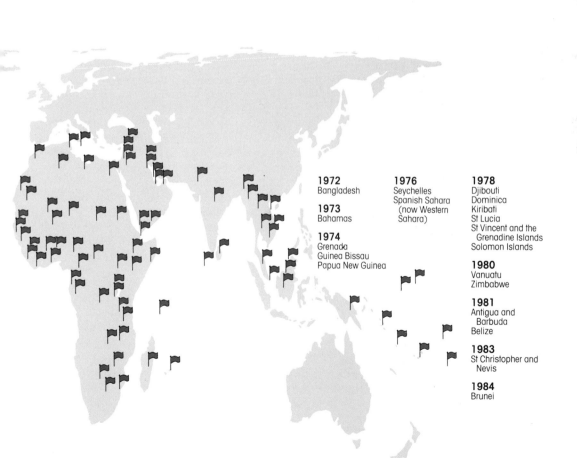

1972
Bangladesh

1973
Bahamas

1974
Grenada
Guinea Bissau
Papua New Guinea

1976
Seychelles
Spanish Sahara
(now Western
Sahara)

1978
Djibouti
Dominica
Kiribati
St Lucia
St Vincent and the
Grenadine Islands
Solomon Islands

1980
Vanuatu
Zimbabwe

1981
Antigua and
Barbuda
Belize

1983
St Christopher and
Nevis

1984
Brunei

largely pre-nuclear World War II are estimated at between 40 and 50 million people, of whom 20 million were estimated as Russian and 6.5 million Jews: that is but a base line for the statistics of war in the second half of the twentieth century. Saturation bombing no less than the concentration camp have witnessed a re-barbarization of civilization. The genocide of the Third Reich has given birth to the running sore of Arab-Israeli conflict which continues to threaten the stability of the world.

Out of the horrors of the war was born the United Nations Organization to secure peace and security, to develop friendly relations among the nations and to achieve co-operation in solving international problems. The initial membership comprised those nations who had taken up arms against Germany, Italy, Japan and other non-colonial nations such as those of Latin America. But other nations were to flood into membership, especially the new countries of Asia and Africa. However, it has lost rather than gained in power as it has grown too big for united action.

Looming over international relations now is the shadow of nuclear war. Its power of annihilation is simultaneously acclaimed as both the greatest deterrent to world-wide war and the greatest threat to human survival. The nuclear scene has changed as all the limitations on the use of nuclear weapons, once so certain, have evaporated. First the American and then the superpower monopoly of weaponry has been eclipsed. Stockpiling has occurred in both East and West. The capacity of carriers has developed with even more sophisticated aircraft, now supplemented by rockets and missiles. Some kind of nuclear-defence programme has been developed.

Thus it needs to be questioned whether the doctrine of deterrence, its roots in limitation of use, can survive in this second generation of nuclear capacity. Does the consequence of nuclear war still remain so certain and so appalling as to prevent nuclear war from ever happening? The response to all this has been the growth of popular nuclear-disarmament movements which have sometimes found it difficult to pursue their conscientious objections within the limits of the law. Internationally there have been conferences about banning tests, limiting arms use, controlling arms and more recently reducing them, but in brutal reality the word 'escalation' has taken upon itself a new and more menacing meaning. All these debates are unresolved; the tensions of the mid-eighties seem nearer to breaking-point. The politicians, strutting behind a façade of mutual toughness, continue to abuse one another, while ordinary people both in the East and West continue to live under the shadow of fear.

The Secular Outlook of Today

DAVID LYON

Whether it is the business person's full diary, or the factory worker's conveyor belt, in the modern world we regulate ourselves by clock-time. And the things we look forward to, even set our hearts on, are part of future planning: the weekend, holidays, retirement. Past traditions, ancient wisdom, we have little space for these in our schedules.

We even have trouble with the present. The seven-to-eleven waking day is taken up with the clock-dominated world, in both work and leisure, so that it is hard to see beyond this horizon of time. And yet without this 'outside perspective' our activities have so little meaning. So we tend to submerge our doubts in more and more frantic activity.

The point is this. The 'secular outlook' of today is in fact a secular way of life. It is not just a matter of the way we think. It is the air we breathe.

'Secular' can be defined as an exclusive concern with the world of the here-and-now, bound by time. Lives wrapped up in calculation and computers, politics and planning, cut themselves off from any wider meaning or purpose, and from any hope that there is more to life than the self-centred pursuit of personal gain. We resort to techniques such as contraception, counselling and clinical care of the elderly. But still this does not help us put birth, marriage and death into a mental framework which makes sense of them. 'Rational' solutions to the classic human problems of hatred, violence, accident and personal guilt also fail to satisfy us.

There is no one 'secular outlook' today; there are many. It is misleading to tar all secularity with the same brush. A great diversity exists, from the tiny minority of serious secular*ists* who wish to remove all trace of 'religion' from school curricula or public law, to the massive majority who are simply indifferent to Christianity, and largely ignorant of it. And neither are secular attitudes and lifestyles new. At the beginning of the eighteenth century Jonathan Swift characterized the mass of English people as 'staunch unbelievers'. It is difficult to discover a time when they were not, although the picture is of course different in the United States. Similarly, non-literate peoples have plenty of 'tradition', but this is not necessarily the same as 'religion'. Such people may also be deeply secular.

WHAT IS SECULAR?

What is important is to understand the secular outlook of *today*. For changes have taken

place, and we must grasp the new challenges thrown up by what has been happening in society over the past 200 years. It does seem that where heavy industry has developed, some practices which are outward signs of religion, such as church attendance, have fallen off. This is especially true of large urban areas. The fact that people move about more (with their jobs for instance) also means that older religious communities break up, and new influences are more easily absorbed. Health, education, welfare and law were all once the work of church agencies, but as they have been taken over by other agencies, especially the state, so people see Christianity as having less importance for everyday life.

Secularization is not mainly about religion declining. It is the process of conventional religion getting cut off from society, having to compete with other world-views and lifestyles. The test of secularity is really whether life is lived as a whole experience, guided by the same set of assumptions. Where it is, that life is at some level religious; where it is not, life is secular. And this kind of religion is especially difficult in the modern world. People rarely justify what they do with an appeal to biblical teaching or church tradition. From the market-place to the marital bed, activities are seldom judged in a Christian light. Religion has no business in the laboratory or labour club, the office or the TV studio. The social space is shrinking in which religion is supposed to survive.

But this prising apart of life and faith is not because religion has somehow been disproved or consciously abandoned. It is because social institutions such as education have ceased to be associated with religion.

Modern societies are held together, not by religion or values, but by impersonal control. People are counted as individuals, but paradoxically that means they are treated as a mass. From the public registration of birth, through traffic-lights, clocking-in, and identity cards, to the careful recording of death, our lives are held in a web of bureaucratic threads. Dull compulsion takes over from responsibility and inner constraint. And yet some sense of goodwill and honesty is still needed for society to function properly. The more individual responsibility is eroded by a mass of bureaucratic regulations, the more we threaten the foundations of a stable and fair society.

A matter-of-fact approach stifles the voice of conscience just as the pragmatic (well it works this way doesn't it?) approach drowns the directives of principle. Cost-benefit analysis shows how foolish it is to waste time searching for one sheep when ninety-nine are safely in the fold. If increased profits are the highest good, then the farmer who pulled down his barns and built bigger ones was entirely right. Persuade myself that my unborn child is really part of my body and I can justify abortion on the same grounds as changing my hairstyle. The constant secular assumption is that there is nothing beyond the matter-of-fact; no one to whom we are responsible except ourselves.

The matter-of-fact attitude has been fostered by the rise of science. The tremendous scientific and technological achievements (and sometimes advances) of the twentieth century have given us human beings a great sense of our power to manipulate the world. This has also extended to social engineering, the 'scientific' effort to create an ideal human environment. Again this is not really new; earlier generations did not in fact spend more time praying for rain than working out new means of irrigation. But now we imagine there are no limits to what we can do to mould the world our way. All problems are reduced to technical dimensions, and can thus be resolved with technological fixes.

DO SACRED AND SECULAR MIX?

All this may make Christians feel somewhat uneasy. Was not part of the drive towards the modern world of industry, commerce and science given an early boost by Christianity? Can these things which were partly stimulated by Christianity also turn out to be Christianity's enemy?

Yes they can, unintentionally. When science or capitalism developed lives of their own, they ceased to be authentic expressions of the Christian curiosity or stewardship which originally motivated them. Modern management is an example. We can recognize in it

the vestiges of Christian teaching on responsible use of 'talents' and resources. And yet its practice also exudes secularity. It is time-tyrannized, output-and-profit-oriented, and aims at ever-increasing control over production and people. Modern managers seldom see their activities in terms of service to others or stewardship of God-given resources.

Unlike oil and water, which refuse to mix, the sacred and the secular merge with each other in a most confusing way. The complexities of secularization abound. The secularization which ends the unholy alliance of church and state earns applause in many quarters. But if this extends to a mental secularization in which religion is

A business executive checks in at an airport passenger terminal. The modern manager must use every moment profitably and get the most out of people. Where does God fit in his scheme of things?

'Today's world is a melting pot. Old frameworks of culture are breaking up. There is confusion, despair and expectancy. God is "shaking the nations yet once more"...All over the world as the Spirit moves, opening up shattered worlds, breaking and remaking God's people, I believe the gospel is a message "whose hour has come".' Simon Barrington-Ward

thought to have nothing to do with politics, many of us regret it. We need to be aware of the main channels of secularization, their ambiguity, and also of the very different patterns of secularization which occur.

Each country has its own religious history, and this means that the secular situation is also varied. The United States, with its deliberate attempts to keep church and state in separate compartments, and its colourful mix of ethnic groups, has a bewildering range of religious and secular options. France, in which church and state were closely intertwined before the revolution, consciously tried to construct a new regime which was as secular as the old regime had been religious. Britain comes somewhere between the two. The state church has never had a monopoly; secularity is not a monopoly now.

Mention of Britain brings us to another source of difference in secular outlook. Class differences are very significant. The secular managerial practice mentioned above is not greatly loved by the working class - they are on its receiving end. So how do members of the working classes in Europe and North America cope with life? Often by falling back on time-honoured myths and superstitions (luck, fate, astrology or whatever). Never fully supplanted by 'Christian' culture, these have proved equally resistant to secularization. The ideas (whether Christian or secular) of the professional intelligentsia, characteristically produced by

See Christians in Eastern Europe; Which Way for a Continent?

modern societies, are not likely to 'percolate down' to other social echelons. A working-class secular outlook is not the same as that of teachers or bureaucrats.

HOW SECULAR A WORLD?
There are challenges to the secular outlooks of today. Secularity is not a trouble-free stance. This book contains plenty of evidence of religious vitality throughout the world. Christian faith burns steadily on in Eastern Europe, long-dominated by official secularity (if not outright atheism). Commitment to Christ also persists despite the seductive affluence and secular practice of countries in the West. Many African countries are experiencing rapid growth in Bible-based religion (plus the apparently inevitable accompanying mixtures of Christianity with tribal religion). Added to this are many non-Christian religions which flourish from Tokyo to Texas, not to mention the resilient undergrowth of folk religions of various kinds. God, and gods, are evidently not yet in exile!

And neither is everything well in the laboratory and government office, those supposed bastions of secularism. Faith in the ability of science to come up with answers to our human problems, or in politicians to sort out our social and economic difficulties, is waning. Corruption and failure in politics; pollution and the sinister threats of nuclear disaster in science; the fear of micro-electronic totalitarianism in both

- these have combined to burst the bubble of optimism inflated in the West at the end of the nineteenth century and resurrected in the l960s. People immersed in secularity have no reason to sleep easy.

Another form of secular outlook involves according an almost religious devotion to someone, something or some process which at first glance has little to do with religion as conventionally conceived. It is hard to deny, for instance, that something approaching religious concern has grown up around sexuality in the modern world. Like religion in general, it flourishes in the private sphere of life. In addition, it has been bombarded by technique-experts and commercialization. Because

of this, many desperately seek 'salvation' in their sexuality. Of course, no one can 'prove' that Eros is a modern secular god, but the idea certainly tallies well both with apostolic teaching on idolatry and with contemporary experience. The same could be said for other 'secular gods', such as faith in the family or belief in technological progress. As people grow dissatisfied with the ability of such gods to produce their goods, secularity itself is challenged.

How then should Christians respond to the challenges of secularization? First, as modern - and modernizing - societies tend to relegate religion to the private domain, we all too easily imagine that life in big business, big government or big military really

THE MARXIST MIND

Marxists are implacably opposed to capitalism because they believe those who produce wealth are always in bondage – the profit from their labour creamed off for the benefit of the few. Only when the system is overthrown will people be free to employ their tool-making and tool-using skills for their own advantage. Christians see this understanding of human life as inadequate, and believe that spiritual as well as purely material factors are important. In many parts of the world Christians and Marxists are at one in condemning exploitation and injustice, but they disagree about the kind of revolution that is needed.

Schoolchildren learn more than knowledge and skills. School is one of the places where we pick up a way of understanding the world. Can our children's education help them keep a sense of the mystery of life?

should run according to its own rules, that Christian faith is irrelevant to those sectors of life. 'The earth is the Lord's,' says the psalmist. Secular outlooks beware!

Second, we should be careful not to be hoodwinked by the dogmas of secularization. It may be a subtle social process, but it is not unstoppable; not all traces of religion have been smothered. Nor is it all for the worse. The secularization of government allows church and society to be seen clearly for what they are, leading to mutual recognition rather than deadly compromise. But the secularization of thought produces a shrunken and shrivelled view of God. Supposedly squeezed out of the scientific picture, he is safely shut up in the private areas of

life, with no contribution to make to operating the rest of his world.

So our resistance to secularization should not be total and undiscriminating. The wistful religious nostalgia which pines for a past age of imagined Christian culture shunts us off into the ghetto. Maintaining the faith of the fathers is one thing. Locking Christian treasures up in a museum is another. It simply confirms the secular societies' suspicions that religion is irrelevant. The prime answer to secularism is to live a life in which all the parts are integrated, held together by a big view of God, creating, and sustaining and redeeming his universe. This redemption, which was won by Christ in his death, makes integration possible once more, both for people and their creation.

Images of Crisis and Chaos

ROGER POOLEY

'Modern literature' had, once, a strong blend of revolutionary self-confidence and regretful atheism. The modernist movement which swept through literature as well as the other arts in the first thirty years of the century was concerned to break the old images, but also to create new ones. This brief survey is chiefly about the novel, but also touches on poetry, drama, television and film.

The formal innovations of modernism - free verse, 'stream of consciousness' and so on - were ways of subverting established ways of perceiving and writing about reality. But the politics of the writers were usually conservative. The poetry of Ezra Pound and T. S. Eliot certainly marked a radical break with the established literary culture. (At the end of *The Waste Land*, 1922, Eliot writes of 'a heap of broken images'; in an essay of 1912 Pound calls for a poetry which is 'austere, direct, free from emotional slither'.) But their energies were at the same time directed towards recreating 'the tradition' (note the singular). They had a nostalgia for the worlds of Dante's Italy, Elizabethan England, even, for W. B. Yeats, twelfth-century Byzantium. These were worlds, so they felt, where ordered government brought justice rather than exploitation; here the true artist had a more respected, less marginal role than the 'accelerated grimace' demanded by twentieth-century Europe and America.

The worlds they hankered after were also worlds of faith, and for Eliot in particular (he was converted to Christianity in the 1920s) there was a crucial need to recover that. We can see this as part of a response to the nineteenth-century crises of faith precipitated by new scientific theories and biblical criticism. Such influences as these, Yeats once remarked, had robbed him of the simple faith of his childhood. His reaction was to find a new system which would not only give him a new faith but also explain the crises of his own history. And so he plunged into spiritualism, magic and myth. The American poet Wallace Stevens went a stage further, arguing that poetry must replace the functions of religion. Franz Kafka was another to lament lost coherences - social, psychological, theological. Perhaps his laments are in part a response to the announcement of Nietzsche's madman: 'God is dead.'

THE LIMITS OF HUMANISM

For many of the fathers of modern literature, then, it was a source of great sadness and perplexity that God appeared to be absent from the universe. If some way could be found to recover him, or to find an acceptable substitute, then that was part of the function of literature. It was a kind of 'atheism of the poets'. But can we sustain such a reading of the literature of today, even that which takes the great modernists as its starting-point?

It seems unlikely. The career of Samuel Beckett is an instructive example. He began by writing in praise of Joyce and Proust, heroes of modernism. The first sentence of his first novel, *Murphy* (1938), parodies

Ecclesiastes: 'The sun shone, having no alternative, on the nothing new.' His best-known play, *Waiting for Godot* (1956), seems to suggest a God whose 'divine apathia, divine athambia, divine aphasia' renders communication impossible. Even waiting - the title suggests an ironic version of waiting for the Lord in the biblical sense - is futile. Not that we give up doing it. Since that play, Beckett's universe has not become less bleak, and there have been fewer of his wonderful jokes, but what he is exploring now are the limits of humanism rather than the limits of theism. He has almost ceased to lament the death, or the inscrutability, of God; he is now lamenting the demise of man.

Beckett, we might say crudely, marks one of the bridges between modernism and postmodernism in literature. This latter movement is most marked in France and the USA, and is a much more aggressively rule-breaking art, typified by the novels of Thomas Pynchon and the poetry of John Ashbery. In modernism the break-up of the old coherences is lamented; in postmodernism it is celebrated.

'Well, it is a good experience, to
 divest oneself of some tested
 ideals, some old standbys,
And even finding nothing to put
 in their place is a good
 experience,
Preparing one, as it does, for the
 consternation that is to come.'
(from John Ashbery, *The Double
 Dream of Spring*, 1970)

The Scream, by British artist Francis Bacon, conveys a sense of destruction and chaos. This same feeling pervades much modern literature.

In Pynchon's novels indeterminacy, the subverting of the crucial certainties of realistic plotting, become central. Carnival, cornucopia, trip, even orgy might be good words to describe the imaginative processes here, though linked to an intellectual delight in inventiveness and wit. But the elements of celebration are almost always tied up with a sense of destruction and chaos in the contemporary world.

APOCALYPSE

'Crisis' is a key word when people discuss the arts today in relation to social and political reality. It corresponds to the Christian anticipation of the 'apocalypse'. Again, the contrast with the first part of the century is instructive. Wilfred Owen's poems (1918) were prefaced by the famous dictum 'the poetry is in the pity'. The literature of World War II, the Holocaust, and the Vietnam War is apocalyptic, almost without the pity - or rather there is a fear that the pity will seem inadequate, out-of-scale. Desolation, numbness is more the mood - or black, anarchic satire, as in Joseph Heller's *Catch 22*. It is interesting that the Vietnam film, *Apocalypse Now*, drew its central myth from Conrad's novel *Heart of Darkness* (1899): a sense of evil portending the end of all things is no invention of the nuclear age. Nor has colonialism and its quizzical, rebellious brother, the fascination with the savage, died out with the European colonial empires.

The spirit of the '68 student revolts brought dreams of liberation on the one hand and doom-laden cults of suicide on the other. These appear to have been taken over by the fashion-conscious. But some important trends have emerged. A greater willingness to listen to the voice of popular music is one - though pop music probably does more to channel rebellion and frustration than to express them. Anyway, pop is no longer simply denounced from the Olympian heights of culture. And an audience for performed poetry grew up at the same time. If much smaller in number than the LP record-buying public, this was stunningly large by the usual standard of poetry audiences.

A second trend, also partly a change in status, is in science fiction. This ranges from the profound 'inner-space' fiction of Doris Lessing, to the moral simplifications and technological heroics of big budget movies - feminists and pacifists are heroes at one end; neo-conservatives zap the aliens at the other.

At the opposite pole from apocalyptic, with its urgencies and crises, is the quiet voice that has characterized much poetry and fiction, particularly in England, since the 1950s. Its rhetoric is of honesty in a rather pessimistic key; its heroes are victims but only in a small way. This style is best seen in the poetry of Philip Larkin. It is not 'confessional' in the melodramatic sense; its studied indirection points to an ironic rather than a Romantic sense of poetry. But it does reflect a suspicion of rhetoric, of the

'I do not believe in any regeneration of a people which does not find expression in their art.' Ananda K. Coomaraswamy

grand gesture, which is the ironic opposite of apocalyptic. It is often an exploration of history, too; perhaps most clearly in the rather richer Irish poetry written at the moment, where such as John Montague and Seamus Heaney swell out from personal reminiscence to a more comprehensive reading of their past.

See The Changing Sexual Scene

For many, the main artistic expression is through pop music. Here it is more than the music that they encounter. The stage effects of the concert, the use of lights, the often highly dramatic persona of the artist, all make up an absorbing experience for the audience.

SEX, CORRUPTION, CLAUSTROPHOBIA

What about sex? Perhaps the best characterization of the literature of the West since the war is to say that it progressively shed taboos about expressing sexuality. Certain trials stick in the mind; but the literature was responding to, as much as leading, general changes in attitude. And, as so often when barriers break, the issues change rapidly. Once it was 'how explicit can you be?' Now the expression of homosexual desire has moved to the centre of critical debate, and the extent to which men's sexuality oppresses women's. While there are plenty of external pressures, one reason why sex has become increasingly important for writers is that it offers a way to express an intense, private, personal desire in an increasingly regulated world. This comes out with delicious irony in the novels of the Czech Milan Kundera, where the limits are those of a totalitarian state.

Contemporary drama may have scandalized by its occasional sexual explicitness, but over the last twenty years two other features come over more strongly. One is that language is a means of betrayal more readily than a means of truth-telling. The work of Harold Pinter adds up to this. And his work on the sphere of private relationships has been matched by many more politically committed dramatists of a more recent generation who have focussed on the fudging and cheating that goes on at a public level. Thus recent Tom Stoppard plays have focussed on Iron Curtain countries; works by John Arden, David Hare and Howard Brenton dwell on the history of Britain.

But theatre is also a visual medium, and the image that recurs most vividly is that of confinement: the prison, the hospital - mental or general. This interestingly echoes the novels of Solzhenitsyn about post-war Russia as well as Ken Kesey's

One Flew Over the Cuckoo's Nest, a patients-versus-institutions novel made into a film.

WHAT COUNTS AS QUALITY?

Of course the largest audience for drama is no longer in the theatre but in front of the TV. Here it is the sheer quantity of the new medium that seems most pressing. But what does that quantity do? It accelerates the spread of information - but tends to centralize and standardize it. Our societies see themselves and others dramatized on a world-wide scale as never before; but more often in terms of formula and melodrama than enquiry and reflection.

And what counts as 'quality' television? A curious pair: radical drama on the one hand, and adaptations of novels from the past, or which express nostalgia for the past, on the other. Every so often one of these plays will by its message, or its violence, or its eroticism, show that television has the power to touch and outrage. But its power to anaesthetize is probably more dangerous.

In attempting a Christian analysis of these trends I have drawn attention to 'pressure points' - atheism, fear of the end, sexuality, images of imprisonment and liberation, the search for truthfulness. Any

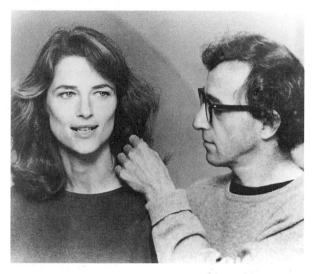

Charlotte Rampling and Woody Allen: two stars among a fairly restricted number who perform in big-budget movies. The pre-war dominance of the film industry has given way to TV and pop music. But occasional block-buster movies become talking-points.

Christian who wants to address the world or study literature should be concerned with these.

But what of Christians writing the literature? After World War II, English, and to a certain extent American, literary and intellectual culture was dominated by Christians, especially High Anglicans and Roman Catholics - T. S. Eliot, C. S. Lewis, Christopher Fry, W. H. Auden, Graham Greene. Even so, they felt they were fighting a rearguard action against secular humanism and existentialism. Now the dominance is gone. There are still distinguished Christian writers; but the compelling stories, images, voices and forms are not, by and large, those of Christians, nor even of a residually Christian culture.

THE ARTS IN THE TWO-THIRDS WORLD

PRABHU S. GUPTARA

The inflated concept of fine art which separates it from craft and design developed primarily in the West. The rest of the world did not make this separation until recently, for a unity of feeling infused everything from the buildings (and the things in them) to the jewellery worn by women and the shoes worn by men.

Though Africa, Asia and Latin America are very different, their arts have gone through similar changes as foreign influences have borne in on them. However, the time when these changes happened, and the order in which these influences came, differed from place to place - and indeed even within the regions themselves. Still, we can try to draw a map of some sort.

Traditional arts are rooted in a traditional world-view, and usually associated with traditional religions. They fulfilled the material or psychological needs of local people. Different forms of art developed for the masses and for specific elites, and sometimes even for a single patron - as in India, where the whims of kings dictated fashions in their courts.

Traditional culture under attack

These traditional cultures were assaulted by three kinds of religious and cultural forces. A good example of a relatively unintrusive influence is Buddhism. Though essentially egalitarian and critical of the contemporary social and religious order, it soon lost this critical impulse and conformed. Chinese Buddhist art differs from Confucian art only in certain minor details.

The second kind of influence on traditional arts was relatively significant, and came from Islam and Christianity. These religions are different in many ways, but they affected traditional society and art in a similar manner: both call for a radical re-evaluation of traditional values and social structures; both invite people to submit themselves, their society, and the fruit of their actions to the will of God.

The result of the influence of these religions was that certain art-forms were discontinued (for example the making of masks for religious dances stopped with the dances themselves), while new art-forms came into being (calligraphy, for instance). But because the followers of Christianity and Islam do not completely live up to their respective faiths, the two religions have not so far exerted a substantial influence on the social and economic spheres of life, nor influenced art and culture as much as they potentially can.

Both religions are concerned about the individual's eternal destiny, but not exclusively so. They are also concerned about this material world, about words and actions and their results - all of which they see as eternally significant. They differ in this way from traditional societies, which see the next world as more important than this one.

This may be the reason why such ideas as secularism, humanism, Marxism, materialism, and science have found more fruitful soil in Western societies. These represent the third kind of impact on traditional societies.

Changing the political, social, and economic framework of the nations in the Two-Thirds World, Western ideas became the dominant influence on their arts. Western values, ideas and attitudes are supported by the vast power of the mass media, as well as by their respectability in universities, educational institutions and among the upper classes, both in the West and in the Two-Thirds World.

Counter-attack

Not all artists, thinkers and ordinary people in the Two-Thirds World have adopted these new ideas. Resistance has come from two sorts of people:

▪ There are **the genuine conservatives**. After the Meiji restoration in Japan, it was argued that the best way of preserving Confucian values was to appropriate what was necessary from the West (rifles, cannon, steamships), but in such a way that Confucianism remained the yardstick for what needed to be adapted. But technology transforms both landscape and lifestyle, so perhaps these conservatives had a naïve view.

▪ There are **'modern' apostles of tradition**. Largely educated in the Western manner, they reassert, not exactly the old values, but a modernized or Westernized version of

them. Some traditional ways and values are recommended, not because they are traditional, not because they have been handed down by the gods or by the ancestors, but because they appear to meet modern Western criteria of what is acceptable or valuable.

Consider 'Negritude' for example, a movement which flourished from the 1930s to the 1960s, and still commands attention. Accepting without question such European concepts as 'race' and 'Africa', it simply stood these ideas on their head to assert the superiority of 'black' values.

Such cultural movements back to the values of the people have themselves received powerful support from European ideas such as those behind the Enlightenment and the Romantic movement - freedom, equality, brotherhood, the noble savage. And it has worked the other way too; some developments in Western thought and art have been provoked by aspects of Third-World societies. Think of Gauguin's primitivism, Picasso's use of African images or the tie-in between some Western psychological thought and Indian yoga and tantra.

European interest in folklore gave these revivalistic movements a certain popularity in Western circles, and this in turn reinforced the appeal of such movements in the Two-Thirds World. Hence the renewed use, in this century, of regional languages rather than of metropolitan languages such as English. Hence also the popularity of ethnographic and documentary films. However, any culture, in the process of borrowing elements from another culture, profoundly reforms and transforms them at the same time.

The popularity of film

Revivalist cultural movements have been keen to use modern technology to propagate their ideas - perhaps the clearest sign of their foreign origin.

This does not make it any less amazing that film, the most technologically-dependent art-form of all, is so very popular in the Two-Thirds World. Film has immediacy, dramatic structure, entertainment. But its traditional content is just as important, expressing and reinforcing certain elements of mass sentiment.

Genuinely traditional values and art-forms disappear with the fading away of traditional society. Societies in the Two-Thirds World are now uneasily poised between a passing tradition and a modernity that they do not wholly like or want. This is also true of their art.

Individually brilliant pieces of work which are produced today may never be properly valued because they lack a discerning public, and appreciative critics and promoters. But where is genuinely great art to be found? It will only become possible, in the Two-Thirds World as anywhere else, when individual brilliance is fed by a genuinely nourishing world-view. This will be one which has a place, however critical, for the traditional as well as for the modern. A few artists and others in the Two-Thirds World are now beginning to discover how effectively the Bible speaks to these issues.

On the far left is part of a study for a mural in Fort Hall, Kenya, painted in 1959 by Elimo Njau, a Tanzanian who is secretary of the Community of East African Artists. Left is a wood carving of the risen Jesus, by Ben Enwonwu of Nigeria.

1.2 WHO ARE TODAY'S CHRISTIANS?

Roman Catholics since the Council

THOMAS F. STRANSKY

The Roman Catholic Church, which numbers about half of the world's Christians, believes itself to be in full historical and doctrinal continuity with the first community of Christ's disciples. The church holds that the divine relevation as contained in the Bible has been safeguarded and made authentic in each generation by its own teaching authority. This authority is exercised especially by the bishops of the local churches (dioceses), all in communion with the bishop of Rome as the successor of Peter. The church thus officially lists Pope John Paul II (from 1978) as the 275th bishop of Rome.

For an understanding of this large and ancient church, with its recent obvious and subtle shifts in theology, attitudes and practices, we need to go back a few decades to the Second Vatican Council (Vatican II). In four long autumn sessions (1962-65), over 2,450 bishops from every diocese in six continents gathered in St Peter's Basilica, Vatican City.

UPDATING THE CHURCH

The last council (Vatican I) had been in 1869-70; at the most 770 bishops took part, mostly European. During the ninety years since then, people had become aware that every frontier of personal and community experience had changed – social,

cultural and scientific, economic and political, intellectual and psychological.

In this context Pope John XXIII (1958-63) convoked Vatican II to 'update the church'. The council immediately became for Catholics and others the public symbol of this church's willingness to accept change with integrity.

None of the previous twenty councils which the Roman Catholic Church counts in its long history had such a wide-ranging agenda. With its sixteen major statements, Vatican II presented to all Catholics the authoritative updating on crucial issues:

● **How the church should understand itself**. This meant

The centre of fellowship and spiritual experience for many Christians today lies outside the main historic churches. The great church traditions, described in the following chapters, still retain considerable importance. But some of the most significant Christian groupings run right across denominational barriers. They include youth movements, evangelistic events and organizations, student groups, Charismatic rallies – often involving great numbers of people.

considering the shared responsibilities of the bishops with the bishop of Rome (pope), of the clergy, of the religious orders, and of the laity;

● **Prayer, worship and the sacraments**, especially the eucharistic liturgy;

● **Relations with 'The Others'**: those of other Christian communions, of the Jewish people, of other world religions, of secular ideologies;

● **The place of Christian faith in the modern world**, with its agonizing and not-so-simple issues: cultural, economic and social life; politics; the solidarity of peoples in one world; marriage and the family; the communications media;

● **The tasks of mission** – evangelization; the fight for religious freedom and the rights of conscience; the struggle for justice and peace;

● **Christian education** of children, youth and adults, and the training of the clergy;

● And in all these renewals, **the stance of the church as a learning and pilgrim people always under the revealed word of God**.

HOW FAR, HOW FAST?

The immediate post-Vatican II mood of Catholics was that of euphoria. It soon waned. Priests and laity were required suddenly to 'own' council statements and to carry out explicit theological, pastoral and missionary demands. Too much came too soon for too many. A secure Catholic identity was at stake.

For some Catholics the stated reforms did not take place fast enough, did not even go far enough. For others, the pace of church renewal was already too galloping, and many changes did not seem to make traditional

Roman Catholics are well represented among the poorest people in the world. In many Latin American shanty towns the local priest's pastoral care is a vital lifeline.

Catholic sense. And in the middle were many who, though they did not regard Vatican II as a big mistake, still deplored what they saw as exaggerations in the interpretation of the spirit and decisions of the council.

The Roman Catholic Church lacked a strong tradition of public self-criticism and calm mutual correction. And so not surprisingly conflicts followed, ranging from mild disagreements to total polarizations, among the bishops themselves, among the priests and among the laity. What to most was a sustaining fresh breeze was to some a faddish, passing ill-wind. For example, very many Catholics welcomed changes in official attitudes towards other Christians, encouraging more collaboration with them. Yet this seemed to other priests and laity to be compromise, even betrayal.

Also, because the church includes Catholics from a vast variety of situations between and within six continents, Vatican II demands were understood and put into effect in an uneven way. London, Boston or a Canadian prairie town is not Dar-es-Salaam, Bangkok or a Peruvian mountain village.

It was the task of Pope Paul VI (1963-78) to bear these conflicts and tensions within himself, and to guide this vast church in giving flesh and blood to the spirit and general directives of Vatican II.

THE LONG-TERM EFFECTS

Although the public Catholic debate has not died out, over the

These Roman Catholic children are making their first Communion. Catholics have always given a high place to the spiritual education of the young.

past few decades the main outlines of the post-Vatican II church are emerging – in theology, church structures and practices. It will help to pinpoint some more obvious examples:

● **The church perceives itself differently**. Its new vision of itself is primarily as a community of baptized disciples who serve God and neighbour as full, equal and responsible members of Christ's body. It is still also an authoritative hierarchical institution, as is needed to guide such a community in its life of faith, worship and service, but this is now the secondary part of the vision.

● **The laity are appreciating that they are the essence of the church**, not its second-class citizens. As people of God, lay

Pope John Paul II, the Polish pope, has earned a very high standing in the world. His directness and spiritual simplicity make him a popular figure and his many travels expose him to pubic view. He is unashamedly on the conservative side in matters of morality and church discipline. The pope called a council in November 1985 for the bishops to review progress in the twenty years since Vatican II.

Christians are responsible for their own faith, for the good of the institutional church, and for the evangelization of the world.

More Catholic women and men are sharing with priests in pastoral ministries, participating more actively in church worship, and giving voice to their own reflections on the word of God and church teaching. The laity are gradually seeing their primary responsibility as being Christian witnesses in their secular tasks – as farmers, business people, politicians, factory workers, students and teachers, military or senior citizens. They are leaven in the dough of everyday life.

● **The traditional Catholic high view of sacramental worship has been enhanced by liturgical reforms**: the use of modern languages (no longer only Latin); wide-ranging Bible readings during the daily and Sunday eucharist; more active lay voices (no longer confined to the choir); more instruction of those who are preparing for baptism, confirmation, reconciliation (still popularly called confession), and marriage.

● **The Bible** which 'teaches without error that truth which God wanted to put into the sacred writings for the sake of our salvation' (Vatican II), **is given a more celebrated place**. This is so not only in the classroom and pulpit but also in the laity's and clergy's use of biblical readings for personal devotion and in prayer groups (often shared with other Christians, as in charismatic groups). Catechisms (in which

young people and adults are taught the Christian faith) are clearly more biblically orientated.

● **Ecumenism**, or concern and work for the promotion of Christian unity, **is reflected in Catholic positive appreciation of Christ's gifts in other Christians and their communities**. This has been given effect in theological dialogues on historically divisive issues with Protestants, Anglicans and the Orthodox; and also in the increasing collaboration in social and charitable works. Former enemies, or at least tolerated strangers, are now being respected as brothers and sisters in the same Christ.

● **The public policy on social concerns is more pronounced**, but not as a suddenly new voice.

See Focus on Worship; Racism, Justice and Civil Rights

The nineteenth century relegated religion to being 'an innocent dedication to personal piety'. Already under the leadership of Pope Leo XIII (1878-1903) an era began of Catholic concern for improving the social order – labour conditions, race relations, and peace among nations. A steady stream of papal letters and bishops' statements has continued, culminating in Vatican II's *Church in the Modern World*. John Paul II continues this tradition, especially in the defence of human rights.

The rationale for these public stances on public issues was condensed in the 1974 statement of the Bishops' Synod in Rome: 'Action on the behalf of justice and the transformation of the world is a constitutive element in the preaching of the Gospel, or, in other words, of the Church's mission for the redemption of the human race and its liberation from every oppressive situation.'

● **'Collegiality'**, a new word on Catholic lips, **is the principle that the universal church is a community or family of local churches** (dioceses). In practice, a mode of decision-making has been introduced which emphasizes the joint responsibility of the pope and his fellow-bishops for the welfare of the whole church.

Before Vatican II, bishops of most areas related to each other only through the Vatican. Now every country or region has a bishops' conference which meets to discuss common concerns and to exercise jointly its pastoral function. Every two or three years representatives of these conferences deliberate in Rome with the pope and his staff during month-long meetings (synods) in response to urgent issues, such as justice and peace, evangelization, teaching in the faith, family life, and the celibacy of priests.

In the dioceses themselves the style of government is shifting. Bishops tend less to issue out-of-the-blue dictates and more to hold prior discussion and consultation. Many dioceses have councils of clergy and laity; most parishes have similar councils.

Popes Paul VI and John Paul II have weakened the traditional influence of one nationality, the Italians, on the Vatican's central administration (the Roman Curia). When Vatican II began, twelve of the sixteen curial

In December 1983 Sigitas Tamkevicius, a Lithuanian priest, was sentenced to six years' strict-regime labour camp and four years' internal exile for his defence of the Lithuanian church. At his trial Tamkevicius said, 'I feel "not guilty". I did everything required of me as a priest. In the gospel it says that when they were trying Christ, he did not defend himself...and I wish to follow his example...Do with me what you will.'

offices were headed by Italians. In 1984, sixteen non-Italians, including two Africans and one Latin American, head the twenty-two top posts. John Paul II is the first non-Italian pope since the Dutch Adrian VI (1522-23).

HOW MUCH DIVERSITY?

With increased collegiality, there are inbuilt healthy, and unhealthy, tensions between the local churches and the Holy See (the pope and his Curia). The church proclaims the principle of catholicity – that there are legitimate and indeed necessary differences in how local churches express Catholic teaching, sacramental life and discipline, and that these enhance, rather than weaken or destroy, the given unity of the church. But how should such authentic diversity within the unity of the faith work out in practice? This has become a never-ending

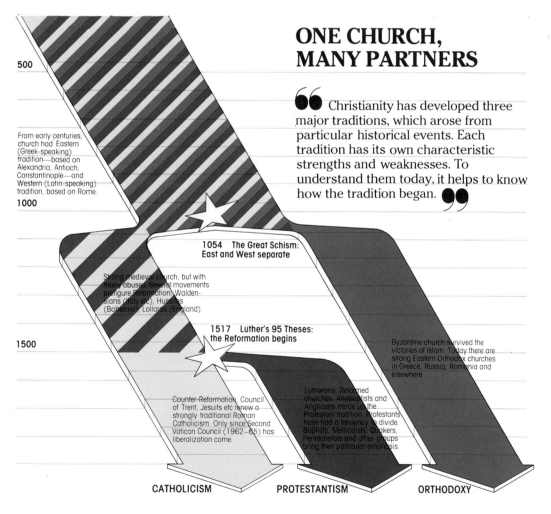

ONE CHURCH, MANY PARTNERS

❝ Christianity has developed three major traditions, which arose from particular historical events. Each tradition has its own characteristic strengths and weaknesses. To understand them today, it helps to know how the tradition began. ❞

500

From early centuries, church had Eastern (Greek-speaking) tradition—based on Alexandria, Antioch, Constantinople—and Western (Latin-speaking) tradition, based on Rome.

1000

1054   The Great Schism: East and West separate

Strong medieval church, but with many abuses. Several movements prefigure Reformation: Waldensians (Italy etc), Hussites (Bohemia), Lollards (England).

1517   Luther's 95 Theses: the Reformation begins

1500

Byzantine church survived the victories of Islam. Today there are strong Eastern Orthodox churches in Greece, Russia, Romania and elsewhere

Counter-Reformation, Council of Trent, Jesuits etc renew a strongly traditional Roman Catholicism. Only since Second Vatican Council (1962–65) has liberalization come.

Lutherans, Reformed churches, Anabaptists and Anglicans made up the Protestant tradition. Protestants have had a tendency to divide. Baptists, Methodists, Quakers, Pentecostals and other groups bring their particular emphasis.

CATHOLICISM   PROTESTANTISM   ORTHODOXY

debate, even though, for Catholics, the pope must be the final arbiter.

This debate will increase as the dominant Catholic population and influence rapidly shifts, and it is hard to predict how it will be resolved.

In the early 1960s, roughly 50 per cent of Catholics lived in North America and Europe. By 1980, 60 per cent were living in Latin America, Africa, Asia and Oceania. It is predicted that by the year 2000, 70 per cent of the over 1,000 million Catholics in the world will reside in these eastern and southern continents. The Northern Atlantic Catholic community is thus being overshadowed by the southern hemisphere, where already creativity, vitality and sheer numbers are pressing the bishops and laity not to be treated as mere receivers of Western Catholic thought and disciplines.

The authority in and of the church, as Catholic teaching believes that authority to be, is under the strain of public dissent.

A specific papal authority-crisis arose from Paul VI's letter, in 1968, on 'the right ordering of the procreation of children'. The letter's positive purpose was to teach the sanctity of human life and the sacredness of marital responsibility – a defence which John Paul II has stressed even more vigorously. But the papal message is remembered, almost exclusively, for its moral prohibition of 'any action which either before, at the moment of, or after sexual intercourse, is specifically intended to prevent procreation'. While many

Catholics immediately rallied behind the pope, others dissented, and many continue to decide for themselves whether responsible parenthood requires artificial methods of contraception.

Dissent is also being publicly registered towards firm papal and episcopal statements on the rights of the unborn, and more recently on the morality of nuclear warfare and the arms race. Very many Catholics, along with others, Christian or not, welcome this strong religious leadership in the midst of so much conformity to society's norms or lack of them. But others attack such hierarchical voices as archaic and self-defeating.

Three other areas are currently provoking discussions and debate: the confining of ordination to the priesthood to men (women, in principle, have always been excluded); the discipline of a celibate clergy in most of the church (the five Eastern churches in union with Rome have always allowed for a married priesthood); the issue, especially in Latin America, of liberation theology.

In 1983 Pope John Paul II published a new set of canon laws – principles and regulations for the life of the church. They had been drafted by a papal commission, and were intended to express the applied theology of Vatican II. They reflect the deep impact the council has had on the Roman Catholic Church. But the process of change cannot be said to have ended with them.

See Dutch Roman Catholics; Good News for the Poor

The Orthodox Families

PAULOS MAR GREGORIOS

All the Eastern Orthodox churches are to be found in the West today, in Europe as well as in America, but still few of their fellow-Christians know them. They are different and seem remote. Yet the Orthodox are one of the three great strands of historic Christianity.

Today, there are 150 million Orthodox Christians in the world. They are in two families, sometimes distinguished as the 'Eastern' and the 'Oriental' Orthodox. The larger, 'Eastern', family consists of some twenty churches in communion with the Ecumenical Patriarchate of Constantinople (in Istanbul, Turkey, where the Ecumenical Patriarch, His All Holiness Dmitrios, lives). The major members of this family are listed in the larger table. The smaller, but more ancient, Orthodox family, sometimes called the Oriental Orthodox, are in five churches, as in the smaller list.

The two families separated from each other in the sixth century, following cultural conflicts and doctrinal disputes about whether the one, united, divine-human nature of Christ should be counted as one or two. Those who said two (now the Constantinople family) called the others 'monophysite', while those who said one (the Oriental Orthodox) called the others 'diophysite'. The conflict was largely one between Asian/African and Hellenic cultures. It focussed at the Council of Chalcedon (AD 451), where a definition of Christ's

See The Orthodox World

nature was formulated which has had wide influence ever since. This was not accepted by the Oriental Orthodox. Today the two families have come to basic theological agreements, but have not yet entered into communion with each other.

RIGHTLY GLORIFYING GOD

What do the Orthodox believe? Their belief is implied in their very name. The very word 'Orthodox' is a creation of theirs. It is made up from the Greek *orthos* (rightly) and *doxadzein* (to glorify). So the Orthodox qualify themselves as those Christians who rightly glorify God. In the history of the Christian church there have been many heresies. One of them nearly engulfed the church in the fourth century, and still persists, especially in the West - the heresy of Arius, the Presbyter of Alexandria, who denied the divinity of Christ.

To Arius and to his followers, who at one time included more than three-quarters of the world church, only God the Father was truly God and to be worshipped as God. So they created a special form of the doxology, different from the one used by the mainline church: 'Glory be to the Father by the Son, through the Holy Spirit.' (The mainline doxology runs '...and to the Son, and to the Holy Spirit.') The Arian formula ascribes glory only to the Father, making both the Son and the Holy Spirit merely channels for that glory, and implicitly denying their divinity. Basil the Great wrote a treatise, defending the divinity of the Holy Spirit and the traditional doxology. Those who used the 'and...and' formula regarded themselves as rightly glorifying God - in short as 'Orthodox'.

The two cardinal teachings, which no Othodox can deny and remain Orthodox, are:

● **The belief in God the Trinity** as Three Persons in a single Godhead;

● **The incarnation of the Second Person of the Trinity**, who is fully God and fully Man.

Set alongside their firm belief in these two aspects of the Godhead is another fundamental Orthodox belief - their understanding of the church. The church to them is not a collection of believers. They use many New Testament images, but the central one is that of the body of Christ. The body of Christ includes Christ and is the dwelling-place of the Holy Spirit. The church is not therefore just an odd collection of forgiven sinners. It is holy 'in Christ', by the Spirit, despite our sins. That is why in the Nicene Creed (central for Orthodox Christians) we confess our faith in the Trinity and in the church.

To the Orthodox, the vision of the church is of one that spans heaven and earth. Jesus Christ is the foundation, for no other foundation can be laid. The apostles, prophets, martyrs and other holy ones are built up on the one solid foundation, forming a growing edifice in which God himself dwells by the Spirit. All the departed Christians are still full members of the body of Christ, and we are never complete without them. That is why the Orthodox Church, in her worship, constantly reminds

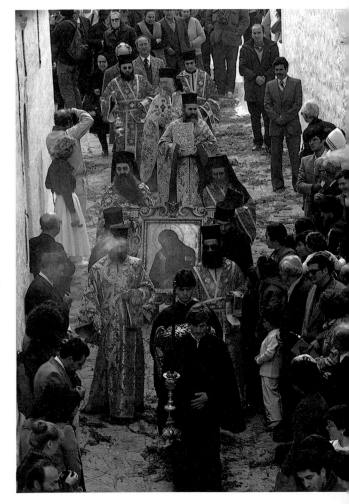

Orthodox Christians on the island of Patmos take part in a Maundy Thursday ceremony of footwashing, which happens only here and in Jerusalem.

herself of the presence of all God's holy ones, living and departed, in our midst.

WORSHIP COMES FIRST

It is a special characteristic of the Orthodox to give priority to worship, even over mission. Mission is understood as the invitation to all humanity to join in the church's permanent, ongoing worship of the Father, Son and Holy Spirit. Preaching and reading the Bible are important to the Orthodox. But both preaching and reading from the Bible must immediately lead to worship, above all. Constantly to acknowledge that God is good and that he alone is good, is to join the company of the angels in heaven who eternally laud and magnify the glorious name of God - to become one, while here on earth, with the eternally worshipping heavenly community. This could be said to be the essence of Orthodoxy.

See Focus on Worship

And central to worship here on earth is the eucharistic worship of the believing community. The eucharist (or holy communion) is, for the Orthodox, not merely a memorial of the death and resurrection of Jesus. It is the actual living out of that saving event in our time and our place. In the eucharist Christ himself is present in a special way, as the High Priest, eternally and once-for-all offering his own body and blood as sacrifice to the Father. It is our participation, here today, in the one, eternal sacrifice of Christ. It is this participation that sanctifies us and makes us worthy to stand in the presence of the awesome throne of God.

The Orthodox hold the Bible in the highest regard, as the direct testimony of the apostles and evangelists who were primary witnesses of the incarnation. They have not accepted all the findings of modern critical studies in the New Testament, though Orthodox seminaries introduce students to modern New Testament criticism. They do not regard the New Testament as just another literary document to be evaluated by the accepted methods of literary criticism. The New Testament is the written apostolic testimony to the event which is always acknowledged in the worship of the church: the life, death and rising again of our Lord Jesus Christ, the incarnate Word of God. The interpretation of the New Testament is not to be taken over by the unbeliever. The church has known the meaning of its true testimony and always lives by it.

COMING TO TERMS WITH THE MODERN WORLD

The Orthodox are not Roman Catholics. They regard the Roman Catholic Church as the Western branch of the world church which broke away from them in the past. They do not regard the pope in Rome as any more than the head of a local church, like their own patriarchs and archbishops. But they also regard the Roman Catholic Church as having deviated from the true faith of the church, in claiming universal jurisdiction and infallibility for the bishop of Rome, and in imposing unnecessary dogmas and rules on Christians. For the Oriental

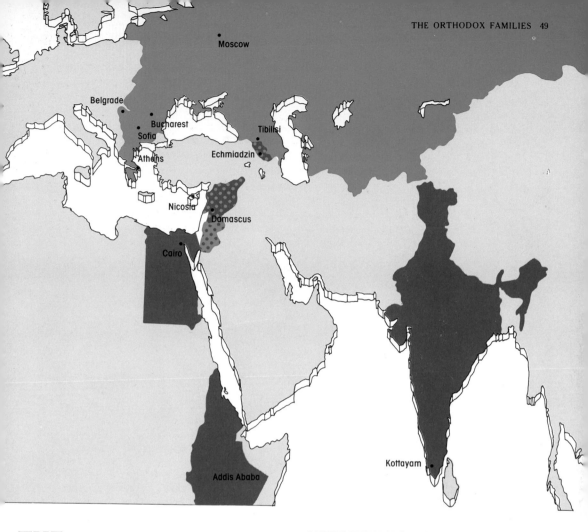

THE
ORTHODOX WORLD

 The Eastern and Oriental
Orthodox churches form one of the three
great Christian traditions, alongside Roman
Catholics and Protestants.

Key:

Eastern
Orthodox

Oriental
Orthodox

EASTERN ORTHODOX CHURCH

Russian Orthodox Church	70 million, growing	Moscow
Romanian Orthodox Church	17 million	Bucharest
Church of Greece	8 million	Athens
Bulgarian Orthodox Church	8 million	Sofia
Serbian Orthodox Church	5 million	Belgrade
Georgian Orthodox Church	2 million	Tibilisi
Orthodox Church of Cyprus	2 million	Nicosia
Greek Orthodox Patriarchate of Antioch	¼ million	Damascus
Ecumenical Patriarchate	5 million	(Europe, America, Australasia etc)
Orthodox Church of America	2 million	New York

ORIENTAL ORTHODOX CHURCH

Coptic Orthodox Church	8 million	Cairo
Syrian Orthodox Church	¼ million	Damascus
Armenian Apostolic Church	3½ million	Etchmiadzin
Orthodox Church of India	1½ million	Kottayam
Ethiopian Orthodox Church	15 million	Addis Ababa

THE ETERNAL LITURGY

At the centre of the life of all Orthodox Christian communities is the liturgy – the intensely beautiful and traditional worship of holy communion. They see the 'eternal liturgy' as a window to heaven and a gate to righteousness. In the service Christians worship God the Father, Son and Holy Spirit, but the focus is on Jesus Christ, whom they believe to be present in the communion. United to Christ in the worship, Christians are thereby united to each other and to all believers who have gone before. The service also involves an act of consecration to live for Christ in the world.

Orthodox, the break with the Roman church is remembered as having taken place in the sixth century (following the Chalcedon controversies), and for the Eastern Orthodox it took place in the eleventh and twelfth centuries, though there was already a major schism between the Byzantine and Latin churches in the ninth century (known as the Photian schism).

For this reason, the Orthodox have never been directly involved in the controversies of the Protestant Reformation. Much of that controversy they regard as mistakenly formulated. They see no conflict between justification by faith and justification by works, or between the Bible and tradition.

Both the Roman Catholic and the Protestant churches have the advantage of being at home within Western civilization, having originated and grown up within it. The Orthodox, however, have great difficulty in adjusting to the modern world and its value system based on rationality, individualism, authority, and truth as proposition. They survive in the modern world with much tension. They have not fully accepted the modern world or fully come to terms with it.

They are under constant pressure to do as the Roman Catholics and the Protestants do. Sometimes they succumb to the pressure and betray their own tradition. For example, they are under pressure to legislate about the use of artificial means of birth control, either for or against. The Orthodox Church only teaches people the moral consequences of using or not using artificial means. It does not legislate about them and lay down that one is right and the other is wrong.

Again in imitation of the West, the Orthodox have started theological seminaries to train the clergy, during the last 200 years or so. They have often imitated the West in methods of teaching and training, in the syllabus and curriculum, and in tests of qualification for the ordained ministry. They have today a dozen or more competent institutions of theological training in the world. Among them are the theological faculties of the Greek universities of Athens and Thessaloniki, the theological academies of Bucharest and Sibiu in Romania, Leningrad and Moscow (Zagorsk) in the Soviet Union, St Vladimir's in Scarsdale, New York and the Greek Seminary in Brookline Massachusetts, St Sergius Academy in Paris and the Orthodox Theological Seminary in Kottayam, Kerala, India. These and other seminaries have begun to make the Orthodox clergy better educated than in the previous few centuries. But the clergy in the Orthodox Church remain, to a large extent, not intellectually competent to deal with the moral and social problems that the laity face.

WITH OTHER CHRISTIANS
Orthodox Christians have been leaders in the unity movement. The idea of a World Council of Churches was first advanced by the Ecumenical Patriarch of

'We know that our life is temporary, and we had better live with Christ and offer ourselves, and have true life in him...The pressures of life have brought us that really deep life of close relation with God.' Pope Shenouda III, leader of the Egyptian Coptic Church

A Romanian Orthodox priest performs a ceremony using hyssop and holy water. This church has its areas of tension with the state, but there are signs of spiritual revival.

See The Unity Movement

Constantinople in 1920. Archbishop Germanos of Thyateira (London), Patriarch Athenagoras of Constantinople, Miss Sarah Chacko of India (a one-time president of the WCC), Metropolitan Nikodim of Leningrad and Archbishop Iakovos of America are among the Orthodox who have given distinguished leadership to the ecumenical movement. The Greek and the Indian Orthodox churches were among the founder members of the World Council of Churches.

The Orthodox churches have suffered greatly in the past from the excessive proselytizing zeal of the Western churches. This made them wary of relationships with other churches. But today agreements have been worked out to stop proselytism, and where these are observed there are good relations between Eastern and Western churches. This affinity is closest with those who retain an uncompromising confession of the full divinity and humanity of Christ our Lord.

Who Are the Lutherans Today?

JOSEPH A. BURGESS

Lutherans are of course Christians first: they follow Jesus Christ, not Martin Luther. Yet they do take Luther's life and teachings very seriously. His translation of the Bible into German shaped the German language and continues in use today. The hymns he composed are still used in worship and celebration. More importantly, for Lutherans – and increasingly for other Christians as well – Luther has become one of the teachers of the church. His Small Catechism is used for instructing most Lutheran confirmation candidates, and more than a hundred large volumes by him have become a source-book for Lutherans and the whole church. Most of all Luther, echoing the apostle Paul, insisted that sin has to be taken seriously and God's grace is the only answer to it; and what Luther insisted on continues to echo in the hearts of many Christians.

Not even Luther wanted the Reformation to be called 'Lutheran', and his opponents created the name as an insult. As time went on, the name became permanent, although today some Lutheran churches continue to call themselves 'Evangelical', or 'Churches of the Augsburg Confession'. Lutherans have not turned Luther into a saint. He was also very much a man of his own time. Much of what he did and thought was simply part of the movement called humanism. Others were reformers before him. His strict approach to spiritual matters simply reflected the spiritual climate of his day. He fell prey to attacks of spiritual depression. His view of society was limited by feudalism. The world would soon come to an end, Luther thought. For this reason, the followers of the pope, the Turks, the Jews, and the left-wing radicals of the Reformation had to be opposed. In none of these things have Lutherans held that Luther is either their model or their guide.

FROM LUTHER'S TIME TO OURS

When in 1517 Luther proposed ninety-five theses for scholarly debate, he started a movement that continues to split the Western church. At first the dispute centred on selling indulgences, but soon the authority of pope and council were at stake. Because the gospel had become distorted in the medieval church, Luther stood firm. His intention was not to break with the church, but in 1521 he was excommunicated. By 1530 the new movement was established and had produced a common statement of faith, the Augsburg Confession. By 1600 the Reformation had spread to most of the northern and middle parts of Europe. It soon took two distinct forms: the Lutheran strand chiefly in Germany and Scandinavia, and the Reformed strand, following John Calvin, mainly in Switzerland, the Netherlands, and Scotland.

Like all renewal movements, Lutherans have gone through certain stages of development. At first, in a period called Lutheran orthodoxy, the Reformation became an establishment in its own right; the pressures of polemics led to hardened fronts with Lutheran opponents. Great theological systems developed. Such systems had a tendency to make religious life external and static, and, as a consequence, at the end of the seventeenth century there was a pietistic reaction. Pietists cultivated the inner spiritual life, Bible study in small groups or by oneself, and abstinence from worldly practices. Often they emphasized actively helping the needy and bringing the gospel to foreign lands.

During the eighteenth century, the Enlightenment, the French Revolution, and the beginnings of industrialization created a new challenge. Yet in the midst of this turmoil, normal church life continued, sustained by worship, the singing of hymns, preaching from the Bible, and the celebration of the sacraments.

In 1817 Frederick William III of Prussia united the Lutheran and Reformed churches. Some welcomed the Prussian Union, and their descendants today still worship in United Churches. Some reacted by emigrating to the United States, by forming another church, or by stressing traditional Lutheran theology. There followed a time first of exploring new ideas and then of widespread optimism.

But all of this was thrown into question by World War I and what followed. Karl Barth, a Swiss Reformed theologian, led in the development of dialectical theology, which was a conservative reaction to the false optimism of the previous period. One key element in dialectical theology was the rediscovery of Soren Kierkegaard, a Danish Lutheran from the first half of the previous century.

When German political and economic conditions became chaotic, Hitler took over both state and church. Many Lutherans in Germany supported him. But a significant minority, together with a significant minority of Reformed church members, formed the Confessing Church, which in turn he severely persecuted. Dietrich Bonhoeffer was one of the martyrs.

JUSTIFICATION BY FAITH

Lutherans understand themselves to be a reform movement within the church universal. In other words, they are not out to split the church, but rather to put before it a theological proposal:

that justification is by faith in Christ alone. Up to this point their proposal has been accepted by only part of the church universal. They do not despair, however, but persist, insisting that their proposal, which gives Christ his proper place, belongs to the very centre of the Christian faith.

Because they stand for this very centre of Christian belief, Lutherans take theology very seriously. But they are not concerned with theology for its own sake – only in that it provides guidance for proclaiming Christ. At times Lutherans have fallen into the trap of believing that salvation depends on holding certain doctrines, but most of the time they have remained true to their central affirmation that salvation depends on faith in Christ alone.

Their seriousness about theology has enabled Lutherans through the centuries to maintain their sense of identity. Their theology, moreover, is very traditional. First of all, they make the Bible their final rule and norm. Second, they hold to the ecumenical creeds: the Apostles' Creed, the Nicene Creed, and the Athanasian Creed. Third, they subscribe to Luther's Small Catechism (1529) and the Augsburg Confession (1530). Other writings from the sixteenth century are held by many Lutherans to be equally binding, or at least to be authentic interpretations of those two statements. In 1580 all these writings were collected in the *Book of Concord*. Furthermore, when Lutherans subscribe to the

Bible and other subsequent writings, they understand this subscription to be a very serious matter.

Yet they are not primarily traditionalists or exponents of systematic theology. Lutherans confess the centre, Christ, not the system. The Word of God is first of all Christ, second, the proclaimed word about Christ, and third, the written word about

Lutherans lay stress on holy communion, taking bread and wine in thanksgiving for Jesus' death for us. In this service they believe they meet the living Christ.

Christ. All words are to be measured by how they point to Christ.

Lutherans have traditionally used two great catchwords, 'Christ alone' and 'the Word alone'. Three other slogans explain what these mean: 'grace alone', 'faith alone', 'the cross alone'. When all is said and done, the five slogans mean the same thing – that we can only find salvation through trusting in Christ. Lutherans, following Luther, are famous for asserting that salvation is not by works. They make this assertion because, as Luther pointed out when he rediscovered the heart of Paul's message, justification is of the ungodly, not the godly, and therefore it is by faith, not by works (see Romans 4:5).

At first these Lutheran slogans may seem like any other body of doctrine, to be believed or not. What is important, however, is not that these affirmations are assented to intellectually but that the promise of forgiveness for Christ's sake truly becomes a promise to the individual person. Through the power of the Holy Spirit this promise proves its own validity. No particular kind of experience or feeling or understanding is required for this kind of faith, although experiences, feelings, and understanding may go with it. This is what Lutherans mean when they insist on 'justification by faith'. At the same time they would be the first to admit that neither in their teaching nor in their practice have they

Preaching is a serious and important matter for Lutherans, like this pastor of a church on a North Sea island. They believe that God's grace to us in Jesus can only be understood when it is explained from the Bible.

themselves always been faithful to that doctrine, but this in itself illustrates what justification by faith means. Although works will follow from such faith, it is not by our works that we are saved: our works are a grateful response to the freedom we have been given.

With this basis, no one should be surprised at the way Lutherans emphasize preaching. They also emphasize the sacraments. Infants as well as adults are baptized, and the Lord's Supper is celebrated frequently. Occasionally private penance is practised. Yet these sacraments are not effective without the promise being proclaimed of forgiveness given by the Lord. The same kind of thinking applies to how Lutherans understand the church. The church is present wherever the gospel is rightly preached and the sacraments rightly administered; in other words, the church is present wherever the promise given by our Lord is proclaimed.

The ministry exists because the promise has to be proclaimed. Lutherans are not committed to any particular structure for the ministry. In some countries bishops in historic succession have continued, but these bishops have no difficulty in accepting as valid Lutheran ministers in other countries without historic succession. More than three-quarters of the Lutherans in the world are members of churches that have ordained women.

Lutherans are very liturgical. Luther translated the Roman Catholic Latin mass into German, and Lutherans have made this the basic format for their worship, using, of course, their own local languages. Preaching and singing hymns are the other key elements in worship.

They also stress education, seeking to train all ages, especially young people, in the basics of the Lutheran tradition.

At times Lutherans have been accused of 'quietism' – being so concerned for spiritual matters as not to be active in helping others who are needy. Some have thought that the reason for this lies at the very heart of Lutheranism, 'justification by faith alone'. Yet although Lutherans would be the first to admit that they have not done what they should for those in need, they can point to a long history of Lutheran social action. One of the great treasures of their tradition is Luther's doctrine of the Christian's calling: every good occupation, no matter how demeaning, is doing God's will for our neighbour in this world. This has kept Lutheran theology constantly earthed in the secular world, as never abandoned by God, but of crucial importance to him.

LUTHERANS TODAY

Lutherans are not generally well known, yet they are the largest Protestant church in the world, numbering about 69 million. Today they are declining in the Lutheran heartland, Germany.

Lutherans, exactly like other groups, followed the paths of emigration and the fortunes of

Youngsters in a Lutheran mission in Papua New Guinea blow on cowrie shells as part of their worship. There are Lutheran churches throughout the world.

See Churches Together

colonial power. Today most Lutherans continue to be those living in northern and central Europe, with a strong presence in East Germany as well as West. But over 9 million are in the United States, and Indonesia, India, Brazil, and Tanzania each have a million or more. For the most part Lutheran churches throughout the world are independent. If they still receive support from abroad, such support is not controlled by the senders.

Almost 55 million Lutherans are members of the Lutheran World Federation, which has its headquarters in Geneva and whose assembly meets approximately every seven years. The assembly cannot legislate or speak for the member churches, but common bonds are strengthened and common concerns are carried out. Many Lutheran churches outside the Lutheran World Federation are not members because they are

more conservative and fear that traditional Lutheran doctrine is being eroded.

Lutherans are concerned for church unity. Most belong to churches that are members of the World Council of Churches. They are carrying on two-way dialogues with many other church bodies; and the dialogue with the Roman Catholics has broken old stereotypes and opened up new possibilities. In Europe the Leuenberg Agreement (1973) has made pulpit and altar fellowship possible between Lutherans and the Reformed. In the United States three Lutheran churches and the Episcopal (Anglican) Church agreed in 1982 to 'interim sharing of the Eucharist'. More steps of this type will soon take place, although to date very few actual mergers have occurred. On the other hand, some, while not denying the need for unity, have asked what shape that unity should take and whether it might not take the form of reconciled diversity, using the analogy of the family, rather than a full church merger.

There is a basic tension for Lutherans: they stress justification by faith and so unity is not the central issue, and yet they understand themselves to be a reform movement within the church universal pressing it towards greater unity. Ultimately, however, Lutherans combine their concern for the gospel with an openness to the future.

Reformed Churches Round the World

KLAAS RUNIA

After the Roman Catholic Church, the Reformed churches are the most widely spread throughout the world. Starting with the Swiss reformers Zwingli and Calvin in the sixteenth century, the Reformed movement spread in all directions across Europe.

In the next century it crossed the oceans and made itself at home in North America, South Africa, Sri Lanka, Indonesia and, for a time, even in Japan. The nineteenth century saw new settlements of Reformed people in Australia and New Zealand. During that same period, new emigration waves carried many more Reformed and Presbyterian people from Europe to North America and South Africa. The nineteenth century also witnessed the planting of new Reformed mission churches in Asia, Africa and Latin America. This process is being continued throughout this century.

But this wide expansion is also due to the fact that no family of churches has suffered so greatly from division and fragmentation as the Reformed family. For instance, the history of the Reformed churches of the Netherlands and of the Presbyterian churches in Scotland is marred by so many divisions that to an outsider it is almost incomprehensible. The positive effect of all this was that every division became a new dynamic to spread the Reformed understanding of the gospel more vigorously.

THE REFORMED FAMILY CHARACTER

What is this Reformed understanding of the gospel? During the creed-making epoch of the sixteenth century, the Reformed churches in the various European countries all made their own national confessions. But interestingly, they have some clear, common characteristics. All place a strong emphasis on the importance of the Bible, on God's sovereignty, his justification and sanctification of the believer, and Jesus' headship of the church.

But the most visible common denominator of the various Reformed churches is probably the way that the churches are

Members of a German-speaking community, who have lived for generations in an agricultural part of Romania, worship in their Reformed church.

run. There are three types of leader at the local level: the minister, the elder and the deacon. Because the elder (or 'presbyter') is the key figure in this system, many Reformed churches in English-speaking countries call themselves 'Presbyterian': that ministers are more properly seen as 'teaching elders' illustrates this fact. These three types of leadership are active at all levels of the churches, right up to the national meeting of the synod or assembly.

In addition to Presbyterian churches, Congregational churches also belong to the Reformed family. They locate authority more within the local congregation than in any national assembly.

CONTINENT BY CONTINENT

The state of the Reformed churches around the world is a study in contrasts. In some areas the church is merely ticking over, and its influence and mission have definitely declined. Other areas have enjoyed an enormous growth in both church members and Christian commitment. Some areas have always placed their stress on personal piety, while others have a tradition of Christian involvement in the political and social arena. So what are the strengths and weaknesses of the Reformed churches in the different continents?

Europe The old historical lines are still very noticeable in Europe. In Western Europe the main Reformed churches are found in Switzerland, the Netherlands, West Germany, France, the United Kingdom and Ireland. In Southern Europe, the Reformed tradition is weaker.

The strength and staying-power of the Reformed tradition can easily be seen in the countries where it first took root. The majority of Swiss Protestants are Reformed, tracing their origin

LUTHERAN AND REFORMED CHURCHES

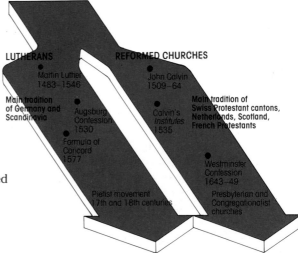

LUTHERANS

Martin Luther
1483–1546

Main tradition
of Germany and
Scandinavia

Augsburg
Confession
1530

Formula of
Concord
1577

Pietist movement
17th and 18th centuries

REFORMED CHURCHES

John Calvin
1509–64

Calvin's
Institutes
1535

Main tradition of
Swiss Protestant cantons,
Netherlands, Scotland,
French Protestants

Westminster
Confession
1643–49

Presbyterian and
Congregationalist
churches

66 Protestant Europe quickly established two traditions, distinct though usually not in conflict. 99

back to either Zwingli or Calvin. The main Protestant church of France is the Reformed Church of France, while there are also some smaller independent Reformed churches. Dutch society still shows many traces of the once-dominant Calvinism. In the late nineteenth century Abraham Kuyper, a Reformed pastor who became prime minister, brought about a renewal of Calvinism adapted to the modern world, and the results of this renewal are still being felt. Today parent-controlled Christian schools are subsidized on an equal footing with the state schools. There are two Christian broadcasting associations. There are several Christian political parties and a Christian trades union movement. Although the impact of secularism on Dutch society is clearly considerable, the Reformed faith here is more than just history.

The same is true of Scotland. The national church is the (Presbyterian) Church of Scotland. Ever since the days of John Knox, Calvinism has been *the* religion of the Scottish people. Although with the Church of Scotland itself the liberal tradition is strong in the smaller Presbyterian churches, traces of the Puritan tradition, with its emphasis on preaching and Sunday observance, are still clearly noticeable.

Wales, Northern Ireland and the Irish Republic each have their own Presbyterian Church, while in England the Presbyterian and Congregational Churches united in 1972 to form the United Reformed Church.

In most of the **Western European** countries the older and larger churches do not encourage a strong commitment from their members. They are churches to which people belong by birth or baptism, rather than through confession of Reformed beliefs or even through regular church attendance. The smaller Reformed denominations in these countries are usually much more strict in their confessional commitment.

Eastern Europe is the home of some large Reformed communities in Romania, Czechoslovakia and Hungary – all dating back to the sixteenth century. The Reformed Church of Hungary, with its 2 million members, is the only Reformed Church that has bishops. The leadership of this church has been rather subservient to the present political regime, with the presiding bishop serving as a member of the Presidential Council.

North America By 1628 the first Dutch Reformed Church was formed at New Amsterdam (now called New York) on Manhattan Island. At about the same time Puritans came to New England and established Congregational churches. In the early eighteenth century, a new wave of immigration brought the Scots and the Irish to America. These last two groups made a great impact, not only religiously, but also economically and politically.

The Reformed churches developed quickly on American soil but, as elsewhere, there were sadly many schisms and

'We in the Reformed tradition believe that God has two servants in the world: one is the state and the other is the church...The church is responsible among other things for reminding the state...that it is not God, that there is a God to which the state itself is subject.' James I. McCord

separations – ethnic as well as theological – that have only been repaired by reunions in this century. The major unions include the United Church of Christ, formed in 1957, and the Presbyterian Church USA (at present the largest Presbyterian body) in 1983.

The two main Reformed denominations are the Reformed Church in America and the Christian Reformed Church, both established by Dutch settlers in the seventeenth and nineteenth centuries respectively. While the Dutch names of most church members still betray their origin, today both churches are becoming more and more Americanized.

Although the Presbyterian and Reformed churches are by no

means the largest church bodies in the United States, their influence is still comparatively strong. This is due to the fact that Calvinism has always been more than an ecclesiastical tradition. It also presents a way of living and acting in the world, encouraging its followers to involvement in social affairs and politics.

South Africa contains the third largest concentration of Reformed people in the world. Today, nearly half of the white population is Reformed.

Being surrounded in their own country by an overwhelming majority of black people, the white Reformed Church has always had a strong sense of calling. Many in the church still believe that God has sent them

A congregation in a Reformed church in Indonesia, where the Dutch colonial history has left this tradition. Christian faith has made great strides in Indonesia in recent years.

to their country with the purpose of establishing a Christian state in a heathen continent. To some extent this also explains the apartheid policy adopted by the government, for the large Dutch Reformed Church has always supported apartheid, even supplying it with a theological justification. In recent years, however, an increasing number of critical voices are being heard within this church.

This sense of calling did not only produce negative results. It has also stimulated the white churches to engage in missionary activities. The Dutch Reformed Church has been particularly active. This has led to the creation of large separate Reformed churches among the coloured, the black and the Indian people. In the same way, Reformed churches have been established in Nigeria, Zambia, Malawi and Zimbabwe.

In seventeen other African countries there are churches belonging to the Reformed family, ranging from 352 members in Algeria to 264,000 members in Cameroon.

Asia In some fifteen countries of Asia, Reformed Congregational or Presbyterian churches have grown up. The oldest is the Dutch Reformed Church of Sri Lanka, dating back to 1642. In India, most Christians of the Reformed tradition now worship with one of the United Churches. The largest concentration of Reformed church life is found in Indonesia (largely due to Dutch mission work) and in Korea. The Korean churches in particular are a miracle of growth. They

doubled in membership during the sixties, and again during the seventies. No one is expecting the eighties to see a slowing of this phenomenal growth. The two largest Presbyterian denominations each have over a million members.

Latin America Reformed or Presbyterian churches exist in twelve countries of Latin America. Most of the churches are small, ranging from 1,000 members to 40,000. The Presbyterian Church of Brazil, however, numbers 168,000.

See Clouds over Southern Africa

REFORMED CHURCHES TODAY

What are the main issues which excite Reformed Christians today?

The search for unity has become a guiding concern for many Reformed churches. In the past, Reformed Protestantism has suffered a great deal from division and fragmentation. But in this century many Reformed churches have engaged in negotiations towards unity, which have quite often issued in actual unions.

Alongside this, most churches of the Reformed family are members of the World Council of Churches and of the World Alliance of Reformed Churches. The latter was established in 1875 and merged in 1970 with the International Congregational Union. There is also a smaller international Reformed Ecumenical Synod, which came into being in 1946 and comprises some thirty-five confessional churches.

An exception to this desire for unity lies with the Dutch

Reformed Church of South Africa, which withdrew from the World Council of Churches and was suspended from the World Alliance of Reformed Churches. It remains a member of the Reformed Ecumenical Synod. The World Alliance of Reformed Churches, whose president is the black South African theologian Allan Boesak, described the situation in South Africa as 'an issue on which it is not possible to differ without seriously jeopardizing the integrity of our common confession as Reformed churches'. It declared the moral and theological justification of apartheid to be 'a travesty of the gospel, and in its persistent disobedience to the Word of God, a theological heresy'. This decision says a great deal about the family relationship within the World Alliance of Reformed Churches. The churches are held together not so much by theological agreement as by involvement in a certain ethos.

The South African churches threatened this ethos, and so were excluded.

Another characteristic of the Reformed churches generally is their deep interest in education and social issues. This undoubtedly harks back to Calvin himself who founded the Academy of Geneva and who also created the 'social' diaconate to underline the church's duty to care for the needy. The United Church of Canada speaks for many Reformed churches when it says: 'Current issues under study include abortion, capital punishment, the right of farm labour to organize, racial injustice, guaranteed annual income, land use, refugees and the massive problems of poverty both at home and abroad.'

Reformed Christians, then, are clearly concerned to be reconciled with other Christians, and also to fulfil their rich heritage of a Christian faith that is alive and active in our world.

MANY-SIDED CHRISTIANITY

Many Christian communities beyond those described in the main chapters are active in the world today. **The Salvation Army** is at work in eighty-six countries. Beginning in nineteenth-century Britain under the leadership of William Booth, Salvationists have always been at war, not only against sin, but against the consequences of social evil in poverty and deprivation. Their relief work is internationally famous. But they are far more than a movement of social concern. Their spirituality centres on a call to personal repentance from sin, and on joyful worship and rousing music.

Moravians are no longer one of the major Christian movements, as they once were. But there are still Moravians to be found in many parts of the world, as at this school in India, and they still retain their missionary zeal. The movement developed among followers of Jan Hus in fifteenth-century Bohemia (part of modern Czechoslovakia). A Moravian community was established in Saxony under Count Zinzendorf, and the movement soon became widespread, having a profound effect on the Wesleys and the Evangelical Awakening in Britain.

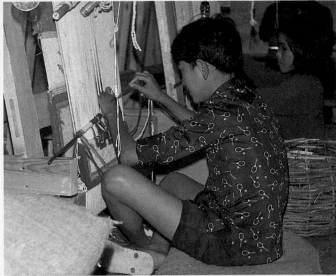

Quakers, often known as **the Society of Friends**, are a powerful force for international peace and understanding. Friends are here seen meeting with Buddhists to promote peace. Their influence is out of all proportion to their numbers. Originating in England through the evangelistic work of George Fox in the seventeenth century, Friends are now found round the world. Their meetings follow no set form, but are essentially silent, with any member free to speak as the Spirit leads. They have a tradition of equality, and of not deferring to rank. Quaker spirituality is marked today by the idea of searching for God; they are suspicious of confident statements of belief.

Make Disciples - Baptizing Them

JOHN BRIGGS

During this century, the number of churches which baptize only those who confess their faith as believers has risen dramatically. The strength of these churches is epitomized by the Baptists of the United States, numbering some 27 million. This is partly because most Pentecostal communities as well as many of the independent churches of Africa practise believers' baptism. While Baptists have been encouraged by challenges to infant baptism made by such eminent theologians as Brunner and Barth, they have more recently felt isolated by the increasing movement towards allowing child communion. Historically, four groups of churches have confined baptism to believers: the Mennonites, the Baptists, the Disciples (or Churches) of Christ, and the Brethren.

COSTLY DISCIPLESHIP: THE MENNONITES

The Mennonites take their name from Menno Simons who organized the Dutch Anabaptists in the sixteenth century. For the Anabaptists, the Reformation did not go far enough. They scathingly described the church of the mainstream Reformers as 'everybody's church', because it did not have any clearly defined membership. Instead, they called for the restoration of what they took to be the New Testament nature of the church of the believers - a church defined by faith and obedience. Their main emphasis on baptism arose out of this understanding of what the church really is; baptism spelt out initiation into both the privilege and the responsibilities of belonging to the body of Christ.

Discipleship for the early Anabaptists meant following Jesus and, regardless of the cost, trying to obey his teachings simply. This entailed an ethic of love - disallowing all taking of life, providing mutual aid within the community of the church, rejecting oath-taking, forming local congregations as bodies of believers separate from state authority, with a clear obligation to evangelize. This evangelistic calling was helped by persecution which drove the movement both eastwards - eventually into southern Russia - and westwards to the New World.

There are about 700,000 (baptized) Mennonites in the world today, but their influence is far greater than their numbers. For their peace witness they have suffered imprisonment in twentieth-century democracies as much as persecution by the authoritarian rulers of the sixteenth century. Their witness in recent years has seen a remarkable twofold commitment to relief and development work, and to establishing a biblical theology for opposing war in general, and nuclear war in particular.

In the past, many Mennonite communities have tended to withdraw from what they regarded as a fatally sinful society. This is still true of some groups. But since World War II American Mennonites have provided a number of distinguished leaders to the radical discipleship movement which has exercised a prophetic ministry to the church and the world. Writers such as John Yoder, Ronald Sider and Donald Kraybill, as well as the magazine *Sojourners*, have been particularly influential in making the whole Evangelical tradition see how radical biblical faith really is. What is the nature of the church? How does the body of Christ become incarnate in the local community? What political principles are implied in the teaching of Jesus?

Closely related to the Mennonites is the **Church of the Brethren**, numbering almost 200,000 and mainly concentrated in the United States. They arose out of a revival among Lutherans in eighteenth-century Germany and were influenced by local Mennonites. As with so many dissenting groups, persecution led to emigration, and they settled in Pennsylvania, retaining their German speech and ways.

The Church of the Brethren practises believers' baptism and is committed to evangelism - planting churches in Nigeria, Ecuador and India. Its members follow a simple lifestyle and oppose all forms of war and violence, advocating instead positive peace programmes.

See War and Peace

BELIEVERS' CHURCH: THE BAPTISTS

Baptists are first cousins to Mennonites and share with them commitment to the idea of the believers' church. The first Baptists were divided theologically into two groups:

● **General Baptists** were Arminian in their understanding of free will, and were influenced by the Dutch Mennonites in their earlier years.

● **Particular Baptists** were Calvinistic. They mainly emerged

Romanian Baptists join in worship. Baptist communities in Eastern Europe have a recent tradition of heroic witness, often against many odds.

Baptists practise 'believers baptism', and do not agree with baptizing children. Once an adult person has professed faith in Jesus, he or she will be totally immersed in water before the whole congregation as a sign that God cleanses us and gives us new life.

out of the separatist wing of English Puritanism and have proved long-lived.

Growth in the seventeenth century was limited first by persecution and later by sectarianism. Many of the General Baptists adopted unitarian beliefs, and too many of the Particular Baptists succumbed to an over-zealous hyper-Calvinism that stressed God's sovereignty to the point where the call to evangelize was almost totally paralyzed.

Both groups of Baptists were reborn in the Evangelical Awakening of the eighteenth century. A New Connexion of General Baptists was set up in 1770, both orthodox and missionary-minded. And a book by Andrew Fuller, *The Gospel Worthy of All Acceptance* (1785), emphasized for the Particular Baptists the missionary nature of Calvinist theology. Out of this renewal of Baptist life came the Baptist Missionary Society in 1792, which heralded the birth of the modern missionary movement. Initially it received considerable support from the Dutch Mennonites, showing the continuation of the kinship between the two confessional groups. This kinship can still be seen in the USSR, where (admittedly under state constraint) Baptists and Mennonites are united in one denominational organization.

While British Baptist and North American Baptists can trace their roots back to seventeenth-century Puritanism and eighteenth-century Evangelicalism, Baptist

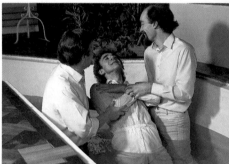

movements in other European countries are more the product of the Revivalism of the nineteenth century. A majority of the European Baptist churches are the fruit of the missionary endeavours of Joseph Oncken's church in Hamburg. Capitalizing on the migration of labour, this enterprising church promoted Baptist churches northward into Scandinavia, eastward along the

Baltic, and southwards into the Balkans, especially among German-speaking peoples.

Baptist strength in the world today is most apparent in North America, where in 1983 there were some 27 million Baptists, of whom 14 million were members of the Southern Baptist Convention while 11 million belonged to the black conventions. The black conventions, as in their most famous spokesman, Martin Luther King, combine warm evangelistic concern with commitment to furthering the civil rights of America's black citizens. Similarly, Billy Graham, a Southern Baptist, has in recent years articulated a more sophisticated appreciation of social problems than many other full-time evangelists, distancing himself from the Moral Majority judgements attractive to the more conservative churches. At the same time he has never hesitated to co-operate with a wide diversity of Christian traditions in his evangelism.

The eighty-year-old Baptist World Alliance, with a membership in 1983 of some 32 million, exists to express the 'essential oneness' of different national groups of Baptists, and to promote programmes of education and evangelism together with a very considerable relief and refugee service.

What are the features that characterize Baptist churches today?
● Baptist churches tend to be more **conservative in theology** than other mainstream denominations.

● Baptists **make their decisions as a congregation**, though one or two small churches have adopted episcopal titles for superintending ministers.
● Baptists stress **the priesthood of all believers** and allow full lay participation in every aspect of the life and work of their churches.
● Throughout their history, Baptists have firmly stressed the **separation of church and state**. They have been committed to the importance of unfettered choice - in matters of religious allegiance, freedom of worship and liberty of conscience. This has made them champions of toleration and campaigners for the protection of human rights.
● Their emphasis on **believers' baptism** wherever in the world they gather, keeps them a missionary and evangelistically-minded family of churches.

Baptists are divided in their attitude to formal ecumenical structures. Less than half of all Baptists are in membership with the World Council of Churches.

UNITY: THE DISCIPLES OF CHRIST
The Disciples (or Churches) of Christ, by contrast, have a special commitment to unity. In the United Kingdom, they had unsuccessful conversations with the Baptists. More recently they sought to express their concern for unity by joining the United Reformed Church, albeit with some dissent. Their roots are among the Scotch Baptists, an eighteenth-century split from the Church of Scotland.

See Churches Together; Evangelicals at a Crossroads

Christian Brethren love the weekly 'breaking of bread' service, in which the simple sharing of bread and wine reminds them of Jesus' death.

At the very beginning of the nineteenth century, Thomas and Alexander Campbell (father and son), took a stand against the exclusiveness of the emerging denominations of their day, and made a bold plea for a return to the primitive unity of the New Testament church. But such was the temper of the times that their efforts simply led to the establishment in 1827 of yet another denomination. Serious in its concern for a high doctrine of the church and sacraments, the Disciples of Christ share with contemporary Baptists a deep suspicion of all credal forms, while remaining deeply committed to the evangelistic power of the gospel story in the Bible. They established their principal strength in North America, with smaller communities in the United Kingdom, Australia and New Zealand.

In 1930 a World Convention of the Churches of Christ was inaugurated with a constitution whose preamble seems to derive from that of the Baptist World Alliance, but with an added commitment to church unity. Their world-wide family strength is approximately 1.3 million. From the days of the Edinburgh Conference of 1910 they have been deeply involved in the ecumenical movement.

IN ALL SIMPLICITY: THE BRETHREN

There were others also at the beginning of the nineteenth century who were disturbed by both the condition and the divisions of the church. Espousing a simple Evangelicalism, they began to hold plain communion services as a means of fellowship across denominational frontiers. But again a concern for unity, in the event, led to an increase in denominational scatter and the **Christian Brethren** emerged. They were also known as the Plymouth Brethren, because of the prominence of that city in their early witness.

In Britain they drew their following both from the Anglican Church and from the different nonconformist denominations. The Brethren soon divided into two groups: the exclusive and the open brethren. Both groups shared a number of attitudes. They were opposed to a separated ministry - although recently something like a ministry has tended to appear, especially on an itinerant basis. They believed that history could be divided into distinct dispensations: law, grace and so on. They also believed that Christ's second coming could not be long delayed. They went for a minimum of structure in the church: they broke bread together weekly; members of the congregation led in prayer and worship; and they practised believers' baptism.

The Brethren are strong in Germany, Switzerland and North America, while their missionary endeavours have taken them to many countries: they are the second largest Protestant group

in Argentina and are numerous in India and Singapore, in Zambia and Zaire, and in New Zealand. They have been very active in non-denominational missions and Evangelical organizations and charities. In recent years the more exclusive Brethren - some of whom have been unpleasantly legalistic - have tended to lose members to other denominations. The more open groups, perhaps now becoming more 'churchy' in the image they project, have given the church some of its most biblically educated lay leaders.

Baptists commonly take communion in an informal way, each taking wine from a separate cup. They do not usually hold this service as often as weekly, but it has great importance for them.

Baptists world-wide

North America	c27 million
USSR	c1 million
India	822,000
Brazil	578,000
Nigeria	386,000
Burma	372,000
Zaire	317,000
UK	220,000
Romania	160,000
Korea	132,000
Philippines	110,000

'My Parish is the World'

HOWARD A. SNYDER

'A Methodist is one who lives according to the method laid down in the Bible.' In words like these, John Wesley stressed life as much as belief. For him, true Christianity was loving God fully, demonstrated by loving one's neighbour as oneself.

Out of Wesley's passion for experimental Christianity lived out in practical holiness has grown a world-wide Methodist community of some 50 million, between 2 and 3 per cent of world Christianity. When the Salvation Army, certain Pentecostal groups and other outgrowths of Methodism are included, the total community with Wesleyan roots totals perhaps 5 per cent of all Christians world-wide.

See Many-sided Christianity

METHODIST BEGINNINGS

Except for a few years in America before his famous Aldersgate experience on 24 May 1738, Wesley ministered almost exclusively in the United Kingdom. But his vision encompassed the world. When Wesley began preaching to large crowds in London and Bristol and was criticized for not staying in one parish, he said, 'I look upon all the world as my parish.' Perhaps no phrase better captures the spirit of Methodism than 'the world parish'.

Wesley's blend of Anglican spirituality and evangelical fervour led to an especially fruitful stress on God's 'preventing, justifying, and sanctifying grace'. God's grace is 'prevenient'; that is, it 'comes before' any human response. Through Jesus Christ God's grace has been unconditionally spread throughout the whole creation and to all persons. No one is totally outside God's grace. Anyone may respond, be converted, and by grace live a life pleasing to God and full of good works. This strain in Wesley's thought and action, which has been called his 'optimism of grace', was the spring for both evangelism and social reform - and it still marks Methodism.

Methodism arose as a renewal movement within the Church of England. But the movement soon spread beyond Anglicanism, partly because from the beginning Methodist evangelists reached the poorer, working people who were often totally unchurched. Nominally Anglican, most early Methodists in fact knew no other church or tradition than Methodism itself.

From the beginning, the genius of Methodism was not merely popular evangelism but also the mixture of close-knit community based on cell groups, preaching services, quarterly love feasts, and a growing corps of travelling lay preachers. Close community was key: 'We introduce Christian fellowship,' said Wesley, 'where it was utterly destroyed.' Through open-air preaching tens of thousands heard the gospel, but the glue of Methodism was the system of societies and smaller groups adapted by Wesley from Anglican and Moravian precedents.

These patterns provided the foundation for rapid growth. By the time Wesley died in 1791, Methodists numbered 72,000 in Great Britain and Ireland.

THE METHODIST EXPLOSION

With the death of the Wesleys and Methodism's subsequent separation from the Church of England, Methodists were in a sense orphaned. Under John Wesley Methodism was a renewal movement; an 'evangelical order' within the larger Anglican Church. What did it mean now to be a separate denomination? Methodists had to face some tough questions about what they believed and how Methodism should be run. Without Wesley's dominant authority, quarrels over these questions provoked several splits. In recent years many of these splits have been healed. Most smaller British Methodist groups combined in 1907 to form the United Methodist Church. This in turn merged with the Wesleyan and Primitive Methodist branches in 1932 to form the Methodist Church of Great Britain and Ireland, with a combined membership of over 800,000. Similarly, the major Methodist groups in the United States reunited in 1939, forming

Methodists have always loved singing hymns, right from the days of John and Charles Wesley, who wrote Christian words to popular tunes of their day which are still sung with fervour in ours.

Like many other Christians round the world, Methodists use all means to worship God. The African dancing is accompanied on a kudu horn, and the Indian soloist is singing in the Malayalam language.

what is now the United Methodist Church (4.5 million strong at the time of merger, now 9.5 million), though there are a number of other Methodist churches in the States including some very sizeable black denominations.

A missionary movement at heart, Methodism quickly spread throughout the world. By Wesley's death there were some 57,000 Methodists in North America. The circuit-riding

Francis Asbury was, until his death in 1816, the chief apostle and evangelist of American Methodism, assisted ably by a growing army of preachers and class leaders.

Methodism grew phenomenally in North America. Its system of circuit riders, societies, class meetings and class leaders were well-suited to the expanding frontier. Methodism exploded from 15,000 in 1784 to 1.5 million by 1855. For the next century, Methodists constituted the largest Protestant communion in the United States, peaking at about 13 million before beginning to decline in the mid-1960s.

INTO THE WORLD PARISH

It is a striking fact that Methodists began sending missionaries to other parts of the world long before the formation of the major Protestant missionary societies in Britain and North America. A key figure in the rise of Methodist missions was the Oxford-educated Thomas Coke (1747-1814). Coke launched Methodist work in the West Indies and Sierra Leone and died while travelling to India. Other Methodist work extended from Great Britain and North America to Africa, Australia, New Zealand, the Pacific islands, Mexico, South America, China, the Philippines, South-east Asia, and elsewhere. Many daughter churches in their turn sent missionaries, carrying Methodism to other countries.

By the late twentieth century most Methodist bodies were loosely united in the World Methodist Council. In several countries, Methodists have

merged into united churches (notably in Australia, Canada, Japan, and south India), but some of these still maintain association with the World Methodist Council.

WHAT IS METHODISM TODAY?

Methodism contains great diversity, but Methodists are held together by a number of things which they have in common.

● **Leadership in the church**. Most Methodist bodies have a system of bishops - although their authority is constitutionally limited and shared with lay representatives. From the beginning, Methodism has made extensive use of lay leaders, both men and women. Wesley involved at least one in ten of the early Methodists in significant leadership. But when Methodism became a separate denomination and lay preachers were ordained, the role of the ordinary member was significantly diminished. In many places, however, Methodism continues to employ local preachers and enlist other forms of lay leadership.

● **Running the church**. Wesley felt that church organization must play second fiddle to the greater aim that the church be God's missionary force in the world. He said that 'The end of all ecclesiastical order is to bring souls from the power of Satan to God, and to build them up in his fear and love.'

Methodists have generally maintained this attitude, changing the structure to meet changing needs. But like other groups, they have sometimes become prisoners to traditions which have outlived their usefulness.

This more relaxed approach to church structure can be seen in the variety of Methodist worship. This may vary from the highly liturgical and sacramental, as in some parts of British Methodism, to the very informal, as in some of the more revivalistic Methodist sects and in some of the newer mission churches. Methodists still use many of Charles Wesley's hymns, which embrace much of his brother's theology, as well as the wider tradition of Christian hymns, together with newer songs and choruses.

● **Belief and living**. Because Methodism first arose within the Anglican Church, Wesley did not develop a doctrinal statement for Methodists. Instead, he affirmed the Anglican Thirty-nine Articles, and designated his sermons and published notes on the New Testament as the doctrinal standard for Methodism.

Wesley's concern was with practical Christian living - and this still marks Methodism. This concern has taken very different forms. The more evangelical strains of Methodism continue to stress the need to be 'born again' and to live a life of practical holiness. A number of Methodist groups still maintain Wesley's emphasis on 'entire sanctification' (living free from wilful sin), though this emphasis has been modified in some areas by revivalistic, Pentecostal and Charismatic influences.

● **A social conscience**. Methodism's focus on the present as well as the future life has

Methodist missions reach beyond evangelism to care for the whole person, including health care.

especially in the homelands of Britain and the United States.

World Methodism, with a century and more of tradition, is in many places a branch of the church awaiting renewal. The renewal of the older Methodist bodies may come from contact with newer, more dynamic Methodist groups. But if present patterns continue, Methodism world-wide will show only modest gains, as significant growth in some areas is offset by losses elsewhere.

With the memory of the evangelical revival and Wesley's world parish still part of her experience, Methodism remains a significant part of the Christian presence in the world and as soil for potential renewal in the years to come.

often found expression in a strong concern for social justice. Wesley himself was an ardent foe of slavery, and though the slavery issue split American Methodism for many decades, many Methodists today oppose injustice and oppression in the world.

● **The world parish**. Methodists continue to have a strong sense of a world parish. Methodists identify themselves as part of Methodism world-wide, and as part of the universal Christian church. The universality of the gospel message continues to be a strong theme in Methodism.

LOOKING TO THE FUTURE
Methodism has not grown over the last century as vigorously as it did in its first century. Today the church is seeing exciting growth in the areas where it is new, and a slow decline in the more established areas -

HOW MANY METHODISTS?
Today Methodism has taken root in nearly 100 countries of the world. Membership numbers about 20 million, with a total community of some 50 million. Approximately 80 per cent of all Methodists are in eight countries.

United States	13,755,000
United Kingdom	960,000
India	750,000
South Africa	532,000
South Korea	435,000
Zimbabwe	187,000
Philippines	171,000
Chile	164,000

A good many Methodists can also be found in Zaire, Mozambique, Australia, New Zealand and Brazil.

Children of the Twentieth Century
RUSSELL P. SPITTLER

Weird Babel of Tongues. New Sect of Fanatics is Breaking Loose. Wild Scene Last Night on Azusa Street. Gurgle of Wordless Talk by a Sister. Such were the headlines that greeted readers of the *Los Angeles Daily Times* on Wednesday morning, 18 April 1906. They described a religious revival underway in the city marked by an outbreak of 'speaking in tongues', a recurrence of a biblical phenomenon in which devotees use unlearned languages or religiously ecstatic speech in praise or prayer to God.

This famed revival meeting continued unabated for more than three years at 312 Azusa Street, in a building reconverted to church use after a period when it housed a livery stable. Thereafter the Azusa Street mission was maintained by urban blacks. In future years, Pentecostals would not again fully recover the interracial character of their origin.

But the Azusa Street meeting was not the first modern incident. In the Welsh revival of 1904, tongues had occurred in meetings held by Evan Roberts. Before that, in 1832, British Presbyterian minister Edward Irving (not himself a tongues-speaker) was defrocked as a Presbyterian minister when such phenomena came to characterize his services.

A LIVING EXPLOSION
Today, Pentecostal believers in over 1,200 of their own denominations number, world-wide, in excess of 51 million. When the newer Charismatics are added (more recent users of the charismatic gifts who, unlike the classical Pentecostals, have not left their mainline churches) the total exceeds 100 million.

These statistics are difficult to comprehend. With no more than a handful of identifiable adherents at the opening of the twentieth century, Pentecostal Christians within three generations have become the largest sector of Protestantism. And in the mid-1980s, close to 10 per cent of the world's Roman Catholics can be identified as Catholic Pentecostals.

The truly striking growth of Pentecostalism has been in the Third World. The three largest churches in the world are Third World Pentecostal churches. The Full Gospel Central Church in Seoul, Korea, records its members at 410,000. Sixteen thousand cell groups meet on Thursday evenings. The Jotabece Church in Santiago, Chile,

See Renewal in the Holy Spirit

numbers 80,000 members. With 16,000 seats it is the largest church structure in the world. It owns and blends into the mother church some fifty-nine 'temples' located throughout the city of Santiago. The parent denomination of this church, the Methodist-Pentecostal Church, claims above 10 per cent of the population of Chile. Congregacao Crista in Sao Paolo, Brazil, reckons its membership at over 61,000.

THE PENTECOSTAL CHARACTER

Setting aside occasional peculiar features of indigenous Third

World Pentecostal groups, the beliefs and practices of Pentecostals clearly resemble those of Evangelicals. They are a part of the Evangelical movement. They believe in the inspiration of Scripture; a trinitarian Godhead (an important exception will be mentioned later); the virgin birth, sinless life, redeeming death, bodily resurrection, and heavenly ascension of Christ – whom also they expect to return at any moment.

But the distinctive doctrine of Pentecostals is their belief in the 'baptism of the Holy Spirit', an

Many black churches are Pentecostal in style. These New Testament Church of God worshippers belong to one of the fastest-growing denominations in Britain; already it is among the largest.

individual experience of God said to enhance and empower the Christian life. Many Pentecostals believe that speaking in tongues is the 'initial physical evidence' of that divine encounter. Though held by nearly all North American Pentecostals, the initial evidence doctrine is not shared by Elim Pentecostals in Britain, the Mülheim-Ruhr group in Germany, nor by the Methodist-Pentecostal Church in Chile.

Pentecostals are often considered to be fundamentalists in theology and lifestyle, but the two movements should not be confused. Both arose in protest to nineteenth-century theological liberalism. Fundamentalism at first represented a corrective theological and apologetic thrust (it later decayed into a negative, pamphleteering and protectionist group). Pentecostalism, on the other hand, located its response in personal religious experience.

This is why Pentecostalism characteristically reflects an anti-intellectual stance. No acknowledged Pentecostal theologian has yet emerged after three generations. Roman Catholic Charismatics, however, who have a rich academic tradition, produced within a decade substantial Charismatic theology. Twice in its constitutional documents one major Pentecostal denomination states, 'No certain amount of education shall ever be required of candidates for the ministry.'

Neither scholarship nor traditional theological education mark the movement. But evangelism and mission efforts do. The Full Gospel Central Church of Seoul has sent missionaries to America, Brazil, Canada, Sweden, and West Germany. Latin American Pentecostalism, which vies with the Roman Catholic Church as the leading religious force on the continent, was largely the consequence of work by missionaries from Europe.

In one type of education Pentecostals do excel: short-term, indigenous Bible schools whose single aim is the rapid preparation of native evangelists and pastors to reach their own people. The rapid global growth of Pentecostalism can partly be explained by the way that missionaries work themselves out of their jobs by training nationals as superior replacements.

WHO'S WHO IN PENTECOSTALISM?

As in any extended family, Pentecostalism includes a wide variety of characters among its different denominations.

● **Wesleyan Pentecostals** Early Pentecostals shared with the Holiness churches (which were dominantly of Methodist origin) a quest for religious fulfilment within personal experience. What Charles Wesley called 'perfect love', came to be termed 'the baptism of the Holy Spirit' among nineteenth-century Methodist daughter churches.

Pentecostalism probably came into being through the merging of this longing for baptism in the Holy Spirit with the phenomenon of speaking in other tongues. Pentecostals also showed a renewed interest in the other

See Evangelicals at a Crossroads; Training the Whole Ministry; 'My Parish is the World'

CHRISTIANS NORTH AND SOUTH

❝ At the beginning of the twentieth century, Christianity was a faith mainly of the northern hemisphere. This is no longer true. During the 1980's Christians in the South will become more numerous than those in the North. ❞

Figures are in millions. They are as people would respond on a census form.

NORTH 1980 SOUTH

East Asia **19**

South Asia **109**

Africa **203**

Europe **416**

USSR **97**

Latin America **349**

Australia and the Pacific **20**

N America **220**

Total 733 700

NORTH 1900 SOUTH

Europe **278**

USSR **105**

N. America **79**

East Asia **2**
South Asia **17**
Africa **10**

Latin America **62**

Australia and the Pacific **5**

Total 462 96

'spiritual gifts' of biblical times – most notably vernacular prophecy and prayer for physical healing.

The oldest variety of Pentecostals can therefore be called Wesleyan Pentecostals. They taught three crisis experiences: conversion, sanctification (understood variously in a Wesleyan sense as removal of radical sin or at least as elevation to the possibility of sinless behaviour), and the empowering baptism in the Holy Spirit.

One American Holiness church which began in the 1890s, for example, was known as The Holiness Church. It absorbed completely the Pentecostal teaching and changed its name to The Pentecostal Holiness Church in 1909. By way of contrast, another major Wesleyan offshoot in 1919 dropped the term 'Pentecostal' from its denominational name and became known thereafter as The Church of the Nazarene. It did this to avoid being confused with the emerging tongues-speaking churches.

● **Baptistic Pentecostals** Other early Pentecostals who stemmed more directly from the Reformed churches were less inclined to pursue personal perfection. For them, the baptism in the Holy Spirit became not a third but a second Christian experience. They believed that this experience had two sides – it enhanced personal holiness and deepened spirituality.

Sometimes called 'baptistic Pentecostals' because their beliefs are similar to Baptists, this offshoot of the family is the largest grouping of Pentecostals. Included are such groups as the Elim Pentecostal Church in the United Kingdom, the Assemblies of God, the Congregacao Crista in Brazil, the movement associated with Nicholas Bhengu in Africa, and the International Church of the Foursquare Gospel.

● **Oneness Pentecostals** During a 1913 Pentecostal camp meeting near Los Angeles, one Pentecostal brother claimed a revelation. Father, Son, and Spirit were merely divine titles: the name of God is Jesus. Out of this incident emerged the non-trinitarian, Jesus-Name Pentecostals, sometimes called Oneness Pentecostals by outsiders. Though ostracized by

their trinitarian brothers and sisters, Jesus-Name Pentecostals flourish within Black Pentecostalism. They dominate Indonesian Pentecostalism, and constitute nearly 10 per cent of all Pentecostals, world-wide. The largest Jesus-Name group is the United Pentecostal Church International.

● **Pentecostal Apostolics** Still another species of Pentecostals affirms the continuing validity of apostolic offices. They identify apostles, prophets and other leaders. There are just short of 4.5 million such Pentecostal apostolics world-wide today.

● **Indigenous Pentecostals** often reflect features of their culture or their founder, or both. The emergence in developing

There is something infectious about the spontaneous worship characteristic of Pentecostals. This crowd meeting near the Sydney opera house raise their hands in a gesture of openness to God.

cultures of such groups, which tend to be highly independent and unrelated to ecclesiastical affairs, accounts for much of the growth of modern Pentecostalism. As with most traditions, extreme forms emerge. There are snake-handling Pentecostals in Appalachian America.

STRENGTHS AND WEAKNESSES

Pentecostals are rightly famous for the vitality of their religious commitment. The high value they place on religious experience makes religion for them an individual, lively and joyous affair. They are people who clearly enjoy their God.

The 'laying on of hands' is practised by Pentecostals and Charismatics in many different cirumstances. Here an Assemblies of God pastor lays his hands on Christians who want to dedicate themselves to particular service for God. But he will do the same as he prays for people to be healed, for example, or to receive the Holy Spirit.

While they are no advocates of a purely social gospel, Pentecostals have made notable applications of the Christian gospel to social ills. An orphanage in Assiut, Egypt. A hospital in New Delhi. A leprosarium in the African interior. Teen-Challenge for ex-drug addicts in Brooklyn. An Hispanic chaplain at a horse-race track in California. A crippled children's work in Germany.

Pentecostals are also innovative in their evangelistic methods. They make use of the printing press. The Assemblies of God church in Springfield, Missouri, mails nineteen tons of religious literature each working day; postal employees report to work on the premises. From Brussels, thousands of correspondence course enrolments are dispensed to hundreds of nations. Televangelism, in America at least, is dominated by Pentecostals and Charismatics. Of the eleven leading American televangelists, six offer distinctly Pentecostal approaches (Jim Bakker, Ken Copeland, Rex Humbard, Oral Roberts, Pat Robertson and Jimmy Swaggart).

But weaknesses can be identified, too. The distaste for anything academic has opened the movement to curious theological beliefs. Claims to high spiritual status all too easily yield an elitist mentality. And tensions have been created with fellow-evangelicals when lofty spiritual experiences are recounted in ways which appear to give second place to all other Christians. With growth and age come institutionalization, a rising interest in self-perpetuation, and a dulling of originally noble spiritual goals. These challenges are being met with varying levels of success by the various Pentecostal bodies.

What future awaits the Pentecostal movement? More growth, assuredly – especially in the Third World. In the West, the Pentecostal churches will be challenged (on a local level if not officially) toward greater co-operation in ecumenical affairs. They also face the task of maintaining vibrant faith in the face of creeping bureaucracy. If greater theological sophistication can be gained, Third World Pentecostals might be spared a repetition of earlier mistakes that may arise from a syncretistic encounter with their cultures.

See The Electronic Church

The Pentecostalism that faces these challenges has come a long way since its beginnings in Los Angeles. David du Plessis, roving Pentecostal ambassador, was once asked to evaluate a report which identified Roman Catholics and Pentecostals as the two greatest threats to the mainline established Protestant Church. His simple comment was, 'They are.'

CHRISTIANS WORLD-WIDE

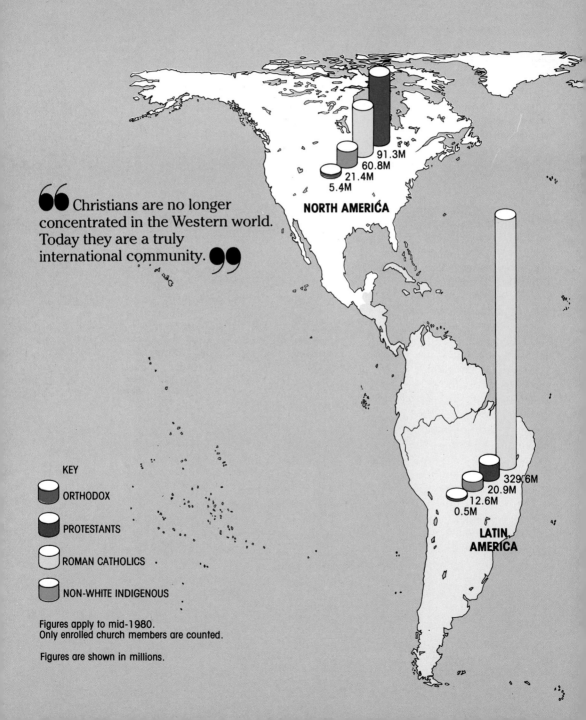

66 Christians are no longer concentrated in the Western world. Today they are a truly international community. **99**

NORTH AMERICA

91.3M
60.8M
21.4M
5.4M

329.6M
20.9M
12.6M
0.5M

LATIN AMERICA

KEY

ORTHODOX

PROTESTANTS

ROMAN CATHOLICS

NON-WHITE INDIGENOUS

Figures apply to mid-1980.
Only enrolled church members are counted.

Figures are shown in millions.

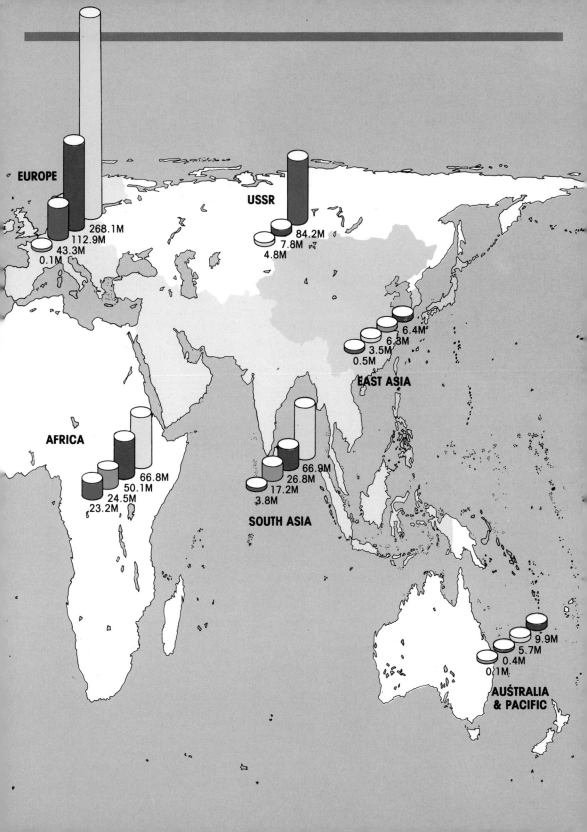

EUROPE
268.1M
112.9M
43.3M
0.1M

USSR
84.2M
7.8M
4.8M

EAST ASIA
6.4M
6.8M
3.5M
0.5M

AFRICA
66.8M
50.1M
24.5M
23.2M

SOUTH ASIA
66.9M
26.8M
17.2M
3.8M

AUSTRALIA
& PACIFIC
9.9M
5.7M
0.4M
0.1M

The Anglican Communion
DONALD COGGAN

It may seem strange that there should be 'Anglican' Christians, with all the overtones of English-ness, in every continent of our modern world. Strange but true. In fact non-Western Anglicans now outnumber those of Western origin, and the Anglican Communion is a truly international family.

The Anglican Communion is a fellowship - within the one, holy, catholic and apostolic church - of those dioceses, provinces or regional churches in communion with each other and with the See of Canterbury.

It is wide-ranging, doctrinally as well as geographically, but yet there are certain beliefs which unite Anglicans. The so-called Lambeth Quadrilateral, set out at the Lambeth Conference of 1888, defines these as:

● **The Holy Scriptures** of the Old and New Testaments, as 'containing all things necessary to salvation'. The Bible is the rule and ultimate standard of faith.

● **The Apostles' Creed**, as the baptismal symbol; and **the Nicene Creed**, as the sufficient statement of the Christian faith.

● The two sacraments ordained by Christ himself - **baptism and the Lord's Supper** - ministered with unfailing use of Christ's words of institution, and of the elements of water and of bread and wine which he ordained.

● **The historic episcopate**, that is, the line of bishops in a carefully maintained succession. The way these bishops carry out their task of oversight and leadership varies according to the varying needs of the nations and peoples God has called them to serve.

There are some twenty-seven provinces within the Anglican Communion, each recognizing a common history deriving from the Church of England. They hold a common tradition of doctrine, discipline and worship; and they are conscious of a shared responsibility for their missionary task. Independent yet interdependent, the provinces owe allegiance to the See of Canterbury, whose archbishop is acknowledged as 'first among equals'. He it is who presides over the Lambeth Conference of bishops (so called because his residence is at Lambeth Palace in London). The first such conference was held in 1867, and conferences have since been held at roughly ten-year intervals, the most recent being a residential one at Canterbury in 1978.

UNITY IN DIVERSITY
It might be thought that, in so far-flung a Communion, the danger of division would be great. But in fact a number of forces work to hold this diverse

Opposite Canterbury in England is the historic centre of the Anglican Communion. This procession in Canterbury Cathedral was part of the enthronement ceremony when Donald Coggan was made archbishop in 1975.

fellowship together. The holding of the Lambeth Conference is one such factor, which also helps to cement an unwritten but none the less real loyalty to Canterbury. The *Book of Common Prayer* has long been another - though now in many different translations and with a wide variety of alternative services, its impact and influence still underlies most Anglican worship. And there are now a number of structural bonds. The Anglican Consultative Council (formed in 1971), with a small staff headed by a Secretary General, now meets once every two or three years in different parts of the world. Still more recently, the 'primates' (or heads) of the member-churches of the Communion have started meeting every two or three years, to help plan the agenda for meetings of the Anglican Consultative Council and the Lambeth Conference, and to consult together on how to implement the Council's recommendations. In addition, a Theological and Doctrinal Commission has recently been formed, consisting of fourteen theologians from different parts of the world, who meet together every two years.

The history of the Church in England goes back long before 597 when Pope Gregory the Great sent Augustine and his company of monks to Canterbury. It is known that there were three British bishops at the Synod of Arles in 314, and Bishop Stephen Neill opens his book *Anglicanism* with the sentence: 'No man knows when the Gospel

Anglican churches are particularly lively in many English-speaking parts of Africa, with strong congregations and diocesan training programmes. More Anglicans now are non-white than white.

immense in extent); and the flock was tended. With the growth of the missionary movement - roughly from the beginning of the nineteenth century onwards - great missionary societies were set up, such as the Church Missionary Society and the United Society for the Propagation of the Gospel. The missionary work of the Anglican Communion has seen the birth of a network of provinces and dioceses from the Arctic to the Equator. Over the generations, and now with increasing rapidity, the leadership of these national churches has passed from English hands and become the full responsibility of national Christians.

RAPID GROWTH

In recent decades the church in the West has felt the chill winds of materialism and, in many parts, has declined in numbers. This is not wholly to be regretted, for the wheat has been sifted from the chaff and the active members of the church have been more easily distinguished from the purely nominal. Such times have been - and are - times of severe testing. In other parts of the world, however, Anglicans have shared in the world-wide Christian growth which has been so rapid as to prove almost embarrassing. Who is to care for the welfare of the tens of thousands pressing for baptism? This is particularly true of Africa and South America. The late twentieth century is proving to be an exciting and challenging period of missionary expansion.

of Jesus Christ was first preached in the British Islands; but there is reason to think that no long period elapsed between the Resurrection and the origins of the Church in England.'

The Church of England claims, uniquely among those churches reformed in the sixteenth century, to have an unbroken continuity with its origins in the Holy Catholic Church. It therefore holds together the Catholic and Reformed elements of Christianity as very few other churches can.

In more recent times this Church of England has provided the nucleus for a world-wide fellowship, now estimated at some 65 million people. As the British Empire spread throughout the world, it was natural that English men and women should look for the episcopal government and the pastoral care to which they had been accustomed in the old country. So bishops were provided; dioceses were formed (often

This growth in the Anglican Communion throughout the world becomes apparent in the Lambeth Conferences: seventy-six bishops attended the first in 1867, 440 came to the most recent one held in the University of Kent in 1978. Whereas the first conference lasted for four days, they needed three weeks to deal with the agenda in 1978.

Membership of the Lambeth Conference is confined to bishops, but elsewhere clergy and laity (men and women) play a full part in the government and life of the church. They take a central role in such gatherings as the Anglican Consultative Council, in the Commissions which are appointed from time to time, and in the Partners in Mission consultations, when groups from all round the Communion visit a particular diocese to help evaluate its life and mission. There has been a renewed insight into the meaning of the people of God, and of lay Christians as the major part of that people. This has led to lay people sharing increasingly in worship, in teaching and in organization. And alongside this, of course, the clergy have had to set a new emphasis on enabling, equipping and instructing all gifted Christians to fulfil these tasks.

It has not always been so. Anglicans have long had a pronounced tendency to leave it all to the vicar, a weakness that still persists in some places. Synodical government - the full participation of the laity along with the bishops and clergy in the government of the church -

has in some quarters only recently become a reality. The Anglican Communion owes much to the insight and determination of George Augustus Selwyn in this regard. He became Bishop of Lichfield in 1868, after twenty-five years as bishop in New Zealand. In both hemispheres he introduced into the life of the church true synodical government. Selwyn held two vital doctrines in balance: the bishop's authority in the church, and also the character of that church as what the New Testament calls the *laos*, the whole people of God. Since his time this balance has become more and more a sign of authentic Anglicanism. True synodical government has come to stay.

A COMPREHENSIVE CHURCH

At its best - this is its ideal - the Anglican ethos seeks to hold within itself the distinctive emphases of what our forefathers rather inaccurately called High, Low and Broad churchmanship. To spell that out a little, it tries to hold together the more Catholic tradition, concerned for historic continuity and liturgical ritual; the Evangelical emphasis on the Bible, on evangelism and personal conversion; and the more liberal openness to new truth and fresh revelation. To hold these distinctive emphases together is necessarily to be involved in tension and sometimes in controversy. But when Anglicanism is functioning at its best these tensions can be creative; they can give an

'We need to be the kind of church which tries to understand and obey the word of God for both rich and poor...The Church is one of the few bridges which can reach across to different sides of our polarized community. It is part of our reconciling task to help different groups to listen to what the others perceive to be happening.' Bishop David Sheppard

See Decline of Faith?

Alongside the practice of infant baptism, in Anglican and Catholic churches, there is the rite of confirmation. In this service candidates publicly confirm their own Christian faith, and a bishop prays that the Holy Spirit will strengthen this faith. Confirmation is the gateway to full membership of these churches.

See The Unity Movement; Renewal in the Holy Spirit

impetus to discovering new truth and fresh depth of meaning in ancient traditions.

This very comprehensiveness gives the Anglican Communion a particular concern for the unity of the whole of Christ's church. It tries to stretch out its hands to such ancient and historic churches as those of Rome and the Orthodox, and simultaneously looks for creative relationships with the churches of the reformed tradition. Its uniqueness as a fellowship both Catholic and Reformed has led it into deep theological conversations with the Roman Catholics, and also local schemes in which Christians of many persuasions combine for joint worship and social co-operation at the grassroots level.

The Charismatic movement has deeply affected the churches of the Anglican Communion in many parts of the world, and one of its results has been to lower the barriers which previously held the followers of the particular tradition apart from one another. The effects of that movement have yet fully to be felt. The revival of religious Orders in Anglicanism and the creation of religious communities have also been a feature of recent years. This has helped to bring about a unity of spirituality and of prayer which overrides differences of churchmanship. It is to be hoped that the coming few years will see such influences strengthening the Anglican Communion in its role as a promoter of Christian unity.

Churches Together
LESSLIE NEWBIGIN

During most of the history of the church divisions among Christians have created breaches which remain unhealed to this day. The twentieth century has witnessed a remarkable reversal, a sustained effort to bring divided churches into unity. Today approximately 20 million Christians are members of churches formed by the union of bodies previously divided by confessional barriers.

And this is not even a fully inclusive figure. It does not include the many churches formed by the reunion of bodies belonging to the same confessional families which had - for various reasons - become divided. This would apply to the Church of Scotland, for example, which was reunited in 1929. In the USA the United Methodist Church came together in 1939, and later broadened to include the United Brethren in 1968. And the Presbyterian Church USA reunited as recently as 1983.

The main factor in promoting unity across old confessional boundaries has been what Dr Visser t'Hooft called 'the pressure of our common calling' as experienced by churches in a missionary situation, especially on new frontiers (as in Canada), or meeting the ancient religious cultures of Asia. The biblical mandate most often appealed to has been the prayer of our Lord 'that they may all be one... that the world may believe'.

Sometimes the pressure to unite has been initiated or increased by the actions of secular governments. The union of Lutheran and Reformed chuches in Prussia (1817) was the result of such pressure, even though there was influential support from theologians. The churches in Japan had already achieved a measure of unity between the denominations before the imperial government in 1940 enforced the merger of Protestant churches to form the United Church of Japan (Kyodan). Similarly, although the former Congo Protestant Council transformed itself into the Church of Christ in Zaire in 1970 because of government pressure, this was in line with a commitment they already had to unite.

These cases of secular pressure are, however, the exception rather than the rule. The great majority of unions between denominations have been entered into in the belief that this was an act of obedience to the revealed intention of the church's Lord.

DIFFERENT WAYS OF UNITING

United churches do not conform to any one type; there is a wide spectrum of models:

● **Complete organic union** in which the old confessional names are simply forgotten;
● **Loose federations** in which old denominational structures continue intact but work together, as in Zaire;
● **Churches retain their identities** but function together as a single entity for certain purposes (as with the old provincial churches of Germany).

See the Unity Movement

Space does not allow us to describe each of the thirty or more united churches which are in touch with the World Council of Churches, but a few examples will illustrate the variety of types:
● The largest group of members is in **the United Churches of Germany (East and West)** consisting of distinct regional churches within which local congregations can be confessionally Lutheran, Reformed or United.
● A large number of united churches combine **Reformed (Presbyterian and Congregational), Methodist and other Protestant traditions**.
● In the United Kingdom, unions in 1972 and 1981 brought into being **the United Reformed Church in the UK**, including Congregational, Presbyterian and Churches of Christ traditions.
● In the USA **the United Church of Christ** has brought together Christians of Evangelical, Reformed and Congregational traditions through unions in 1934 and 1959.

We may end the list by mentioning the smallest of all the united churches, that which brings together twenty or thirty Lutheran and Reformed Christians as they seek to bear witness in the difficult environment of south Arabia.

Only in the Indian subcontinent has the movement for unity brought Anglicans into full union with other heirs of the Reformation. The Church of South India (1947) and the Churches of North India and Pakistan (1970) embrace Anglican, Methodist and Reformed traditions, the last two including also Disciples (Churches of Christ) and smaller numbers of Baptists and Lutherans. (The creation of Bangladesh as a separate state in 1975 meant that the single Diocese of Dacca in the Church of Pakistan became the autonomous Church of Bangladesh.)

It will be obvious that these united churches are immensely diverse in background and experience, but they have also much in common. They have steadily refused to form a global organization analogous to the eighteen globally-organized 'Christian World Communions', since to become merely another denomination would contradict the purpose of their being. They have, however, held occasional consultations (1967, 1970, 1975, 1981) to share their experience and to take counsel together on common problems and opportunities. The reports of these meetings give some indication of both their strengths and their weaknesses.

DYING TO LIVE

The experience of union has, in the words of the 1981 consultation, 'forced the churches to open themselves to change and renewal'. The experience of union 'does mean a kind of death which threatens the denominational identity of its members, but it is dying to receive a fuller life. That is, literally, the crux of the matter' (*Faith and Order Paper 118*). Moreover 'united churches have been freed through their union to respond more directly to their national and cultural contexts'. United Churches in the Third World, while having their main international contacts through the World Council of Churches, can still retain their relationships with the globally-organized world confessional bodies. But they are generally grateful to be relieved of the pressures which can arise from the fact that these bodies have their power-centres in the First World.

The representatives of the united churches affirm that 'the very act of union has, in a number of cases, enabled churches to be more outward-looking, more conscious of their mission to the countries of their birth, and better able to undertake mission beyond their own borders'.

In its opening paragraph, the South India 'Basis of Union' states a test of all local schemes of union. It is that they should express locally the principle of the great catholic unity of the body of Christ. The leaders of the united churches are aware that they are far from meeting that

In the 'Cathedral of Reconciliation' at Taizé in France, young people of many denominations and of none meet to pray and to grow in understanding each other and God. They come for limited periods from many countries, in the hope of re-discovering the spiritual dimension of life.

THE ACHIEVEMENT OF UNITY

66 Quite a number of 'united' churches have come into being this century, reversing centuries of division. Most have involved Methodist, Presbyterian, Congregational and other Protestant churches, but in India and Pakistan Anglicans also were included and in Germany Lutherans and Reformed have come together. Roman Catholics and Orthodox have not yet joined in union schemes. 99

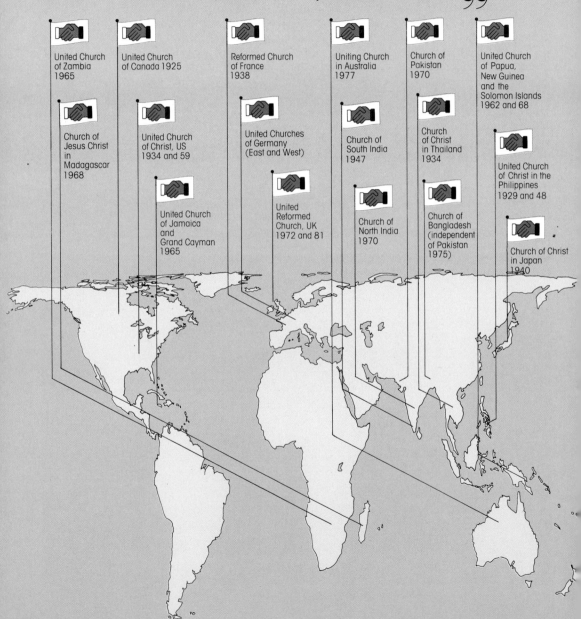

United Church of Zambia 1965

United Church of Canada 1925

Reformed Church of France 1938

Uniting Church in Australia 1977

Church of Pakistan 1970

United Church of Papua, New Guinea and the Solomon Islands 1962 and 68

Church of Jesus Christ in Madagascar 1968

United Church of Christ, US 1934 and 59

United Churches of Germany (East and West)

Church of South India 1947

Church of Christ in Thailand 1934

United Church of Christ in the Philippines 1929 and 48

United Church of Jamaica and Grand Cayman 1965

United Reformed Church, UK 1972 and 81

Church of North India 1970

Church of Bangladesh (independent of Pakistan 1975)

Church of Christ in Japan 1940

test. Roman Catholic and Orthodox churches have not been involved, although the Churches of North and South India are in very intimate relation with the Mar Thoma Syrian Church. The united churches acknowledge that they need to keep a dialogue going with the Christian World Communions so that their catholicity may not be distorted by excessive concentration on local issues.

The act of union by no means eliminates sin, and united churches continue to be plagued by the evils which always threaten the integrity of the church. Sadly the life of the united churches of the Indian subcontinent has been marred by the zest for going to law which infects other Christian bodies in India. This has been given many openings by failure to deal adequately in advance with all the legal and property issues which are involved in the union of churches.

Yet the acknowledged evils which corrupt the life of united churches are those which are common to all churches. They do not arise from any reopening of the old wounds. The evidence is that, even where there are vigorous disagreements, mutual commitment to a shared life in Christ has not been in question. It is the general testimony of the united churches that human sin has not destroyed the blessing which followed the act of union, an act of obedience to the clearly expressed will of the Lord.

The movement for unity continues, and at the time of writing (1984) about a dozen union negotiations are in progress. The twentieth century has been, in effect, the first century of Christian reunion. It will not be the last.

1.3 CHRISTIANS ON THE MOVE

Tomorrow's Church Today
BRIAN C. STILLER

Anywhere you walk you will see them: on the crowded streets of Hong Kong, jungle paths of central Africa, sun-scorched beaches of Australia, congested sprawls of Mexico City, night spots of Europe, and university halls of countries all around the world. Young people. Some are ignored, some are politicized, while others are just wooed for their money.

As this planet pushes to a population of almost 5,000 million, young people are influenced by the many changes in society. Hunger, poverty, militarism, consumerism, nationalism and materialism define and darken the boundaries of their world. One fifth of the world is aged between thirteen and twenty-three. For many of them, the adult world has come too quickly. Their idealism has been tarnished by the reality of a changing world.

And they are caught in the middle. Like generations before them, they find refuge in conformity. But this time it is world-wide. Regardless of ideology, tribal instincts, economic theories, political rhetoric or religious ideals, a world youth culture is forming. The symbols of this youth culture can be seen from Holland to Irian Jaya. Radios pump out common themes and styles as music fills the air in a Chinese village or a Canadian disco. Denim jeans, rock stars and sports heroes are part of the mystique as today's young people dream their dreams.

During Jesus' youth, Greek culture pervaded the Mediterranean world. Today's dominant world culture is Western. A common bond has been formed between young people of various cultures, helped in many places by economic prosperity and almost everywhere by the music and film industry. Sophisticated marketing has shaped the ideas of fun, pleasure and success. Clothes, records and video have become the bread and wine of the god of today's youth: materialism. The high priests are the stars of the record and film industry. Old cultures, striving vainly to hold on to their traditions, are often no match for the power of Western youth culture.

Many people today, young and old, want to make a new start. Christians are often not content simply to repeat the patterns of previous generations. They want to explore different ways of living out their faith.

WHAT DO YOUNG PEOPLE BELIEVE?

What are the elements that make up modern youth culture? What forces shape the minds of young people? Who calls them to build a future? Who offers hope of translating today's disorders into dreams, today's failures into successes? Youth culture is marked by at least four different elements:

● **The information revolution**

The world of computers, lasers, space travel and machines can dominate today's modern young person. When asked to list the natural resources of his small country, a young Singaporian replied, 'our minds'. But gone is the idealism of the 1960s generation. Replacing it is the resource of technical information which is designed to improve the

CHRISTIANITY AT COLLEGE

MICHAEL GRIFFITHS

The universities and colleges of the world are a uniquely strategic mission-field - for Christians as much as anyone else with a message. In some countries there may only be one or two universities training the elite. Others may have many institutions for higher education, though a few prestige universities may still take the best students destined to be future leaders in politics, economics, sciences, medicine, the arts and the media.

Students, often free of parental control for the first time, are encouraged to read and think for themselves. Even in traditional Buddhist or Muslim countries, a spirit of free enquiry means that the Christian world-view can be considered on its own merits. Students of English literature or European music inevitably try to understand the Christian background and biblical allusions involved.

Universities are where the thinking is done. This is where political revolution and informed protest against injustice frequently start. As I write, Ghana has closed its universities to silence criticism of the present regime. In South Africa white student leaders of Christian Unions are going to prison as conscientious objectors refusing to bear arms against their black fellow-citizens. South Korean governments have been overthrown in the past by student protest demonstrations.

Students get together

The strength of Christian witness in universities varies greatly from country to country. Singapore University has 20 per cent of its students in Christian groups; this makes it one of the strongest. The Christian Union at Cambridge, more than 100 years old, has had a membership of 1,000 students in recent years, 10 per cent of the university. At the opposite end of the scale are countries with a tiny handful of Christian students or no officially-recognized group at all.

Yet, even small Christian minorities can be significant. At the University of the Philippines, at a time of militant student demonstration, Christian students insisted that violence was not the way; this helped to cool tempers. They produced duplicated handouts suggesting Christian solutions to injustice which appeared in the national press.

There are different approaches to making the gospel known among students. Churches have sometimes attempted to do so from outside the campus. In areas where Christianity carries some official status, university chaplains are appointed. Some para-church groups have erected students' centres close to the campus. But the most fruitful work has followed the best missionary principles, insisting that Christian work on the campus be undertaken by students themselves. If they are capable of organizing politically then they are equally capable of organizing Christian witness. Young people rarely find much opportunity for leadership in the churches, but the Christian campus group provides training and experience which has developed embryo church leadership for the future. When many students are being converted, students learn to expect results from Christian work. Being a leader, planning advance and taking pastoral responsibility for other Christians is a stretching experience.

Student Christianity, good and bad

Christian student groups vary from place to place and time to time - in their militancy, enthusiasm and effectiveness. Sometimes they become a holy huddle: a ghetto concerned merely to preserve the faith of those

material base of the world. The heroes of today's youth are not Plato or Bertrand Russell, but Einstein. But the application of information technology has practical consequences. It is welcomed in many democracies, but where the state demands to control information, even the home computer is already a political threat.

● **Individual rights** The

horrendous treatment of dissidents in both left- and right-wing countries has highlighted the concern for human rights. But for young people the issue goes deeper – to a search for personal equality. Yet even this idealism often leads to grouping people at a lower level of common experience as the search for equality continues. The result is sameness.

See The Secular Outlook of Today; Racism, Justice and Civil Rights; Evangelicals at a Crossroads

already Christian, often preciously pious and with a wet, wishy-washy reputation among other students. Longer-established groups may become hopelessly programme-orientated and fail to maintain their original gospel aims.

Others pray together for an impact on the whole student body and are graciously aggressive in reaching out to other students with the gospel. Such groups often know how to define their convictions effectively, and win many to their ranks. The best of them are concerned about social issues and elect gifted Christians to university student government, earning respect for the relevance of their faith.

Work is always easier to sustain in residential universities and harder in smaller colleges, where students commute from home and are limited to lunch-hour activity.

While denominational groups are occasionally effective, it is the para-church and interdenominational movements which have shown most promise in reaching non-Christians. The Student Christian Movement (internationally the World Student Christian Federation) was fruitful during the nineteenth century, but it made links with theological radicalism and lost its effectiveness at student level. The Inter-Varsity Christian Fellowships (usually known locally as Christian Unions and affiliated to the

International Fellowship of Evangelical Students) have been, for all their faults, the most effective student-led movements.

In recent years two new groups exporting North American methods have entered the field with some success. The Navigators have been outstanding in basic training, in devotional Bible reading and evangelism, while Campus Crusade for Christ has been an effective movement for Christian outreach in some countries. Both movements suffer somewhat because they are led from outside the campus by a team of professionals, not themselves students. But they will make progress, to the extent that they can liberate

themselves from outside control and become more truly campus-based. Whatever their affiliation, student Christian groups are being raised up in more and more universities around the world.

Student years, then, are times when many people begin on the Christian way, and many grow towards more mature faith. This represents a call for student Christians to throw in their energies wholeheartedly with groups that aim for these goals.

Consensus becomes the style, eliminating courageous action or healthy individualism. What started out as a search for individual freedom can often end up in conformity.

● **Personal values** One modern writer claims that during the sixties young people studied sociology to change the world. In the seventies they studied psychology to change themselves. Today, however, they line up for courses on modern management to ensure prosperity. The Western dream of personal peace and well-being has become an important influence again. Young people of the Third World put their hope in Westernism, believing that fulfilment can be found in its standards and opportunities.

● **Religion** The pursuit of materialism and trust in scientific achievements has created a spiritual vacuum. And the failure of world economic systems, governments and education to meet youthful aspirations has triggered an interest in the non-material. African independent church movements, the explosion of Islam, Eastern gurus, Christian fundamentalism and the popularity of Pope John Paul II, along with a fascination in astrology, all point to today's interest in the metaphysical.

Young people take part in a service in Warsaw, Poland. In many parts of the world youth movements have a great deal to teach their elders about wholehearted Christian commitment.

NEW CHRISTIAN ACTION

On every continent, young people are facing the challenge of youth culture by initiating new, creative ways of presenting the Christian faith. The approaches are many, but common to all is the historic faith in Jesus Christ as Lord. Many different examples can be quoted.

Competing for the hearts and minds of non-churched youth in Hong Kong, a Chinese medical doctor has launched a popular youth magazine. Young blacks in Soweto, South Africa, are finding hope and inspiration through the ministry of Youth Alive. Huge crowds of European students gather every few years in Lausanne to be challenged by the needs of a world largely

untouched by the good news. Sports celebrities in North America publicly declare their faith. *The Herd*, a popular television show in New Zealand, reaches out beyond the borders of the church.

Across South Korea, young ministers are building massive churches. The missionary conference 'Urbana' in the United States attracts 20,000 college students every second year, all in the interest of world missions. Fast-growing church movements throughout Africa are led by younger leaders. 'Spring Harvest', which attracts over 20,000 each year, has set a new pattern for youth mobilization in Britain. In the centre of civil wars, churches in Central America are experiencing unprecedented growth.

Along with the growth of churches, large international youth movements network the world, generating youth conferences, innovative outreach and discipleship training. Youth with a Mission, Campus Crusade for Christ, the International Fellowship of Evangelical Students, Youth for Christ, the Navigators, and Operation Mobilization, along with many regional movements, continue to challenge today's generation with courageous commitment to Christian service.

BEYOND 2000

Today's young people are determined to shine the light of biblical faith on their generation. But what can we expect the churches to look like as we get closer to the twenty-first century?

● Less and less will Third World churches rely on their Western counterparts. Nationalism will dictate **a more indigenous style of activity and leadership**.

● **Theology will take on a local flavour**. The Bible will be interpreted out of local experience.

● **Music** tells us a great deal. Already new musical forms in the church have announced a new day. This will continue as the music of the West is replaced by sounds and ideas common to the home soil.

● Many believe that the big challenge will be the gigantic task of **integrating new Christian believers into the church** and encouraging personal Bible study and spiritual growth.

● Young people will expect their leaders to address **local and international social issues**. This will stretch the current definition of evangelism. Also, new types of ministry will be created to address the changing needs of people.

● **House churches** will spring up, countering the large mega-churches, providing intimacy and nurture. Also, the high cost of today's new cathedrals will lead to more inexpensive settings for worship.

● Christians will continue to express their faith in **varying art forms** – in drama, music, television, film, journalism and other forms of creative writing.

Young people are often the first to feel the winds of change. Thus their culture reacts, swinging from one extreme to the other. The search for success and prosperity is the climate of today. But the cycle of change will continue. Once today's generation has moved into adulthood, the following generation may revert to an idealism reminiscent of the sixties. There are too many unknowns to make strong predictions. But one thing is certain: the heart of a young person honestly searching for life will only be satisfied by meeting with the King of creation, Jesus Christ. It is this certainty that will motivate the church of tomorrow.

See Spirituality Today; The Church at Home

Renewal in the Holy Spirit

MICHAEL HARPER

In all the main denominations there are congregations and groups of Christians who show an uninhibited exuberance about their faith. This is the 'Charismatic movement', a movement for renewal in understanding and experience of the Holy Spirit.

Charismatic worship is marked by spontaneity and joyfulness. Worshippers often clap hands or raise their arms. During the services, different participants may lead in prayer, or in giving 'a word from God', or in 'speaking in tongues' – as the Spirit leads.

This first emerged and hit the headlines in the early 60s and it was from California that the shock-waves spread out. It was evident that the Pentecostal movement, which had developed separately, was now breaking out within the mainline, historic denominations, and the same experiences of the Holy Spirit and spiritual gifts were being claimed by Anglicans, Lutherans,

Presbyterians, Baptists and others. The new movement was soon labelled 'Charismatic' to distinguish it from the already-existing Pentecostal Church. (The name comes from the Greek word for 'gifts', referring to special abilities given by the Holy Spirit.) Later it became more usual to call it 'Charismatic Renewal' or just 'the renewal'. Although some later left their denominations, the majority have remained as spiritual ginger groups within them.

THE MOVEMENT DEVELOPS
In the first two decades of its life, this movement has passed through several phases of development:
● **The personal phase (1960s).** The early development was intensely personal and found expression in 'testimonies', or accounts of personal spiritual experience. These were given at conferences and meetings held in hotels and homes rather than church buildings. From the first it has been a lay movement. The earliest pioneers in the United States were the FGBMFI (Full Gospel Businessmen's Fellowship International) whose headquarters are in Los Angeles. Ministers were brought into

meetings, to testify, not to preach. The movement spread rapidly, carried by the new charismatic jet set of business-men, who did their business during the day and gave their testimony at breakfasts, luncheons and evening meetings.

● **The corporate phase (1970s)**. In 1967 the first Roman Catholics joined the movement and their numbers grew phenomenally in the next few years. The 'testimony' phase was beginning to lose its momentum; people realized its limitations. The Roman Catholics gave a new stimulus to those wanting a church or corporate expression of renewal. An Episcopal church in America, the Church of the Redeemer, Houston, became in the early 70s a model of this new phase. The emphasis switched to church renewal, and testimonies gave way to teaching. Testimonies had been able to unite the movement, but teaching tended to divide it. New denominations began to form such as the house church movement in Britain. People began to assert that the new wine of the Holy Spirit could not be contained in the old bottles of the historic churches.

● **The global phase (1980s)**. The early stages of the movement were almost exclusively taking place in the Western world. Then Roman Catholics pioneered renewal in Latin America and the first World Conference for Roman Catholics was held in Rome in 1975, attended by many from Central and South America. Anglicans soon followed with their first

HEALED

Liesl Alexander was in a British hospital, acutely mentally ill. Friends came and prayed for her, laying hands on her as they prayed.

'Something within me was being moved towards an encounter with light. I was face to face with that light. I was being held within it. I knew it to be creative and positive, loving and peaceful, totally the opposite of the darkness I'd just left. I was completely enveloped by it, unaware of anything else, aware only of this wonderful presence...I saw so clearly that I'd been ill, that for years I'd existed in a hell of mental illness, that I was now cured of that, suddenly, miraculously, in the space of a few moments...And the biggest thing was that there was hope now...They believed God had done something in my life, and as I heard that, I realized clearly how very far from normal my life had been up to that point.'

World Conference in Canterbury in 1978 and shortly afterwards SOMA (Sharing of Ministries Abroad) was set up to encourage the renewal in the world-wide Anglican Communion. The Lutherans have also developed a global strategy. The 80s have witnessed many signs that the Charismatic movement in the Third World is eclipsing that in the rest of the world.

In twenty years the Charismatic movement has become a major Christian force numerically. It has spread into every major denomination and every country of the world, and it is still increasing rapidly - especially in the Third World. The largest numbers are Roman Catholics. The greatest impact on bishops and clergy has been in

See Children of the Twentieth Century; Roman Catholics since the Council

CHRISTIAN HEALING TODAY
MORRIS MADDOCKS

The present century has seen a remarkable and universal revival of Christian healing. From the first decade of this century, pioneers in this field of ministry have recalled the churches to Jesus' commission: 'Preach the gospel, heal the sick.' The work of the pioneers influenced the churches' leadership. For instance, in 1944 William Temple founded the Churches' Council for Health and Healing 'to afford a recognized basis for the co-operation of doctors and clergy', and also 'to bring the work of healing into closer relation with the regular work of the churches'.

In 1968, the Roman Catholic Church restored the sacrament of anointing with oil as a sacrament of healing. Today most congregations of all denominations have a healing emphasis within their work and teaching, their worship and evangelism. There is also a more widespread consultation and working together among the healing professions.

God's power to heal

The quotation in the right-hand margin comes near to expressing the mind of the church on Christian healing. It is more than curing symptoms. It is Jesus Christ setting free all the forces of health on every level of a person's personality - body, mind, spirit, emotions and bio-energy. It is a process that restores harmony and balance between the different levels, within a person and between people.

Christians believe that Jesus Christ is both source and agent of this healing. The name Jesus means Saviour/Healer and carries the idea of spaciousness and freedom, of growth and enlargement. Through his cross and resurrection he has unleashed a divine power to heal, and he has commissioned his church to proclaim the good news by preaching and healing, aided by the gifts of the Holy Spirit.

The two gospel sacraments of baptism and the eucharist contain within them the basis of Christian healing. Baptism declares a new birth; it speaks of a person sharing in the dying and rising of Christ, of a life redirected away from brokenness and disease towards integration and wholeness. In the eucharist Jesus is present to heal in his 'timeless potency'.

But Christians use a number of other specific means to bring Christ's healing to those who need it:

■ **Anointing with oil** or Holy Unction, has been commended as a sacramental means of healing grace from New Testament times. The service (sometimes formal and sometimes unstructured) includes prayer with the laying-on-of-hands, used by the churches after Jesus' example for commissioning, blessing and healing. The patient is then anointed with oil by the priest or elder (in Episcopal churches with oil previously blessed by the bishop). The minister makes the sign of the cross on the forehead and sometimes on the palms or affected part. The laying-on-of-hands is also ministered separately, often happening during an act of worship or times of prayer.

■ **Confessing sin**, before a priest or before other fellow-Christians, is also a vital part of healing.

■ **Counselling** is often used to help minister healing. Many Christians are trained counsellors and do valuable work with patients, as well as teaching their fellow-Christians to be good listeners and befrienders. Some Christians are pioneering ways in joint work with the medical profession, especially in conjunction with local group practices.

■ **Healing meetings** have been a feature both of American revivalism and of the newer Charismatic movement. Many churches now have a special part of the regular service devoted to prayer for healing of people present. Some claim that it is God's will that all should be healed as part of the salvation Christ has won for us. Others see this as still future, when the whole creation is to be re-made without sin, suffering and death: healing is a declaration of God's kingdom here and now.

■ **Hospice care** is basically a Christian movement. Hospices offer specialist care for the dying, in the context of Christian love. They have helped many people to find healing from their fears about dying and death.

None of this important Christian work can be undertaken without deep prayer. There are an increasing number of Christians who are being called to the work of prayer and who, in various cells and groups, are undergirding the work of Christian healing today. Usually these groups cross denominational boundaries and so contribute to the healing of the churches themselves. Prayer is vital because Christian healing is not a technique; it is a spiritual ministry.

the Anglican Church, in which over 100 bishops were active in renewal by 1983. The emphasis in the Roman Catholic Church has been on lay communities and prayer groups (in France alone there are over 700,000 Catholic Charismatics, most of whom are involved in such groups). The emphasis in the Anglican and Protestant churches has been on local-church renewal, and hundreds of churches have been affected throughout the world.

HAS IT STRENGTHENED THE CHURCHES?

How have these great numbers of Charismatics affected the Christian scene spiritually? Certainly they have brought significant advances.

● It is essentially a **lay movement**, particularly in the Roman Catholic Church. It could be called the 'lay lib movement', as it has witnessed the release of lay people into a great variety of ministries in the church which were previously regarded as the preserve of ordained ministers - leadership, healing and exorcism, preaching and teaching, evangelism and travelling ministries. Perhaps this is why it has grown so fast - by thawing out what were once called 'God's frozen people'.

● It is a **singing movement**, which has seen the creation of a whole new style of worship, free, spontaneous and bodily (especially lifting hands in worship). It has majored on worship which is enthusiastic, often lengthy and usually congregational. It has produced a rich variety of songs and hymns which are now sung and enjoyed by people who may never have heard of the movement.

● It has **ecumenical dimensions** which are unique in the world-wide church, particularly the bridging of the gaps between Catholics and Protestants and Pentecostals. The Charismatic movement has provided one of the very few bright spots in the otherwise dismal story of sectarian bitterness in Northern Ireland.

● It has given new understanding and dynamic to the **community side of the church**, as Christians have learnt what it is to be part of the body of Christ and to function harmoniously with others.

● Above all it has injected **enthusiasm** into millions of Christians at a time when the fortunes of the churches in the Western world were definitely flagging.

'The pastoral and sacramental ministry of the church brings an assurance to the patient of God acting both within their innermost being and through those who are treating them. It helps to break down barriers deep in the personality which stand in the way of healing.'
Archbishops' commission on healing, 1958

See Focus on Worship; The Agony of Ulster

Christians have always prayed that sick people will be healed, whether physically, mentally, spiritually or emotionally. Belief that God heals through prayer is growing today.

But there is another side. We know something about the problems of Charismatic churches through reading Paul's correspondence with the church in Corinth. The problems do not seem to have changed very much.

All enthusiastic movements have been weakened by internal squabbles and divisions, and the Charismatic movement is no exception. It remains shapeless and largely structureless, partly because it is a reaction against over-structured and institutionalized churches. New churches and denominations have come into being, often themselves re-dividing at a later stage. Some other weaknesses are common to most renewal movements in their early years: in some parts of the movement a strong emphasis on authority has produced serious problems; personality cults have developed, new ministries built around dominant personalities sometimes encouraging unhealthy individualism. As in Corinth, the misuse of spiritual gifts has not always been checked, and there has been an insatiable thirst for the unusual and exotic, especially in the area of prophecy. Perhaps more serious still, there has sometimes been a lack of commitment to the causes of social injustice and economic deprivation. The movement has also failed to attract theologians and has produced few deep thinkers. Its tendency has been anti-intellectual.

ITS CENTRAL EXPERIENCE

You can recognize a Charismatic Christian by two closely-connected emphases which he or she will hold as centrally important. First, the experience which has been called 'the baptism in the Holy Spirit'. Second, the recovery by the church of the charismatic gifts. There is not total agreement on how to interpret the experience on its biblical foundations. But the heart of this movement is to be found here - in a spiritual release, a coming to fresh life in the Holy Spirit. Charismatics claim to have experienced a personal Pentecost and often to have received the gift of speaking in tongues. Charismatic churches use in their church life the gifts of the Holy Spirit, such as healing, prophecy, tongues and their interpretation.

The Charismatic movement has many aspects. The churches influenced by it often grow in numbers, sometimes spectacularly. They are always enthusiastic about evangelism, and also about spreading 'the renewal' and testifying to their experience of the Holy Spirit. Charismatics are very gregarious - they love meetings and groups for worship, witness and teaching. They testify at the drop of a hat. Their worship is loud and long. But the source from which all this flows is a new encounter with Jesus Christ, who said, 'I will baptize you with the Holy Spirit.'

Evangelicals at a Crossroads

WALDRON SCOTT

The title 'Evangelical' means different things to different people; for some it just means 'Protestant', or even 'Lutheran'. But during the past generation or so it has come to be used specifically to identify more than one in six of the world's Christians. These Christians are conservative in questions of belief, and hold a distinctive threefold emphasis: the primacy of the Bible as the inspired word of God, the need for a personal relationship with Jesus Christ through conversion and new birth, and a strong commitment to evangelism and missionary endeavour.

Evangelicals are among the fastest-growing branches of Christianity in our time. Best estimates are of nearly 270 million world-wide in 1985.

This impressive figure includes four main sub-groups (although there is some overlap between them):
● **Conservative Evangelicals** are formally united within the World Evangelical Fellowship (WEF). They are keen to maintain a distinct identity, and in certain important ways constitute the core group of Evangelicalism. Many of them maintain their membership in churches belonging to the World Council of Churches. (Anglican Evangelicals represent one such long-recognized group.)
● **Fundamentalists** (here taken to include Southern Baptists) comprise an independent 'right wing' of the broader Evangelical movement. They do not, on the whole, join in with non-evangelical bodies.

● **Black Evangelicals** were essentially an American phenomenon, but now include many of the independent churches of Africa.
● Most **Pentecostals** (though not all in the Charismatic renewal movement) identify themselves as Evangelicals.

Although Evangelicals make up a significant minority within the total Christian community, their size is not as important as their overall contribution. They have

Students study the Bible in Sarawak, Eastern Malaysia. Belief in the Bible as the 'word of God' is central for Evangelicals. They take its teaching extremely seriously, and try to work out how it applies to their lives in the modern world.

contributed and are contributing substantially to the quality of Christian life during the twentieth century. In an age when much Christianity is only nominal, they have preserved the warm, pietistic values of earlier generations. In an age when everything is held to be relative, Evangelicals have maintained a rational theology firmly grounded in the Bible. In an age of social activism they have continued to demonstrate the effectiveness of gospel proclamation. And in an era of religious pluralism they have not forgotten that the church has a mission to all people.

RESPONDING TO THE WORLD'S NEEDS

All this is to be expected, perhaps, given the conservative nature of the movement. Less predictable has been the way Evangelicals have responded creatively to the special challenges of our generation. Among these challenges and responses, seven are particularly notable.

● **Wycliffe Bible Translators**, an Evangelical agency founded in 1934, has become the largest Protestant missionary society in the world. Under its aegis more than 2,500 missionaries are at work reducing unwritten languages to writing and translating the Bible among 700 'people groups' round the world. Theirs is a major contribution to global Christianity, despite the fact that nearly 3,300 languages and dialects remain to be translated.

● For the past fifty years

Billy Graham has been an Evangelical leader since the 1950s. His evangelistic campaign meetings have drawn huge crowds in most nations of the world. He has a simple, direct and challenging style of preaching which has caused millions to think hard about what Jesus Christ means for their lives. Campaign evangelism is only one way of spreading the gospel, but it continues to be effective.

Evangelicals have both pioneered and excelled in exploiting the potential of **electronic mass media,** first radio and more recently television. Today the gospel message is broadcast to the so-called Iron- and Bamboo-Curtain countries: its effectiveness attested by countless letters. Radio has also become an important resource in the teaching and evangelistic ministries of Third World churches. In the West the ubiquitous 'electronic church' has become an object of both praise and criticism, but its influence is unquestioned.

● Evangelicals have also developed highly contemporary approaches to **church planting.** The relatively soft science of sociology has been used creatively here, in establishing the 'homogeneous unit principle' - people convert more easily to Christian faith when cultural barriers are minimized. This has been part of a new effort to evangelize previously unreached 'people groups' - a people group being defined as a significantly large collection of individuals and families who perceive themselves to have a common affinity to one another. The Lausanne Committee for World Evangelization and the US Center for World Mission have been prominent in promoting the drive to reach unreached peoples.

● **Third World missions** are another creative response arising from within the world-wide Evangelical community. The term refers to members of the Evangelical churches of Asia, Africa and Latin America crossing cultural barriers within their own regions in order to make disciples from other groups. Such endeavours have mushroomed in recent years. Now numbering more than 32,500, Third World missionaries are expanding their areas of service rapidly. Some see them as the missionary wave of the future. The World Evangelical Fellowship has been instrumental in bringing together key Third World missionary leaders to help each other and to work together.

● **Disaster relief and community development** has been another important reaction to the demands of modern life. Evangelical agencies such as Tear Fund, World Vision and World Relief are among the significant private voluntary organizations at work in the world today.

● Evangelicals have also made substantial progress in **reintegrating social action and evangelism.** This has partly been spurred by the pressure of Third World concerns. The Lausanne Congress of 1974, when Evangelicals from the Third World succeeded in bringing this issue to the forefront, was a watershed. The relationship between evangelism and social action is still being hotly debated among Evangelicals, but a lot more agreement was evident at the Consultation on the Relationship between Evangelism and Social Responsibility (at Grand Rapids in 1982), co-sponsored by the World Evangelical Fellowship and the Lausanne Committee for World Evangelization. This trend toward

See Translating the Bible;The Electronic Church; Reaching New Peoples; Bread for the World; Telling the World

A young woman found society empty, tried Confucianism, then Zen Buddhism and then drugs. At last she encountered Jesus Christ. 'I learned how to take him into my heart and trust him with my life. Then the change began...almost in spite of me...I began to know inner peace and the reality of God's love.' Quoted by Billy Graham

Evangelicals are found throughout the world, in many different denominations. And so from time to time great international gatherings are held, like this all-denominational consultation at Lausanne, Switzerland, in 1983, to consult together about priorities and strategies for Christian mission.

a more holistic understanding and application of the gospel is welcomed by many; it seems a true reflection of Jesus' way of ministering to people.

● Evangelicals have made positive contributions in the area of **international co-operation**. The Billy Graham crusades continue to unite Christians across denominational lines in major cities in all six continents. The Lausanne Congress, in 1974, the fruit of three decades of

growing co-operation between Evangelicals in Europe and North America, also introduced a new generation of Third World Evangelical leaders to the public. The congress spawned a host of joint evangelistic enterprises.

Going beyond evangelism, the World Evangelical Fellowship has brought leaders together, especially during the past ten years, from the West and from the Third World. Theologians, communicators, development

specialists, missiologists have met in a variety of forums. At the same time WEF has expanded its grass-roots network to include national Evangelical associations in more than fifty countries.

Evangelicals have also been reaching out, rather tentatively, to Christians in other sectors of the world church. Small ad hoc groups have taken part in dialogues with representatives of the World Council of Churches. Serious theological discussions have been held, without publicity, between Evangelical and Roman Catholic leaders.

So Evangelicals are growing and highly active. They can claim to be a significant clan within the world-wide Christian family. In certain respects they are stronger now than at any time since the 1910 Edinburgh Conference on world evangelization. Their colleges and seminaries, though not as well-endowed as some, are

See The Missionary Inheritance

bursting at the seams. They are producing a limited but growing number of highly respected Third World leaders. They are more socially conscious than previously. Their future seems assured.

WHERE NOW?

Evangelicals are at a crossroads. They have to decide which way to move ahead from the strong position they have reached. And there is not agreement as to which road to take.

One way is to keep the Evangelical ship watertight: restrict co-operation to other Evangelicals only, work within purely Evangelical bodies, concentrate on evangelism and social caring and keep out of politics. This way has the great benefit that traditional Evangelical beliefs can be kept intact: the primacy of the Bible, the news that individual lives can be changed by conversion and new birth - these vital truths will not be lost to the world.

Others argue that they should have more creative interaction with the other Christian communities, and accept that, while the world still desperately needs the gospel of Christ, many people also need to be liberated from oppressive social structures.

In mid-1980 the World Council of Churches (WCC) held a major international conference on world mission and evangelism in Melbourne, Australia. Just three weeks later the Lausanne Committee for World Evangelization (LCWE) sponsored an international consultation on

unreached peoples at Pattaya, Thailand. Evangelicals were present and active at the WCC gathering in Melbourne, and at least twenty-five went on to participate in the Pattaya conclave. There they made vigorous attempts to relate the major emphases of the Melbourne meeting to the main thrust of Pattaya. But they met with a cool response on the part of the LCWE leadership.

Pattaya was concerned with the millions of people still unreached by the gospel. Melbourne had focussed on the fact that the overwhelming majority of these unreached people are *poor*, in the many-sided biblical sense of that word, and wrestled with the relevance of the gospel to such people. The struggle to bring together these vital insights was a hard one, and it was not really successfully resolved.

Some argue that for Evangelicals to be as influential as they should be in the whole Christian scene they need to get their house in order, develop a stronger dynamic of inner unity, and reach a consensus on issues such as the balance of social action and evangelism. That is, they must relate to others from a position of strength rather than weakness. It is doubtful whether the first Christians worked on this basis. And anyway Evangelical numerical strength and the vitality of their work for the kingdom has aroused the interest of World Council and Roman Catholic leaders who welcome their participation in the larger arena. It is largely due to Evangelical influence that the WCC is now more convinced than for some years of the centrality of evangelism.

SOMETHING TO GIVE, SOMETHING TO GAIN

At the sixth assembly of the World Council of Churches in Vancouver, Canada, in July 1983, a number of Evangelicals were present. Most of them were happy to find that the WCC had moved significantly in the direction of a more biblical and spiritual Christianity. Others disagreed, feeling that too many Christian distinctives were blurred at the frontiers with Marxism, for example, and with the other major faiths. There will probably always be this conflict among Evangelicals, between those who want to have full interplay with other Christians and those who believe the only way to renew Christianity is to separate from those with unbiblical presuppositions and preach a better way.

And yet the greatest contribution Evangelicals can make to the church and to the world may not be primarily in official conferences and matters of high policy. Perhaps, above all, what they have to offer is the very soul and ethos of their movement.

Evangelicals have always placed central stress on applying the Bible to current social conditions. They have prayed together simply and freely, and taught that every believer has access to God through Christ. These emphases can be seen reflected right across the Christian scene now in a more biblical, informal and lay-centred Christian practice.

Above all, they have always believed that the gospel of Jesus, dying and rising to give us new life, can transform people in every situation. Much work remains to be done, often alongside other Christians, to give this belief practical effect in all the different cultural and economic contexts of the world. But believing that the good news of Jesus contains the dynamic to change everyone who receives it with faith is what makes a person an Evangelical. And maybe simply holding true to that faith, while retaining the humility to learn from anyone who can help them apply it more effectively, remains Evangelicals' most important calling.

See The Church of the Poor; The Unity Movement; Does the Bible Speak Today? The Gospel in Today's World

All Things In Common

KEITH HARDER

A vision for community is capturing the hopes and imaginations of many Christians in the last decades of the twentieth century. Community has become an expression of renewed Christian commitment and a sign of renewal in church and society. The steady erosion, especially in the Western world, of shared values, confidence in social structures, vitality of family life – and the related increase in violence, fear and isolation – make this concern to re-establish community particularly important.

Many people gave community living a try in the 1960s, and quite a few still do. Christian communities have a history stretching back to the third-century desert monasteries, and the community movement today is giving new shape and life to this tradition.

But in all too many places the church has lost its community character and become an impersonal institution touching people only on the fringes of their lives. Jim Wallis, editor of *Sojourners* magazine, explains the church's conformity to the values of our age as being due to a 'fragmentation of her common life'.

In reaction to this, thousands of Christian 'intentional' communities have emerged in the last two decades. Christians and non-Christians alike encountering this new social environment are 'intentionally' choosing different forms of life, embodying co-operation over competition, integration over fragmentation, relationships over institutions. People are realizing that in the modern Western world living in community will need to be an intentional choice requiring deliberate changes in their patterns of living.

COMMUNITIES AROUND THE WORLD

The United States has always been a fertile ground for community experiments, and in the 1970s an explosion of communities occurred there. One estimate suggests that more than 10,000 communities were formed,

most of which were short-lived.

While the emergence of new counter-culture communities has slowed considerably in the mid-1980s, there continues to be a lively interest in community as an expression of renewal in church and society. Presently at least seven networks of Christian communities operate in the United States, embracing over 100 separate communities. There are also other communities with no particular alliance. While they include only a small fragment of American Christians, they may indicate a significant force for renewal on the American scene.

Community is not only a contemporary concern in the West, however. The natural community of many traditional societies in the Third World is being threatened by the inroads of modernity. A Bolivian church leader visiting a community in the United States noted that the Inca community he came from embodies many of the values and patterns of living which that community was struggling to develop. He also lamented the slow loss of these values in his home community.

Thousands of 'base communities' have emerged throughout Latin America as a grassroots expression of spiritual renewal and of the need for social justice. In their typical form, base communities are small groups of Christians gathering around the Bible, sharing concerns vital to their physical and spiritual well-being. It is calculated that in Brazil there are 80,000 small Christian communities and approximately 150,000 in all of Latin America. By 1983 there were 10,000 communities in East Africa.

Also, the perseverance of the church in China has often taken the form of small, house churches. As Jonathan Chao notes: 'The church in China has been transformed from a timid, foreign-coloured institutional church into a bold, indigenous, institutionless church...'

WHAT ARE COMMUNITIES FOR?

As a world-wide phenomenon, there is also a diversity among these communities reflecting different needs and a wide range of concerns.

For some, community is a way to restore and preserve traditional values and life-patterns that are threatened by modernity. For others, community is the way to be freed from traditional values. For some, community is a chosen lifestyle in the context of affluence. For many, community is the only possibility in the face of a poverty of other options or direct government oppression.

While there is no organized world-wide community movement, there are important areas of common concern and common witness:

● **Relationships characterized by commitment, unity, trust, sacrificial service and shared life** are central in these communities. The words of Jesus, 'A new commandment I give to you, that you love one another, even as I have loved you', have a new importance and urgency.

'In our time, when there are...so many people who have not been faithful to their vow, more and more communities need to be born as signs of fidelity.' Jean Vanier

See The Secular Outlook of Today; Good News for the Poor; The Church in China

● Most communities are not the product of bureaucratic planning. **They have emerged from common folk** and reflect new-found lay initiatives. Many new communities have close ties with the institutional church. Others do not.

● **Some communities are associated with churches that have long traditions of community witness**. A number, for example, are from Anabaptist groups; others spring from the Charismatic renewal among Roman Catholics; yet others are connected with the Reformed and Episcopal traditions.

● Most communities have emerged in response to particular historical situations. The analyses of the world situation may vary and particular forms may vary, but **all communities share an awareness of profound needs in the church and the world**.

● **These communities also share the calling to embody the teaching and the spirit of the Bible**. Biblical interpretations may vary: many communities espouse pacifism, some do not; some communities espouse full community of goods, many do not. And there is considerable variety in form and structure. Most have well-defined patterns of leadership, but vary in the balance between authority vested in the leaders and the members. Some communities function as local churches; others as communal groups within a larger parish church. But the theme of discipleship and faithful obedience to Scripture is basic to these Christian communities.

The teaching of Jesus has taken on new relevance and urgency. The example of the New Testament church is energizing many Christian communities.

For some, living in community has no particular goal or purpose beyond obedience and faithfulness to God. As Eberhard Arnold, founder of the Society of Brothers, wrote: 'All life created by God exists in a communal form and works toward community. Therefore we live in community.' Reflecting this conviction, some communities see their primary task in being an alternative society reflecting the vision of the kingdom of God.

For others, like the Gospel Outreach and Bethany Fellowship in the United States, community is seen as an effective means for evangelism and mission. Still others, such as Sojourners and L'Arche, see community as the most effective way to witness for justice and to serve the poor,

See The Church at Home

L'Arche communities are shared between those who are handicapped and those who are not, in the belief that each member has something vital to bring to the whole.

handicapped and oppressed.

The communities in these networks are composed mostly of fairly well-educated whites between twenty-five and forty years old. There are also communities in the United States which are predominantly black. People from a wide range of church backgrounds as well as many with no church background make up these communities, most of which are located in cities.

Community has become a symbol, a sign, an expression, a parable of what God is doing in the world. Whether the primary motif is restoration or renewal, liberation or survival, community has become a vehicle for many twentieth-century Christians throughout the world to embody their concerns and their commitments.

WHAT IS COMMUNITY LIFE LIKE?

Jean Vanier opens his book *Community and Growth*: 'Community can appear to be a marvelously welcoming and sharing place. But in another way, community is a terrible place.'

This paradox is the testimony of most experienced communitarians. The vision and the experience of community as a haven of peace and sacrifice is well attested to. The other is also true. As Vanier tells it, 'When we were alone, we could believe we loved everyone. Now that we are with others, we realize how incapable we are of loving, how much we deny life to others.'

Since community is supposed to be a place of harmony and love, the encounter with pain and suffering can be disappointing and disillusioning. This is why people often conclude that, given the realities of sinful human nature, community is too idealistic.

True enough, there has been suffering born of communitarian idealism. Communities have been prone to the tyranny of anarchy on the one hand and of authoritarianism on the other. Most communities that have lasted have endured extremes in the search for balance in form and structure. Intense, close relationships are difficult to sustain.

Communities of the old monastic orders still thrive in many places. At monasteries such as Prinknash in England, a regular pattern of work and worship links the present monks to generations who have lived this way before them.

Continued on p.120

THE CHURCH AT HOME
ROBERT BANKS

Since the early 1970s a new phenomenon has appeared on the Christian scene. In increasing numbers people have begun to meet in homes or secular premises to worship and learn together, rather than in church buildings. This has happened before. Some of the Anabaptists met in a similar way during the Reformation; Wesley's class meetings were held in homes, the early Brethren meetings too. But such 'house churches' have rarely become a normative feature of Christians' lives together.

Why have home churches emerged again just at this time? Several factors have been at work. In North America, some of them have resulted from the conversion of people through the Jesus movement and from the influence of encounter and other small groups on the church. In England, many have arisen out of a Charismatic background. In Third-World countries, and particularly in Latin America, many home- or work-based churches have stemmed from ordinary believers' attempts to do something about their poverty and oppression. In certain countries, such as China and to some degree the USSR, political constraints have forced large numbers of Christians to gather in less public ways. Elsewhere, as among many groups in Australia, they have come into being as people have begun to reassess biblically what the church really is.

But there is a more basic reason for this phenomenon. For a long time many Christians have been frustrated with traditional church life. They have found it formal, rigid, passive and unreal, and so have looked for a more intimate, flexible, vital and relevant relationship with God and with their fellow-believers. By meeting together for church in smaller groups they have begun to experience this.

Such groups go under several names. Frequently the people within them simply refer to themselves as 'the group' or 'the meeting'. Some call themselves 'house churches', others 'neighbourhood churches', 'small churches', or 'base churches'. In other circles they are generally talked about as 'basic' or 'grassroots' communities. All go beyond the 'small groups', 'home fellowships' and 'family clusters' that have also sprung up in large numbers over the past two decades. While churches in the home generally do not have a written basis of faith, a few do possess a covenant defining the quality of commitment involved. The whole phenomenon is not identical to what is often called the 'house church movement', though it has many points of overlap with it.

What makes a home church?

There have been different influences on these groups, they have sprung from varied church backgrounds and thrived in divergent social, political and cultural settings. This makes it difficult to generalize about their basic principles. But it would be usual for them to show many of these features:

■ **God** is most vividly and concretely **present among a small company of believers** who seek his presence and direction in an open, wholehearted, practical way.

■ The gospel requires Christians to have a specific, and sacrificial **commitment to a limited group of fellow-believers**. This leads to the establishment of an extended Christian family, in which children are members as fully as anyone else.

■ The group's most central activity is its **regular common meal**. In eating this meal together they celebrate Christ's death and resurrection, but also, through fellowship, they enter into each other's concerns and bear each other's burdens.

■ **Every part of their lives, and every aspect of society should be radically affected by the gospel**. This drives them to desire not just personal change but social and cultural transformation as well, especially for those who are most disadvantaged.

■ **God gives gifts to each member and to women as much as men** to share with the others. The Spirit, rightly discerned, draws these together into valid and helpful forms of worship and service.

■ **Every member of the church should have a share in basic decisions** affecting the group's life, even if some have greater wisdom, pastoral awareness and spiritual experience than others.

■ They stress **function rather than office**, tasks rather than titles, example rather than position. This gives them a respect for those who play a more visible part in the church's life though not necessarily uncritical agreement with them.

■ God reveals his truth and guidance chiefly as Christians come together to **survey their problems and aspirations in the light of the Bible and shared experience**. Understanding of society and of people play an important part, as do the gifts of the Spirit, and they lead to the kind of prayer that listens as well as asks. Home churches in a particular city or region also regularly meet together, often across denominational boundaries, to celebrate together and encourage one another.

A new denomination?

How do these groups relate to the mainline denominations? There is no one answer, but at least four main patterns can be found.

Many of them began independently of the institutional church. Some of these groups see themselves as an interim arrangement until congregations establish sufficient home churches themselves and give them the priority they deserve. In the meantime, members of these independent groups try to avoid any sectarian attitudes and to maintain good relationships with other Christians. Some keep up membership in a local church. Most take part wholeheartedly in interdenominational activities.

Some home churches commenced as distinct break-offs from a denomination, but have since developed into larger churches in a more traditional sense, complete with special buildings and formalized ministry. These see themselves as a permanent alternative to the existing denominations and are beginning to establish more organized 'connections' with other similarly-minded groups.

Home churches have also begun to appear in a small way within the mainline churches themselves. These are strongest where they have equal priority with the Sunday services. Where they are simply one among the usual plethora of church organizations, or are regarded as an evangelistic strategy or temporary phenomenon, they do not have the same impact. So far only a small number of congregations seem to have developed churches in the home in a serious way.

In a few cases, a congregation has decentralized itself completely into home churches, sometimes selling its building in the process and having only occasional larger or regional meetings for its members in hired premises. Sometimes this happens with a denomination's approval, sometimes not.

Small groups, big influence

The number of Christians involved in home churches is still relatively small, though it seems to be growing fast. But whatever the numbers, this is one of the most significant Christian developments in recent years. Within such groups, people are making discoveries - modest as yet, but vitally important. They are finding out what Christian community really is. They are learning how to give children a new kind of Christian education. They are coming up with fresh ways of carrying out evangelism and fulfilling civic responsibility, new and revitalized rituals for family and urban life.

The mainline churches are being painfully slow to take up the challenge of home churches, and so independent groups are bound to increase for some time to come. Only if these avoid becoming sectarian in attitude and remain in fellowship with denominational churches will they make the impact of which they are really capable. Home churches will also grow within the institutional church, but for the most part they will operate under greater constraints and so take longer to realize their potential. Both sets of groups need each other if they are to fulfil their vision.

The influence of home churches, for all its limited character at present, will continue to grow out of all proportion to their size. Without making too much of the analogy, we should remember that the first Christians met for a century and a half in a home-church way. And look at the effect they had on their religious and social environment! They remind us how far-reaching the effects of small but committed groups of Christians can be.

One family among many who have practised Christian communal living, learning to share their possessions, found that 'the mere fact that our faith actually touched our money was much, much more impressive than that we sang certain songs or prayed certain prayers. David Watson

See Spirituality Today

Most people growing up in the modern West are not well equipped for the encounter with poverty and suffering in community. Materialism and isolation have created illusions of self-sufficiency that will need to be changed. The capacity to suffer, to persevere, to reject the temptations of affluence will mean much change and learning. The church in the Third World has much to teach Christians in the West about the spiritual qualities necessary for living in community.

The encounter with sin and suffering in community also creates conditions for healing and growth. Facing one's sin is the first step to forgiveness and grace. Embracing one's poverty is the first step to justice.

While living in community can be difficult, there is so much more that is rich and fulfilling. To live with the close support and love of others is a great gift. Sharing life with others committed to the way of Jesus enables faithful discipleship. The ready availability of honest counsel and loving forgiveness is indispensable for Christians in any age.

Another challenge facing most Christian communities is how they relate to the wider church. Is a Christian community a church? Is it a para-church organization? a religious order? a renewed remnant? part of the larger church? Is communal life in some form incumbent on all Christians or is it the special calling for some? These questions have faced the church throughout its history.

Communities over time must also face the issues of institutional life and tradition. Since many communities emerged in reaction to impersonal formalism and dry tradition, it is sometimes difficult for them to accept the need for structure and the inevitable emergence of institutions. The care of the young, the training of youth, the care of the aged, the human need for order, the rhythms of life all require tradition and institutions that will themselves need revision and renewal.

Living in community also includes the call to mission and service. A consistent criticism of communities is that they tend to be ingrown and self-absorbed. No one would deny that this is a potential problem. The search for wholeness, the struggle for unity and the quest for simplicity require much time and energy.

At times the search for love and acceptance can itself be self-defeating. Parker Palmer has identified an 'ideology of intimacy' afflicting many intentional communities. He says this search for intimacy has resulted in an unhealthy depreciation of relationships that are less than intimate, and this has particularly limited the contribution of communities in the public sphere.

But many communities have also effectively marshalled resources for significant ministry:
● **Sojourners community** initiated and maintains Sojourners magazine which now serves over 50,000 readers;
● **Word of God community** has

spearheaded an international missionary effort;

● **Reba Place Fellowship** has touched the lives of hundreds through a ministry of counselling and inner healing;

● Communities have had significant impact on deteriorating neighbourhoods in **Detroit, Houston and Chicago;**

● **The Communities of Celebration** in Colorado and Scotland have produced worship and music resources that have enriched many;

● **L'Arche communities** serve hundreds of handicapped people who have been placed on the margins of society.

Considerable resources of Christian communities continue to be channelled into evangelization, church renewal, peace witness and projects for justice. Community has been an effective vehicle to call forth and mobilize human and economic resources for the renewal of church and society.

In Europe, Taizé continues to serve as a symbol of hope and a catalyst of commitment for thousands, especially young people who feel disenfranchised by the church.

Many people living in community are over-extended to the neglect of relationships, prayer and family. But they are working to counteract this and to find better rhythms of worship and work, prayer and witness.

COMMUNITY IN THE FUTURE?

As the world becomes a global village and the human needs

PILGRIM PEOPLE

The American 'Community of Communities' recently put out a statement that included these words:

'We see the people of God as pilgrims and sojourners in this world because of our loyalty to the kingdom of God. Our identity in this world grows directly out of the positive vision of a new order which commands more loyalty and obedience from us than we have toward any of the world's systems.

There is a deep hunger in us for restoration of our covenant with the poor, with our neighbours of different races and nations, with our marriage partners and our children, with unborn lives, with whole populations we now call enemies and threaten with nuclear destruction, with God's earth, with our sisters and brothers in Christ as we build community, and, at root, with God who loves us and is calling us back.

A new style of life is emerging in our communities that is a clear alternative to the political and economic status quo. Our commitments have taken the form of creating marriage and family patterns based on fidelity, mutuality, living among the poor, organizing for economic justice, labouring for peace, and evangelizing ourselves and others with the good news of the gospel. Together we are seeking to forge a new shape for the church's life.

The renewal of faith is finally the only thing with the strength to resist the economic and political powers now in control and to provide an adequate spiritual foundation for better ways to live.'

Christians do not live in community chiefly for their own benefit. A community in Detroit, United States, staffs a school in a poorer area of the city.

being unmet in modern technological society become more apparent, there will be increased concern for interdependence and co-operation. If it is true that the current Western indulgence in materialism simply cannot continue, interest in alternative patterns of living will increase. For concerned Christians, the need for community in some form will become evident.

This is not to say that the transition will be painless or that people will flock into the existing communities. New wineskins will be needed to accommodate a major change in consciousness and lifestyle. There will likely be considerable trauma – even conflict and much failure – in this transition.

The Christian communities in North America, Western Europe and the Third World will have a role to play in the development of these new structures. What role remains to be seen. Partly it will depend on breadth of vision, partly on the willingness to change to serve the need of the hour.

Focus on Worship

GEOFFREY WAINWRIGHT

In our century all the churches have been seeking a renewal of Christian worship. Starting from many different points of need and opportunity, they have joined in a 'liturgical movement' which has brought the different traditions closer in fundamental patterns of worship, while yet allowing a great diversity in the style of their celebration.

In the **Roman Catholic Church**, Pope Pius X (1903-14) started to encourage lay people to take communion more frequently. The ecumenically-minded Belgian Benedictine, Lambert Beauduin (1873-1960), after ten years' experience in an industrial parish, began to press home the worship-assembly as the place in which Christians learned their faith. In Germany, the monks of Maria Laach explored what the early church taught about the sacraments. The French took the lead in reintroducing the people's mother tongue into the liturgy of the 'Latin Church' and in engaging the whole congregation in active participation at mass. When the biblical theology movement spread from Protestantism into the Catholic Church, priests began to preach from the Bible. The fruit and official sanction of all this is found in the new services that followed on the Second Vatican Council.

If the Roman Catholics had to prune some of their medieval and more recent accretions, **Protestants** have rather needed to move the other way. They have been recovering riches from an earlier tradition (which has, incidentally, brought them closer to the intentions of the Reformers). They appear gradually to be making the eucharist more central to their worship, as witness the success of 'parish communion' as the main Sunday service in many parts of Anglicanism. The use of the calendar and lectionary for regular set Bible readings and prayers has gained ground in areas of Protestantism that were earlier suspicious of the yearly round. The life and worship of the Taizé Community has greatly influenced the corporate prayer of many Protestants.

WORD AND SACRAMENT TOGETHER

The sixties and seventies saw many denominations producing revised service books. They testify to the now widespread agreement that Sunday worship, in its fullness, calls for a service of scripture and sacrament, word and table. Liturgical scholars have returned to the church that

See Roman Catholics since the Council; Does the Bible Speak Today?

Opposite When the pope travels to a city, the focal point of his visit is usually a great service of eucharistic worship, like this one in Bogota, Colombia. This testifies to the belief that, whatever else may be urgent, the most important thing Christians can do together is to worship God.

existed before the Emperor Constantine made Christianity official Roman religion, and found there a model of the Sunday service. Justin Martyr, around AD 150, records how Christians from town and country gathered to hear readings from 'the memoirs of the apostles and the writings of the prophets'; these were then interpreted by the president of the assembly; prayers were said; bread and wine were brought to the presider, who 'to the best of his ability' gave thanks to God the Father over them 'in the name of the Son and of the Holy Spirit'; the bread and wine, as tokens of Christ's body and blood, were then distributed for communion, the deacons taking

them also to the absent members.

This ancient rite clearly forms the backbone of the new forms of service, which have the same elements:

● **readings from Old and New Testaments**;
● **the sermon**;
● **prayers for church and world**;
● **the presentation of the gifts**;
● **the prayer of thanksgiving for Christ's saving acts**;
● **the sharing of bread and wine**.

Other elements in the Sunday service are secondary, though they can often threaten the principal structure. Many

THE CHANGING BALANCE OF WORSHIP

PRIEST PERFORMS, PEOPLE WATCH
In medieval times, priests performed the mass, while the people looked on, often from behind a screen.

MINISTER AND PEOPLE KEEP THEIR DISTANCE
Church buildings still kept the medieval lay-out. So until recently the minister led the worship, often far-removed from the people. Congregations sang hymns, said 'Amen' to prayers and took communion, but were otherwise rather passive.

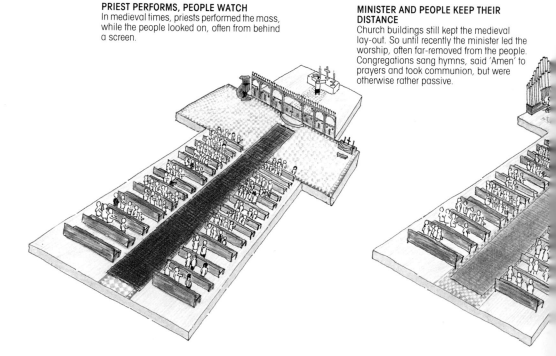

Protestants have grown frustrated with a service that stops short after the sermon. The Eastern Orthodox have still to catch up with the Roman Catholics in restoring regular lay communion.

EACH MEMBER TAKING PART

Another principle on which the modern liturgical movement agrees is the need for active participation in worship by the whole congregation, all with their varied ministries. For a time it was fashionable to interpret the Greek behind our word 'liturgy' as meaning 'the work of the people': worship as a corporate act, with each member playing his or her part. This remains a

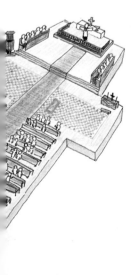

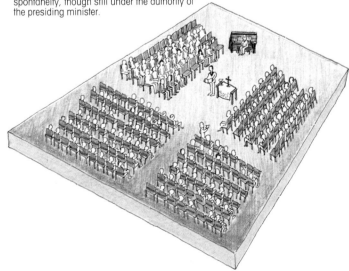

ALL TAKE PART TOGETHER
More and more today, the people take part in the worship—reading lessons, leading prayers (often from the body of the church), announcing hymns, helping administer communion... In Pentecostal and Charismatic worship, people may join in with complete spontaneity, though still under the authority of the presiding minister.

Styles of worship cover an enormous range. At the other end of the spectrum from the formality of much Catholic and Orthodox worship is the spontaneity and informality of the Pentecostals and the house church movement.

See Renewal in the Holy Spirit; The Orthodox Families; The Anglican Communion

true insight, even though 'liturgy' is now understood as a 'public service' which the church offers to God on behalf of the world: the worshipping church holds the fort until all humanity has the chance to be brought into the community of God's glory in response to the church's prayers and evangelism.

Yet one more feature common to the liturgical movement is an attempt to combine order and freedom, structure and spontaneity, tried traditions and spiritual innovation:

● **The Charismatic movement** has had a liberating effect on the worship of many hidebound congregations, with its songs, its testimonies, its extemporary prayers, its employment of gesture.

● **Free churches** have learned the value of ancient rites and ceremonies, of prayers hallowed by centuries of use.

● **Prayer-Book Anglicans**, at least in the United States, may now, with the 1979 book, experience the presider making the eucharistic prayer of consecration into a free prayer, providing certain themes are respected and the words of institution are included.

The old distinction between 'liturgical' and 'non-liturgical' denominations is tending to break down.

With so many old church traditions moving closer to each other, it is not surprising that the liturgical and the ecumenical movements should have intertwined, worship and unity coming together. The most notable product of this so far has

been the Lima text on *Baptism, Eucharist and Ministry* (1982), which is part of the help given by the Faith and Order Commission to the churches as they seek 'visible unity in one faith and in one eucharistic fellowship'. There the Lord's Supper is presented, in word and sacrament, as 'thanksgiving to the Father', 'memorial of Christ', 'invocation of the Spirit', 'communion of the faithful', and 'meal of the kingdom'.

WORSHIP IN DIFFERENT CULTURES

The emphasis on positive features should not be taken to imply that everything in the liturgical garden is lovely. In the First and Second Worlds, twentieth-century secularism has brought a massive defection from the church and its worship, returning the church in some respects to a situation where practising Christianity is no longer the norm. In such a situation, the Orthodox churches have started to talk of mission and service as the necessary 'liturgy after the Liturgy'. In **the Soviet Union**, and other communist countries where evangelism is prohibited, the sheer radiance of the worshipping congregation, whether Orthodox, Baptist or Pentecostal, bears its own testimony.

In **Western Europe**, the churches have tried to adapt to the 'modern spirit'. While the human sciences have cast some light on the place of ritual in all our lives, a more 'human' liturgy

CHURCH FOR THE WHOLE FAMILY

JOHN TIGWELL

Everything was ready for the service to begin, but where was the vicar? Suddenly, with a loud roar, the vicar appeared mounted on a shiny new motorbike. He thundered down the aisle, between the rows of his surprised congregation, stopped the motor and parked the bike at the front of the church. Not a happening in some trendy suburb, but the first few minutes of a family service for Pentecost in an English country church.

Or take the case of a small church in Western Australia. The temperatures were in the 40 degrees Celsius and people were wearing their lightest clothes, but everyone, young and old, was engrossed in what was happening. A large mural was being prepared from newspaper pictures to form the focus for a family worship service on the theme of prayer. This church had seen its Sunday evening congregation grow from very few to hundreds by the new emphasis on the family.

All round the world congregations are seeing numerical growth from a discovery of family worship. But why concentrate on the family aspects of worship? Isn't what we have always done good enough?

Celebration

The world in which we live is not religiously neutral. It is a battleground on which the forces of evil are pitted against the power of Christ. As we gather together to worship, the family of Christ does so in confidence that he is the winner in that battle. Worship is not a fantasy world in which we can escape, but the celebration by God's people of Jesus' victory over sin and death. In worship the Christian fellowship demonstrates its Christian world perspective.

Because of this, it is vital that everyone - children and adults - should share in this experience. The celebration of God's people should be a genuine meeting of each person with their Lord in the particular situation where he has put him or her. And the whole community of the church has the opportunity in worship to experience the presence of God and to be enriched by learning more about him and his saving acts.

As churches have rediscovered the joy of worshipping together, they have learnt something else, too. They have found that the vitality of worship is not just for adults, but for all age-groups in the church. The attitude of many churches towards the participation of children in the worship of the fellowship has so often been out of keeping with Jesus' attitude. He showed this clearly when he took a little child and warned the disciples not to prevent children in their innocence and humility coming to him.

The most important aspect of any group is its rituals, because they make that group distinctive. Worship is central to church life. If the next generation is to experience the essence of Christian life, they must be participants in all the rituals of the Christian community. Churches are now waking up to the idea that young

people should not simply be in the church, but that they should be allowed to express the liveliness and vitality which is their gift to the community. This natural joy and wonder needs to be brought out if families are to participate fully in the worship of the church. Increasingly, the language churches use, the hymns, readings and activities are chosen with great care, demonstrating clearly that everyone there is important and is included in what is happening.

Kids' stuff?

There are, of course, dangers in this trend towards family worship. What must be avoided at all costs is making a family service only a children's service. The average person in the street still believes that religion is good for kids. When uncommitted parents come into our services and then find only children's material, their assumption that religion is for kids and has no relevance to their life at all is confirmed. They will leave the church with a smile on their lips but nothing in their hearts.

Similarly, family worship should not just be about families. It needs to include single people, and those who feel isolated in society. The key feature of family worship is not the family, but the fact that it includes people of all ages and all conditions. All generations can learn to express themselves in worship and praise to their Lord and Saviour. Only as this happens will we experience the reality of God's alternative society and celebrate Jesus' victory over sin and death.

In worship Christians offer themselves and their gifts to God. Sometimes this includes such gifts as dance and drama, as well as music and verbal communication.

See New-world Faith; Gospel and Culture; African Independent Churches

has, some 'old believers' feel, forfeited the sense of transcendence and mystery. How should modern people meet with God in worship? We are still looking for more adequate ways to express this encounter.

It is in **the United States** that the churches have gone furthest in accommodating their liturgy and life to the surrounding culture. The result is a polarization between extreme liberals and the numerically-stronger fundamentalists, with great tracts of blandness in between; none of these has much sense of the importance of sacraments. Somewhere in the United States, a church which is Evangelical, Orthodox and Catholic is waiting to be born.

In **Latin America**, prayer, Bible study and mass undergird the livelier 'base communities' which are striving to establish a counter-culture which will transform their society.

In **the Third World**, the goal has been to find forms of worship which will genuinely respect the local culture. In black Africa, the churches founded by Protestant missions were slow to take the risk of Christianizing native music, poetry, art and so on. By contrast, the 'independent churches' sometimes appear to have gone overboard in their desire to achieve a fusion with African traditional religion. When, fifty years after the ministry of

Simon Kimbangu, the Kimbanguists in 1971 introduced the Lord's Supper, they employed 'bread' made from potatoes, maize and bananas, and the drink was honey and water. It was a serious attempt to ground the sacramental meal in local custom, but it raised the question of what it is about the Lord's Supper that has been unchangeably instituted by Christ.

In **India**, the Roman Catholic Biblical Catechetical and Liturgical Centre at Bangalore published in 1974 two *New Orders of Mass for India*. These orders adopted Indian ways of honouring the ministers, the Bible and the sacramental elements, using flowers, lights and incense. They were later withdrawn by Rome after protests from other Indian Catholics, particularly because in the eucharistic prayer thanks were given for the religions of India.

Christians in countries with or without a Christian tradition must alike confront the issue of how far their faith can be culturally adapted without losing the distinctiveness of the universal gospel. Worship is often the place where questions such as this are most sharply posed and where there is an opportunity to explore and solve them in an attitude of prayer and reflection.

The Unity Movement

JOHN BRIGGS

There are three strands in the ecumenical movement. The movement commits the one church of Jesus Christ throughout the world to a threefold quest for unity, evangelism, and service in the world. This means that the movement is at once international, and interdenominational. It seeks to aid the churches in making manifest the kingdom of God among all peoples, and to working out God's purposes of redemption and salvation throughout the world.

Brother Roger, founder of the Taizé community, and Dr Philip Potter, until recently General Secretary of the World Council of Churches, join in worship with a child. Christian unity operates at the personal level as well as at the level of denominations – whenever different traditions meet in Jesus' name.

The first move towards united Christian witness began in the nineteenth century. The Evangelical Alliance was formed in 1846 and the World Alliance of YMCAs nine years later. In 1889 the Sunday School movement held its first international convention and in 1895 the World Student Christian Federation came into being, with its clear and important missionary imperative: 'Evangelize to a finish and bring back the king.' This message was sent around the world from conference to conference at the beginning of the twentieth century. However, the birth of the modern ecumenical movement is normally dated to the World Missionary Conference held in Edinburgh in 1910. There, the scandal of a divided church and the crippling effect this had on evangelism was urgently explored.

The strong emphasis on evangelism led to the founding of the International Missionary Council in 1921. Four years later, the Life and Work movement, under the leadership of Archbishop Söderblom of Sweden, sought to help the churches to work out more effective ways of witnessing in the secular world. In 1927 the first Faith and Order Conference was held at Lausanne, and explored ways of breaking down the differences between churches, in doctrine and church organization. Just before World War II, plans were being worked out to bring all these concerns together in a World Council of Churches – but this was not formally constituted until the Amsterdam Assembly of 1948.

THE WORLD COUNCIL OF CHURCHES

The basis of the World Council of Churches (WCC) is that it is a 'fellowship of churches which confess the Lord Jesus Christ as God and Saviour according to the Scriptures and therefore seek to fulfill their common calling to the glory of God, Father, Son and Holy Spirit'.

See Roman
Catholics since the
Council; America's
Black Churches;
Clouds over
Southern Africa

By 1984 the World Council had within its fellowship over 300 churches representing more than 400 million Christian people around the world: at Amsterdam in 1948 where the World Council had already begun to engage in reconstruction and refugee work in post-war Europe, there had been 146 churches, but more than three-quarters of these were from the Western world.

Six assemblies of the World Council have been held since its beginnings:

● **Amsterdam**, as the first assembly, was characterized by the determination of those present, that having discovered one another, 'we intend to stay together'.

● The second assembly met at **Evanston** in the United States in 1954, in a world where reconstruction had given way to recriminations, the suspicions of the Cold War and MacCarthyism. But it took as its theme, 'Jesus Christ, the Hope of the World.' However, even within the fellowship of the WCC it was necessary to hold separate Free

Church, Lutheran, Anglican and Orthodox communion services at the assembly. (By the Vancouver conference, all except the last group met around a common table with male and female clergy celebrating together.)

● In 1961 at **New Delhi**, the first assembly in the Third World, the work of the International Missionary Council was integrated in the WCC. The Orthodox (and other) churches of eastern Europe were also received into membership.

● Perhaps the most critical of assemblies since the first was that at **Uppsala** in Sweden, which in 1968 witnessed the World Council trying to grapple with the radical challenges of the 1960s: the problems of racism, the growing gap between rich and poor nations, the ambiguity of scientific and technological progress. These were not easy issues to handle and there was a danger of leadership and constituency becoming divorced from one another.

● The subsequent assemblies at **Nairobi** (1975) and **Vancouver** (1983) both witnessed an attempt to hold in tension all the different strands of the ecumenical movement – life and work, faith and order, evangelism and education.

THE CATHOLIC-PROTESTANT DIVIDE

During these same years, dramatic changes of attitude occurred within the Roman Catholic Church, stimulated by the initiatives taken by Pope John XXIII (1958-63). In 1960 he

Christian leaders from Canada, Fiji, India and England join to celebrate a communion service during the sixth assembly of the World Council of Churches in Vancouver, Canada, 1983.

THE PROGRAMME TO COMBAT RACISM
ROGER WILLIAMSON

For its Uppsala Assembly in 1968, the World Council of Churches invited Martin Luther King as a main speaker. But exactly three months before the assembly opened, King was shot on the balcony of his hotel. For many black people at the time this was confirmation that white-dominated power structures would never willingly allow black equality. James Baldwin, the black American novelist, spoke as a replacement for King and delivered a blistering attack on white oppression. These events led directly to the World Council of Churches' Programme to Combat Racism - the most controversial of its initiatives.

All one in Christ Jesus

For many years there has been a consensus among Christians that discrimination on grounds of colour is sinful - particularly *inside* the churches. This condemnation of racism has its roots in the Bible, where Paul said, 'There is neither Jew nor Greek, there is neither slave nor free, there is neither male nor female; for you are all one in Christ Jesus.' From 1924 onwards, the ecumenical movement issued a series of declarations against any form of racism, including the racist doctrine of Nazism, which was condemned in the 1930s.

There have been many steps taken in the modern campaign against racism. Perhaps the oldest was the Christian initiative to secure the abolition of slavery. Gandhi's protests, beginning in South Africa, mark another. Yet another was the civil rights movement in the United States, led by Martin Luther King. In the 1950s and early 1960s the movement for civil rights for black people was exclusively non-violent - but it was often met by violence from those with

power. In South Africa, the exclusively non-violent approach lasted from Gandhi's early campaign (1910 onwards) to 1960 and the Sharpeville Massacre, when sixty-nine people in a non-violent demonstration were shot and killed.

Grants for liberation movements

In 1969, following the Uppsala Assembly, the World Council of Churches decided to go beyond merely condemning racism. It was agreed, during a consultation held in Notting Hill, London, that positive encouragement should be given to liberation movements. One year later, the first grants were made to liberation movements such as the African National Congress (South Africa), Frelimo (Mozambique), and SWAPO (Namibia). There was instantly a hostile reaction from the South African government and the white churches in that country, and also from the conservative media in North America and Western Europe - accusing the World Council of Churches of supporting violence and terrorism. The World Council of Churches and its supporters pointed out that the grants had been given for non-military purposes such as health care and education in the areas under the control of the liberation movements. They added that the grants had been made from a 'special fund', given expressly for this purpose.

The programme has concentrated on southern Africa, but has taken up the cause of oppressed racial groups world-wide.

In 1971, the World Council of Churches Committee passed a resolution in favour of economic sanctions against the countries of southern Africa whose form of government was based on racial

discrimination. This economic pressure was an entirely non-violent technique of the type used by Gandhi, Martin Luther King and the black South African Christian leader and Nobel Peace Prize winner, Chief Albert Luthuli. Once more there were protests in South Africa and the West.

Bishop Desmond Tutu, also a Nobel Peace Prize winner and the General Secretary of the South African Council of Churches, visited Europe in 1974 and preached a sermon in Westminster Abbey. He asked why Bonhoeffer is regarded as a saint in Western Europe for trying to kill Hitler and rid Germany of the Nazi system, when black South Africans who take up arms to defeat the apartheid system are regarded as terrorists. Apartheid has now been condemned as heresy by the World Alliance of Reformed Churches - a severe blow for the white Dutch Reformed churches of South Africa.

Many black South African Christians argue that if it is right to have army chaplains for white South African soldiers, it is right to have chaplains for those in liberation movements. They point out that those who oppose grants to liberation movements and who also reject economic pressure leave no hope of change.

As far as black people are concerned, the importance of the Programme to Combat Racism cannot be overestimated. Many black South African church leaders openly support the programme. They do this in spite of the fact that expressions of support for liberation movements or economic sanctions against South Africa can carry heavy prison sentences. They are willing to take the same risks and make the same sacrifices that their predecessors have made in the struggle against injustice.

See Renewal in the Holy Spirit; Focus on Worship; Telling the World; The Church of the Poor; Stewards of Creation; War and Peace

established the Papal Secretariat for the Promotion of Christian Unity and soon after summoned the innovative Second Vatican Council which met from 1962-65. Since 1965 a joint working group has met annually with members appointed by both the WCC and the Vatican.

More of the division between Protestants and Catholics was broken down when from 1967 the Charismatic movement was seen to be influencing Roman Catholic as well as Protestant churches. In 1969 Pope Paul VI visited the WCC headquarters and fifteen years later Pope John Paul II also visited Geneva. The relationship between the Vatican and the WCC at present is one of mutual respect and co-operation in specific areas, but it seems unlikely that the Roman Catholic Church will apply to join the World Council, even though in specific countries and areas (such as Brazil and in the Caribbean) it may already be a full member of associated national and regional councils of churches.

SETTING TARGETS FOR THE CHURCH

The actions and concerns of the World Council of Churches reveal the main emphases of the ecumenical movement, as it looks inside the church and outside to the world at large.

● **Bringing Christians together**
Following the assembly at Vancouver, the WCC put two important documents to its member churches for discussion. The first was on the sacraments

and the church's ministry, entitled *Baptism, Eucharist and Ministry*. This was produced after much study and consultation, including participation by Roman Catholic theologians. Although some of the difficult issues remain unresolved, it witnessed to more agreement than earlier seemed possible. Most member churches have responded by looking seriously at their own theologies of ministry and sacrament. Alongside this there have been talks between a number of world confessional families which have resulted in agreed theological statements. These show how much common ground there is in the profession of the Christian faith today.

● **Evangelism and the poor**
The second document was entitled *Mission and Evangelism, an Ecumenical Affirmation*. It was produced to make clear the WCC's continuing commitment to evangelistic enterprise, following criticism that the council had sacrificed evangelistic concern to political action. Another signal of this commitment to evangelism was the appointment in 1984, for the second time in succession, of the director of the WCC's Commission on World Mission and Evangelism to be its general secretary. The Uruguayan Methodist, Emilio Castro, took over from Philip Potter, a fellow Methodist from the Caribbean.

This emphasis on evangelism, however, had to start by taking the earth's poor seriously. Raymond Fung, a first-generation Christian and Baptist layman whose experience has been in urban mission in Hong Kong, spoke for many in the WCC when he said, 'We cannot be serious, and do not deserve to be taken seriously, if we claim to be interested in global evangelization - of Asia, of Africa, of Latin America - and yet refuse to take as central to our evangelistic commitment the masses of the poor in the cities and villages all over the world. A middle-class church in a sea of peasants and industrial workers makes no sense, theologically and statistically.'

Since the Vancouver assembly, a new study of the relationship between gospel and culture has been launched, with a view to aiding practically the churches in their witness. The study aims to help churches to discover the bridges between the Christian message and local or national culture, and to remind them that the gospel both judges culture and stands above it.

● **Hard cash for those in need** The World Council undertakes a sizeable programme in inter-church aid, refugee relief, and also in development work. In 1983, it handled more than $44 million in project funds for the emergency relief and development work of the churches around the world, while it spent just over $5 million on its own programmes in those areas. But the WCC recognizes that aid is not enough; the attitudes of people and of governments have to be changed if justice is to be available to all.

● **Biblical action in a desperate world** In what

appears to be a deteriorating world situation, the WCC has committed itself to struggling for 'justice, peace and the integrity of creation'. This commitment is made against a background of the alarming increase in world hunger, a world refugee crisis, the widespread erosion of human rights, the increasing preparation for war, the belligerence of the super-powers, and an

increasingly rapacious exploitation of the earth's resources coupled with the alarming pollution of the environment. Issues like these put peace firmly on the agenda of the Vancouver assembly, but the Third World delegates were particularly anxious that the peace issue should not be divorced from the total issue of justice. They claimed that the biblical concept of *shalom* did not signify the fragile peace of politicians - a mere absence of war - but rather the deep peace which made for the wholeness of

Members of different denominations forget their difference in many of today's movements and not just in the formal 'unity movement'. These Charismatic Christians combine dignity and joy in their worship.

all people. For them the crisis was not in some maybe tomorrow, but was present today; therefore peace and justice have to be held together.

Alongside this commitment to justice and peace is that to 'the integrity of creation'. The developed world's use of technology and the Third World's inability to control population growth are in danger of creating an economic system and pattern of life that cannot be sustained. Together they are rapidly exhausting the earth's limited resources, increasingly polluting the environment, making ever-greater demands of land and sea. The WCC gives a much-needed call to respect the integrity of creation and to develop styles of living, as nations and individuals, that respect the created order rather than violating it. It is a call to recognize that the gifts of creation are for all of God's children, both in this generation and in generations yet to come. Here is theology in action, the

FROM AMSTERDAM TO VANCOUVER

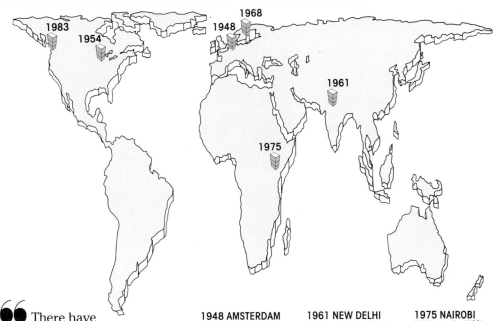

66 There have been six assemblies of the World Council of Churches since its foundation in 1948. Each has had its own particular focus. 99

1948 AMSTERDAM
The council inaugurated: 'we intend to stay together.' Post-war reconstruction: aid and relief programme. 146 churches represented, only 30 of them from Asia, Africa and Latin America.

1954 EVANSTON
Appeals for international toleration at the height of the 'cold war'. Confession of 'our oneness in Christ and our disunity as churches'. Stress on the ministry of laypeople.

1961 NEW DELHI
First assembly in the Third World. The work of the International Missionary Council integrated with WCC. Orthodox churhces from socialist countries and some Latin American Pentecostal churches join the council.

1968 UPPSALA
Some radical challenges of the 1960s confronted: racism, growing gap between rich and poor, ambiguity of progress in science and technology.

1975 NAIROBI
Holding together WCC's radical leadership and representatives of member churches. Working towards 'a just, participatory and sustainable society'. Concern for 'holistic evangelism'.

1983 VANCOUVER
Assembly centred on worship of God's pilgrim people. West's concern for peace under nuclear threat not to be divorced from Third World's search for justice.

Bible leading Christians to adopt an urgent ethical stance.

AREAS OF DIFFICULTY

Some of the work of the World Council has provoked controversy, especially the distribution of money contributed to the 'Special Fund' (of gifts specifically earmarked for this purpose) operated by the Programme to Combat Racism. These grants demonstrate World Council solidarity with all who oppose racial oppression. They are made to the humanitarian work of liberation organizations, some of which use military means to secure their ends. These have been widely criticized in the West, but have been well received throughout the Third World. The task of dialogue with other living faiths is another difficult area which has caused argument, where activity has to be undertaken with great care and watchfulness.

Actions such as these have offended Christians who are unhappy about church involvement in politics, especially politics of a radical kind. Similarly, there are churches which will not join the World Council because they believe it to be compromised by the breadth of the council's membership, by a lack of particularity in its doctrinal basis, or because of its positive attitude towards the Roman Catholic Church.

BEYOND THE HEADLINES

The less sensational work, though often ignored by the press, is no less important. For example, the council undertakes an immense amount of educational work on a number of fronts: through the Ecumenical Institute at Bossey, near Geneva; through the WCC scholarship programme; and through the Programme on Theological Education. All the time it is working to deepen and extend an awareness of ecumenical issues. Other WCC programmes are designed to enrich the life of its member churches by sharing experiences which can give new life to their work and witness. Activities such as these, which do not attract publicity, are crucial, because the ecumenical movement must always remain something more than the activities of the World Council itself, which is the servant of the movement, not its incarnation.

PART TWO
In Every Place

2.1 WHICH WAY FOR A CONTINENT?

Christians in Africa

TITE TIENOU

People often think of Africa as if it were all very much the same, from Egypt to Namibia or from Senegal to Mozambique. But it is not. It is a continent of great diversity. The conditions, beliefs and practices of Christians in Africa are as varied as the continent itself. If we want to understand these Christians, popular generalities must give way to a view which takes full account of this diversity and variety.

Geographically and politically, the variety of Africa can be seen in the fifty-nine or so nation-states, each peopled by a diversity of ethnic groups of pre-colonial origins. Religions such as Islam or Christianity (*imported* religions, as some call them) add to the diversity of Africa by their multitudes of sects and denominations. It is important to recognize the diversity of Africa at the outset because there are all kinds of Christians in Africa.

The purpose of this article is to provide a guided tour of this rich and varied scene:
● **taking in the full impact of the variety of Christians in Africa**;
● **looking at the growth of Christianity in this continent**;
● **examining the paradoxes of Christianity in Africa**;
● **asking about its prospects for the future**.

A RICH TAPESTRY
Observers of the religious scene generally divide Africa into two sections: north of the Sahara Desert and south of the Sahara. The countries north of the Sahara, from Morocco to Egypt, are generally classified with the Arab world. They are essentially Muslim in religion and Arab in ethnic composition. The rest of the continent, south of the Sahara, is thought to be the area where traditional religions are strongest. It is also the part of Africa where Christianity has enjoyed its most remarkable growth. Consequently, Africa south of the Sahara is thought to be more pluralistic than north Africa in religious terms.

Yet this distinction should not be drawn in too sharp a way. There is a Christian presence in North Africa. Egypt was one of the four poles of Christianity in its early centuries. Today's

How will African Christians meet the new challenges of an independent, increasingly educated continent?

The image of a largely peasant culture in Africa, with a tiny educated elite, is becoming out of date. A generation is coming up in some countries of which a significant proportion are well-qualified, sometimes at African colleges and universities. In future outside expertise will be less essential, both in industry and in church.

Coptic Church in Egypt, though a minority, testifies to the fact that this North African country is not totally Muslim. Similarly Christians in Sudan, though not direct descendants of the old Nubian Christians, are recognized as a significant minority, particularly in-southern Sudan. Though the other North African countries have proportionately fewer Christians than Egypt or Sudan, there are still isolated Christians in the general population. The Christians of North Africa, facing their own particular pressures, contribute to the variety of Christians in the continent. The perspective of Christians in a predominantly Muslim society is quite different from that of Christians in a largely Christianized population.

As we move from North Africa to the countries south of the Sahara, we begin to leave behind a situation where Christianity is submerged and sometimes suppressed by Islam, and to find places where Christians have a more siginificant position.

Islam is still the most important religion in the countries immediately south of the Sahara: Mauritania, for example, or Senegal or Niger. But as we move still further south, the religious picture becomes more complex. In some countries, such as Burkina Faso (Upper Volta until August 1984), Guinea, Chad, Mali or Sierra Leone, Christians are still a very small percentage of the population, but here traditional religions, the third element in the African religious scene, are important. In other countries, as for instance the Central African Republic, Kenya, Malawi or Zaire, Christians seem to be the majority of the population. Christians are unevenly distributed across Africa.

But the variety of Christians in Africa lies in more than mere geography. Political situations, colonial history, the particular history of Christianity in the various countries, each contribute to the diversity of Christian experience in the continent. For instance, the political situation in the Republic of South Africa colours the Christian experience of blacks as well as white South Africans in ways which are not readily understood in West Africa. Likewise, Christians in countries such as Mozambique and Angola, whose colonial histories were so distinctive, must deal with issues not normally raised in Kenya. In general terms, Roman Catholicism is the dominant form of Christianity in so-called French-speaking Africa, while Protestantism displays more vitality in so-called English-speaking Africa. There are, however, exceptions to this general trend. In Zaire, for example, the Kimbanguist movement, with its clearly Zairian roots, is very important. Colonial history and policies account for the geographical distribution of many mission-founded churches. By contrast, the rise of African Independent Churches is most clearly seen in Southern and Central Africa and in some of the coastal countries of West Africa.

All this rich variety of Christian experience in Africa makes it rash to generalize. What is often presented as African Christianity is seldom more than a local reality applied to the continent as a whole. If there are common characteristics of Christians in Africa, they are so general as to be true of Christians anywhere. But there is one feature which seems to be specific to Christianity in Africa south of the Sahara: phenomenal growth.

See Islam Encounters Christianity

CLOUDS OVER SOUTHERN AFRICA

Members of an African Independent church worship on a Pietermaritzburg hillside – many in Southern Africa are Christians. Ian Smith supported a white Rhodesia for the sake of 'Christian civilization', when most of the future Zimbabwe's Christians were black. Some Christians, including many from Independent churches, keep clear of politics. But many others feel in Christian conscience they cannot do so.

Black South African protest meetings often include prayer and hymn-singing, though other politically-conscious blacks have rejected Christianity. Afrikaaners enforce apartheid (separate development of the races) for reasons stemming from their Dutch Reformed Church's interpretation of the Bible. They genuinely believe these policies will sustain a Christian community. But black Christian leaders such as

Allan Boesak and Bishop Desmond Tutu warn of violence to come if injustices like the immigrant labour system continue, with families forced to live hundreds of miles from the white areas where the wage-earner must work. Any attempt at reconciliation has to be concerned with the structures which divide people.

GROWTH

Some have described Africa as the most fertile soil for Christianity in this century. Others have predicted that Africa will be a largely Christian continent by the year 2000! How credible are such statements? First, it is worth noting that the prediction of complete success for Christianity in Africa is not as recent as some believe. Back in 1956, Roland Oliver was very optimistic about Christianity's prospects in Africa. In a broadcast talk he indicated that there had been a geometrical progression of Christianity in Africa south of the Sahara since 1912. And he added: 'If things were to go on at the same rate, there would be no pagans left in Africa after the year 1992.'

But we must remember that social institutions do not function according to mathematical formulae. There are many factors which can increase or decrease this rate of growth. We are seeing today a resurgence of African traditional religions, while Islam is developing more missionary zeal. This could slow down the growth of Christianity in Africa. Also, the countries of Africa, together with the rest of the Third World, have a very high population growth. Unless the growth of Christianity is significantly greater that the growth of population, there will be plenty of people left to convert in Africa in the foreseeable future!

Still, the optimistic observers of the progress and growth of Christianity in Africa are not mistaken. The numbers of people identifying themselves with some form of Christianity in the continent is unprecedented. David B. Barrett's *World Christian Encyclopedia* (1982) shows that only 9.2 per cent of Africa's population was Christian in 1900. In mid-1980, 44.2 per cent of the continent's population was Christian. Barrett's projection for the year 2000 is that 48.4 per cent of all Africans will be Christian! Remembering that these figures apply to the whole continent, the growth-rate of Christianity south of the Sahara has been quite remarkable.

These sort of statistics encourage everyone interested in Christianity's evangelistic success. They show the great vitality of Christianity in post-independence Africa. Millions of Africans have not been persuaded that Christianity is a 'white man's religion'.

Some people are suspicious of such stress on statistics. They believe our concern should be to measure real Christianity or the depth of Christian maturity. This is a valid warning, even though it can lead to counting only those who fit one's own category of Christian. And that does not work in contemporary Africa, which defies classification into pre-established categories. Whether it is Egyptian Coptic, Ethiopian Orthodox, Mission Church or so-called African Independent Church, Christianity in Africa has aspects which sometimes baffle the outside observer.

But if we take numbers and a desire to celebrate in worship as signs of vitality, then African

An Afrikaner Christian, Beyers Naude, expressed his surprise at how black Christians in South Africa act towards him. They have 'a feeling that bitterness will achieve nothing, a removal of feelings of personal revenge, but still the same determination to end the system of apartheid. Their Christian witness humbles me.'

Christianity is indeed vital. Millions of Africans, approaching nearly half the population of the continent, openly identify themselves with some form of Christianity. They fill cathedrals, temples and church buildings week after week. They attend countless religious ceremonies in the name of Christ. Yes, Christianity has found a fertile soil in Africa and it has grown.

But being a Christian in Africa is by no means easy. It means living with the frustrations and paradoxes which are currently present in the continent. These aspects of the 'African condition' tend to weaken Christianity.

CLASH OF CULTURES

According to Ali A. Mazrui, a well-known Kenyan political thinker, the current situation in Africa can be described in one word: paradox. He described one such paradox in a broadcast lecture, *A Clash of Cultures*, in which he explores the result of

Continued on p. 146

A RELIGIOUS MAP OF AFRICA

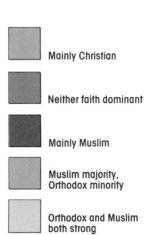 Islam and Christianity compete for Africa's allegiance. Tribal religions are also widely practised, but their pattern is too complex for this map. The Orthodox churches of Egypt and Ethiopia go back to the early Christian centuries. **99**

Mainly Christian

Neither faith dominant

Mainly Muslim

Muslim majority, Orthodox minority

Orthodox and Muslim both strong

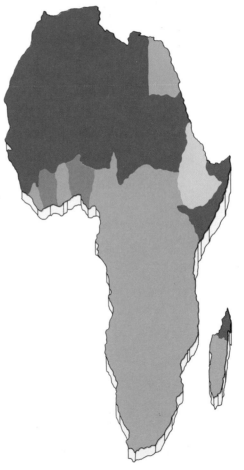

AFRICAN INDEPENDENT CHURCHES
DAVID SHANK

Hundreds of thousands of sub-Saharan Africans live out their faith in a wide variety of churches, unrelated to foreign church traditions, structures, leaders, doctrines or discipline. These African Independent Churches have developed under African initiative, in response to the needs and understanding of Africans. Together they form an extensive movement of rich creativity and astonishing diversity.

Breakaways from mission churches in all areas of the continent during the last third of the nineteenth century marked the beginnings of the movement. By 1967, one survey reported 5,000 such independent churches, totalling 7 million adherents among 290 tribes in thirty-four nations. Twenty years later the numbers of churches and adherents have probably more than doubled. They range in size from several congregations to churches with more than a million members. The African Independent Churches are a dynamic, major dimension of African Christianity.

But why have these separated churches formed?

■ One cause of this unexpected development was **the identity of Western missions with European colonialism**. Africans experienced a 'lack of love' from their European brothers and sisters. African responsibility for the church was thwarted by colonial missionary policies which controlled church government, finance and discipline. Because of these restrictions, African Christians responded with breakaway churches which, nevertheless, reflected patterns of church life they had received from the missionaries.

■ More importantly, **many Western founders of churches in Africa were scarcely aware of African religions** and their powerful vitality, which offered a religious climate in which the teaching of Jesus could be experienced in a new way. When African Christians dealt with these unhindered, new religious break-throughs occurred. Spiritual liberation and protection, spiritual healing, prophetic guidance, and understanding through dreams were just a few of the hallmarks of what followed. The independent, charismatic leadership of African men and women had become a vital feature of the African church.

Multi-coloured faith

Throughout the twentieth century in different parts of Africa, remarkable spiritual leaders have emerged with new patterns of piety, ethics, government and practice. They have created a new shape for African Christianity.

■ In West Africa in 1913-14, the Glebo prophet, William Wade Harris, sparked a mass movement which created **the Harrist Church** on the Ivory Coast. This became the forerunner of several hundred '**spiritual churches**' in Ghana and Liberia.

■ In the Niger Delta area, Garrick Braide began a similar movement, which became **the Christ Army Church** in 1918, when the Anglican Church could no longer contain it.

■ This anticipated the appearance of '**aladura' (praying) churches** among the Yoruba in western Nigeria in the 1920s. These churches began under leaders like Orimolade, the young prophetess Abiodun, Babalola, Oshitelu and others, who responded to the failure of Western medicine during an influenza epidemic.

■ In South Africa after 1915, numbers of **Zionist churches**, influenced by Western Pentecostals, accented the power of the Spirit, spiritual healing, and immersion baptism. White racist and elitist policies helped them to mushroom into a movement of hundreds of '**prophet healing churches**' among the dispossessed blacks, who exported them to countries to the north.

■ Among the Bakongo in Zaire in 1921, a former Baptist teacher, Simon Kimbangu, set off powerful spiritual waves in Central Africa. The largest has become the '**Church of Jesus Christ on the Earth by the Prophet Simon Kimbangu**', with its 'New Jerusalem' at N'Kamba in lower Zaire, and its claim of more than 2 million adherents.

■ In Kenya among the Luo a similar movement in 1916 evolved within the Anglican Church until a split occurred in 1934, followed by another in 1958, to form **the Church of Christ in Africa**.

■ A massive exodus from Luo Roman Catholicism in 1963 led to **the Legion of Mary Church**, under the inspiration of the prophetess Gaudencio Aoko. This is one of several independent churches with a Roman Catholic background.

Such are among the outstanding independent Africans and their churches, which are giving a permanent stamp to the character of African church life.

What marks the independents?

While Westernized churches have put a priority on literacy and education, many African Independent Churches have grown by exploiting the popular oral culture with its language of symbol and ritual. Biblical and

Members of the Kimbanguist church in Luanda, Angola, perform a play about the events of their founder's arrest and imprisonment.

appear to drown out the person of Christ. Many of the churches combine ritualism and a hierarchy of apostles and prophets with evangelical doctrine and charismatic experience.

It is particularly significant that large numbers of independent Christian communities are reading, interpreting and applying the Bible for themselves. The availability of the Bible in local dialects has even been cited as another cause of African independency. This seems convincing in the case of churches that use the Bible in a radical, literalist way to criticize the mission-established churches, and which try to recreate the church found in the New Testament.

Western-trained African theologians are pleased to see this spontaneous and dynamic application of the Bible as authentic raw material for a developing African Christian theology. Despite this, some independent churches accept training from the established churches, or invite Western Christian teachers to train their leaders.

National and international councils, both evangelical and ecumenical, have admitted selected African Independent Churches into membership. Many other independents have created among themselves local organizations for mutual counsel. Others are exclusive and relate officially to no other church organization. At the continental level, a fledgling Organization of African Independent Churches, based in Nairobi, has existed since 1978.

However, the heart of these new churches is not found in writings or councils. Rather, it is in the rediscovery of the power, liveliness and truth of the Christian faith for African life today.

Christian themes are also expressed through song, dance and preaching, following the intuitions of the first leaders and their successors.

Alongside Western doctrinal traditions, many independents seem poor in biblical and Christian content and have often been described as syncretistic. But there are great differences among the churches in their approaches to healing, the ancestors, polygamy, female circumcision, the use of dance and drama, and in borrowing from Western churches.

Many have important doctrinal foundations, while others stress right religious practice. For some independent churches Christ is the Light which disperses the power of the occult, while for others he is especially the Giver-of-Life and Healer. In numbers of them, Jesus is openly confessed as powerful Lord and Saviour, while for some the here-and-now power of God the Spirit may

Western influence in contemporary Africa. Because of the very rapid pace of Westernization, Mazrui claims, 'Africans are caught up between rebellion against the West and imitation of the West'. Political developments in Africa confirm that this paradox is indeed a reality. Unfortunately, Mazrui's clash of cultures is also seen in African Christianity. On the one side there are calls for an African theology, and the deeply African practices of the African Independent Churches. But at the same time Western church architecture and Western clerical vestments continue to be highly valued by many African Christians, who therefore resist moves towards more authentically African expressions of worship and Christian lifestyle.

Other paradoxes, such as Africa's underdevelopment and hunger in spite of its vast resources, its fragmentation and its lack of significance in world

affairs, also help us to understand the current situation of African Christianity. They explain why, in spite of its great numerical strength, African Christianity is little understood outside the continent and only very few African leaders are significant in world Christianity.

While some paradoxes of African Christianity are related to the situation in the continent, others are more specific to African Christianity itself. While thousands gather at religious ceremonies, this does not always mean zeal and commitment. We should never forget that the state of being non-religious, or even atheist, is a rather recent phenomenon in Africa. People are generally expected to be followers of some kind of religion. Religion then becomes a form of social identification. Consequently the great numbers who crowd Christian cathedrals, temples and churches may do so because they attach a special significance to the festive and social aspects of religion. If that is so, then the real increase of Christianity in Africa may be less than the numbers indicate.

When people understand Christianity as little more than a form of social identification, the result is that Christians tend to live an outward piety, a religion which lacks real substance. That in turn leads to rigidity, conservatism and legalism. All of these are present, in varying degrees, in African Christianity. The paradox here is that some Western Christians tend to look at Africa as the land of Christians with simple faith, less

Bishop Desmond Tutu, the Anglican Bishop of Johannesburg, received the Nobel Peace Prize in 1984. He was in the United States when he heard, and immediately returned home, saying that the prize belonged to all those working for peace in South Africa. Bishop Tutu had made clear to the World Council of Churches assembly in Vancouver that the North's concern for freedom from nuclear threat must not obscure Southern Christians' longing for freedom from oppression.

encumbered with forms and traditions. While this is true in one sense, it is equally true that such simple faith often exists alongside a deadly legalism – an emphasis on do's and don'ts rather than on the vital heart of Christianity.

Another paradox of African Christianity is seen in the way African Christians view themselves in relation to Christians from other continents, particularly to Western Christians. Much of present-day Christianity in Africa is the result of the modern missionary movement, which, rightly or wrongly, has been related to European colonial expansionism. One of the lasting effects of the European colonial domination of Africa is that Africans generally perceive themselves as inferior to Europeans and Westerners. That explains why, despite numbers and vitality, African Christians continue to view themselves as being on the receiving end of missions. Somehow the growth of Christianity in Africa has not yet produced the self-confidence we might expect. Consequently, the influence of Western Christians in Africa remains great while Christianity is decreasing in the West and rapidly increasing in Africa.

African Christianity has great potential. And yet it has serious areas of weakness and it experiences itself as poor and insecure. This weakness alongside strength shows in the relatively small missionary outreach of African churches. African Christians display a remarkable zeal in evangelism

within their own cultures. A spontaneous ability to share their faith largely explains the rapid increase in the numbers of Christians in recent years. But the crossing of significant linguistic and ethnic barriers is still largely neglected. There are exceptions, such as the vigorous mission programmes in Nigeria of the Evangelical churches of West Africa or those of the African Inland Church in Kenya, but these should not be taken as the norm. Rather, the opposite is true. Most churches in Africa have turned inwardly towards themselves. This, coupled with the fact that many churches are ethnically based, means there is a real danger of moving away from Christ, the centre of Christianity, into a religion based on local culture.

The weakness of African Christianity may also be attributed to problems in leadership. It is a well-known fact that the development of leadership has not kept pace with

A Shona choir sing Christian music in Harare, Zimbabwe. African Christian singing has a beauty all its own, whether it be Western hymns given an African cadence or songs set to traditional tunes.

See Gospel and Culture; The Missionary Inheritance

'The Christian faith is not just a private bank account which the holder uses secretly or privately. It is public property which has to be shared through service and proclaimed through evangelism. It is at the very heart of what our Lord himself did; he went about preaching the gospel, healing the sick, raising the dead, feeding the hungry.' John Mbiti

the explosive growth of Christianity in Africa. This is often a problem associated with rapid expansion: the many new Christians put great pressure on those responsible for Christian nurture. This includes the untrained leader of a congregation as well as the graduate of a Bible institute or of a theological college or seminary. At all these levels leadership is sorely lacking in African Christianity.

It is not uncommon to see one person in charge of several congregations or a self-proclaimed prophet lead people away from generally accepted biblical truth. In either case the result is the same: the vast potential of new Christians is diverted away from strengthening the Christian cause. African Christianity is in desperate need of leaders gifted and trained to care for new Christians. Only so can its growth be sustained.

TODAY'S CHALLENGE
Christians in Africa are faced with a double challenge: consolidating their gains and sustaining their growth.
● **In order to consolidate the gains of Christianity in Africa, the various church bodies will need to plan, develop and implement a vigorous programme of leadership development**. Only mature, well-instructed Christians will be able to resist the various anti-Christian influences and options now present in the continent.

AFRICAN THEOLOGY

African theology is concerned to express the Christian gospel against an African cultural background, and to take as positive an attitude to African traditions as is possible while remaining true to the gospel. This is sometimes in reaction to the opposition to those cultural traditions on the part of Western missionaries. African theologians want to interpret Christian faith in a way that the rapdily increasing number of educated Africans can relate to, without losing contact with their African heritage. In South Africa the emphasis is more on 'black theology' – seeing the political implications of faith in a form that has parallels with black theology in the United States.

● **The growth of Christianity needs to be sustained in Africa through a deliberate cultivation of missionary expansion across cultural divides, coupled with a conscious effort at de-Westernizing**. Current church practices, as well as the way the faith is expressed and taught, need to be made authentically African.

In other words, the various church bodies in Africa must, at the same time, be concerned with inner strengthening while boldly looking beyond their own selfish interests. These are the essential conditions for Christianity in Africa to fulfil its vast potential.

It is entirely possible that this potential will be realized; the opportunity is there for a tremendous Christian impact on the life of the whole continent. But it could all go wrong. Christians in Africa would do well to temper their present almost excessive optimism by remembering the fate of Christianity in North Africa and in Nubia in the early centuries of the faith. We know that in spite of its early gains in the present-day Maghreb (Morocco, Algeria, Tunisia and Libya), Christianity failed to survive the pressures of Islam. We also know that although Nubian Christianity managed to keep itself alive until sometime in the fifteenth century, it also faded out. Furthermore, the present situation of the Coptic Church in Egypt and the Orthodox Church of Ethiopia should give us warnings concerning the future of

Christianity in the African continent. The Coptic Church in Egypt has dwindled into such a minority position that, with exciting exceptions, it is mainly interested in survival and self-preservation. In the long term, such a limitation of concern means self-destruction. Although there are recent signs of life and revival in the Orthodox Church of Ethiopia, it has moved from a position of state religion (under the rule of Emperor Haile Selassie) to a position where the

See The Historic Churches of Africa

present regime sees it as suspect and linked to the feudalism of the old imperial order.

The history of Christianity teaches us that Christianization is never a complete process. There is never a point where Christianity is fully and finally established in a given situation. It must always maintain the vitality of faith. History also teaches us that an inward-looking church sooner or later loses its vitality,

Christian marriage and family life have just as important a job to do in Africa as anywhere else, as witnesses to the different quality of love and faithfulness Christians can find.

Pope Shenouda III is leader of the Egyptian Coptic Church. At a time of communal unrest he was confined by government decree to a desert monastery. But in January 1985 he was released to take up his duties as pastor and leader once again.

Christianity was essentially a Latin religion. It did not make inroads into the largely Berber population, nor did it really seek to do so. Consequently, as Roman civilization was pushed out of North Africa, Christianity disappeared with it.

We see today similar dynamics operating in Africa south of the Sahara. Many still claim that Christianity is a Western religion, which has to be rejected together with Western imperialism. This is the argument used by those opposed to Christianity as well as by those interested in establishing an African cultural identity. As long as church leaders, particularly those of the denominations founded by mission organizations, continue to maintain Western Christian forms and structures, they unwittingly contribute to the possibility of Christianity being rejected by the ordinary people of Africa.

The solution is not to fit Christianity into a traditional African culture, because that is rapidly disappearing everywhere in the continent. Rather, the challenge for Christianity in the coming years is how well it will meet Africans in their current ambiguous situation. If it succeeds in doing so, Christianity will lose the stigma of a foreign religion imposed on Africans, and be able to provide just that spiritual focus which a developing continent needs.

credibility and even sound doctrine: it becomes a system of rituals. That is the present danger faced by the Coptic Church in Egypt and the Orthodox Church of Ethiopia.

There is another lesson that today's Christians in Africa can learn from early Christianity in North Africa. It is this: when Christianity is viewed as the religion of an elite with alien connections, it does not survive strong outside pressure. In early Christian North Africa,

AFRICAN SELFHOOD
A few years ago, there was a call for a moratorium on outside

Christian personnel and finances into Africa. It originated in the All Africa Council of Churches. For those who proposed it, moratorium meant a temporary stop to the flow of outside missionaries and money into Africa. The reasoning was that the large number of missionaries and the great amount of foreign money were an obstacle to Christianity really taking root in the continent. The purpose of the moratorium was to allow Africans, by themselves, to Africanize Christianity as best they could. The purpose of the moratorium, then, was to make Christianity fit contemporary Africa. Although no longer a hot debate today, moratorium is still a vital issue for many African churches, and will continue to be so as long as Christianity is perceived as foreign to Africa.

Moratorium is one factor in the African Christians' quest for selfhood. This is a political quest as much as a theological statement. Moratorium does not automatically exclude evangelization – Africans are very good at that. But whether they focus on evangelization or not, Christians in Africa must live their faith in a highly politicized continent. That fact inevitably affects the churches. It is a vital part of the picture as Christians in Africa look into the future.

Churches in Southern Africa are much more aware of the political implications of their faith than those elsewhere in the continent. In the Republic of South Africa itself, both black and white Christians must deal with an increasingly violent situation.

There the oppression of blacks by the white minority has already produced the largest number of African Independent Churches. These churches are clearly a quest for selfhood. In this quest some Christians in South Africa and Namibia may come increasingly to use Marxist categories for analyzing and understanding their situation, and consequently, the theology produced may reflect Marxist influence.

Christians in countries which themselves are more or less Marxist will be less attracted to Marxist ideology as a basis for their theology and action. That is the case for Christians in countries such as Angola, Mozambique, Zimbabwe, Burkina

'We must take what Jesus did in first-century Palestine as a series of pointers to what he is doing amongst us – and that is what God has always been doing since Moses led the Israelites out of Egypt – freeing men and women from every form of slavery, political as well as spiritual'. President Kenneth Kaunda of Zambia

AN AFRICAN MARTYR

Janani Luwum became a Christian while a young schoolteacher in a northern Uganda village. He began to preach and was imprisoned for disturbing the peace. He told the warders: 'We love you, and our master, Jesus Christ, loves you too. The wooden bars at the window of this cell cannot separate us from the love of God, nor stop us proclaiming his message of salvation.'

Luwum later became Archbishop of Uganda during the Amin presidency. A government worker said: 'People these days say there is no God...when we can see things like fellowship between races and tribes, and people getting cured of their leprosy, none of which would happen if there was no God.'

He was eventually killed by the regime, and his funeral was held on Easter Day 1977 outside Namirembe Cathedral in Kampala - round an empty grave as the body had not been released. The Easter hymns declared a faith stronger than death.

'THE EVIL OF RELIGION'

A secret tract, published by the Ethiopian Ministry of Information and National Guidance, was smuggled out of the country during 1984. It said: 'There cannot be a more urgent task than the immediate launching of a campaign to remove the evils of religion. This can be effectively done through the skilful propagation of materialism in a carefully orchestrated campaign.'

The document, quoted by *The Times* of London, acknowledges that there is a revival of religion which 'is fast becoming ground for counter-revolution'. It suggests turning monasteries of the Ethiopian Orthodox church into museums, and confiscating priceless books and treasures. Regular church-goers, identified by a network of informers, should be discouraged by financial incentives and use of jobs. A propaganda campaign should emphasize the material side of life and promote the view that religion is 'always an obstacle to the liberation of oppressed people'.

Faso (formerly Upper Volta) and Ethiopia. For them the quest for selfhood will take different forms.

There is a common factor for Christians in South Africa and in the more or less Marxist countries of the continent. It is this: Christians will increasingly find themselves in open conflict with the political authorities of the various countries. The issue of church and state will become focal in the years to come. Once again Christian faith will have to be lived dangerously. That is one of the prospects of Christianity in Africa. It is one element which Christians there share with Christians in the rest of the world in this latter part of the twentieth century.

One final future Christian development in Africa needs to be mentioned here. The traditional categories for distinguishing kinds of Christianity will become more and more meaningless. Categories such as Evangelical, ecumenical, or even African Independent will become less and less helpful in understanding African Christianity. What we call African Independent Churches are really a group of churches which are very diverse. Evangelicalism in Africa, generally identified with the Association of Evangelicals of Africa and Madagascar, also includes churches with diverse dynamics. In the same way, the Unity Movement, represented in the continent by the All Africa Council of Churches, is more diverse than it is generally perceived to be in the West.

Issues of Christian living and theological development are better ways of determining the direction of African Christianity. In that regard, the different 'families' of Christianity in Africa are closer to one another than we think. The quest for authentic selfhood, the need to develop viable African Christian theologies and the desire to fit Christianity into contemporary African cultures – these are some of the unifying factors of Christianity in Africa. It is unlikely that the organizations mentioned above will disappear or fuse into one. But the features which tend to distinguish them sharply from each other will probably become less important.

It is right to conclude by returning to the great

possibilities lying before Christians in Africa. Though they are as diverse and varied as the continent itself, there are nevertheless some general characteristics which are applicable to Christianity in Africa as a whole. One such characteristic is the swift growth of Christian faith in Africa south of the Sahara, which is rapidly making Christianity a truly universal religion. Christians in Africa like to belong to wider church bodies. That spirit of solidarity is seen as Africans participate in world denominational bodies as well as the World Council of Churches and the World Evangelical Fellowhsip.

In spite of the rapid progress of the past years, there is still much to do to secure a solid implanting of the gospel in contemporary Africa. In one sense, the symphony of gospel communication is still unfinished in Africa. That is why foreign personnel and money will continue to be necessary in the foreseeable future. But this will only be truly useful if it genuinely contributes to making Christianity fit into the African situation of flux.

These are challenging times for Christians in Africa. In great numbers and more than ever before, African Christians are both taking up the challenge in their own continent and taking their place in world Christianity.

Africans are just as much missionaries in this generation as people from outside the continent used to be. Christians from one region of a country must cross real cultural barriers to take the gospel to totally different circumstances in another region.

An Ethiopian
Orthodox Christmas
Service. This is one
of the most ancient
national churches.

THE HISTORIC CHURCHES OF AFRICA
ROGER COWLEY

The two historic churches of Africa, in Ethiopia and Egypt, are under increasing pressure today. Although each has been a fact of life in its country for centuries, they are tolerated, rather than valued, by their governments.

The Ethiopian Orthodox Church

This church traces its founding to the fourth century AD, when Frumentius and Edesius preached the gospel in the kingdom of Axum. Frumentius went to Egypt, where Athanasius made him bishop of Ethiopia. From that time until 1950, monks were sent from the Coptic Church in Egypt to be head (abun) of the Ethiopian Church. Since 1950, the abun has been appointed from within the Ethiopian Orthodox Church.

About 15 million Ethiopians (approximately half the population) are attached to the Ethiopian Orthodox Church rather than to any other religious group. Church services are held early on Sunday mornings and on festivals. The main service is one of holy communion, and the language of the service is Geez, with Amharic increasingly coming into use for parts of it. Geez is the ancient language of northern Ethiopia, and Amharic is the official, modern language of the whole country.

The principal annual festivals are Easter and the Baptism of Christ. Saints' days (especially those of the Virgin Mary) and days of fasting are widely observed. Church buildings are usually circular, with a roof of thatch or corrugated iron. Many of the books kept at the churches and monasteries are hand-written on vellum (scraped animal skin); printed copies of the books in frequent use are available today.

Since 1974, under the military government, the Ethiopian Orthodox Church has lost many privileges. In 1976, the head of the church was deposed by the government, and others of its leaders have been imprisoned or transferred to other places. Its youth organizations have been closed down. Religious publishing and broadcasting have been severely restricted. In some areas, far worse things have happened.

The government, in following a Marxist policy of encouraging the decline of religion, is proceeding cautiously against the Ethiopian Orthodox Church because of its large popular following. However, conditions for this church can be expected to worsen rather than improve.

The Coptic Orthodox Church

This Egyptian church was traditionally founded by St Mark, in the first century AD. Alexandria became a major Christian centre, linked with leaders and teachers like Origen, Clement, Athanasius and Cyril. The deserts of Egypt were important early centres of monasticism, where Antony, Macarius and others lived.

The Coptic Church did not accept the decisions of the church Council of Chalcedon on the nature of Christ in AD 451. For this reason, it is one of the 'non-Chalcedonian', or 'Oriental Orthodox' churches. (These churches are also sometimes called 'monophysite', but reject the name themselves.) From the Muslim invasion of AD 642 onwards, the Coptic Church came under heavy pressure from Arab Muslim rulers, and many Christians became Muslims. This persecution continued under the Turks, throughout medieval times.

Today there is officially freedom of religion in Egypt, but there is much unofficial discrimination, and the church still feels itself threatened by the Muslim majority. Recently, the activities of the head of the Coptic Church, Patriarch Shenouda, have been restricted by government order. There are difficulties over permits for building churches. In the educational system there is a bias towards Islam, as in many other areas of social and political life. Sporadically, Coptic Christians and churches have been attacked.

Government statistics appear to minimize the church's membership, showing it as between 2 and 3 million, while actual membership lists total between 6 and 7 million (out of a population of over 30 million). There is a steady loss in numbers through conversion to Islam, and through emigration.

In spite of these problems, the church has undergone many refreshing changes in recent years. Coptic, the language which gives the church its name, was spoken in Egypt from about the third to tenth centuries AD, but today the services are in Arabic. There has been an increase in the numbers of church schools offering Christian instruction on Fridays. Many young Christians have become monks, and the production of Christian literature has increased. Encouragingly, the laity of the church is active and anxious to involve the church in new enterprises.

2.2 CRADLE OF FAITHS

Christians in Asia

VINAY SAMUEL AND CHRIS SUGDEN

Asia has by far the largest population of all the continents. And of its 2,000 million people, 95 per cent still have no meaningful contact with Christians. Extreme and increasing poverty stalks the continent. The gulf between rich and poor within Asia and between Asia and advanced countries yawns ever wider. As Asian countries struggle for bread, they feel constrained to limit freedom. Human rights have suffered. Ancient religions, after repelling Christian witness for centuries, are now reasserting themselves.

This increasing self-awareness in the great religions of Asia showed itself in **India** when a Freedom of Religion bill in 1979 asserted Hinduism. **Iran's** revival of fundamentalist Islam toppled a government and has influenced neighbouring nations, leading to a stronger emphasis on Islamic faith in **Pakistan**.

What of Christianity in the continent where it began? 1984 saw the centenary of the church in **Korea**, and in many ways the Korean church is representative of the different aspects of Asian Christianity. It has its great successes. Billy Graham's largest crusade meeting ever, attended by over a million people, was held in South Korea's capital, Seoul. The largest congregation in the world is in South Korea, with over 350,000 members. Yet Korean Christians also have struggles and hardships. The general secretary of the Presbyterian Church in South Korea has been imprisoned for his strong commitment to human rights. While the idea is resisted by many Christians, there is a need for the church to enter into dialogue with Communism in North Korea and with Buddhism within its own borders.

Triumph, struggle, Communism, other faiths – these mark the Christians of country after country in the vast, complex, fascinating world of Asia.

THE SOUL OF ASIA

Asians are a people with a tremendous thirst for God. We express this thirst, and seek to satisfy it, not only with our intellect and ideas but also at an

Christians worship together in a church in Canton, China. The greater freedom for Christians in China since 1979 has shown that this great people, along with many other Asian peoples, contains a significant minority of Christians.

A MAP OF ASIA'S RELIGIONS

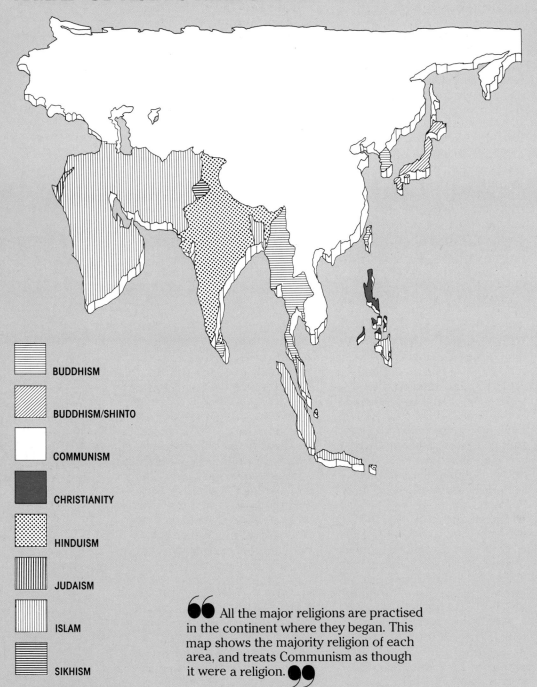

BUDDHISM

BUDDHISM/SHINTO

COMMUNISM

CHRISTIANITY

HINDUISM

JUDAISM

ISLAM

SIKHISM

66 All the major religions are practised in the continent where they began. This map shows the majority religion of each area, and treats Communism as though it were a religion. **99**

emotional level with deep feeling. Asian Christianity has to be taught and lived within the atmosphere of this Asian soul.

Our religions are **culture religions**. This means that religion is bound up closely with the way we see the world, with our family life, our sense of identity and our national histories. We Asians do not separate religion from our social, political, economic and personal lives.

Within this overall religious experience of life it is also important to distinguish between **high religion** and **folk religion**. High religion is the belief system of Hinduism, for example, or Islam: their teachings about the origin of the universe and of life, about the nature of God and the destiny of humankind. The religious worship of temples and mosques is all part of high religion.

But running parallel with this is a vast reality of folk religion. When an Indian villager loses his bullocks, or his baby is ill, he prays to local goddesses, and consults diviners and soothsayers.

To adapt a model used by Paul G. Hilbert:

● **High religion, being other-worldly, is concerned with cosmic gods, spirits of other worlds;**

● **Folk religion, being this-worldly, treats in local gods and goddesses, ancestors and ghosts, demons and evil spirits, dead saints.**

● **High religion is based on impersonal cosmic forces, such as fate;**

● **Folk religion deals with magic and astrology, 'mana', charms and magical rites, evil eye, evil tongue.**

It is folk religion which is the religious reality for everyday life and its problems; it is the more immediate religious experience for poor people.

FATALISM AND FEUDALISM

Asian life is dominated by a sense of fatalism. No change is possible because of the decree of the gods. Many people's experience of poverty teaches them that any change will only be for the worse. This acceptance of their lot is the Asian way of discouraging change; it has enabled people to survive great hardships. But it works against efforts to alter bad circumstances. Muslims, too, believe in an unalterable 'will of Allah' which determines their fate.

The Christian hope that God is active to bring change which redeems human life is a powerful ingredient in such a context. The encounter can be explosive between the kingdom of God and Indian fatalism.

Asian life and society is also often feudal in structure. Power rests not in social organization but in individuals, to whom power has been handed over because they are sons of parents who have demonstrated the ability to use power for the benefit of those they rule.

The feudal pattern survives because it creates dependency in the powerless. Leaders create

It is estimated that in India over a quarter of all medical care is provided by Christian agencies and church-based hospitals. Although Christians form only 3 per cent of the total population of some 730 million, about three-quarters of the country's nurses are professing Christians.

this dependency as they act as gatekeepers of an Aladdin's cave of scarce resources and coveted positions. People know that to keep the gate open they must support the dominant and prominent, mouthing whatever ideology is appropriate. The Asian tradition is one of deference to others who are older, wiser and appointed by the destiny of birth, allowing them to determine the course of common people's lives.

Against this background, Christians are given a tremendous challenge through Jesus' teaching that leaders should be servants. Sadly, churches are often affected by the feudalistic pattern of leadership so powerful in the surrounding society.

Patrick Sookhdeo has summarized the Asian religious world-view. Asians long for:

● **Prosperity**: they often seek God for the blessings he can confer.

● **Power**, as in the attempts of folk religion to control a disordered world.

● **Patronage**, in the whole apparatus of feudalism.

ISLAM ENCOUNTERS CHRISTIANITY

A Muslim mother brings her children to a Christian hospital in Pakistan. Islam began as Christianity's next-door neighbour; Arabia was surrounded by Christian countries. The Eastern Christians established a reasonable relationship with Muslims, but Western Christians ruined all that with the Crusades. Centuries later the missionary movement established small churches in central Asia, the Indian sub-continent and Indonesia.

The recent Islamic resurgence in some countries has made things hard for the churches, reducing their freedom to evangelize. But sometimes the hard legalism of fundamentalist Islam makes people want to look at the Christian gospel of liberation.

In many other lands, minority Christian churches are respected as communities serving people's needs. And dialogue continues over points of agreement and difference.

● **Peace**: rural Asia has been called 'a tranquil culture'. This is the peace of personal well-being.

The contrast of this with Christianity is at certain points very marked. It is based on quite different understandings of what salvation means and of how God created and sustains our world. And it knows little of the Christian grace of being a servant, nor of the positive power of suffering, nor of the peace of God's 'shalom'.

PRESSURES OF THE CITY

An increasing number of Asia's people live in towns and cities. The proportion varies considerably from country to country. In **India** and **China**, the majority of the population still live in the countryside, while countries such as **Singapore** and **Hong Kong** are virtually city-states. Some projections estimate that by AD 2000, 69 per cent of Asia's population will live in cities.

Cities have a profound effect on people's lives. They promote secular values and push religion to the margins. The office-block replaces the temple at the heart of the community. The purpose of the city is business, and anything which does not promote business and industry has a hard time surviving. The city breaks up community, because wider families are often prised apart by economic factors.

Cities act as magnets to rural populations. As numbers expand and become too great for the land to support, the rural poor flock to the cities, which are growing in Asia at the rate of 7 per cent every year. These rural people try to recreate in the cities the communities they knew in their villages.

Pentecostals and Roman Catholics are the most flourishing Christian groups in the slum areas to which these migrants gravitate. They offer that strong sense of community, authority and spiritual power which characterizes the religious and social life of the village. The mainline Protestant churches are found more in middle-class areas. The attractiveness of their programmes of ministry to poor people is that they are carried out by people who have made a success of city life.

Asia's cities present a strong

See The Global Village

A STORY FROM NEPAL

Kamala, a Nepali woman married off at the age of eleven, was unhappy in her marriage. Then her husband, Lakshmi, became ill. Kamala recounted how they were invited to a weekly Bible study at the hospital:

'We both attended and began to grow spiritually. Lakshmi's health improved, and so did our marriage. Later that year we were baptized. The village people and our family still hate us though, and perform *puja* (a Hindu ceremony) against us. We keep a hostel for hospital patients and their families, and at night we often sing and read the Bible...Some come and listen and want to know more. I like to explain the gospel to them...So much has changed in our lives: before we had so much trouble but now we are happy and have found peace.

CHRISTIANS IN THE MIDDLE EAST

 The region where Christianity began is now riven by conflict between people of different faiths. The central confrontation is between Jew and Muslim, as Israelis and Palestinians battle for a homeland. But Christians also face Muslims in Lebanon. Who are these Christians?

ARMENIANS
The Armenian Apostolic Church is another 'Oriental Orthodox' confession. The Armenians of the Catholicate of Cilicia separated in 1956 from those in the Soviet province of Armenia. They are found in Lebanon, Cyprus, Syria and Iraq.

COPTIC ORTHODOX
A large minority group in otherwise Muslim Egypt, they are 'Oriental Orthodox' Christians. They number about seven million, and there is a degree of spiritual renewal among them.

COPTIC EVANGELICAL
A Presbyterian church in Egypt, they are the largest Protestant community in the Middle East.

JEWISH CHRISTIANS
In Israel a number of congregations are emerging of Jews who accept Jesus as their Messiah.

PALESTINIAN CHRISTIANS
Drawn from several Christian confessions, they are a large majority of the Christians in Israel.

MARONITES
The largest Christian group in Lebanon, they played a central part, with the Druzes, in the rise of their country. Originally the church of the old Syriac culture, they have been Roman Catholic for many centuries. There is at present much tension between Maronites and Muslims.

MELKITES
Sometimes known as 'Greek Catholics', the Melkites turned to Roman Catholicism from Eastern Orthodoxy during the eighteenth century. Probably the largest of several groups originating in this way, they play an important inter-denominational role. They are found in Lebanon, Syria, Jordan, Palestine, Egypt and Israel.

SYRIAN ORTHODOX
Like the Coptic Orthodox in Egypt, they are among the 'Oriental Orthodox' churches, and so distinct from the Greek Orthodox Christians in the area. Their centre is Damascus, but most are found in northern Syria.

GREEK ORTHODOX
Christians of the Patriarchate of Antioch, they are 'Eastern Orthodox', and the main church of the Arabs—their liturgy is in Arabic. Living mainly in Lebanon, some of them are strong Arab and Palestinian nationalists.

ASSYRIANS
A small community dating back to the 'Nestorian' Christians of early centuries, they are found mainly in Iraq.

EXPATRIATE CHRISTIANS
Working largely in the Arabian peninsular in the oil industry, there are thousands of Indian, Pakistani, Korean, American and European Christians living in the region.

PROTESTANTS
Protestants do not form a majority of the Christians anywhere in the region. But there are groups in most countries and thousands of them have a significant witness.

challenge to the churches. They need to make real in their church life a vision of community which can resist the pressures the city exerts to individualize and commercialize every part of life.

PAST AND PRESENT
Christians have been in Asia from the very earliest days of the church. Christianity in **India** traces its roots back to the apostle Thomas, reputedly martyred in India. The Christians reached **China** in AD600 – before Islam or Buddhism.

The first missionaries to Asia were Roman Catholics, in the sixteenth century. These missions tended to put social institutions in a separate compartment from religion, and to be more concerned with individuals than with transforming society. As a result, they perpetuated values in Asian society which worked to support the caste system and other forms of oppression.

With the exception of the

church in the **Philippines**, Asian Christians are in a distinct minority. In most countries it is only in the last thirty years that they have emerged from Western rule into a new self-understanding.

Many Asian Christians now find themselves aliens in their own cultures. This has happened because missionaries taught converts to be Christian as they understood 'Christian', expecting that they would then somehow become 'Asian Christians'. The missionaries also expected that if they could only convert enough people, Asian society would change. But this has not happened.

Asia is the continent with the lowest percentage of Christians. Yet today the church is growing there, faster than the biological birth-rate.

The church in Asia is marked today by a tremendous commitment to evangelism, to human rights and to bringing about social change. A vast number of Christians are poor, yet in certain countries Christians are found in the wealthiest sector of the population.

The continent suffered in the colonial era from an excessive emphasis on missionaries from outside. But now in post-colonial days missionaries are being replaced in certain places by strong national churches and national missionary movements. Far from being left-overs from a colonial past, these churches have a strong sense of identity and a strong commitment to their task.

THE NATIONS OF ASIA

We have written of 'Asia' as if it were a single entity, and indeed the continent has certain common features. But in such a vast area, national circumstances vary greatly.

Japan

The Japanese consider themselves to be irreligious: a recent survey showed that most Japanese disclaim any religious affiliation. But according to a leading Japanese pastor, 30 per cent of the population say that if they were ever to choose a religion it would be Christianity. So he calculates that there are 32 million latent Christian seekers in the country, which might explain why the Bible is a best-seller at over a million copies a year.

Group solidarity is a major feature of Japanese life. There is tremendous loyalty to one's company and work, and also loyalty across the generations to one's ancestors and grandchildren. Maturity, for a

A lady minister in Hong Kong greets her congregation.

Japanese, is to be able to co-operate and work creatively in a group. This communal life gives great stability. People work for the same company for life, absenteeism is unheard of and unemployment is currently 2 per cent. The police do not carry guns; cars and houses are left unlocked. The pay differential between a teacher and the chairman of Toyota is only 1:3, as

against 1:20 in the United States.

But for all the strength of communal life, sometimes a Japanese grows tired of it and likes to be alone. He wants to be alone so as to look at his situation and at himself. There are many devices for doing this: keeping a diary, practising judo or the martial arts, the tea ceremony, fine arts. Fishing is one of the most popular

CHRISTIANS, JEWS AND MUSLIMS
JOHN M. CLARK

The Middle East is the birthplace of Christianity. Christians have lived and worshipped there from the time of Christ. It is easy for those outside the area to overlook the fact that some 12 million Christians live there today and that the great majority of them are Arabs.

Challenges for the churches
Christians form 10 per cent of the peoples of the Middle East. Over centuries they have learned to live as minority communities, 'protected citizens' under the Muslim majority. It was only with the development of the modern states of the Middle East after World War II that greater freedom came. Now they face many challenges.
■ The first and most serious is **emigration**. The instability of the area and the resurgence of Islamic values have caused many Christians to emigrate, usually to the West. Others remain, believing that as people of the Middle East they are called to live and witness to their historic Christian faith among Muslims and Jews.
■ To make their traditions come alive, the churches face **the call to renewal**. Many are seeking to

rediscover their spiritual roots in the Bible and the early Fathers. In Egypt there is a continuing revival of the spirituality of the desert monasteries that is influencing the whole church. All communities stress the renewing effect of Christian education in family, church and school, and emphasize the need for effective theological training of the clergy.
■ Middle Eastern Christians also face **the challenge of witness**. Traditionally witness has taken the form of *diakonia*, or service. 'The quiet, spontaneous witness of daily life,' as one bishop has put it. Schools, medical work and community development are all aspects of witness by service to the whole community.

The Coptic Evangelical Organization for Social Services is a fine example of integrated service and witness in Egypt. The Department of Service to Palestinian Refugees of the Middle East Council of Churches has expressed practical concern for Palestinians (both Muslim and Christian) since 1948. But can the modern media also be used to provide an authentic Arab Christian voice?
■ **Christian divisions** pose another

challenge. Gradually churches are learning to work with each other. The Middle East Council of Churches has developed since 1974 from being a focus only for Protestant churches to providing a forum for Orthodox and Protestant (including some Evangelical) churches to work and grow together.

A region of conflicts
Christians, like Muslims and Jews, are caught up in the political, social and community tensions of the region, of which the State of Israel is a part. For Jewish people around the world, the establishment of Israel as a Jewish state in which Jews can live in dignity, free from persecution, has been an event of the profoundest significance. The survival of Israel is of paramount importance for the future of Judaism.

But for many Christians and Muslims in the area, the new state reintroduced the idea of a nation based on a religious identity. It also displaced many Palestinian Arabs, some of them Christians. With support for Israel coming from Western 'Christian' nations, indigenous Christians can often be made to feel in some way disloyal to their wider

pastimes. People know in their spirits that solitude is essential if they are to continue to grow and mature.

Religion in Japan is a factor of this solitude. The Buddhist religion is constituted so as not to get in the way of family and work. And among Christians there is a strong non-church movement, which adopts a Zen Buddhist lifestyle with the Bible as its holy writing. People stay at home, read the Bible and pray. They regard church-going as less pleasing to God, since at church people will dislike the pastor or disagree with an elder. By worshipping alone they feel they will be better Christians.

The question in Japan is whether Christianity is to be shaped to meet the Japanese religious ideal of the solitary Arab communities.

The years of civil war and foreign occupation in Lebanon, the one country where Christians and Muslims have lived side by side in constitutional equality, have seriously affected attitudes throughout the Middle East.

In the last twenty years, oil wealth has spread widely. Christians, like other Middle Easterners, are learning to live with the problems of consumerism. Yet areas of great poverty and under-development contrast with others of great wealth.

One area of possible conflict is the reassertion of Islamic values and the possible return of minority communities to the second-class status of 'protected citizens'. For three centuries the Muslims of the Middle East have felt dominated by the pressures of Western power. Islamic self-confidence has gradually grown following political independence in the 1940s, the power bestowed by new oil resources, and the stimulus of the 1979 Iranian revolution.

Perhaps the basic issue facing the Middle East for the rest of the century is how the followers of the three great faiths born in the region can learn to live together and yet bear witness to their most deeply-held beliefs.

An Armenian priest.

individual, or whether this is too great a distortion of the faith.

Korea
Here the church has developed a strong commitment to human rights and a theology of people under oppression. But there is also a very optimistic and even aggressive version of Christianity which claims that by AD2000 over 50 per cent of the country will be Christian.

One reason why Koreans respond positively to Christianity is that it did not come to them as the religion of a colonial power – quite the reverse. In the first part of this century Korea was a Japanese colony. As Christians, and especially Christian women, refused to participate in worship of the Japanese emperor, Christianity became a focus of the country's resistance and sense of pride.

The number of Christians has doubled every decade since 1940. Before 1945, Korea had the

second largest Christian population in Asia, but things changed as a result of the Korean War in 1953. As the Communists advanced, Christians fled from the north and most churches were closed in North Korea. In South Korea a significant percentage of Christians see the country's economic growth as part of God's blessing and enabling to reach Asia for Christ. So missionaries are being trained and sent in increasing numbers to other countries in Asia.

Indonesia
This network of islands is the largest Muslim country in the world. But Islam has proved more amenable to Christian witness in Indonesia than anywhere else. The church now includes 11 per cent of the population. There are records of Roman Catholics on the island of Sumatra in the seventh century, but in 1605 the Dutch Reformed Church expelled the Catholics and was the sole Christian presence in the islands for 300 years.

There has been remarkable Christian growth since 1966. A number of Indonesian missionary societies now send missionaries, both to other Indonesian islands and outside Indonesia.

Philippines
The only Christian country in Asia, Philippine Christian history goes back to 1521, when a priest landed with Magellan's round-the-world voyage. He made these islands the base for mission to

In South Korea there is rapid growth in the number of Christians. Some churches are packed, and the city of Seoul has a church with one of the largest memberships in the world.

the rest of Asia. Most, though by no means all, Philippine Christians are Roman Catholic. They have a deep spirituality and desire for God, mixed with a lot of spiritism and churches full of statues and patron saints.

Christians here also take a firm stand for justice, under the leadership of Cardinal Sin.

Cardinal Sin, the leader of Roman Catholics in the Philippines, takes a strong stand for justice. When opposition leader Aquino Ninoy was murdered in 1984, the cardinal said on television that protest demonstrations should reach beyond students and poor people to include the business community. His influence is such that business people demonstrated in strength, defying the President's initial refusal of permission.

China

Half of Asia's people live in China, the most populous nation on earth. Estimates of the number of Christians vary from 10 million to 50 million. The church has grown in spite of persecution – during the 1920s, the time of Communist take-over in the 1940s and the Cultural Revolution in the 1960s. We wait to see this church's contribution, based on this experience, to a rapidly changing and modernizing China.

Franciscan missionaries reached China in 1294; in 1907 there were over 1,000 Protestant missionaries. All missionaries were expelled by 1949, leaving behind 3,251,347 baptized Christians. The most conservative estimate is that the church has tripled in size in the thirty-five years since then.

Some Christians belong to the officially-recognized Three-Self Church. Others belong to house churches, which have no official recognition, though they enjoy a degree of protection through the government's recognition of the Three-Self Church. Despite this, many still suffer persecution.

Post-Mao China is opening up to the West in its policy of 'four modernizations': agriculture, industry, science/technology and defence. But Chinese Christians warn Western Christians that this is not an invitation to bombard China with radio, television and other forms of evangelism. The burden of evangelizing China will fall on the many Christian Chinese outside mainland China, and in 1997 the Christian population will increase considerably when Hong Kong is reabsorbed, with its half-million Christians.

The key question Chinese leaders ask of Christians is whether they can make a significant contribution to shaping a modern China.

Overseas Chinese

The Asian church is not just growing among the poor, but also in affluent societies such as Singapore. The vigorous Christianity among the largely Chinese people there is mirrored among Chinese migrant populations elsewhere in East Asia – in the Philippines, Malaysia and Indonesia, for example. Although Chinese are a minority in these countries, they

A MESSAGE OF RECONCILIATION

During 1983 race riots broke out in Sri Lanka. Some of the Sinhalese majority attacked Tamils in retaliation for a guerrilla ambush.

Bishop Lakshman Wickremesinghe, himself a Sinhalese, called his fellow Christian Sinhalese to confess their guilt, since 'as Sinhalese we share in the total life of our people'. He quoted the example of Jesus: 'In the midst of brutality and suffering...he apologized for all those who did not know the moral evil they were doing, so that he might begin the process of setting right what was wrong in broken relationships.'

Looking to the future, the bishop continued: 'Christians will know that in setting right a broken relationship with Tamils who suffered unjustly, they would be setting right a broken relationship with God.'

Kwok was a young Chinese living in Hong Kong, who at twenty was involved in a murder. While awaiting trial he heard about Jesus loving everyone, no matter how bad his or her past. He lost his fear and found a new hope. He dedicated his life to telling his fellow-prisoners about Jesus, delighted that in spite of his past he could have work to do for God. Told by Jackie Pullinger

have a powerful hold on business.

In Malaysia and Indonesia, they are subject to a certain amount of discrimination. But there is no bar to evangelism among Chinese, as there is among Malays. The Chinese communities are very receptive. Their faith tends to be individualistic and to neglect social justice, perhaps because of their tenuous position in these societies as 'the Jews of Asia', tolerated but not fully accepted.

Taiwan

This island has seen an 'economic miracle' since 1949 when it became the home of the Chinese government in exile. The church is increasing in size and in commitment to support minority groups. Many Christians feel the need to be cautious here, for fear that commitment to justice might be seen as crypto-Communism in a situation where the people dread that Taiwan might fall to mainland China.

Kampuchea and Vietnam

In Kampuchea Jesuits and Dominicans arrived in 1555 and Protestant missions in 1922. Many Roman Catholics were massacred after the 1970 coup and all expatriates expelled in 1975.

In Vietnam Franciscans came in 1580 and there was rapid growth in Roman Catholic numbers. By the time South Vietnam fell, there were 3 million Catholics and significant Christian growth among tribal peoples. No statistics are available on how many Christians there are now, but stories have trickled out of heroic witness to Jesus Christ despite fierce persecution in both these countries.

Malaysia

The official religion here is Islam. It is an offence to try to convert Malays, who have a strong identity as 'sons of the soil'. Most Christians are among the Chinese and Indian (largely Tamil) communities. A growing indigenous missionary movement is developing among the Chinese and Indian Christians.

Thailand and Sri Lanka

These are Buddhist countries,

Continued on p.172

THE CHURCH IN CHINA

When the Communists took over China in 1949, there was a significant but relatively small Christian community – 700,000 or 800,000 Protestant communicant members; a Roman Catholic Church some 2 million strong.

During the years that followed, and particularly during the Cultural Revolution, it became increasingly difficult for anyone to know what was happening to Christians in China. Government-controlled media put out disinformation on many subjects, and virtually none on this one. Some people even thought Christianity had virtually died out in the world's most populous nation.

Then in 1979 the official churches started to open for public worship. To the surprise of government and church officials, they were filled beyond capacity with young and old. Gradually the picture began to unfold of churches that, far from dwindling, were now larger and more alive than thirty years before. Through all the difficulties and suffering of the Mao era, the church had grown.

Yet the Christian scene in China is still a very hard one to interpret, and there are several different analyses of it. For example, just how many Christians are there now? In 1983 the China Christian Council estimated 2 million Protestants and 3 million Roman Catholics, but this was widely thought to be too conservative. Jonathan Chao, of the China Church Research Centre in Hong Kong, estimates 30 million believers, or 50 million 'if the border regions and secret believers are included'. These larger figures were put by a recent visitor to official pastors, who deemed them 'over-generous but not impossible'. China has a population of a 1,000 million, so we are still talking

about a small minority. But given the recent history, the size of the Christian presence is remarkable.

Part of the difficulty in understanding the Christian picture in China is that there are three distinct strands, each with its own problems:
■ **The Three-self Patriotic Movement**, the officially-recognized Protestant Church, relates most easily to official churches in other countries;
■ **The house church movement**, particularly strong in the countryside, is seen by many Evangelicals as the more authentic Chinese Christianity;
■ **The Roman Catholic Church** has a particular difficulty of relating to the Vatican.

Official church

The Three-self Patriotic Movement was started in 1951. It is the state-recognized non-Catholic church, and is intended to ensure that Christians remain patriotic and independent of foreign influences. The Chinese church is to be something other than a legacy of the missionary endeavour

of the nineteenth and early twentieth centuries. The three-self principles are to be self-supporting, self-administering and self-propagating.

The internal affairs of TSPM are managed by the China Christian Council, a sister organization whose leader also leads TSPM. The leaders of TSPM suffered along with leaders of other Christian groups during the Cultural Revolution. Since 1981 branches have been set up provincially and nationally. The church has reportedly printed 1.3 million Bibles since 1980. And it operates a four-year undergraduate theological college in Nanking, affiliated with four regional training centres in Foochou, Peking, Shanyang and Chengtu. Branch TSPM offices also conduct short-term leaders' training courses.

So there is much to be thankful for

Chinese people stream out of church. When churches re-opened in 1979, after years of suppression, there proved to be many more people with Christian faith than in 1949.

in the Three-self Patriotic Movement. Yet its very official recognition provides constraints and limitations which are familiar to all state-recognized churches. And these constraints are more tightly drawn in a situation where other non-Catholic groups have to register through TSPM. A delegation from the British Council of Churches visited China in December 1983, and reported that 'the church's relationship with the state is interesting and complex. The state...probably prefers to deal with a centralized, disciplined church, rather than with a dispersed movement which it might suspect of being subversive...It is clear, however, that the acceptance and freedom which Christians currently enjoy could disappear overnight.'

House churches

Christian groups meeting in homes are not a recent development in China. There is a tradition of such meetings going back to the nineteenth century. But in the special conditions of the past thirty years such groups have been highly important. There are a great number of them – some estimate 100,000.

Their growth during years of persecution is understandable. House churches gave support and fellowship in such times, and many still value this. Some are chary of joining TSPM, which they see as an arm of the government. Some belong both to a house church and to an official church. Their greatest strength is in the countryside, and it is among the great mass of rural Chinese that the main uncertainties about numbers persist. It is a highly fluid movement, free from dominant structures, whose leaders give great importance to prayer. Members are taught to follow the way of the cross by accepting suffering.

In 1982, the TSPM introduced a 'three-designates' policy, allowing only designated places of worship, designated pastors and designated areas for each TSPM pastor. House churches were asked to register with the TSPM or with local authorities.

Jonathan Chao reports that those who refused to register became targets for closure and their leaders liable to arrest. Since the summer of 1983, several hundred house church pastors have been arrested, and many more are at large as fugitives. Those groups that have been disbanded are regrouping in smaller numbers and once more have to meet at different places at unannounced times. But this situation may change again soon, and any description of official policy towards the churches runs the risk of dating quickly.

One positive effect of leaders being arrested is that younger leaders come up to take their place. And when these men are arrested, young women come forward to take evangelistic and pastoral responsibility, which can involve long treks to reach remote mountain communities. As a result of these treks, new congregations are being formed.

Roman Catholics

A church which has a world-wide allegiance to Rome is plainly going to have difficulty with a policy of freedom from foreign connections. In 1957 the government-sponsored Catholic Patriotic Association was formed in an attempt to create a continuing Catholicism in China independent of the Vatican. This led to a split; some have not joined CPA and have been persecuted as a result.

Largely insulated from outside developments, CPA has remained pre-Vatican II in its outlook, conservative in liturgy and theology. Most of its bishops now serving have been consecrated without Vatican approval. In this situation of tension within their own community, Catholics have not had much contact with Protestants.

The new China

Christians in China today have certain marked advantages over their brothers and sisters in pre-revolutionary China. They have been impelled to throw off any sense of superiority to or isolation from their fellows in the new China. They are no longer weighed down by denominational differences.

In the shared experiences of the new China, simply to be faithful in worship can be a powerful sign. Raymond Fung has written: 'In a highly uniform and totally authoritarian society, the only regular corporate-life experience different from what the state and its apparatus can provide, and yet accessible to the people, is the Christian church – more specifically, the weekly gathering of Christians for fellowship and worship.'

The goal of believers in China is both the evangelization of the Chinese people and that Chinese society should be permeated by Christian influence. A remarkable start has been made. The story of Christianity in China in the coming years will be of profound importance for Christians world-wide. And it may well have importance for the world as a whole.

HARDSHIP AND GROWTH

Era of foreign missions

1949
Communist take-over

Clergy removed from pastorates.
Various church functions put to an end.
Institutional church brought under
control of Three-self Patriotic
Movement. Catholic Patriotic
Association formed (1957).

1958
Pressure on churches intensifies

Few churches open (8 in Shanghai,
4 in Peking). Christians scattered.
House church meetings multiply.

1966
Cultural Revolution begins

Red Guards storm believers' homes.
Bibles, hymn books publicly burned.
Church leaders exposed to 'struggle' —
ridiculed and paraded in streets.
House churches grow in spiritual
power.

China begins to open up to the outside
world. Religious persecution slackens
off. House churches hold semi-open
meetings in countryside.

1977
Death of Mao Tse-tung

Newly re-opened churches packed
with people, young and old. Three-self
Patriotic Movement holds national
conference (1980). Official church
and house churches co-exist, but
since 1982 'three-designates' policy
has hampered house churches.

1979
Churches start to re-open

since that religion was forced out of India where it arose largely as a protest against the Hindu caste system.

In Thailand there are 44,000 Protestant Christians among a population of 44 million. There is, however, an openness to the gospel among refugees from Kampuchea and Laos.

In Sri Lanka there is a sizeable minority of Tamils, brought across by the British from India to work in the tea estates of the old Ceylon. They live mainly in the north of the island, and that whole area is a diocese of the Church of South India. There is also a population of descendants of the Dutch and Sinhalese who are largely Presbyterian. The main body of Christians are Roman Catholic (from the Portuguese colonial era; 7 per cent of the population), and Anglicans and Methodists from the British imperial days.

Burma

This is the third (mainly Buddhist) country on the borders of India. Christian witness came to Burma which was a closed country through a North American missionary, Adoniram Judson. His work over thirty years produced very little fruit among the majority of the population who were Burmese and Buddhist. But it produced fruit among the other tribes, especially the Karems and Chins. Strong and committed churches were planted among these hill tribes which continue to bear courageous witness in difficult situations today. Burma has been completely closed to outside influences for years, since missionaries were expelled and Christian institutions nationalized in 1965. Yet the Baptist Church was able to celebrate its centenary by sending 300 young people on evangelistic treks throughout the country.

Most Christians are found among the tribal peoples in the hills along Burma's borders. In common with other tribal people, they feel oppressed by the Buddhist ruling group who live in the plain along the Irrawaddy river and who remain resistant to the gospel.

India

In this ancient land the church is not only holding its own but growing. It has an influence in society out of all proportion to its size. In India, as in other parts of Asia, the church in many ways reflects society with Christians at all levels of the social scale.

The main entry point for Christianity was among the outcaste, to whom Christian faith offered a place in the sun. The outcaste was taught by tradition

A leper in Thailand reads his Bible.

that his or her state was a judgement from God. Their longing for dignity as children of God was met, not by an endless cycle of rebirths, but by new birth in Christ. But the very success of Christianity among the lowest castes shaped the character of the Indian church. As outcastes had no place in traditional Indian religion, they felt that no aspect of that culture could be brought in and used in Christian worship and lifestyle. So new converts necessarily embraced a culture which was Western rather than Indian.

The advent of Christianity produced changes in Indian society, but these worked to block the further expansion of the church. Hindu reform movements made Hinduism more socially aware and relevant to people's lives. Through finance and favour the wealthy and powerful exploited for their own benefit Christian institutions (schools, hospitals and so on) which were founded for the sake of the poor. Thus they used service which could have threatened their dominant position to bolster it.

Hindus have seen the improvements which Christian faith brought to outcaste people, and have generally not liked what they have seen. Since independence in 1947, the government has instituted economic benefits for outcastes which are forfeit if people become Christians. There has also been an attempt to make conversion from Hinduism illegal.

The Indian church provides an example of the tremendous growth of national missionaries in India. From 1977 to 1981, the number of expatriate missionaries in the country fell from 1,200 to 900, but the number of missionaries with national missionary societies going from one part of India to another rose from 700 to 2,300. There is a tremendous ebb and flow of people throughout Asia. Korea has eighteen missionary agencies with 260 missionaries overseas, and there are many Indian and Filippino Christians employed in the Gulf States, as well as Koreans in Libya.

A most outstanding area of growth has been among the tribal people of north-east India, including the Nagas. Here whole tribes which a century ago were headhunters have embraced Christianity. The proportion of Christians in the seven states which form north-east India rises as high as 80 per cent, most of whom are Protestant. Roman Catholics are increasingly active in this area.

Pakistan

This is another strongly Muslim country. Nearly all Pakistani Christians come from Hindu origins. The church is found mainly among Punjabis, where the Church Missionary Society began work in 1850. New constitutions in the last thirty years have proclaimed Pakistan an Islamic republic with freedom of religion. Even though church properties have been nationalized, the church continues to grow and is found attractive.

In Asia a very high proportion of people, like this porter in Darjeeling, India, are teenagers. Christians face a great challenge to win the allegiance of many of these young people, by showing them a faith that will match their aspirations.

In 1974 in Bangladesh six Christian organizations launched a programme for health, education and economic development, which included hospital care for over 700 leprosy sufferers, the introduction of farming improvements and a scheme offering a guaranteed market for locally-made handicrafts. Ten years later weavers, crochet-workers and wood-carvers working under the scheme were earning some £200,000 in export sales.

In many parts of Asia a rural culture still prevails, with its old unhurried ways. A Japanese Christian, Kosuke Koyama, has written of a *Three Mile an Hour God*, who travels at the walking pace of an Asian villager and meets him as he is.

The Muslim revival is challenging Christians not only to evangelize Muslims but also to articulate a social order based on the will of God as revealed in Jesus.

Nepal

The Hindu kingdom of Nepal was closed to the gospel for many centuries. Nepalese who lived outside Nepal, however, were reached with the gospel. In 1951 the ruling Rana family were overthrown with the help of the Indian government, and religious freedom was proclaimed.

Foreign missionaries were then able to enter the country under the United Mission to Nepal – one of the first co-operative ventures in mission. This body carries out social and humanitarian work in conjunction with the Nepali government. Though no direct evangelism took place, this kind of ministry was meeting people's needs, and the church has grown remarkably as a result. Recent estimates suggest that since 1954 the number of Christians baptized in Nepal has risen from none to 17,000.

This growth has happened even though it is still an offence to change one's religion and be baptized. Christians face prison sentences of up to three years for becoming a Christian, and up to six years for baptizing another person. But, with Afghanistan, Nepal is an example of Christian perseverance penetrating societies thought to be closed.

There is in effect no country which is totally shut off from the gospel.

West Asia

The region in which Jesus lived continues to be the hardest place to fulfil the Christian task. The Orthodox are the largest Christian community in this area. In **Lebanon** Christians are under great stress. In **Israel** they face a certain amount of persecution. In **Iran** and **Iraq** the small churches have been decimated by persecution and pushed underground. In **Turkey**, the land of the churches in many of Paul's letters, the number of Christian believers is less than a hundred.

ASIAN CHRISTIANS SURVEY THEIR TASK

Many vital issues face Christians in this continent with all its needs. What are the most crucial?

First, vast masses of people in the continent know nothing of Jesus at all. These are by and large the poor people of Asia. They do not even know that Jesus lived. The continent of Asia is the greatest mission field in the world.

Second, the church must address the questions of social justice with which it is confronted. These are days of rapid social change throughout the Third World, Asia not least of all, and such transitions inevitably throw up points of conflict, of class warfare and of desperate poverty. How should Christians address these? How

A PALESTINIAN CHRISTIAN

Elias Chacour is a Catholic priest. A Palestinian Arab now absorbed into Israel, his family were driven out of their home when he was a small boy by Jewish soldiers during the setting up of the state of Israel. He nonetheless feels no hatred for Jews, but rather 'a kind of pity for the blindness they have', and this attitude means he is sometimes taken as an enemy by his compatriots.

He bases his life on Jesus' Sermon on the Mount, 'where human dignity comes before land consideration or ideology or any other considerations, even religious ones.' His view of life was formed early on: 'I was educated in a family where violence did not have any place and where faith in God, who is the protector of the weak and the poor, was very strong.'

can they witness to reconciliation in the middle of social agitation? Should they be in there promoting civil unrest to get wrongs admitted and put right? Is part of the Christian's mission to be an agitator for the rights of poor people?

Asian Christianity started with the poor but has always been upwardly mobile. Can it nonetheless be involved in movements of social change on behalf of the poor? Can it take a preferential option for the poor while itself increasingly growing elitist? Or must such involvement be left to the Marxists?

The Asian church has often been a provider of relief – from a position of strict neutrality. But relief, by its very nature, comes from outside a situation. Poverty

See Racism, Justice and Civil Rights

is the result of definite decisions made at a social, political and economic level: Who makes what for whom? How are the results to be distributed? Christians, called to show God's justice for the poor, cannot avoid being involved from the inside in these decisions and choices.

Closely linked to this is the issue of human rights, which in Asia really means rights for the poor, as they are the victims of the deepest human rights violations. The church is closely engaged in the struggle to recover these people's rights – to exist, to apply for jobs, to be treated fairly.

CHRISTIANS AND THE OTHER RELIGIONS

All the major world religions are strongly present in Asia.

PUTTING THE GOSPEL IN ITS CONTEXT
WAYAN MASTRA

Bali is one of the islands that make up Indonesia. Ninety-eight per cent of its 2.5 million people belong to the Bali Hindu religion, which is a mixture of Hindu beliefs, animism and ancestor worship. I was raised as a Balinese Hindu. In 1952 Christ came to dwell in me through a deep religious experience when he answered my prayers in a crisis. Through that process, many Christians expected me to become a Westerner in my thought and culture. Such expectations have a long history.

Christ is my life but Bali is my body

The early Christians successfully planted the seed of the good news of Christ in European cultures. The gospel put on the cultural clothing of Europe. For example, the pagan word 'Gott' was given the meaning of the God of the Bible, Yahweh. The pagan day for worshipping the sun, Sunday, was used by Christians for their day of worship. They used the pagan symbol of new life (or eternal life), the fir tree, to celebrate the birth of Christ and to adorn their churches in the form of spires. All of these examples, and many others like them,

can be seen as a legitimate 'translation' of the Christian faith into European culture.

But by the twentieth century, European Christians had completely identified Christianity with Western European culture. When European missionaries came to Bali fifty years ago, they made the Balinese Christians abandon their cultural heritage and accept Western Christian culture. Such transplanted culture is like a pot plant which cannot grow beyond the size of its pot. Like the Japanese bonsai tree, it remains stunted and fruitless. But when the gospel is placed in a culture like a seed, it will bring forth new fruit and flowers.

A Balinese-shaped faith

Since 1971, the Bali Protestant Church has been trying to understand the Bible through Balinese thought and express it in Balinese terms. This follows the way of Jesus who became incarnate as a Jew. It follows the tradition of the early Christians in Europe who, like Asian Christians today, were a minority in their societies.

Christians in Bali use the Bible,

Christian tradition and the local situation as their guidelines. We seek the Holy Spirit's help to discover where God has already been at work

Christians cannot live their faith in a way that pretends these other faiths do not matter. They need to talk with people of other faiths, to enter into dialogue with them. But what kind of dialogue should this be?

Is dialogue a process by which Christians and people of other faiths share their insights in a common search for truth? Is it discussing personal religious experiences? Or is it a matter of Christians and those of other faiths listening carefully to one another, so that they can appreciate each others' understanding of God and human life as far as possible without prejudice, each understanding the other as they would like to be understood?

Dialogue has tended to be on the subject of belief systems and

in the good things of our culture for us to build on. At the same time, we try to learn from and share with Christians from other cultures to ensure we remain true to the Christian family.

We share the water of life in a Balinese coconut of religious experience rather than in a European cup of rational argument. In this way, we lead the Balinese on from what they know to a deeper understanding of Christian faith.

■ The Balinese offer animals and flowers at a temple in the mountains to calm angry ancestors or deities. I told a woman that Christians do not have to bring offerings because they had already made their offering on Mount Golgotha in Palestine when Christ died. My explanation met her need for security. I encouraged her to grow in faith by moving beyond that need to offer her own life in service to God and, like Abraham, to be a blessing to others.

■ Ancestor worship promotes respect for elders and unity in society. Balinese Christians try to build on this by teaching that we bring honour to our ancestors and our family by living a good life.

■ Similarly, spirit worship is an attempt to experience God. So it is appropriate for Christians to teach that as Jesus is God become human, he is the closest that God has ever come to us. We can experience him through the Holy Spirit in a direct encounter.

■ The visual aspects of life are very important to Balinese Hindus. Our church buildings preach sermons in stone by using Balinese art-forms. The Balinese associate the mountains with the presence of God and the source of life, so churches are built to resemble a mountain. The Balinese see a temple gate as a symbol of coming into God's presence. So behind the communion table is a traditional temple gate with a cross in the middle to show that Jesus is the way to God's presence.

■ Since the Balinese love drama and music, traditional Balinese dance and gamelan orchestras are used to tell the dramas of the Bible.

■ Most Balinese are poor. They need to see the love of Christ demonstrated. The church stresses practical help to people through education, loan funds and employment training.

The gospel transforms every aspect of a people's life so that the good news of Jesus can be rooted in the soul of a society. Jesus comes to us from outside, but he does not remain an outsider. He lives among a people so that each nation can feel that he is their Saviour.

personal religious experiences. But some Christians are exploring dialogue over a wider area, asking and discussing such questions as: How do poor people, women, or the oppressed experience the way the dominant religion operates in their area? How do the various religions account for people's experiences of poverty, illness, oppression by the spirits and exploitation by others?

In the context of a plurality of religions, how can the gospel of Jesus Christ be shared without giving an arrogant impression? There is a particular problem with Hinduism here. Its religious atmosphere pervades much of Asia, and it is very tolerant of other beliefs. For Hindus, religion is a matter of personal religious experience. It is not possible to evaluate whether any one religious experience is better or more valid than any other. If a Christian says to a Hindu that he believes Jesus is the unique and supreme Lord, he appears to be showing such arrogance that he cannot possibly be living close to God, whatever he claims.

This dilemma represents a challenge to Christians to be humble about their personal testimony of faith, and to focus not on their own spiritual experience but on being disciples of Jesus who is God at work to redeem mankind within the world we know. Thus discipleship and witness can never be simply words: it must be the witness of a community living out God's redemption in the public arena of life.

RELIGION AND CULTURE

Many of Asia's religions are culture religions. **Iran** is an Islamic republic; so are **Pakistan** and **Bangladesh**. **Indonesia** proclaims *Pancasheela*, the equality of the five religions on its shores: Hinduism, Islam, Roman Catholicism, Protestantism and Buddhism.

Nationalist movements have been very strong in the recent past of many Asian countries. This puts great pressure on national churches to express, for example, an Indian Christianity or a Chinese Christianity. But what aspects of Indian or Chinese culture can be fittingly expressed in Christian life and witness to the gospel without fundamentally denying crucial features of the gospel? This is a critical question which Christians in Asia are working out.

Mother Teresa of Calcutta and her Sisters of Mercy have caught the imagination of the world. A Yugoslavian Roman Catholic, she has devoted her life totally to the poor and dying, of Calcutta and now of other parts of the Earth.

Another issue is as important for Christians in Asia as those anywhere else: that of Christian unity. The first united church in the world was in Asia. In 1947 the Church of South India was formed, uniting Presbyterians, Congregationalists, Anglicans, British (not American) Methodists and some Lutherans. Then in 1970 the Church of North India was formed on a slightly different basis. The significance of these unions is hard to overrate. In a society which is fragmented, of diverse races, with constant religious tensions between different groups and castes, Christians were able to demonstrate unity.

This remains a major challenge. There is still not total Christian unity, in India or anywhere else in Asia. How can the church so demonstrate unity that it can call the peoples of Asia to be united?

THE MISSION OF THE KINGDOM

These are some of the key questions confronting Asian Christians. Not all churches have come to the same conclusions. Some have a longer history of wrestling with the problem than others. There is great diversity, and a number of the conclusions are interesting.

Asia continues to be a field where Western missionary societies which have worked in Asia for decades continue ministry in partnership with the national churches they have helped to form. A vast number of Western missionary societies,

relief and development agencies and Christian mission groups working in radio, language translation and literature, continue to consider Asia as a mission field and work in it. They have benefitted Asia greatly.

They have prevented some languages from dying out by reducing them to writing and by producing literature. This has enabled a whole group of people to develop their identity through literature. Relief and development agencies have responded magnificently in times of calamity, famine, flood and fire. They have also initiated development work among the poorest people in urban and rural areas. Medical missions continue to pioneer in remote areas and provide models of health care. Education continues to benefit from the effort of mission, especially as mission efforts address the needs of those who are bypassed by local governmental education efforts.

Apart from direct missionary activity, churches in the West continue to transfer substantial financial resources to enable national churches to address socio-economic needs in these countries. The human and material resources of the West are being increasingly made available for the task of mission in Asia.

Some Western Christian mission agencies work independently, some employ national Christians and many work with Asian partner churches and agencies. It must be noted that Christians in Asia are speaking with one voice

See Defending the Faith; The Unity Movement; Gospel and Culture

'There is a village in Nepal in which the majority of the people have become Christians. The difference now seen in the quality of life there – in caring, sharing, working together – is a testimony not to any physical work of development, but to the power of God to change lives in all aspects. That change is complete development.' Richard Clark, chairman of Nepal Bible Ashram

Girls in the print collating room of the Christavashram in India. Ashrams were essentially Hindu communities, but some Christians are adapting the idea to express their own community life.

concerning the nature of partnership with Western Christians. 'Let us spell out the good news of Jesus Christ in words and in community life that is true both to Jesus and to our own culture. Share this task with us, and we will join hands to share with you from our rich treasure of Asian Christian heritage.'

The mission of Christians

CHRISTIANS IN ASIAN COUNTRIES

	Congregations	Christians	Percentage of population	
Bangladesh	2,030	449,960	0.5	Predominantly Muslim; tribals most responsive
Bhutan	60	850	0.1	Evangelism forbidden; most Christians are Indian or expatriate Bhutanese
Brunei	19	12,840	8.0	Mostly Roman Catholics; Chinese or expatriates employed by Shell
Burma	7,300	1,970,900	5.6	Mainly Baptist churches of Karen, Chin and Katchin tribes
China	50,000	1,800,000	0.2	Figures hard to get, but church growing rapidly
(Taiwan)	4,300	1,288,430	7.4	Largest denomination Presbyterian; mountain tribes becoming Christian
Christmas Islands	5	515	15.6	
Cocos Islands	2	254	36.3	
Hong Kong	990	800,400	17.7	Many independent Chinese churches; Roman Catholic, Baptist and Church of Christ are largest groups
India	91,000	27,078,000	3.9	Many churches linked in church unions; most Christian state is Manipur
Indonesia	28,500	17,069,900	11.0	Christianity spread under Dutch rule; since 1960s further rapid growth
Japan	17,000	3,526,400	3.0	Great interest in Bible, but not a religious people
Kampuchea	150	56,000	0.6	Church decimated by persecution
Korea, North	1,900	161,900	0.9	Most Christians flee south
Korea, South	29,600	11,409,800	30.5	Presbyterian church largest, but Pentecostals growing; some Christians socially active
Laos	200	67,000	1.8	Some well-established churches; mountain tribes responsive

everywhere is Jesus' mission of the kingdom of God. God's kingdom challenges human kingdoms, and brings new, right relationships between people and God, and between people and people. It must be expressed within a community, and in terms that are relevant to particular societies and cultures.

The kingdom does not come only to individuals. Jesus addressed the people of Israel. And Christians must speak not only to individuals but to cultures – showing by their lives together how God judges those cultures and longs to redeem them. To do this in Asia we need churches that will grapple with Asian religious world-views and social and political situations in a way that brings authentic Christianity to bear.

See The Missionary Inheritance

	Congregations	Christians	Percentage of population	
Macao	36	36,330	12.4	
Malaysia	2,500	861,800	6.2	Strongly Muslim country; Christians among Chinese and in east Malaysia
Maldive Islands	2	170	0.1	
Nepal	105	5,570	less than 0.1	No religious freedom, but church growing
Pakistan	3,950	1,475,500	1.8	Church of Pakistan formed in 1970
Philippines	36,200	49,201,700	94.3	Mostly Roman Catholic; some Protestant groups; Christians lead fight for social justice
Seychelles	37	64,560	97.8	
Sikkim	51	6,510	2.4	Dependent on India; Christians contribute in education
Singapore	390	208,630	8.6	Religious freedom; half church services in English; all dialects respresented
Sri Lanka	1,270	1,283,600	8.3	Buddhism supported by government; Christians mainly Tamil; strong national leadership
Thailand	4,900	521,400	1.1	Most Christians expatriate or tribal; Christian-Buddhist dialogue
Timor	90	293,800	38.9	Almost exclusively Roman Catholic
Vietnam	3,700	3,627,000	7.4	Figures hard to get; some Christians become refugees

	Christians in 1985	% of population	1970-85 growth rate
East Asia	22,324,690	1.4	4.04
South Asia	125,914,645	8.1	3.35

2.3 A WORLD OF OUR OWN

Australia and the South Pacific

ROBERT BANKS

Christianity came to Australia primarily from the United Kingdom along with its first white inhabitants. It came predominantly in a Protestant rather than Roman Catholic form and with a stronger Evangelical than broad or high church flavour. In the two centuries since, this transplanted British Christianity has been supplemented by other varieties of Christian expression imported from Europe, the United States, and most recently, Asia. This has happened chiefly through migration.

By the 1980s, about one quarter of all Australians claimed to be Anglican, one quarter Roman Catholic, one eighth Uniting Church of Australia (comprising most Methodist, Presbyterian and Congregational churches), and one eighth from other Christian groups including the Orthodox. Approximately one in ten Australians have no religious allegiance and about the same proportion refuse to answer any questions on the issue. Only 1.5 per cent have non-Christian religious affiliations, Muslims, Jews and Buddhists being the most numerous of these.

Since World War II, with some fluctuations, the Roman Catholic Church, many of the smaller independent Christian groups, and the older Pentecostal denominations in Australia have registered a growth of religious allegiance relative to other bodies. Meanwhile, Anglican and other mainline Protestant groups have witnessed a steady decline. Over this period, the number of people describing themselves as Christian has declined by 10 per cent, and the number aligning themselves with a non-Christian religion, though still statistically small, has risen.

There is no established church in Australia, and on the whole a strict distinction is maintained between secular and religious affairs at the political and educational level. The opening of each parliamentary session with prayer, the exemption of churches from paying rates, and the granting of government· financial aid to church schools are among the few exceptions to this rule.

City life in Sydney and elsewhere in Australia is as secular as anywhere else in the world. Australian Christians face the challenge of presenting to their compatriots a full-blooded modern Christianity.

MEASURING CHRISTIAN COMMITMENT

As in many other countries, there is a considerable gap in Australia between professions of denominational allegiance and such things as actual attendance at worship, use of Christian rites, and the significance of the church in society at large. Looked at in turn, these three areas can tell us a great deal about the current state of play of Christianity in Australia:

● **Church attendance** Today, about half the Australian population rarely, if ever, goes to church, and almost another quarter attend only irregularly. On any one Sunday only one in five Australians will be found in church, though there are wide denominational differences. (Roman Catholic attendance is approximately twice as high as Protestant attendance.) There has also been a gradual decline in numbers among irregular churchgoers, a noticeable move away from the church on the part of younger people and young adults, and a growing drift to smaller religious groupings at the expense of the mainline denominations.

● **Christian rites** The number of people requesting religious rites for funerals has remained fairly constant (around 97 per cent). But the number of marriages celebrated in churches over the past fifteen years has dropped from 90 per cent to 64 per cent. This decline is also reflected in the number of infant baptisms, Sunday school pupils and confirmation candidates – all of which have dropped markedly.

● **The significance of church in society** The influence of the church upon social and political life has waned considerably over the last few decades. But this does not mean that Christians have disappeared entirely from national life. Some of the newer Christian or Christian-based lobby groups, though not always acting in a fully informed way, have exercised political influence from time to time, and religion has recently been attracting more media attention. More importantly, the brunt of voluntary activity in the social work area is still carried on by denominational and other religious organizations. In some cases, church organizations act

See The Secular Outlook of Today

Christians from the Tuamotu archipelago in the Pacific go into a church.

as agencies for government services as well. In education, there are now a number of religious studies departments and boards of divinity in various Australian universities and colleges, whereas previously these scarcely existed.

NEW ZEALAND'S FAITH

The Christian message was first taken to New Zealand by a convict chaplain and two tradesmen missionaries from Australia, with a touch of American influence as well. This meant that there were some Maori Christians before settlement began. Unlike Australia, distinct Anglican and Presbyterian settlements were then established in two different parts of the country, leaving regional religious differences which persist to this day.

However, there are many similarities between the situation in New Zealand and Australia. According to New Zealand's 1981 census, Anglicans form about one quarter of the population and are declining proportionately. The Roman Catholic population is smaller however (about 14 per cent of the population), and declining at a slower rate than the Anglicans. Presbyterians, stronger in New Zealand than in Australia (almost 17 per cent of the population), are also decreasing in numbers.

New Zealanders who say they have no religion are on the increase (about 9 per cent). But there is only a very slight rise among those who are involved in a non-Christian religion, possibly because the immigration rate is lower than for Australia. There has been a slackening in religious adherence among the under thirties, but a noticeable strengthening of allegiance among smaller newer religious groupings. In spite of all this, New Zealand is said to possess the highest ratio of Christian bookshops to size of population.

The Australian pattern of church attendance is very similar to that for New Zealand. In New Zealand, the main denominations are attracting fewer people than they used to, without suffering major losses, while smaller religious groups with a more Charismatic or informal character tend to be growing. Younger people display significantly less religious interest of any formal kind than older ones. Though the independent Ratana Church gained many social reforms for Maoris at one time, the impact of the denomination upon social and political life has not been conspicuous.

WHY THE DECLINE?

Why is there an increasing lack of interest in Christianity in Australia and New Zealand? In part it is simply a public admission by many people of what has been the case privately for some time. It has now become socially more acceptable to take an openly non-Christian or non-religious stance. This has happened for several reasons:
● In some measure it is due to the growing alienation some people feel from the **outmoded overseas cultural forms** in

which Christianity still comes to them. This probably affects only a minority who have become more conscious of their national roots and identity.

● To some extent the decline stems from the **recognized pluralism of modern life**. Many people are now more aware than ever, through the media and their own encounters, of the competing nature of religious convictions, all of which are now seen as in part culturally conditioned.

● In the main, however, Christianity has been weakened because of **the increasing industrialization and bureaucratization of modern life**. The weakening of established forms of Christianity is a phenomenon that can be seen in all advanced Western

TOWARDS AUSTRALIAN CHRISTIANITY
JIM STEBBINS

The style of Christianity in Australia stems from the English, colonial and convict origins of the European society established almost 200 years ago. Australia achieved political independence in 1901, but the larger vision of a new start was lost on the main Christian denominations: solid, cramped and traditional, they continued to compete against one another. However, the rapidity of social and technological change in recent decades has provoked many Christians to seek a new role, true alike to their faith and to the land and the age in which God has placed them.

In the beginning...
The first chaplains in Australia worked in a hostile situation, with unsympathetic governors, apathetic home churches, and a population divided in its religious outlook. Although they were employed by the state, the chaplains received only grudging state support in building churches and schools.

Anglicans, Roman Catholics, Presbyterians and Methodists, together with the smaller denominations, strove to carve out their own spheres of influence. Competing for state funds, preaching against one another, they became rivals as the outer settlements developed.

This rivalry continued through the nineteenth century. As secularism overtook society and denominational bickering engaged the churches, the denominations gradually received less financial aid from the state, and the functions of church and state became distanced.

Australian Christians have always had a strong emphasis on private morality. The early clergy assumed that one of their main tasks was to raise the moral tone of society. They regularly preached against such sins as lying, whoring, covetousness, drunkenness, stealing and insubordination. The convicts did not see Christianity as a source of new life or genuine community, but as an extension of the gaoler's repertoire of compulsion and admonition. This stress meant that for later generations, Christian conversion was often identified with the rejection of alcohol, smoking, gambling and so on.

Another legacy from the early days was the failure of the churches to adapt to their new circumstances. The clergy assumed that what was right for Britain was also right for Australia. Church government, ceremony, architecture and dress were exported around the world to Australia, lock, stock and barrel. This reproduction of the detailed habits and customs of 'home' was continued well into the twentieth century.

Responding to Australian needs
But in an important respect, there were signs of hope. Australian Christians and churches showed a vitality and imagination in their practical service to others that took notice of some of the particular needs of Australian society.

■ In the 1840s, **Caroline Chisholm**, a Roman Catholic, became virtually a one-person unofficial immigration agency as she set about redressing the imbalances she identified in the composition of the country's population.

■ In the 1920s and 1930s, the Presbyterian **John Flynn** developed an innovative and effective 'flying doctor service': a pedal radio, small plane and bush hospital network covering 5 million square kilometres

societies. The growth of industry and bureaucracy has certainly taken much of the mystery and precariousness out of life, dimensions for which religion has traditionally provided answers. Because of this, the place of intuition, imagination and passionate commitment, as well as belief in realities beyond the detection of our physical senses, has lessened. Yet all these elements are crucial to religious belief.

But if traditional Christianity has declined, what has taken its place? Where the religious aspect of people's lives comes to the surface, it tends to focus on contemporary idols rather than the living God of Christianity. For some, politics, health, sex, material well-being, family and the environment have become

of the outback.

- In the early 1960s, the Methodist **Alan Walker** began in Sydney the Lifeline telephone crisis counselling agency that quickly became a model for cities across the world.

Finding a national Christian style

How has Christianity in Australia changed over the last twenty years? Can it now be said that there is a genuine Australian expression of Christianity?

- One of the big changes is **the remarkable drop in rivalry and bitterness between the denominations** in recent times. Most of the Presbyterian, Methodist and Congregational churches merged in 1977 to form the Uniting Church. Although smaller denominations

continue, many of them co-ordinate action on social issues, and in evangelism. The different churches appear to have become reconciled to a more limited influence in a pluralist, technological, welfare society, and are seeking to define their roles in it.

- Among Christians, **the public morality nerve remains sensitive** on issues such as abortion, pornography, and the structure of social security benefits.
- But what of the church traditions inherited from Great Britain, or more recently, the United States? Although dissatisfied voices have been raised, **overseas agendas still dominate the Christian scene** in Australia. Issues such as ecumenism, Pentecostalism, biblical authority and international disarmament arrive pre-packaged on Australian shores, limiting the scope for developing the

debate in terms of contemporary Australian concerns.

Today there is a widespread recognition of the need for a specifically Australian angle in theology, apologetics, evangelism, liturgy, music and lifestyle, and some important first steps have been taken. This need is underlined by growing contacts with neighbouring nations in South-East Asia, and an increased community awareness of Muslim, Hindu and Buddhist viewpoints.

- It is encouraging, too, that the Australian Christian emphasis of **care for the community has continued and grown**. Interest in innovative social service programmes continues strongly. The churches have participated in government reviews of social service issues and have been to the fore in implementing new approaches to refugee settlement, overseas aid, care for the elderly, and school-to-work transition.

The altering face of modern Australian life calls for greater changes in the church in Australia. The development of a truly Australian Christian faith is vital for Christians to be effective in the society they seek to reach.

A baptism on a Sydney beach. Australian Christians are looking for genuinely national ways of living their faith.

The Charismatic movement has been in Australia and New Zealand for some time, bringing a new spiritual dimension into many cong-regations.

the objects of ultimate concern, though most people are content to preoccupy themselves with the demands and opportunities of the moment.

Christian leaders have reacted differently to this process. Some have suggested that the loosening of religious adherence has only pruned the churches of their nominal membership. But this overlooks the facts: many mainline churches have an ageing population; the denominations have little witness in industrial and inner city areas; even committed Christians no longer go to church because they cannot identify with the churches' ethos and superficiality.

Other religious leaders believe that New Zealand and Australia are on the verge of national religious revivals. There are signs of a new Christian vitality, but in the absence of any deep and widespread upheaval in Australian and New Zealand society – whether from within or

without – revival on the scale they expect seems very unlikely. Others talk of the church being in the trough of a cycle which will soon return to normal. In view of the picture world-wide, and the length of the downward curve in the mainline churches, this is too glib and passive a view.

SOURCES OF NEW LIFE
However, in both countries there are real signs of continuing and new life. In some places traditional churches possess a genuine vitality, and also make an effective contribution to the wider society around them. In para-church and inter-denominational groupings as well as in experimental forms of Christian community and more informal church life, there is also evidence of a revitalization of Christian vision that augurs well for the future. These movements, however, contain certain ambiguities and inadequacies as well as important discoveries and potential.

● **Evangelistic work** In the late 1950s and 1960s, new life was breathed into many of the mainline churches through the evangelistic crusades led by Billy Graham and others. This led to a temporary increase in church attendance and growth in the number of men and women who came forward for full-time ministry. But since the 1970s, such activities have no longer had the same impact. Where they have been held, they largely renew the faithful and challenge nominal Christians to a greater commitment, rather than solve the problem of reaching outsiders.

Other evangelistic approaches have been tried in order to overcome this difficulty. Home dialogue meetings, the recent introduction of church growth principles from America, and a return to longer-scale missions have had some results. But they do not appear to have generated the same impact as their counterparts of a generation ago.

One exception to this is the work of Australia's best-known evangelist, John Smith, who has conducted highly innovative and extremely fruitful meetings in several Australian states. His genuinely indigenous style, use of existing communication frameworks, and commitment to long-term mission have helped here.

● **The Charismatic movement** A more lasting impact upon mainline church life has come through the Charismatic movement. This is now nearly two decades old and scarcely any denomination has remained untouched by it. While it has created divisions in some churches and religious organizations, where it has been responsibly expressed and openly weighed it has brought new life. There has been a deeper commitment to other Christians, a greater sense of the importance of each person's contribution, a stronger desire to study the Bible, a more generous approach to giving, a more joyous approach to worship.

Along with certain Reformed groups, the Charismatic movement has also been the catalyst in the formation of Christian schools (over 120 now in Australia), though many of these have developed a Fundamentalist, 'accelerated-learning' character, with all the problems these outlooks contain.

The Charismatic movement, as in other parts of the world, has also shown a tendency to dogmatism, an insistence upon a certain uniformity of experience, and a naivety about what is happening in the world. The Charismatic influence now seems to have largely run its course in Australia and New Zealand so far as introducing genuinely new impulses into church life. Unless it can translate some of its concern into more thoroughgoing institutional reforms, make a more profound theological contribution and develop a more realistic analysis of modern life, it will not remain a significant force in church renewal.

● **Radical discipleship, social justice** A third source of new life in Australian and New Zealand Christianity comes from the so-called radical discipleship and social justice movements. From their different perspectives, these have sensitized many Christians, particularly younger ones, to discover a more distinctive Christian lifestyle, corporately as well as individually, and to express a greater commitment to social justice.

There are now many experiments in communal living alongside or within local church life, and the relationship between such communities is growing.

See Telling the World; Renewal in the Holy Spirit; All Things in Common

The continuing growth and impact of house churches, at first outside but now also inside the denominations, has also pioneered a form of church life and developed a quality of Christian commitment that may well become the standard for the church at large. Some of these experiments in Christian community have a well-defined outreach into more disadvantaged social groups, and others seek to help their members to relate their faith very specifically to their work, leisure, political and cultural life.

There are also new resource centres helping Christians to understand and relate more effectively to their society. The National Catholic Research Council and the Zadok Centre are good examples. The Social Responsibility Department of the Uniting Church in Australia and the Catholic Commission for Justice and Peace, among others, have exhibited strong, if at times doctrinaire, social concern over the problems of minority groups, unemployment, and issues of war and peace. More than half the well-known aid organizations in Australia and New Zealand also have either Christian foundations or strong Christian elements, while Christian groups like the Brotherhood of St Lawrence continue to be a source of social research and policy recommendations as well as providing much-needed social services.

● **Revitalized spiritual traditions** Another source of new life, still emerging, comes from a revitalization of older

Many New Zealand Christians have gone from the thriving suburban churches to missionary assignments in the Third World. Australian and New Zealand churches are sending out an increasing number of missionaries.

Catholic or Anabaptist spiritual traditions. A growing number of Protestants are coming to see the importance of meditation, dreams and more imaginative approaches to the Bible, and organizations like the Anglican-based Eremos Institute in Sydney are helping them to do this in quite practical ways. Since the Second Vatican Council, many Roman Catholics have also come to see the

importance of traditional Protestant spiritual emphases.

But only as these new impulses are thoroughly integrated with, and not just complemented by, a concern for social issues, will they result in any real transformation of personal, church, or social life. One encouraging sign of this is the growing publication of books by Australian authors seeking to combine a concern for theological freshness, contemporary relevance and practical spirituality. A number of agencies are also seeking to do this in some journals as well.

CHURCH UNITY AND MISSIONARY OUTREACH

Two other important dimensions of Antipodean church life

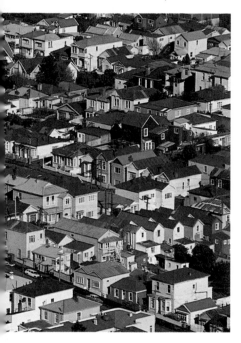

concern church unity and missionary work. The most ambitious move towards **church unity** in the region was the attempt, in the 1970s, to unite the Presbyterian, Methodist, Congregational and Anglican denominations in New Zealand. While this attempt failed to reach agreement, the first three groups became the Uniting Church in Australia in 1976 (with 33 per

cent of Presbyterians and 15 per cent of Methodists not joining). Although this has led to a re-modelling of the structures of the church, it has not as yet led to significant renewal in these denominations. On the contrary, their membership appears to be both ageing and declining.

In theological education, increasing co-operation between Roman Catholics and Protestants, as well as between Protestant groups, has had a range of quiet, but nevertheless valuable effects. While the Australian Council of Churches does not have Roman Catholic or Lutheran participation, there are moves to establish a National Council of Churches in New Zealand in which Roman Catholics will be fully involved. However, the most important ecumenical endeavours probably take place at the grass-roots level in Christian communities, home fellowships, social action projects, working groups and so on. Such projects, organized on an ecumenical basis, are likely to play an increasingly significant role in the future.

Missionaries from New Zealand and Australia can be found on all six continents, but especially in the Asian and Pacific areas. Numerically they are on the increase even in these days of declining church allegiance. A higher percentage of the Christian population in the two countries respond to this call than in societies like the United States where church attendance is more than twice as high. Apart from people sent out by official missionary organizations, many,

See Spirituality Today; Churches Together

Continued on p. 194

AUSTRALIAN ABORIGINAL CHRISTIAN MOVEMENTS
ROBERT BOS

In March 1979, a remarkable Christian movement began among Aboriginal people at Galiwin'ku, in Australia's isolated Arnhem Land on the northern tropical coast. It soon affected not only their entire community of 1,600 people, but spread to neighbouring towns and eventually across the state borders to other Aboriginal communities thousands of kilometres away.

The movement was marked by nightly fellowship meetings, sometimes lasting until one or two o'clock in the morning. These meetings consisted of much singing of choruses and hymns, some in local dialects, and some in English. Early in the night the singing was relaxed, but joyous and exuberant. Later, it became fervent and intense as people were deeply moved by the Spirit of God.

After a period of Bible teaching by one of the leaders, worshippers (usually several hundred people) formed a circle and continued to sing with arms raised and eyes closed in adoration. Those wishing to commit their lives to Christ or seeking healing for some problem quietly knelt in the centre of the circle for prayer and the laying-on of hands by the church elders.

A victimized people
Australia's Aboriginal people are a small, 2 per cent minority in their own country. Many have been displaced from lands for which they hold strong religious and emotional ties. Some state governments have now begun to recognize traditional land tenure in European law, where such land has not yet been alienated by white settlers. Unemployment, disease, alcoholism, infant mortality

and prison statistics for Aboriginal people are many times greater than those for the white population. Discriminatory legislation persists in some states.

Yet in spite of all this, Aboriginal people have begun to find new confidence in recent years. The fact that in the Christian movement God has dealt directly with them has increased this sense of self-confidence. No longer does Christianity have to be mediated by white missionaries.

Aboriginal theology
Missionaries have worked among Australia's northern tribal people since early this century. But it was not until the 1970s that the Aborigines had opportunities for church leadership training. The Anglican and Uniting churches jointly established Nungalinya College in Darwin, and a small stream of graduates has begun to provide trained, sensitive, indigenous leadership for the Aboriginal congregations.

A few Aboriginal men who have been initiated into the traditional ceremonial life of their own people and who have also had a thorough theological education have actively begun to develop an 'Aboriginal theology'. They believe that the Spirit of God was with their forefathers before the missionaries came, and that there is much of value in the ancient wisdom. At the same time, knowledge of Jesus through the Bible is recognized as the ultimate revelation of God, and the authority against which all else is measured. But parallels between traditional beliefs and practices and biblical truth are eagerly discussed, with each illuminating the other.

The emerging Aboriginal Christianity in the tribal communities of the north is marked by:
- A deep commitment to personal evangelism
- A style of worship which is participatory and dynamic (influenced by the Charismatic movement)
- A sympathetic re-examination of traditional pre-Christian beliefs and practices in the light of the gospel
- A deep sense of the spiritual dimension pervading all of reality
- A sensitivity to the social justice implications of the gospel (there has been some influence from liberation theologians)
- A sense of oneness among people who were previously separated by distance and language.

Frustration with the 'white' church
As the Christian movement among Aboriginal Christians gathers momentum, there is a growing

frustration with the 'white' church in Australia, which is seen as cold, intellectual, and preoccupied with structures, rule books and finances. They also believe that large sections of the white church are unable to hear the cries of suffering of the Aboriginal people. There are almost no Aboriginal people in white congregations.

It is not surprising then that Aboriginal Christian leaders are calling for their own church structures. The Uniting Aboriginal and Islander Christian Congress (UAICC) is in the process of formation. The aim of this is to link Aboriginal congregations together, to build a church organization which will recognize their freedom to worship in their own way, and to make decisions about evangelism, social justice issues, finance, and the placement of ministers.

In almost every part of Australia where church bodies meet, Aboriginal people are in the minority. Not only do they feel intimidated by the fact

that all discussions are in a foreign language (English), but everything that is done presupposes a European world-view, European assumptions about the nature of the church, and European procedure. Aboriginal people do not, for example, discuss things by debating for and against. They prefer the slower but ultimately more effective way of permitting everyone to voice an opinion, and then gradually allowing people to modify their positions until a group mind is reached. Nobody goes away dissatisfied because they have 'lost'.

Aboriginal Christian leaders do not see the UAICC as a separatist movement, but rather as claiming their freedom in Christ to worship and make decisions in their own way, and so be able to relate to white Christians with integrity and dignity.

The Congress hopes to include in its organization not only northern, tribal people, but also southern, urban Aborigines. Although many of these people are of mixed-race descent, they nevertheless see themselves as

Aboriginal people over against the wider European Australian population.

In 1970 the Aboriginal Evangelical Fellowship was formed, also out of frustration with white-dominated church structures. Although this organization shares the evangelistic concerns of the northern movement, some members are more suspicious than their northern counterparts of religious and cultural traditions that go back to the time before European contact. They also wonder whether land rights (the primary political goal of Aboriginal people across the nation) is a legitimate Christian concern. Despite these differences, they have been invited to be part of the UAICC.

God chooses the weak

Aboriginal Christians see themselves as being open not just to the renewal of their own people and communities, but also to bearing testimony to the life-changing power of Christ to the wider Australian society and beyond. They see growth resulting from their own deep relationship with God, and look for fraternal relationships with the Maoris of New Zealand, the indigenous churches in Melanesia, and with black Americans and Africans.

As they search the scriptures, they find assurance that in the past God has used 'what the world looks down on and despises, and thinks is nothing'. To fulfil his purposes, they want to make themselves available for that to happen again.

In recent years a surge of new Christian life has begun among Australia's Aboriginal people.

inspired by missionary motives, go through government agencies like Australian Volunteers Abroad or as private citizens carrying out professional responsibilities in the land of their choice.

CHRISTIAN FAITH IN THE SOUTH PACIFIC

Jesuit missionaries first brought the Christian faith to parts of Melanesia, but it was through the efforts of Protestants from Britain, France, Germany and Holland in the nineteenth century that the first real breakthroughs came in the South Pacific as a whole. Some of these led to genuinely indigenous missions, which were without parallel anywhere. The social and political framework of Islander life led to some strange alliances between church and rulers, as in the 'Christian' kingdoms of countries like Tonga and Tahiti. It also led to community agreements with particular denominations which resulted in a largely Presbyterian Vanuatu, a Methodist Fiji and a Lutheran (northern) New Guinea.

In the wake of unresolved tensions between Christianity and European influences on the one hand, and traditional culture on the other, some successful indigenous movements and churches have sprung up. Political independence has now been granted throughout most of the region, the denominations have attempted to hand over control of the churches to national church leaders. But despite this, in many places there is still a definite European influence on church affairs.

What problems are faced by South Pacific Christians?

● One arises from the continuing pattern of migration to the towns and cities or outside the country altogether. The resulting **break-up of traditional family life** and the **dire social effects of too rapid urbanization** bring many difficulties in their wake.

● Another concern is the **widespread nominalism in many churches** on the part of third, fourth, or even fifth generation Christians. Evidence for this state of affairs is widespread in Fiji, Tonga and other countries.

● A further difficulty stems from the long period of dependence upon Western church models and financial resources. In many places **worship still reflects northern European styles of dress and liturgy**, and local support of pastors and denominational structures is weak.

● Another problem has its roots in the **materialism of denominations** in many rural areas and the new **competitiveness among denominations** in the towns. In Samoa, for instance, many church officials are preoccupied with questions of plant and organization, while in the burgeoning urban areas in all countries the range of churches available often creates confusion and division.

● A final hazard faced by all the inhabitants of the aptly-named South *Pacific*, is the impact on these peace-loving people of **the**

nuclear policies of the Western powers. They have every reason to object to being dragged into the power-politics of the northern hemisphere and to their peoples being subjected to radiation hazards as a consequence of nuclear tests in the region (for example in the Marshall Islands).

Despite these problems, there are many signs of life among Christians in Oceania. There is generally a sense of unity and openness which transcends traditional and denominational barriers. This is reflected in the formation of the Pacific Theological College in Suva, in the composition of such groupings as the various National Councils of Churches and especially in the Pacific Conference of Churches which has Roman Catholic, Protestant and Independent membership. Also, many national leaders of the Pacific island nations in politics, education, law and the professions are committed Christians. Under the direction of the South Pacific Leaders Fellowship, which organizes retreats and regional gatherings, these leaders are brought into regular contact with one another.

Several generations of Pacific Christians have undertaken pioneer missionary and evangelistic work across national and cultural boundaries. Today

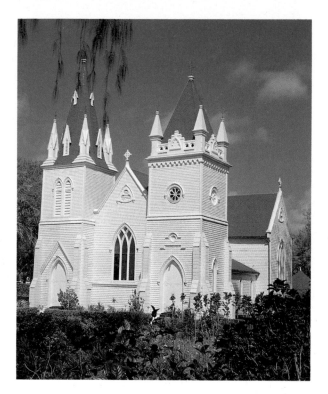

these endeavours range from work in large congregations in Western capitals like Sydney, to village outreach teams in the remotest islands. In some places very innovative and successful ministries directed to major social problems like mobility and unemployment have been developed. In these respects particularly, South Pacific Christians have much to teach their more technically advanced Western neighbours in the region.

The royal chapel on the island of Tonga, where the great majority are members of Christian churches.

2.4 THE DECLINE OF FAITH?

Christians in Europe

KLAAS RUNIA

When the apostle Paul received the vision of a man of Macedonia calling, 'Come over to Macedonia and help us', he immediately obeyed the vision and crossed over into what is now Europe. Most probably he did not then realize that this was the beginning of the Christianization of a whole continent. In the following centuries the gospel of Jesus Christ was brought to all the tribes and nations of Europe.

By the end of the fourteenth century most European countries had been reached by the gospel and most nations had embraced the Christian faith. For many more centuries Europe remained the centre of Christianity. From the sixteenth century onwards most mission work was carried out by European Christians. As late as 1970 the majority of Christian missionaries still came from Europe.

In the meantime great changes had begun to take place. Industrialization and the accompanying urbanization deeply influenced the state of Christianity in Europe. The traditional structures of the church appeared unable to cope with the new urban situation, and city life itself easily led people to give up all religious practices. Today secularization affects all spheres of public and personal life. Even though officially the national churches of Europe still have a large membership, the reality is that the number of people attending the weekly services is going down in most churches. The role of the churches in public life is becoming smaller and smaller. A long article in the French magazine *L'Expres* in 1981, for example, deals with the many changes in the life and thought of the French people. But it contains no reference to the church or to the role of religion and faith.

We are faced with a bitter but undeniable fact: Europe itself has become one vast mission-field, and missionary work in this mission-field appears to be very difficult. The sons and daughters, the grandchildren and great-grandchildren of the prodigal son are hard to reach. They seem to be inoculated against the Christian faith.

Cross-country skiers pass an Austrian church. For many in Western Europe the pattern of work and leisure leaves little room for the spiritual side of life.

See The Anglican
Communion

Does this mean that there is no hope for Europe? Most certainly not! In spite of all the negative side, which we cannot ignore, there is still much for which to be thankful. The Christian churches in Europe still show many signs of vitality, and many congregations make a strong impact on their neighbourhood. European culture has been deeply influenced by the Christian faith. Nearly everywhere in Europe, and this is true even of large parts of eastern Europe, people can attend church services if they wish. There are indications of interest in the Christian faith among young people, intellectuals, artists, and so on.

A survey of Europe is not an easy matter. Europe has gone through such a complicated history that the situation is virtually different in every country. It may help to divide Europe into four main regions.

WESTERN EUROPE

In **England** the Church of England is still the national church, with the queen as its titular head. In many ways this church continues to be very influential, even though both membership and church attendance have dropped considerably. It contains a wide variety of views, from the ritualistic through the more liberal to the evangelical. In recent years the Evangelical wing has grown in numbers and strength.

Alongside the Church of England there are many free (non-established) churches, such as the Union of Baptists, the Methodist Church, the United Reformed Church, the Salvation Army, the Society of Friends, and so on. Unfortunately, in the last thirty years the membership of the free churches has dropped from about 1.7 million to a million. A number of independent Evangelical congregations flourish, however, and West Indian Pentecostal churches show startling growth. The Roman Catholic Church, with a large contingent of descendants of Irish immigrants, is generally rather traditional in theology and attitude. In 1973 the overall picture of the British religious scene was frankly described by the Anglican bishop of Truro in these words: 'A majority of people in this country are neither practising Christians, nor draw upon a capital of Christian moral standards.'

In **Scotland** the dominating church is the (Presbyterian) Church of Scotland, while there are also a number of smaller Presbyterian churches (Free Presbyterian, Reformed Presbyterian, United Free, and so on). The **Irish Republic** is over 95 per cent Roman Catholic, with a very high religious practice. The Roman Catholic Church of Ireland has always been, and still is, very Rome-oriented and mission-minded. **Northern Ireland** is a sorely divided country, with Protestants and Roman Catholics embroiled in constant battle. **Wales** has a strong free-church tradition, but spiritual life has declined.

The three Benelux countries

THE AGONY OF ULSTER
CECIL KERR

Ireland, once known as 'the island of saints and scholars', has sadly become in the eyes of many a dark blot on the map of the Christian world. Puzzled onlookers ask: 'How can a country that professes so much Christianity be so divided?'

The roots of the present conflict go back several centuries, to the settlement in Ireland of many people from England and Scotland in the seventeenth century. The settlers who occupied large areas of the land were mostly from the Reformed or Protestant traditions, while the native Irish owed allegiance to Rome. The barriers of resentment, fear and mistrust that were erected then, persist until the present day. This explains why, generally speaking in Ireland, political and religious allegiance follow parallel lines: Roman Catholic people aspire to a united Ireland, while Northern Irish Protestants favour union with Great Britain.

Centuries of separate development have led to two distinct communities divided by religion, education, culture and politics. From the roots of ignorance, fear and suspicion the weeds of prejudice, hatred and violence have grown. The fruits appear in the awful suffering and agony of the last two decades, in

which over 2,000 people have been killed and many thousands more severely injured. Almost every family in Northern Ireland has been personally affected by the continuing violence.

The challenge to the Christian church in Ireland is to release people from the prison houses of their history into a new experience of mutual forgiveness and brotherhood. Yet the churches themselves are deeply infected by the history of division. Tribal loyalties are strong and the temptation in leadership is to speak for one's own side rather than declare the prophetic word of truth.

Healing the wounds

Despite the legacy of violence and behind the newspaper headlines there are, thank God, many signs of hope.

■ Since the beginning of the present troubles there has been in Ireland, north and south, **an unprecedented moving of God's Spirit**. This has influenced Roman Catholics as well as Protestants. A true awareness of God's mercy and love in Jesus Christ has led to some breaking down of centuries-old barriers of suspicion and fear.

■ The leaders of the four main churches have, in many instances, given **a clear and united Christian**

witness in the face of considerable opposition. This was particularly marked in 1981, when they called for prayer for the nation:

'We need a truly repentant spirit and a sorrowful penitence for our failures. We must...become aware of the many ways in which we have come short of the Christianity we have professed'.

■ Many Christians have recognized **the urgency of working together** to heal the deep wounds that scar the church in Ireland. Courageous initiatives have been taken to draw both sides together for mutual understanding. Experiments in shared education are being made, notably at Lagan College in Belfast. Centres of reconciliation such as Corrymeela, Glencree, Columba House, Cornerstone, the Columbanus Community and the Christian Renewal Centre at Rostrevor (on the border between north and south) have made significant contributions towards healing the divisions.

■ Perhaps the most remarkable feature of all in the agony of Ulster is **the truly supernatural power to love and to forgive** that so many have shown in the face of terrible injury and suffering. Nothing could bear more eloquent testimony to the true Christian influence in Ireland than these thousands of unrecorded acts of love. For those of us who live and work in Ireland this true Christian spirit of love gives us inspiration to continue the costly work of reconciliation. We believe that Ireland can still, under God, be a visual aid to God's healing power.

In this procession in Dublin on the Day of Pentecost, Roman Catholics and Protestants march together for peace in Ireland.

See Reformed Churches round the World; Roman Catholics since the Council; Churches Together; Who are the Lutherans Today?

show quite a varied picture. In the **Netherlands** the northern part is largely Protestant and the southern part largely Roman Catholic. Nearly all the Protestant churches belong to the Reformed tradition. Unfortunately there have been so many divisions that a few years ago a booklet could be published with the title *Ten Times Reformed*. The Roman Catholic Church is perhaps the most open and progressive in the world. On the whole Dutch theology is very vigorous, grappling with the issues raised by modern secularization. However, a recent poll indicated that 42 per cent of the Dutch people professed to be unaffiliated to any church.

Belgium is largely Roman Catholic. Ninety per cent of the population are baptized Roman Catholics. In the post-war years there has been a sharp decline in church attendance. The same is true of **Luxembourg**.

France is also predominantly Roman Catholic. About 85 per cent of the population are baptized in the Roman Catholic Church. The decline in church attendance is very sharp, especially in the age group of thirty-five to forty-five and among young people. In some regions half the young people abandon church attendance immediately following their first communion. The main Protestant churches are the (Reformed) Church of France and the (Lutheran) Church of Alsace and Lorraine. The Protestants have a fairly strong representation among business people and intellectuals and are therefore comparatively

influential. However, they are no longer the second largest religious force in France. They have been overtaken by the Muslims who have come to France in great numbers during the post-war years, mainly from North Africa.

The position in **Switzerland** is almost the same as in the Netherlands. Protestants and Roman Catholics are almost equal in numbers, with some cantons historically Protestant and some Roman Catholic. Although the majority of the original Swiss population is still Protestant (mainly Reformed), since 1970 the Roman Catholics have had an overall majority, in particular due to immigration of workers from Roman Catholic Mediterranean countries. The Roman Catholic Church is rather open and progressive. The headquarters of the World Council of Churches and of some confessional world communions (such as the World Alliance of Reformed Churches and the Lutheran World Federation) are in Geneva.

The overwhelming majority of people in **Austria** are Roman Catholic (88 per cent). The Protestants (6 per cent) are largely Lutheran.

The ecclesiastical scene in **West Germany** is very complicated. Officially 92.8 per cent of the population (totalling 57.5 million) are Christians, of whom nearly 29 million are Protestant and just over 27 million Roman Catholic. Evangelicals are estimated to number 6.5 million.

The majority of the Protestants

belong to the seventeen *Landeskirchen* (territorial national churches), which are all members of the Evangelical Church in Germany (EKD), a loose federation that was formed after World War II. Seven of these territorial churches are Lutheran, two are Reformed and eight are united Lutheran-Reformed. The EKD is a rich church, due to the official church tax, virtually unique to this country, whose annual income is 3,000 million dollars. Because of this income it is able to maintain a huge administrative apparatus and to perform a world-wide ministry through missions, through pastoral, social and medical work, and through development aid. For all these reasons it is

still rather influential, even though only 6 per cent of nominal church members attend services regularly. Next to the EKD there are also a number of Lutheran, Reformed and other free churches.

The Roman Catholic Church has grown considerably since 1945, mainly due to the influx of 15 million refugees from East Germany and eastern Europe. But it also suffers from a sharp drop in church attendance and in ordinations. The theological unity of the past has been replaced by diversity. There have been many cases of theological friction between theologians and the hierarchy, the most famous case being that of Hans Küng, who in 1979 was dismissed from his post *Continued on p.204*

DUTCH ROMAN CATHOLICS

Although the Reformed Churches are strong in the Netherlands, 40 per cent of Dutch people are Roman Catholic. And Dutch Catholics have been good missionaries, with world-wide influence. However, over the last twenty years or so they have been at loggerheads with Rome over the degree of independent authority a province should have.

Many Dutch Roman Catholics want a shared authority with Rome. They have advocated an independent line on such matters as clerical celibacy, and have worked closely with Reformed churches. Rome's response has been to put in conservative bishops and try to enforce central authority, and some Dutch Catholics agree with this. But the central question of authority remains unresolved.

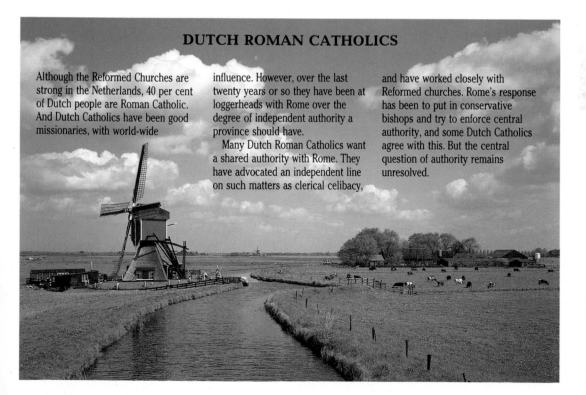

LUXEMBOURG
Roman Catholic

IRELAND
Still very much a Christian island. In Northern Ireland, Protestants predominate over Roman Catholics (about 60:40) and there is conflict. In the Irish Republic, Roman Catholicism is very strong, largely traditional.

WEST GERMANY
About half Protestant, half Roman Catholic. Protestants mainly in federations of Lutheran and Reformed churches. There is a church tax. Evangelicals generally strong. Many influential theologians.

PORTUGAL
Very conservative Roman Catholicism. Some anti-clerical feeling, especially in south.

ITALY
Strongly Roman Catholic, though attendance not high. Ancient Waldensian church and active Pentecostals. Charismatic influence among Roman Catholics.

BELGIUM
Strongly Roman Catholic, though attendance decreasing.

SPAIN
Roman Catholic country. More progressive Catholics gaining over traditionalists since death of Franco. Small Protestant groups now have more freedom.

GREECE
National Eastern Orthodox church. To proselytize an Orthodox Greek is forbidden. Small Protestant and Roman Catholic churches.

ENGLAND
National church is Church of England. Smaller nonconformist and Roman Catholic churches. Rapid growth among West Indian Pentecostals and independent Evangelical churches. Mainstream decline seems to have halted.

WALES
No national church. Strong nonconformist tradition, often Welsh-speaking. Smaller, non-established Anglican church. Many attend church, but not the revival spirit of early twentieth century.

SCOTLAND
National church is (Presbyterian) Church of Scotland. Smaller episcopalian, nonconformist and Roman Catholic churches. More attend church than in England, but numbers declining.

MALTA
Strongly Roman Catholic, in dispute with state about education.

ALBANIA
Was mainly Muslim with some Christians. But now atheistic state with total repression.

YUGOSLAVIA
Some republics Orthodox (including Serbia), some Roman Catholic (including Croatia and Slovenia). Orthodox the most influential. Small but lively Protestant churches. Generally there is religious freedom. Strong Muslim presence.

FRANCE
Mainly Roman Catholic, but many have abandoned church in recent decades. Protestants (mainly Reformed) few but influential.

SWITZERLAND
About half and half Roman Catholic (mainly progressive) and Protestant (Reformed). Most cantons are historically one or the other.

AUSTRIA
Strongly Roman Catholic.

EUROPE'S CHRISTIAN HERITAGE

66 For many centuries Europe was the only Christian continent. Only in the twentieth century has the balance changed. As a result, Europe has a rich legacy of Christian traditions. The pattern is different in each country. **99**

HUNGARY
Over half are Roman Catholics, but also strong Protestants (mainly Reformed). Roman Catholic relations with state improving; Protestant relations good, with considerable freedom.

EAST GERMANY
About half the people belong to churches, mostly Protestant but some Roman Catholic, but numbers decreasing. Interest among young people. Reasonable church/state relations, but still much pressure.

POLAND
Strongly Roman Catholic, with great spiritual fervour. State has to come to terms with church's influence. Small Protestant churches.

BULGARIA
National (not established) church is Orthodox. Nominal freedom but tight control. Strong Muslim presence.

FINLAND
Two national churches: Lutheran is larger, but Orthodox church is significant. Very active Pentecostal churches.

USSR
Long Orthodox tradition, which remains strong despite severe pressure. Devoted Roman Catholics in Lithuania and Ukraine. Protestants are mainly Baptist, with some Pentecostals and others. Some Baptists refuse to register and are arrested. Widespread spiritual interest despite atheistic education.

NETHERLANDS
Northern part largely (Reformed) Protestant, southern part (progressive) Roman Catholic. But many not affiliated to either.

DENMARK
Lutheran national church, to which most belong but not many go.

SWEDEN
Automatic membership of Lutheran state church. But highly secularized society. Ten per cent of the people belong to free churches.

ROMANIA
Largely Orthodox country, though some Roman Catholics and Protestants. Some revival among Orthodox, Baptists and Pentecostals. Some religious freedom, but church/state relations often strained.

CZECHO-SLOVAKIA
Roman Catholics strongest, but significant Protestant churches, and some Old Catholics. Very tight state control.

NORWAY
State church is Lutheran, but attendance is low. Religious but not church-going people. Strong student work.

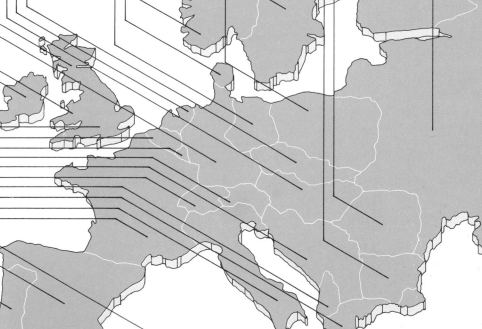

as an ecclesiastically-recognized professor of theology in Tübingen.

Evangelicals are very active in West Germany. They have some fairly strong organizations, such as the Gnadauer Alliance, the No Other Gospel Movement, and the (German) Evangelical Alliance.

NORTHERN EUROPE

The four countries which make up Scandinavia have developed in similar ways. All four countries (Denmark, Norway, Sweden and Finland) are predominantly Lutheran and have an established Lutheran Church. In most cases this means that the final legislative and financial authority resides in parliament and that bishops are appointed by the king or government. Nearly the whole population is nominally Lutheran. Most people are married in the church (a family affair rather than a religious ritual) and have their children baptized, but the percentage regularly attending church is very low. In all four countries the Roman Catholic Church is on the small side.

In **Denmark** the Evangelical Lutheran Folkekirke (National Church) comprises 95 per cent of the total population. Although the numbers of practising adherents is low, there are very few official withdrawals. The free churches are small, the Baptist Union (7,000 members) being the largest.

The Church of **Norway** (96 per cent of the total population) has an attendance of 3 per cent. This is due partly to traditions of the past when people could not go to church because of the vast distances, partly to modern secularization. Yet half the people appear to listen regularly to religious broadcasts, half claim to pray daily, 85 per cent claim to teach their children evening prayer, and 95 per cent support religious instruction in the state schools. There are several free churches, the Pentecostal Church (39,000) being the largest. There are also some Lutheran free churches. The Mission Movement and the Evangelical Student Movement are both strong.

Sweden is one of the most secularized countries in Europe, with a sophisticated culture and a socialist welfare state. Yet there are many disillusioned people, as appears from the fact that alcoholism and drug abuse are on the increase and the suicide rate is one of the highest in the world – between 1962 and 1971 death from suicide outstripped death by traffic accidents. While 98 per cent of the population belong to the Church of Sweden (one is automatically a member by birth!), only 0.8 per cent attend regularly.

Nearly 10 per cent of the

Cardinal Hume, leader of Roman Catholics in England and Wales, with other Catholic bishops. Roman Catholics form a significant minority of British Christians.

people belong to the free churches, which are characterized by pietism and evangelistic fervour. The largest of them is the Swedish Mission Covenant Church (over 200,000 members). Recently a 'free synod' has been formed within the Church of Sweden, in protest against being forced to accept the ordination of women. (The Synod of the Church of Sweden had decreed that men unwilling to co-operate with female colleagues could not be ordained.)

Finland has two national churches: the Lutheran Church (4 million) and the Orthodox Church (nearly 57,000). There are several free churches. The 40,000 Pentecostals send out more missionaries than the entire established Lutheran Church. Evangelicals are fairly strong and active within the state church.

EASTERN EUROPE

This is the sector of Europe which is hardest to survey and assess. We can definitely not speak of *the* church in *the* Communist world. The situation is quite different from country to country. In Albania all religious life is suppressed, but Poland is the most Roman Catholic country in Europe. In Russia, a number of believers are imprisoned because of their religious practices, but in the German Democratic Republic this hardly ever happens. Alongside Protestants and Roman Catholics there are Orthodox national churches in many countries, often surrounded by sects and smaller movements

that can hardly be traced.

In each country the historical position is different. In Bulgaria the church was the rallying-point for resistance against Turkish occupation for more than four centuries, while the Russian church worked hand-in-glove with tsarist suppression. The Croatian region of Yugoslavia is an old stronghold of Roman Catholicism, while in Hungary, ever since the Counter-Reformation in the sixteenth century, the Reformed Church has opposed Roman Catholic dominance.

Nearly all Communist countries have in their constitution an article guaranteeing freedom of conscience and religion, but in nearly all countries a rider is added, limiting this freedom in the interests of the state. A good example is the Hungarian Constitution of 1972. It guarantees to all citizens freedom of conscience and the right of

A Swedish couple bring their baby for baptism in a Lutheran church. Most Swedish people have nominal church membership but attendance is rather low.

See The Orthodox Families

Continued on p.208

CHRISTIANS IN EASTERN EUROPE
PETER KUZMIC

In the late 1960s when many in the so-called Christian West carried the slogan 'God is dead', a Marxist philosopher wrote a bestselling book in Czechoslovakia, an East European country governed by the atheistic Communist Party. The book was entitled *God is Not Yet Dead.* The church in Eastern Europe, despite the circumstances, not only persists, but in certain areas flourishes.

Christians in Eastern Europe live, worship and witness in an ideological environment that is more or less hostile to their faith. This differs from country to country, and the degree of opposition or toleration changes at times. General descriptions are hardly possible, though it is true that all of the east European countries, except for the non-aligned Yugoslavia and the totally closed Albania, receive ideological direction from Moscow. Albania claims to have created the first full atheistic society in the world, as it has brutally exterminated all religious institutions and outlawed all religious activity.

Why the opposition to Christian faith? The Communist governments claim that Marxism-Leninism is the only proper and scientific understanding of the human race and history. Religion is viewed as a superstitious and false view of reality, and despite massive indications to the contrary, the need for it is expected to disappear gradually under the onslaught of scientific progress, education, and the new social order. At times administrative measures are used along with atheistic propaganda to speed up this process.

Christians can also come under suspicion as the reactionary remnant of the old society. In some countries, Protestants are looked upon as an infiltration of Western influence.

The Soviet Union
Since World War II, the Soviet state has used the hierarchy of the 1,000-year-old Russian Orthodox Church to promote various Soviet policies abroad, notably the policy of 'peace'. In return, the state has allowed the church some institutional life. But there are still wide-ranging restrictions on tolerated religious activities.

In the last twenty years, the Russian Orthodox Church has grown in strength and numbers, despite the limitations and repression of the state. There has been a significant turning to Orthodoxy among young people who have experienced personal conversion. In many cases this has been in reaction against Communism and represents an exciting, first-generation turning to the Christian faith. The revival has resulted in unofficial gatherings of young people to study the Bible and other religious writings, and in calls on church leaders by their flock to be more robust in resisting state pressure.

There has also grown up within the Orthodox Church a movement for religious freedom. This had its beginnings in the mid-1960s and has involved priests and laity. In 1976, Father Gleb Yakunin founded the Christian Committee for the Defence of Believers' Rights in the USSR, which sent over 3,000 pages of documentation to the West, listing infringements of the constitutional rights of Orthodox, Roman Catholics, Baptists and other Evangelicals to practise their faith. The committee was one victim of a comprehensive wave of arrests of dissidents.

Outside the Orthodox Church, there has been an Evangelical movement in Russia for over a century. At the time of the revolution of 1917, there were

close to 200,000 active Evangelical believers. The revolution was followed by a decade of the most astonishing spiritual revival of modern times. By 1928 the Evangelical groups in the Soviet Union already had a constituency of 3 to 4 million. This phenomenal growth resulted from the movement's evangelistic fervour, and was externally facilitated by Lenin's tactical toleration of the 'sectarians'. Since that time, Evangelicals, like the Orthodox, have experienced waves of persecution and toleration. Periods of relaxation marked by increased church activities and growth, have usually been followed by persecution and stricter control.

In the Soviet Union there are today registered and non-registered Evangelical churches. The largest registered body is the All-Union Council of Evangelical Christians and Baptists, which also includes Pentecostals and Mennonites. They number over half a million believers (unofficial sources claim 2 to 3 million) who are obliged to operate within the restrictions of Soviet law. Large groups of unregistered Baptists and Pentecostals refuse to do so, preferring to worship, teach their children the faith, evangelize and produce literature in a clandestine way, for which they often have to suffer. Both the registered and non-registered churches are growing.

Warsaw Pact countries
Romania is marked by an awakening of the Christian faith more than any other European country, east or west. The Evangelical free churches number over half a million active members, Baptists and Pentecostals being the strongest and fastest-growing.

In the Romanian Orthodox Church, a revivalist group, 'The Lord's Army',

A young couple come on their wedding day in Leningrad to lay the bridal bouquet at an eternal flame. Those who try to live without religion still need rituals and symbols in their lives.

is at least half a million strong. This movement, founded in 1923 for lay renewal within the Romanian Orthodox Church, has suffered intense persecution since the Communists came to power in 1947. Traian Dorz, its most prominent leader, also a poet and hymnwriter, has spent seventeen years in prison, followed by years of house arrest, searches and state surveillance. Despite the pressures, the Lord's Army continues its prayer, Bible studies, preaching and printing of Bibles and Christian literature.

A similar renewal movement known as 'Oasis' or 'Light and Life' activates thousands of young people in the strong, traditional Polish Catholic Church.

Czechoslovakia, like Poland, has a large Roman Catholic Church. The Czechoslovakian state has traditionally treated Catholic priests as its own employees, demanding from them obedience to the state's political line. But the Vatican, under the present pope, has been putting pressure on priests to reassert their independence from state control. Meanwhile, an increase in anti-Vatican propaganda from the Kremlin shows how worried the Soviet authorities have become about a pontiff

experienced in Eastern European church affairs, and who is now exercising his influence from outside the Soviet bloc.

Protestants are small minorities in most of the East European countries. Hungary and Czechoslovakia have larger Protestant communities. They tend to be theologically more conservative than their West European counterparts. Evangelical free churches in all these countries and in Poland, Bulgaria and Yugoslavia are rather small, though experiencing some growth.

East Germany is the only East European country with a Protestant majority. The Protestant churches here are traditionally strong and have had historic links with their sister churches in West Germany. They adopt an attitude of 'critical solidarity' towards the state. In recent years there has been a considerable rise in religious commitment among young people. In particular, the Protestant churches have sheltered a growing, independent 'peace movement', marked by a high level of moral responsibility and political even-handedness.

Christianity under pressure

Christians in most of the Soviet-bloc countries are marked by a theology of the cross. External pressures have purified and strengthened the church. Their spirituality now is marked by a strong emphasis on prayer and clean ethical living. Church membership and discipline demand serious commitment. Personal evangelism is effective because of the quality of life evident in believers and their families.

Christians are at a great disadvantage as they face the challenge of Marxist atheism.

Possibilities for providing Christian education for their young people are limited or outlawed, and Christian literature is hardly available. They can also be isolated from the broader international church community and lack information about it.

■ **The Orthodox churches** of the Soviet bloc have been experiencing tremendous surges of new life and vitality, but at the same time are compromised by their alignment with state authority. This has led to polarization in the churches between the unofficial renewal groups, and the official church leaders who have found it difficult to speak out openly for those who are persecuted. Despite this, the large numbers of new Christians continue to keep alive the true expression of the Orthodox Christian faith in difficult times.

■ **The Roman Catholic Church** has the advantage that its headquarters are outside the Soviet bloc. Under the present pope, the Vatican has followed a more robust policy towards state efforts to control Catholic priests in Eastern Europe, and believers have responded positively to this stimulus.

■ **The Evangelical churches** in Eastern Europe are also alive and growing – but the limitations and pressures of their situation have forced some of them to retreat into the defensive position of barely-tolerated and irrelevant minorities. In many places there is an increasing generation gap between the older, more legalistic believers, and the younger generation in search of a more innovative and intelligent approach to Christian faith. Evangelicals must find ways to overcome widespread theological illiteracy, secure the authentic independence of their churches and develop a new base of leaders. And most importantly, they need to grasp creatively the many new opportunities for the gospel.

free exercise of religion. But these rights are qualified by the words: 'The Hungarian People's Republic guarantees freedom of speech, of the press and of association, as long as this freedom does not interfere with the interest of the working masses.' Such a qualification offers the state every chance to interfere with or to suppress the church, whenever this proves convenient. Indeed, in many countries the church's situation

A lady lights a candle in an Orthodox church in Zagorsk, historic centre of Russian Christianity. Many in communist countries continue to believe, despite an atheistic education.

is quite different from what the constitution seems to indicate.

People from the West should be very cautious in their assessment of the attitude of the churches in Communist countries. They should always bear in mind that these churches find themselves in a situation in which two totalitarian claims oppose each other. Both the state and the church make such

claims. The state, however, cannot bear such a rivalling claim and so it tries to reduce religion to the private sphere. The church cannot accept this, but cannot ignore either that the claims of the state are backed by force. The leaders of the church in particular are always balancing on a razor's edge between these two opposing claims. They need not only the wisdom of serpents but also the innocence of doves.

All east European churches share this basic problem in their relationship with the state, and yet the actual relationship in the various countries differs markedly. In Albania, all religious practice in whatever form is prohibited. In East Germany there are regular contacts between state and church. A large traditional Orthodox church occupies a place in society quite different from a small Baptist Union. A centrally-structured church is much easier to manipulate than a union of independent congregations.

The **German Democratic Republic** has a total population of 17 million, of whom 43 per cent are Protestant and 7 per cent are Roman Catholic. Up until 1968 the eight Protestant *Landeskirchen* (territorial churches; three Lutheran and five united Lutheran-Reformed) still belonged to the all-Germany EKD (Evangelical Church of Germany). In that year they withdrew at the urging of the government.

In the years since the war church membership has decreased sharply, from 92 per cent in 1950 to 50 per cent today. There are many vacant parishes and the number of theological students is far too small. The Roman Catholic Church faces similar problems: too many priests of advancing age and too few young ordinands. The only good point is that many lay-helpers come to the fore, some of whom receive ordination as deacons.

The relationship between state and church is better than in most east European countries. Especially since the meeting of party-leader Honecker and Bishop Schönherr in 1978 the relationship has improved, although even then the agreements made received no legal backing. Nevertheless the churches still own much property and land, have their own educational and social services, and even receive some subsidies from the state. Yet the pressure from the state is still real and unrelenting, as is shown in particular by the introduction of socialist ceremonies to take the place of religious ceremonies (notably the so-called 'consecration of the young') and by the introduction of military education in the schools. Generally Christians have difficulties in obtaining a position of real importance and their children are often thwarted in their educational aspirations. And yet many young people in the GDR show a deep and genuine interest in the Christian message. Often they say, 'This is the only place where we can talk openly and honestly about the real problems of our lives.'

In **Poland** we meet with quite a different situation. It is largely a Roman Catholic country (82 per cent). The church is very popular: the percentage of practising Roman Catholics is much higher than in western and southern Europe, and there is a growing number of priests. The next most important church is the Orthodox Church with about 600,000 members. The Protestant churches (Lutheran, Reformed, Pentecostal) are very small. In the controversies surrounding 'Solidarity' and its leader Lech Walesa, it has become clear that the communist state cannot afford to ignore the Roman Catholic Church; it is too deeply embedded in the life of the nation. Most Polish people believe that there is a special link between God and their nation. The election of a Polish pope has strengthened this belief.

Czechoslovakia has a

RUSSIA ON THE CROSS

A Russian Orthodox pastor, Dmitri Dudko, made this comparison between Eastern and Western spirituality:

'It has been said that, if there is light anywhere, it is coming only from Russia. Why? Because Russia is Golgotha (the hill of the cross), and where the cross is, there too is resurrection...'

'If we compare our spirituality with that of the West, the balance will fall on our side. Why? Simply because Golgotha is here, and not there. Can an abundance of material goods bring about a religious rebirth? They say that the Catholics don't know what to do in order to keep people in church. They have everything: books, churches...But the people, if they believe at all, do so only weakly. We have nothing. But if people believe here, they are ready to die for their faith.'

population of 15 million people. Forty-nine per cent of them are Roman Catholic, 16 per cent Protestant, 5 per cent Old Catholic and 1.6 per cent Eastern Orthodox. To all outward appearances it is a Roman Catholic country. There is a Roman Catholic church in every town and in nearly every village. Yet this church lives under severe strains. Many parishes are vacant and the number of theological students is very limited. The Protestant churches are mainly of Hussite, Lutheran or Reformed background. All churches are effectively controlled by the state through the Federal Office of State for Ecclesiastical Affairs.

In **Hungary** the Roman Catholic Church (65 per cent of the total population) was for many years involved in a deep conflict with the state. Since 1971, when Cardinal Mindszenty left the American embassy, relations have improved, even though the church remains under constant pressure from atheistic propaganda by the state. The main Protestant church (19 per cent) is the Reformed Church (with four bishops). In Debreczen, the 'Rome of the Calvinists', there are seventeen Reformed church buildings against one Roman Catholic building.

In many ways the Reformed Church is flourishing, being able to have regular church services, to operate two theological schools, to give religious instruction in state schools (before or after regular school hours) and to publish its own newspapers. There seems to be a situation of peaceful coexistence. But this is possible only because the church, and in particular its leadership, has failed to establish a critical distance from the state. Its leaders seem uncritically to accept the objectives of the socialist society.

There is also a Lutheran Church and there are several small Orthodox churches. It is further interesting to note that the state allows regular religious broadcasts on the state radio.

Yugoslavia is politically a federation of six republics. Religiously it also shows a varied picture: Orthodox (7 million, many of them in Serbia), Roman Catholic (6 million, many of them in Croatia and Slovenia), Protestants (150,000) and Muslims (2.5 million). The Orthodox Church is still the most influential, although its former privileges have been taken away. The Protestant churches are comparatively small: Lutheran (90,000), Reformed (35,000), Baptist (3,000), Methodist (2,000). There are several Pentecostal bodies, which are all very active,

Christians gather outside a Roman Catholic church in Czechoslovakia. The many churches throughout the country are under pressure, partly through a lack of new priests.

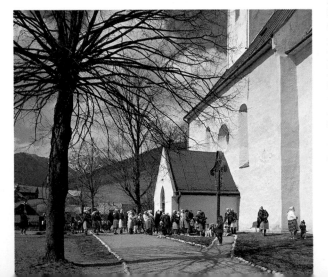

while there is also a Charismatic movement within the Roman Catholic Church. On the whole the churches enjoy a great measure of liberty, but repression is never far away. In recent years several priests have been imprisoned and teachers have been dismissed because of their religious convictions.

Albania is quite different again. The majority of the people were Muslim (1959: 700,000). There was an Orthodox Church (300,000) and a Roman Catholic Church (150,000). In 1967 the government proclaimed Albania as 'the first atheistic state in the world'. All mosques and churches were closed. All worship, even the showing of religious feelings, was outlawed. Many church leaders were executed. In 1973 an old priest was summarily shot, because he had baptized a child.

Of the **Bulgarian** population of 8.5 million, 85 per cent are Orthodox, 10 per cent Muslim, 0.7 per cent Roman Catholic and 0.2 per cent Protestant. The Orthodox Church is the national (though not established) church. Since 1953, when it pledged loyalty to the regime, it has received a small measure of liberty. It even receives some subsidies from the state. In actual fact, however, it is barely tolerated and is very restricted in its activities. The 120 monasteries, many of them most beautiful, house only 200 monks and 200 nuns. This poses quite a problem, since the members of the hierarchy have to be chosen from among the monks. The Protestant churches (largely springing from the work of American missionaries in the nineteenth century) feel the pressure of the atheistic regime even more.

Romania is largely an Orthodox country (82 per cent of a population of 21 million), although there are also Roman Catholic and Protestant churches (6 per cent and 5 per cent respectively). Especially since Nicholas Ceaucescu came to power the churches have been comparatively free. The Orthodox Church is a live church with a highly-educated clergy. There is much interest in religion among young people and working-class people. The largest Protestant church is the Reformed Church (about 500,000). Of late there is a revival going on in many churches, including the Orthodox Church but especially the Baptist and Pentecostal churches, which are growing rapidly (together about 500,000).

In spite of the relative freedom the relationship between state and church remains strained. At present the government is severely restricting the number of theological students and from time to time there are problems over church buildings. In 1983 the Orthodox Church was allowed to accept fifty of a hundred applicants, the Reformed Church only six of seventy and the Lutheran Church only one.

The Soviet Union is the country with the longest communist tradition. For over sixty-five years it has had a communist regime and for just as many years the churches have suffered under this regime. At times they have had to go

Continued on p.214

FERMENT IN POLAND
ALEXANDER TOMSKY

The one thing which marks Poland out on the map of Eastern Europe is her church. The present strength of Polish Catholicism is an inheritance from the nineteenth century, when the country, shared out among the neighbouring empires of Russia, Prussia and Austria, survived as an entity only through the church. It was from the pulpit that Polish culture, patriotism and a longing for freedom could be preached with relative impunity. The situation is practically the same today, except that the conflict between Christianity and totalitarian mendacity is much sharper than in the days when the oppressors had only traditional means and no universal ideology at their disposal.

utopia, is bent on the destruction of everything real – faith, hope and charity in particular. Cardinal Wyszynski put it this way: 'This juggling of words like progress, peace, justice etc. is nothing but a screen for its real aim...which is essentially to correct God himself. Instead of Christian love, this evil promotes conflict...'

This ideological victory, however, was not in itself sufficient to alter the political situation of Poland, which is ultimately determined by the Red Army. Yet in a politically hopeless situation it provided people with hope. Throughout the 1970s, people began to express their convictions without fear, and groups of human rights activists attempted to force

their government to respect the integrity of the individual. Both found refuge in the church.

Then, unexpectedly, on 16 October 1978, the election of Karol Wojtyla as Pope John Paul II, altered the balance of power between church and state. The church's prestige was enormously strengthened and thousands began to return to the fold. The church, still excluded from public life, was now in everyone's thoughts and conversations. Christianity as an ideological alternative now surfaced as a political reality.

Yet it was not until the return of the pope to Poland a year later that this newly-found unity could manifest itself. The millions who then gathered found a new strength and freedom

Battle for the Polish soul

As a Communist country Poland is a paradox. It has a weak government, toppled three times since World War II, and an incredibly homogenous civil society, since the war practically deprived it of its ethnic and religious minorities. This numerical strength helped the Catholic Church to survive as an independent institution during the time of Stalinist terror in the 1950s. Subsequently, Cardinal Wyszynski recognized the inevitability of the status quo, but fought an incredible spiritual battle against the official ideology and the policies aimed at secularizing the country. Following his ingenious leadership, the church has won the hearts and minds of the new generations.

The Poles, even if aided by a sense of nationalism and anti-Russian sentiment, have been able to recognize Communism for what it is: a primitive, secular religion of hatred which, for the mythical cause of social

through their religious experience. Psychologically, the communist government fell by the wayside. It was from this experience that the free trades unions were born in Gdansk in 1980.

Solidarity

Solidarity's peaceful revolution was unprecedented in the entire history of Communism. The workers, who wrested their own unions out of the hands of the state, knew what they were up against. Yet they renounced violence, hatred (and even drink) in a society where the pent-up sense of injustice could have become a deluge. Lech Walesa expressed this religious dimension of the movement clearly when he said, 'If I did not believe in God, I would become a very dangerous man.'

This moderation and pacifism, supported by church leaders,

disarmed the government in August 1980 but also led to Solidarity's eventual downfall sixteen months later. During this period of great national revival, concessions were wrested from the party only when the workers threatened a general strike.

The party, its back to the wall, was disintegrating. But nothing, it seemed, could force it either to share out its executive power or to come up with constructive political and economic reforms. The bureaucracy fell back on its own administrative inertia and the country's economy began to disintegrate.

Martial law

The military takeover on the night before 13 December 1981 plunged Poland into a deep political and psychological crisis. The shock of the overnight suspension of all public life, together with the mass arrests of Solidarity activists and intellectuals, not to mention the various forms of intimidation in every sphere of life, would have been sufficient to subdue any secular society. But in Poland the stumbling-block was the church. It organized immediate help for prisoners' families, collected money for those dismissed from work and provided a psychological and spiritual refuge for those in distress. Many who had not found their faith at a time of national euphoria found it now at a time of despair.

The Polish episcopate, backed by the powerful voice of the Polish pope, has called untiringly for the release of prisoners and an end to martial law. The conflict between government and society has assumed a new subterranean dimension. While the

A Christian choir sing in the open air in Poland. The influence of the Roman Catholic church in this country cannot be ignored, and Christian spirituality is deeply woven into the fabric of Polish life.

Solidarity underground is gradually losing its ability to mobilize people, hundreds of new journals and books are clandestinely printed with the help of the workers. The new clandestine groups are formulating Polish aspirations for freedom and independence by providing both an alternative framework of information, and a platform of discussion which breaks the state monopoly.

Their task is daunting: to remain hopeful in the absence of political hopes. Christianity provides the answer: simply by being true to ourselves, by rejecting lies and propaganda, through the spirit of love and charity in our immediate daily surroundings. As public demonstrations begin to subside, every church service is becoming a protest. However, this should not be surprising. After all, Christianity and slavery are incompatible.

So far the Catholic Church is the only institution that has survived the state's pogrom, but it faces many dangers. Already the pressure on the cardinal and the episcopate to remain neutral in the conflict between the government and Solidarity has decentralized the church. Poland has become a sort of confederation of parish republics.

The government hopes that the church will also give up its role as a mouthpiece for society and remain silent on moral, social and economic issues. For this reason it has allowed almost 600 new chapels and churches to be built. There is a danger that priests will become absorbed in material activities at the expense of their pastoral work. The new generation of priests, however, is not easily intimidated. They have been brought up in opposition and personal trials and they know that without faith there is no future for either the people or Poland.

through severe persecution. In fact there have been four such periods: 1917-25 (under Lenin), 1927-41 (under Stalin), 1960-64 (under Krushchev), the years after 1970 (under Brezhnev). And yet there are still many Christians. Since no official figures are given by the state, only an estimate can be made: 50 million Orthodox Christians, 10 million Roman Catholics and 3 million Protestants.

The state itself takes on many of the aspects of religion, so its attitude towards the churches is at best one of repressive toleration. At the same time the state uses the church wherever it can (especially the Orthodox Church with its many ecumenical contacts) to influence churches in the satellite countries, to promote the state's foreign policy and peace offensive, in short to improve the image of the Soviet Union abroad.

The attitude of the churches towards the state is ambiguous to say the least. The bishops, and the clergy generally, of the Orthodox Church have grown up within the Soviet system and have learned to be strictly loyal to the state. Most of them undoubtedly do this with the best of intentions. They want to support the state in its efforts to be a world power and they want to protect the church. But such an attitude easily leads to uncritical conformity to the political system.

The situation of the Orthodox Church is still very difficult. It is estimated that only between 4,000 and 7,000 church buildings are open. There is a serious shortage of priests, since there are only three seminaries left. Four-fifths of those ordained have had no theological training at all. Among the common believers there is much ignorance. Many have never seen a Bible, prayer books are not available, and yet the Orthodox Church is going through a kind of regeneration. This is seen on at least three levels: an increasing number of people offer themselves for the priesthood; there is increasing activity among lay people, and there is a revival of the Orthodox-oriented culture. The church is winning people's hearts more readily and more rapidly than in the last 100 years.

The Roman Catholic Church, mainly found in particular regions of the USSR, such as Lithuania and the Ukraine, has no central leadership and no official contact with the Vatican. Yet it is reported that in Lithuania particularly there is a very live and active Roman Catholic Church.

The main groups among the Protestants are Baptists, Brethren, Pentecostals and Mennonites. Baptist congregations are found throughout the entire Soviet Union. In the last five years 200 new congregations have been established, and over 35,000 people baptized.

There are many unregistered groups in the Soviet Union. Some refuse to be registered (among them several Orthodox groups!), others are refused registration by the state (some Pentecostal groups). One cannot but have deep respect for these Christians.

'It doesn't take much to become an atheist today. Master a few prepared phrases, swim with the current, and you're an atheist! On the contrary to be a believer you have to know a lot. You have to bear a lot of difficulties, you have to swim against the current..It's not an accident that believers today are heroic people.' Dmitri Dudko

It would be wrong, however, to conclude that all registered churches are unfaithful and hypocritical.

It is a striking fact that even after more than sixty-five years of official and repressive atheism, there is still a people of God in the Soviet Union. Michael Bordeaux wrote in 1978: 'In a country where it has been tried over a period of sixty years, [Communism] seems to the younger intellectuals to be a god that failed – whereas the Christian church is providing evidence about a God who is active and is not failing the people in a country where the church has been so bitterly persecuted.'

Another widespread phenomenon in nearly all the countries of eastern Europe is the growth of so-called 'peace movements'. Usually they are instigated by the party and the churches are expected to join in and follow the party line. The Christian Peace Conference (CPC) of Prague was started in 1958 by the Czechoslovakian Council of Churches, under the leadership of Professor L. Hromadka. When, however, in 1968 the CPC praised the Russian armies for crushing the 'Prague Spring', Hromadka withdrew. Since that time the CPC has increasingly become a tool in the hands of the Communists, extending its activities even to the Third World. H. Basarak, vice-president of the CPC, declared: 'Today opponent number one in the struggle for peace is imperialism.'

In recent years a peace movement has started in the

churches of East Germany. It opposed the escalation of nuclear arms in both camps, and so got into trouble with the state. It seems that 'peace' in eastern Europe easily becomes a political instrument of the Communist state and the churches are required to serve the state's ideological propaganda. It is symbolic of the church's ambivalent position. However there are also promising signs. Early in 1984 the largest Protestant church in Czechoslovakia protested against the government-approved stationing of Soviet SS-20 missiles in its own country.

A group of Christians from an unregistered Soviet Baptist church meet to worship. Churches that refuse to register with the authorities have to conduct their activities in a clandestine way.

SOUTHERN EUROPE
In **Greece**, 97 per cent of the population belong to the Orthodox Church, which is the official state church. The parish priests generally have had little education. There is a great number of bishops, because the dioceses are small. The Roman Catholic and Protestant churches are comparatively small (together not yet 100,000 members).

Evangelistic work is almost excluded by a strict rule forbidding proselytism.

The other three southern European countries, Italy, Spain and Portugal, have much in common. All three are predominantly Roman Catholic, yet in each of them church attendance is generally poor and there is much ignorance and even superstition among the common people.

In **Italy** 99 per cent of the population are counted as Roman Catholics, but only 6 per cent take communion every Sunday. In the last election 30 per cent of the vote went to the Communist Party (the largest in western Europe). Forty per cent of these voters are estimated to be professing Catholics. The church has lost much of its traditional authority, as shown in 1974 by the strong popular 'No' vote against the repeal of the existing divorce law. The Protestant churches are generally small. The oldest is the historic Waldensian Church (dating back to 1173); the largest are the Pentecostal churches (782 congregations in 1976). In the Roman Catholic Church there is also a strong Charismatic movement.

Since World War II a struggle has been going on in the Roman Catholic Church of **Spain** between traditional, national Catholicism and progressive, conciliar Catholicism. During the Franco era the traditionalists still prevailed. In recent years, greatly helped by Vatican II, the more progressive element has been more influential. In the meantime the number of vocations and

ordinations is sharply declining, and there are many vacant parishes – particularly in the south.

Protestants, who are small in numbers and widely dispersed throughout the country, have long suffered repression and persecution. In recent years, however, the Constitution has been changed, providing religious liberty for all. Recently the Spanish government even decided to grant free television time to Protestants.

In **Portugal** the Roman Catholic Church is very conservative and fearful of the modern world. Because of the church's association with the dictatorial regimes of Salazar and Caetano there is a strong anti-clerical mood in the country, especially in the south where church attendance is very low.

Looking back over this survey it is plain that the situation of the Christian churches in Europe is very complicated. On the one hand, traditional historical lines are continued. In all countries we still find the major denominations as they have come into existence since 1051 (the schism between the Eastern and Western churches), the sixteenth century (the Reformation period) and the nineteenth century (when many separations or disruptions occurred). On the other hand, there is a blurring of these traditional lines. This is partly due to increasing secularization and the national churches losing their privileged position, and partly to advances in church unity. Persecution and repression have also played a part. Gradually, the religious map of Europe is changing.

Some of these changes are very much to be regretted, such as the sharp decline in the membership in many of the large national churches, and the even sharper drop in church attendance. At times one cannot help wondering whether Europe is moving to a post-Christian paganism.

But there is also another side to the picture. Secularization can bring with it a purification of the churches. The pruning of the vine also means that it will bear more fruit. Christians are becoming more aware that post-Christian secularism is a new challenge to the church. The churches in eastern Europe may well be more aware of this challenge than those in the rest of Europe. The Conference of European Churches provides a useful arena for co-operation and reflection on this common challenge, as does the Fellowship of European Evangelical Theologians on a smaller scale.

When the apostle Paul was sent to Europe a new future was opened for this continent. There is still a future for it, even in this time of secularization, whether of the Communist or the Western kind. But this requires that the churches do not lose confidence in the gospel of Jesus Christ. The last thing Christians need is a superior, condemning spirit. They need the love of Christ, who can make them alert to every opportunity to preach the message of God's kingdom of peace and justice. There is only one message for the world of today as there was for the apostolic church who took the gospel into the heart of the far more alien Roman Empire. The centre of that message is Jesus himself, who is just as powerful and attractive in Europe as in Africa or Latin America today.

The Ponte Veccio in Florence. Italy has a unique Roman Catholic tradition and many beautiful churches and monasteries. But church attendance has declined.

2.5 GOOD NEWS FOR THE POOR

Christians in Latin America
RENE PADILLA

Christianity has been one of the most important factors which have shaped human life and institutions in the continent of Latin America. This teeming continent has a population of 350 million (as compared with 200 million in 1950) and the highest rate of population growth in the world (3 per cent annually). Despite the advance of secularism, a high percentage of people in Latin America continue to regard Christianity as a living option. Because of that, the future of the Latin American nations is largely dependent on the extent to which Christians are able to respond to the many challenges posed by growing social, economic and political problems.

The sword and the cross
Christianity was introduced in Latin America by the Spanish and Portuguese conquerors at the turn of the fifteenth century. At the time of the conquest, it was practically impossible for Spanish and Portuguese people to think that a Christian could be anything else than a Roman Catholic. The conquest itself was seen as a co-operative effort through which a new world was to be brought into subjection to both the (Roman Catholic) church and the (Roman Catholic) state. A year after Columbus's 'discovery of America' (1492), Isabel and Ferdinand of Spain sent, alongside their civil representatives, priests and soldiers whose task was to conquer the lands and nations for Christ and the king. The church and the state that had spawned the Crusades thus imposed their structures on Latin American society from the beginning.

The Indians (amongst whom were numbered several higher civilizations, such as the Incas, Aztecs and Mayas) were conquered within a relatively short span. The problem was then, as the *conquistadores* saw it, to work for the establishment both of the Spanish and the Portuguese crowns and of the Roman Catholic Church.

This political and ecclesiastical enterprise had the enthusiastic

A Bolivian Indian lady sells wool at a market. She lives in a highly religious continent, where Christianity sometimes gets mixed up with folk religion.

support of Roman Catholic kings and religious orders (mainly Franciscans, Dominicans and Augustinians) who understood the extension of Christendom as their divine mission. Thousands and thousands of Indians were baptized *en masse*; they were incorporated into the church as well as into the European labour system. Later on, during colonial times, the Jesuits gave special attention to education and founded 'reductions' (Indian villages organized as divine communities, with the Jesuit fathers at the top of the pyramid) in an effort to develop a Christian civilization.

It is now generally accepted, however, that the end result of the Spanish and Portuguese mission was a 'popular

This Brazilian boy is growing up in a country with many economic and social problems, yet with vast untapped potential. His is the largest Roman Catholic nation in the world, but there are also increasing numbers of Protestants, especially Pentecostals.

religiosity' – a sort of mixture of Christianity and pagan customs. Roman Catholic scholars today admit that the evangelization of colonial times failed to accomplish a lasting spiritual transformation. In the words of David Auletta, 'Latin America is a continent of people who have been baptized but not evangelized'. It therefore needs to be 're-evangelized'.

A NEW ELEMENT
Until quite recently the Protestant presence was almost nil in Latin America. There are historical records that show that in the sixteenth century there were two or three Protestant colonies in Venezuela and Brazil, but those were isolated cases and in no way did they change the fact that this was a Roman Catholic continent. For this reason, as recently as the Edinburgh Missionary Conference in 1910, all reference to this region of the world as 'mission territory' was excluded.

The first Protestant churches, established in the nineteenth century by European immigrants, were glad to limit their work to catering for the needs of their respective ethnic groups. These immigrant churches did not evangelize but confined themselves to more or less private explorations and initiatives.

The first Protestant missionary to Spanish America was James (Diego) Thomson. He was sent by the British and Foreign Bible Society and arrived in Argentina in 1818. His main concern was to spread the knowledge of the Bible. This he did by promoting the Lancaster method of education and using the Bible as a reading text. He visited at least nine of the recently-founded Latin American Spanish-speaking republics and established Bible distribution centres in various key cities.

At this time, new government elites were searching for ways of consolidating national independence from Spain. They were open to the influence of the Anglo-Saxon (Protestant) countries, which were gaining power all over the world. They regarded Roman Catholicism as an obstacle to modernization and adopted a favourable attitude towards Protestantism, which stood in their minds as a religion of freedom, education, morality and individualism. Benito Juárez, president of Mexico, has been quoted as saying: 'The future happiness and prosperity of my country depends on the development of Protestantism.' During the second half of the nineteenth century, many governments opened their doors to Protestant immigrants and even missionaries. In this way, Protestantism accepted the role that the liberal elites assigned to it within their modernizing programmes.

The main methods used by the earlist missionaries were public preaching and personal witness aimed at personal conversion. Methodists and Presbyterians established primary and secondary schools, but the emphasis was generally on preaching and instruction rather than on works of caring. Except for the work of the South America Missionary Society in Argentina, Bolivia, Paraguay and Chile, not much activity was undertaken during this century among the Indians. Only nine medical institutions were established in Latin America during the nineteenth century as compared with ninety-four in Africa, and 415 in Asia.

Evangelical churches grew considerably in the period between 1880 and 1916. The common people found in them a living faith that stood in sharp contrast to a religion of ritual and traditions.

By the time of the first Protestant Congress in Panama in 1916, Protestant churches in Latin America had approximately 300,000 members. A very high percentage of those participating in the Panama Congress, however, were foreign missionaries and leaders representing churches in the United States, Canada, Britain, Spain and Italy. Evidently, Protestantism still remained feebly rooted in Latin American soil. And it was constantly subject to discrimination and persecution on the part of the Roman Catholic Church, with the result that it developed strong anti-Catholic tendencies which continue up to this day.

END OF THE CLOSED SOCIETY

In many Latin American countries, Roman Catholicism continues to be regarded as the official religion, even today. At the same time, religious freedom

At an open-air gospel meeting in Chile one of the audience experienced a dramatic change in his life as he heard the good news of Jesus. He went up to the speaker and to demonstrate his desire to change he handed over his suitcase. Inside were a machine-gun and a bomb.

is recognized as a constitutional right. In a few countries (notably **Ecuador, Chile, Uruguay** and **Brazil**) there is separation of church and state, but the Roman Catholic Church often receives state subsidies and enjoys special privileges. (**Mexico** is a notable exception to this general trend. As a result of the 1917 revolution, all church properties were taken over by the government, many priests were deported and the Roman Catholic Church lost its role in education.)

Since approximately the middle of the nineteenth century, however, Roman Catholicism has slowly lost much of its influence all over the continent. Already at the turn of the century the first plenary Latin American Council (at Rome in 1899) analyzed the evils affecting the Roman

THE COCKPIT OF CENTRAL AMERICA
PABLO E. PÉREZ

The six republics of Central America have been headline news throughout the world in the 1980s. Acute deprivation for the majority of the population, political conflict, guerrilla warfare, refugees crossing frontiers and interference from outside the region have conspired to make the region one of the major trouble spots of the globe, where life is cheap and war is an ever-present reality. Yet, in spite of the violence and instability there is hope in many quarters, as people make valiant efforts to defy the trends toward decay and ruin.

Both the uncertainty and the hope are reflected in Central American churches. The churches have always enjoyed a high degree of religious liberty. They have shown consistent growth and a desire to be counted as integral parts of their own societies. The Roman Catholic Church, traditionally predominant in the region, has taken an active part in the present crisis. Evangelical Christians have attained increased visibility and are now quite influential in the mainstream of life.

One example of the increase in Evangelical influence was the coming to power of General Efraín Ríos Montt of Guatemala in 1983. He became president when Lucas García's government was toppled by the armed forces. Some critics have said that Montt's rule, because of his public Christian identity, has lowered the reputation of Evangelicals. They point to his mistakes, particularly the continuance of brutal political murders and public executions, and the fact that he was deposed after little more than a year in office. But it can be argued that this ignores many of his genuine accomplishments, including his fight against corruption in high positions of power. Moreover, it would be wrong to expect swift and spectacular changes in the country, just because he claimed to be born again in Christ. Other complex and intractable social factors which he inherited have to be considered.

Polarized churches
The churches in Central America represent a wide variety of origins. Although the Roman Catholic Church has been in the region for centuries, faith missions from the United States are vigorous and growing at present. Great zeal for evangelistic work and the Bible training of many believers has resulted in strong churches.

Training centres for the churches' ministry are numerous, and Christian work to alleviate and eliminate suffering, as may be expected in lands where the material needs of the majority are overwhelming, is also strong.

Nevertheless, a traditional pietistic theological stance has produced Christians who, having a purely individualistic faith, refuse to face the real troubles of Central America. Many Christians have not been adequately prepared to face the social and political convulsions of the present decade.

Others, especially in the Roman Catholic Church, have become outspoken critics of the political oppression of the poor, among whom they live and work. While most Evangelicals have been influenced by a highly conservative North American theology, this radical wing gains its inspiration from the South and its theology of liberation.

These two different stances have led to polarizations in many churches of Central America:
■ The dictatorial rule of Somoza in **Nicaragua** eventually became unbearable and he was overthrown in July 1979 in a popular uprising. Many

Catholic Church: superstition, paganism, liberalism, socialism, Masonry and Protestantism. The new century was to see different traditions and ideologies existing alongside each other. A secularistic society has emerged, especially in the big cities.

Quite definitely, Latin American society has ceased to be a 'closed society' in which the Roman Catholic faith and values could be easily transmitted from one generation to the next. As Juan Luis Segundo has written: 'The closed, unanimous milieu that provided for Christian rootedness is gone.'

Even though Roman Catholicism has lost much of its institutional support, Latin America is by no means a totally secularized place. 'Popular religiosity' still plays an

Christians from all sections of the churches gladly joined the revolutionary forces to bring about the radical changes that were needed. They have accepted many of the political tenets and policies of the ruling junta.

However, since many in the churches have reservations about some of the more obviously Marxist beliefs of the Sandinista government, tensions among Christians are evident. While the constitution guarantees full religious liberty, there are several instances of what appears to be the harassment of Christians. At the same time, where violence or victimization has occurred, it has been repudiated by the government. In addition, permission is often given to hold large evangelistic crusades. The situation is, at best, unstable and unpredictable.

■ Conditions are similar in both **Guatemala** and **El Salvador**, although their respective governments claim to be middle-of-the road politically. However, Christians, Evangelicals among them, have a particularly strong voice in Guatemala and they boldly denounce persecution and defend their constitutional rights.

In El Salvador, Christians are more polarized, partly because of the influence of liberation theology, which some embrace and many others reject, and partly because of the long-drawn-out civil war. Those who reject liberation theology and its political implications claim that there has never been such spectacular church growth and such hunger for the gospel – in spite of mass emigration, the ruthless violence of the extreme political right, and the constant threat posed by guerrilla activity. These all result in a persecuted church, suffering in the midst of its rapid growth.

■ Polarization is probably at its highest point in **Honduras** where most people want neither war with Nicaragua, nor Marxism, nor the military presence of the United States. Some of the churches are vocal in their views, while others prefer an uneasy silence. Both tactics separate members from one another.

■ In **Costa Rica** and **Panama**, there is also absolute religious freedom, but the situation seems ripe for an outburst of political dissent that could cause a deeper split in the churches.

Shaping the future

It has often been said that persecution, within certain limits, leads to a stronger church. This has certainly been true in Central America. Persecution, despite its terrible cost in human suffering, has provoked deeper commitment and faithfulness to Jesus Christ and his church.

The stark realities of Central America call for radical action and prophetic denunciation by the church of oppression, poverty, exploitation and alienation. But if, at the same time, the church can avoid polarization in its midst in favour of a fusion of the views which presently divide it, then a more mature church will grow up.

Central America became the context for a model of evangelistic outreach in the 1960s. Many now feel that it is being prepared by the Lord as it passes through a time of deep disturbances for greater contributions to the church world-wide. The present church leadership bears a great burden of responsibility to understand and follow the direction of the Holy Spirit and thus to provide an example to Christians elsewhere of how Christ requires them to act in similar circumstances.

important role among many millions of people. They *feel* Roman Catholic, but have little knowledge of or interest in Christian doctrine or discipline. Thus, for instance, in **Brazil** – the largest Roman Catholic nation in the world – it has been estimated that one third of all Roman Catholics are affiliated in some degree to a mediumistic religion such as *Umbanda* (a mixture of Christian and pagan rites of Afro-American origin).

See Children of the Twentieth Century

Latin American Christianity is very unlike that in Western Europe, for example, where a majority of Christians are middle-class. In a country such as Mexico many poorer people and peasants are deeply religious.

PROTESTANT GROWTH

During the last half century Protestantism has experienced a fantastic numerical growth, due mainly to the expansion of Pentecostalism – especially in **Chile** and **Brazil** but also in many other countries. Today there are approximately 18 million Protestants in Latin America, out of whom two-thirds are Pentecostal.

In **Chile**, Pentecostalism traces its origin to 1909 when W.C. Hoover, a Methodist missionary,

was repudiated by his own denomination and helped establish the Methodist Pentecostal Church (IMP). In 1933 this church was divided and the Evangelical Pentecostal Church (IEP) was constituted as a result. At present the IMP and the IEP are the largest non-Catholic church bodies in Chile. The IMP in Santiago (commonly called the Jotabeche Pentecostal Church) is the largest Evangelical congregation in Latin America, with over 90,000 members.

Pentecostalism was introduced in **Brazil** in 1910 by Luigi Francescon, an Italian Waldensian, and by the Assemblies of God from the United States. By 1940 this latter denomination had churches in all the states of the country. Most Pentecostal churches, however, have been formed since 1945. The Assemblies of God are said to be the largest Protestant denomination in the country, with three-quarters of a million adherents.

A high percentage of Pentecostals come from the poorer classes, the common workers or the unemployed. Their phenomenal expansion has attracted the attention both of sociologists and church-growth experts, whose studies show that such growth is often related to the identity crisis and the sense of lostness caused by internal migrations and urbanization: the people in the city feel marginalized, but in their churches they find a friendly group that preserves traditional values and provides a buffer against a society which is new to them. Be that as it may, the fact remains that Pentecostals are an important popular movement – self-supporting, self-multiplying and self-governed. Most of their leaders have no formal theological training, but their educational level has been rising in the last few years.

The so-called 'transplanted churches' (Anglican, Lutheran, Presbyterian, Reformed and so on), representing immigrant groups that came in the nineteenth and early twentieth centuries, have been largely dedicated to preserving religious and cultural traditions from their respective homelands. Some of them, however, have lately begun to adapt themselves to the Latin American situation and have begun to nationalize their ministry.

The 'missionary churches' (Methodist, Baptist, Plymouth Brethren, Salvation Army, Disciples of Christ and others), which came into existence through missionary activity supported by churches abroad, have grown mainly among people of the middle- and lower-middle class. Their rate of growth is far below that of Pentecostalism. Many of them, in fact, are middle-class enclaves with little outreach.

Since World War II there has been a dramatic increase of Protestant missionaries, many of them representing 'faith missions' (conservative, mostly from the United States). In 1903 there were 1,438 missionaries; in 1938, 2,951; in 1949, 4,488; in 1969, 11,363. The increase was thus of 690 per cent, compared with 283 per cent

for Africa and 39 per cent for Asia in the same period. The personnel working with 'faith missions' constitute about a third of the total foreign Protestant missionary force in Latin America, yet they are related to churches including less than 2 per cent of the total communicant membership. This is in sharp contrast with the Pentecostal movement, which has less than 10 per cent of all Protestant missionaries working in this area of the world.

The increase in Protestant missionary activity has been parallelled by the growth of United States economic and cultural penetration into Latin America during the same period. Consequently, in most countries Protestantism is often regarded

Continued on p.228

'Martyrdom is a grace of God that I do not feel worthy of, but if God accepts the sacrifice of my life, my hope is that my blood will be like a seed of liberty and a sign that our hopes will soon become a reality.' Oscar Romero, then Archbishop of San Salvador, a month before he was shot dead in 1980.

NEW LIFE IN BRAZIL

Celso Franco de Oliveira is pastor of a church in Rio de Janeiro. The services were very dull, until in 1978 he was challenged through his child's illness:

'I began to experience in a new dimension what the Christian life really means. To my amazement, I discovered that everyone I met needed the salvation which comes in Jesus. A passion for evangelism swept the church. We wanted to present Jesus as someone alive and personal. As we did so, lives were saved, drug addicts transformed and spiritists freed from the powers of darkness. Our congregation opened up to include the poor, the coloured, the illiterate and even beggars, bringing wonderful enrichment to our church life. Bibles sold like hot cakes. Prayer became the backbone of church decisions, and tithing became the norm as a result of the transformation of people's lives by the power of Jesus.'

LIBERATION THEOLOGY
SAMUEL ESCOBAR

During the 1960s a radical change took place in the political stance of many Roman Catholics in Latin America. In the face of the poverty, instability and violence in the continent, clergy and lay people started to work towards a socialist model of society and a revolutionary approach to political life. Under the influence of pastoral experiences in France, Belgium and Spain, the methodology and conclusions of the social sciences became crucial in designing a strategy for a pastoral work.

For a church that had traditionally been part of feudalistic social order, this was a significant change. But it was a change that followed the trends set by the Second Vatican Council in the areas of biblical scholarship, liturgy and church affairs.

A growing influence
By adopting socialism as an aim and Marxism as a tool for the analysis of society, the new political stance could be described as a struggle for liberation. Biblical themes like the exodus, the social attitudes of Jesus, the love of God for the poor and the attack on injustices by the prophets have given deeper meaning to the ideas of the social sciences, and have given birth to what is known as *liberation theology*.

Such biblical themes, often ignored by the church in the past, have also become part of liturgy, preaching and popular literature. The books of priests like Gustavo Gutiérrez and Juan Luis Segundo, and former priests like Hugo Assmann and Severino Croatto, have achieved widespread fame as theological and biblical expositions on what is taking place. Bishops like Helder Camara in Brazil,

as well as others in other Latin American countries, have become symbols of the growing influence of liberation practices and ideas among the hierarchy of the Roman Catholic Church. And the documents produced by the Conference of Latin American Bishops in Medellín (1968) reflect clearly the extent of official church acceptance of liberation ideas.

Ministry to the poorest
Liberation theology is not, like many Western theologies, about academic thinking, but about action on behalf of the poor. Identification with the poor and progressive politics were pioneered by orders like the Maryknollers (the Catholic Foreign Missionary Society of America) in the 1950s. But a whole new generation of nuns and priests now live among the poor in the growing slums of great Latin American cities or among the despised and usually exploited rural Indian communities in the highlands and the jungles. They have tried to follow closely what they understand to be a biblical pattern of ministry:
■ Following Roman Catholic tradition, this ministry tends to concentrate on the **mobilization of communities** of baptized people rather than on the preaching of individual conversion to Jesus Christ.
■ Service to the poor is understood as **understanding their plight, defending their rights and organizing them for social activism**. Such mobilization tends to make poor people more socially aware. It follows the line taken by Brazilian educator, Paulo Freire, who proposes education as 'consciousness raising' rather than 'domestication'.
■ Ministry to the poor tends to major on **achieving social aims through**

confrontation rather than helping the rich give hand-outs to the poor. Justice rather than charity is the order of the day.
■ **Theology and liturgy** express the spirit of this militancy.

Theology in a harsh climate
Between 1968 and 1973, a wave of socialist-inclined governments came to power in South America. This set the scene for some of the most dynamic moments of liberation theology. But after 1973, these governments fell to a succession of authoritarian regimes, which represented conservative views of society that were very close to fascism. The Roman Catholic Church, influenced in a radical direction by liberation theology, came into tension with the military in power, especially in Brazil, Argentina and Chile, where this tension led to many victims among followers of liberation theology.

But it also produced tensions and division in the church itself. These came to the surface in the more conservative Conference of Latin America at Puebla (1973), which stood out in marked contrast to the Medellín conference of 1968. The internal polemics became acute in 1984 with a publication by Cardinal Ratzinger of the Holy Office in Rome. Ratzinger accepted that service to the poor and commitment to the change of society could be a Christian calling, but he clearly opposed the use of Marxism as a tool for understanding society and reflecting on the faith.

The Protestant minorities
But what of the Protestant churches? The Protestant minority in Latin

A group of Nicaraguan national leaders meet to discuss policy. Some priests who have espoused liberation theology are closely involved in Nicaraguan political life.

America has itself been an element of social change since its appearance in the early part of the nineteenth century. It has usually been vocal about the need for reforms in society, and has sometimes been allied to progressive political groups resistant to Marxism.

However, its commitment to individual conversion and its dependence on ideals, models and theological books from the English-speaking world has made it resistant to liberation theology. However, a small, vocal elite of intellectuals in historic Protestant churches adopted liberation theology views even before Roman Catholics, especially those related to the 'Church and Society' movement sponsored by the World Council of Churches since 1961.

Evangelicals in the region are searching for a position to take. On one hand, some conservative Protestants, including Pentecostals, have too easily given their support to conservative authoritarian regimes. On the other, many Evangelicals relate evangelism and social responsibility in a way that takes positive account of the contribution of liberation theology. The Latin American Theological Fraternity, and men such as René Padilla, Orlando Costas and Emilio A. Núñez, fulfil this latter role.

Liberation theology, which was born out of the concern to act against suffering and oppression, is well adapted to the harsh climate of Latin American life. Unlike academic theologies, its true test in the years to come will not be whether its ideas remain fashionable, but whether it continues to act on behalf of the poor and trampled.

'This is a theology which does not stop with reflecting on the world, but rather tries to be part of the process through which the world is transformed.' Gustavo Gutierrez, on liberation theology

as the religious expression of 'American imperialism'. The fact remains that Protestantism concentrated its efforts on spiritual conversion; its role in relation to the 'modernizing programme' was an unintended result of its mission. By inviting people to a personal decision before Jesus Christ, it promoted inidividualism; by emphasizing personal morality, it promoted such values as hard work and honesty. In that way, it helped to create a new mentality, more in accord with modern society.

THE NEW CHRISTENDOM

At the beginning of the twentieth century the Roman Catholic Church revived its interest in education in Latin America, and this led to the signing of educational agreements with governments in a number of countries. As a result, many Roman Catholic primary and secondary schools were established. Later on, this effort was completed with the opening of universities in Bogotá (1937), Lima (1942), Medellín (1945), Rio de Janeiro and Sao Paolo (1947), Quito (1956), Buenos Aires and Córdoba (1960), Valparaíso and Guatemala (1961). Several other Roman Catholic universities have been established during the last two decades.

Under the influence of the French philosopher Jacques Maritain, the Catholic Action movement took root in Latin America, beginning in 1929. This lay movement, promoted by Pope Pius XI, was instrumental in shaping a new social

See Roman Catholics since the Council

consciousness, particularly among the upper class. It became the organizational core of several labour and peasant groups working on development projects and people's co-operatives.

Roman Catholic efforts to regain political power were channelled through the Christian Democratic parties, which were organized in various countries to reinstate Christendom as an alternative to Marxism. The Christian Democrats promised a 'revolution in freedom' (a phrase coined by one of their most outstanding leaders, Chile's president, Eduardo Frei). They seemed to offer a solution to social injustice through 'development'. As a result, they were able to attract sizeable segments of the working class. Their position found further support in Pope John XXIII's encyclicals, *Mater et Magistra* (1961) and *Pacem in Terris* (1963). At the beginning of the 'First Development Decade' (thus defined by the United Nations), these papal statements favoured the development of the poorer nations.

Yet this 'revolution in freedom' has largely failed. Contrary to predictions, the development projects of the sixties did practically nothing to improve the situation of the poor. Far from it – the gap between the rich and poor continued to grow. The only development that took place was what has been called 'the development of under-development'.

But this increasing Roman Catholic interest in the poor did have an important by-product.

Catholic Action actually got involved with the poor. And so an important sector of laity and clergy gradually became politically radical. That was the time when guerrilla warfare, inspired by the Cuban revolution, was becoming a serious problem in various countries. Many radical Christians were tempted to violence as the only means to bring about structural change. One of them – Camilo Torres, a Colombian priest – joined a guerrilla group and was killed in the jungles of his country. Simultaneously, the way was being paved for a new pastoral approach characterized by 'the preferential option for the poor'.

A Colombian bishop gives a boy his first communion.

PREFERENTIAL OPTION FOR THE POOR

Latin American Roman Catholicism has been accorded great importance on the world scene in the second half of the twentieth century. This was evidenced by the presence of 601 bishops and experts from this region at the Second Vatican Council (22.33 per cent of the total, second only to Europe which had 849 participants or 31.6 per cent of the total). The fact was recognized that Latin America is the continent with the highest percentage of Christians and that the future of the church universal is therefore bound up with the future of the church in Latin America.

In the last three decades the unity of the Roman Catholic Church throughout Latin America has been greatly strengthened by the Latin American Episcopal Conference (CELAM), which met for the first time in Rio de Janeiro in 1955. Despite its rather small beginnings, CELAM has virtually become the intellectual powerhouse linking the bishops from different nations and providing guidelines for pastoral action all over the continent.

The second CELAM General Conference was held in Medellín (Colombia) in 1968 for the purpose of analyzing the implications of the Second Vatican Council and of Pope Paul's encyclical *Popularum Progressio* (1967) for Latin America. This conference has been regarded as a watershed in the history of the Roman Catholic Church in the region. The Medellín Conclusions, signed by the 130 prelates present,

Continued on p.232

LATIN AMERICAN PENTECOST
NORBERTO SARACCO

Pentecostalism is the youngest Christian denomination and, at the same time, the one that has grown the most in Latin America. By the end of the 1980s it will have more than 10 million members and will be the largest denomination in every Latin American country.

Pentecostalism arrives

The Pentecostal movement reached Latin America during the first decade of the twentieth century. Its arrival was not the result of planned missionary expansion, but rather the consequence of the 'Pentecostal revival' experienced in many sectors of Protestant Christianity. This revival emphasized what was called 'baptism in the Holy Spirit', combined with the sign of speaking in other tongues. Pentecostals believe that this experience has its roots in the account of the Day of Pentecost in the book of Acts, chapter two.

Chile and Brazil have the largest Pentecostal communions. Brazilian Assemblies of God include more than 2 million members. In Chile, the Pentecostal movement can be traced back to 1909 when the Methodist Episcopal Church in Valparaiso, pastored by W.C. Hoover, was shaken by a series of manifestations such as speaking in tongues, dancing and ecstasy. This was interpreted as God's response to their desire to become a church like the primitive church. Those who participated came to the conclusion that they had received the 'baptism of the Holy Spirit'.

The Pentecostal movement reached Brazil in the following year, with the arrival of Daniel Berg and Gunnar Vingren, both Swedish, and Luigi Francescon, an Italian American. Berg and Vingren made contact with the

Baptist church in Belem, and a short time later some Baptists received the gift of speaking in tongues and other Pentecostal phenomena. Berg, Vingren, and their followers were soon excommunicated, accused of falsifying Baptist doctrine. From this group sprang the Brazilian Assemblies of God.

Francescon founded what today is known as the Congregacão Crista do Brasil. At first it was limited to Italian residents, to the point that during its early decades only the Italian language was used in its services.

In the rest of Latin America, Pentecostalism arrived in very similar ways. It sprang up as a movement of openness to the Holy Spirit within the traditional denominations. Each group contributed something from its own background (Methodist, Baptist,

Presbyterian, Nazarene, and so on), and to this was added the uniting experience of the 'baptism of the Holy Spirit'. This variety and diversity has been a constant cause of internal division, to the extent that today there are more than 1,500 distinct Pentecostal organizations.

Effects of the movement

Pentecostalism has mainly spread among the poor, lower classes. Because of the freedom of worship and the dynamic of organization, each new convert finds in the Pentecostal churches the possibility of self-realization. He or she passes from anonymity to playing a leading role, and becomes part of a community that shares collectively in the mission of the church. Studies of the

Pentecostal phenomenon agree that its extraordinary growth is due to this ability to mobilize each and all of its members.

In Latin America, Pentecostalism has been instrumental in the social ascent of the lowest classes. Its rigorous ethics and dynamic faith have served to organize, orient, and put into action the possibilities of the most marginalized, helping them to progress slowly. It has also improved the condition of women. In a society as male-dominated as Latin American society, this is a major achievement. It is common to see women preachers, pastors and missionaries. The whole area of the Argentine Patagonia, with its inhospitable climate and difficult living conditions, has been evangelized – especially by Pentecostal women.

Marks of Pentecostalism
■ **Personal experience** plays a leading role in Pentecostalism in Latin America, as in other parts of the world. Preaching and teaching emphasize what God can do in the individual's life, satisfying his or her physical, spiritual or material needs. Testimonies of healing, liberation and prosperity are common in Pentecostal services.

■ **Manifestations of God's supernatural power** are experienced as part of daily life. With good reason one sociologist has called Pentecostalism 'the refuge of the masses'. Pentecostal churches frequently organize huge meetings for healing and liberation. They draw thousands of people to halls and stadiums seeking miraculous healing for the sick. They also pray for people to be freed from the influence of demonic powers. This approach to the miraculous and supernatural has found an echo in an extremely needy continent, one with animistic ancestral traditions.

■ **Pentecostal worship is very free**

and easily adapted to different cultures. This has meant that the most varied national musical instruments have been used, making possible a faithful expression of people's experience. During religious services, the participants live an atmosphere of freedom, enthusiasm and joy, fully participating in prayer and worship.

■ **The pastor is the central figure** and the unchallenged leader. His personality is generally strong and dominant. He follows the model of leadership inherent in Latin American society (the chief, the commander, the 'caudillo'). There are no academic requirements for ordination to the ministry. Promotion to the pastorate is nothing more than a confirmation of what has already been demonstrated in service to his neighbour and zeal for the church's mission.

■ **Pentecostal ethics** is characterized by its opposition to everything that is to do with 'the world'. This is the religion of what should not be done. It isolates people from their surroundings, either by filling all their free time with church work or by imposing strict regulations that make them break every tie with the world.

Seeds of freedom
In the midst of situations of deep pain and hopelessness such as those in Latin America today, the affirmation made by Pentecostals of the presence and the power of the Holy Spirit contains the seeds of freedom and is a call to hope. Perhaps this is Pentecostalism's greatest contribution.

interpreted the Latin American situation as a 'situation of sin', openly condemned the 'institutionalized violence' fostered by capitalism and neo-colonialism, and encouraged the promotion of popular education and organizations, especially through *communidades de base* (Christian grass-roots communities). Medellín thus marked the beginning of a definite 'preferential option for the poor' – and this on the part of the Roman Catholic hierarchy, which has traditionally been identified with the powerful. They had clearly seen that in this region of the world 'the alternative is not between the status quo and change, but between violent change and peaceful change'.

The Medellín Conclusions became the basis for social activism. Some sections, especially those dealing with justice, peace and poverty, provided the framework for the development of 'the theology of liberation'. This theology has been defined by Gustavo Gutierrez – one of its best-known representatives – as 'a new way of doing theology'. It works to liberate the poor and the oppressed from all servitudes, including that related to socio-economic dependence. One of its key words is 'praxis', which means practical action aimed at social change, but with reflection on, and for the sake of, that action. Liberation theologians use social sciences in the analysis of Latin American realities. They see the common people as active makers of history, and they

'The church is, and will continue to be, persecuted as long as it does not accommodate itself to the whims of totalitarianism whether of the right or of the left.' Arturo Rivera y Damas, Archbishop of San Salvador

understand the mission of the church as bearing on the struggle for justice for the poor. The most outstanding representatives of this theological movement are Gustavo Gutiérrez (Peruvian), Juan Luis Segundo (Uruguayan), Hugo Assmann, Leonardo Boff and Clodovis Boff (Brazilians), José Miranda (Mexican) and Enrique Dussel (Argentinian). Some of their works have been translated into several languages, including English.

In a continent where the upper 20 per cent of the population receives 66 per cent of the total income while the lower 20 per cent receives 3 per cent, the Medellín meeting and the theology of liberation could hardly pass unnoticed. The Medellín Conclusions, with their strong social criticism, became the object of heated debate not only in Latin America but also in North America and Europe. As a result, a good number of the bishops who had signed them preferred to draw back from that commitment.

The theology of liberation, in the same vein, was either enthusiastically received or passionately rejected both within and outside the region. Shortly after Medellín, for instance, a Belgian Jesuit, Roger Vekemans, described liberation theology as a 'theology of violence' and requested funds from a German agency to support a 'redeeming crusade' against it. His efforts culminated in a meeting of the so-called 'Church and Liberation Circle of Studies' held in Rome in March 1976. This meeting was sponsored by the Roman Curia and by Adveniat – the German bishops' aid agency for the church in Latin America, led by Bishop Franz Hengsbach, military bishop of the German armed forces. Serious questions were raised about liberation theology. In 1977, however, Adveniat was denounced by over 100 German theologians for financing a 'not very brotherly attack...which endangers autonomous church evolution in Latin America...and is causing divisions between theologians and bishops in the national churches'.

Against the background of the so-called cold war, the seventies saw the establishment of anti-Marxist and neo-Nazi military 'national security' governments in several Latin American countries. According to the ideology adopted by these governments, the task of the state was defined in terms of geopolitical control, and total and permanent war as a means to national security. The economic aim was capitalist expansion from the centre and preserving foreign investments through military defence. The net result of this 'decade of captivity' was the violation of all human rights, with hundreds of thousands of political prisoners, refugees and exiles, and with tens of thousands of people who were tortured, executed or assassinated, or who simply 'disappeared'.

In this political context, the clergy who wanted to implement the Medellín Conclusions had to face a double reaction: from the conservative constituency of the

TRAIN WHERE YOU LIVE

A grass-roots leader of a church in Latin America is called to train for ministry. How to train him? Take him away to college for a few years and lose his contact and leadership where he is? The alternative is Theological Training by Extension (TEE), a system to train him in his own locality, to prepare for the same exams as college students.

TEE began in Guatemala in 1963 and is strongest in Latin America, but it is spreading fast in Asia and Africa too – by 1980 there were thought to be 100,000 students round the world. TEE has grown alongside other types of extension studies, but it has particular Christian importance. It challenges an elite ministry and affirms the significance of local leaders on the New Testament pattern.

See Racism, Justice and Civil Rights; The Church of the Poor

Local people take part in a fiesta outside a chapel in Peru. Much Latin American social and communal life is linked to popular Catholic religion.

church and from the repressive regimes in their respective countries. The 'cost of prophecy' was exceedingly high! It has been estimated that between 1968 and the third CELAM General Conference (at Puebla in Mexico, 1979) approximately 1,500 priests, nuns and active lay-persons were arrested, kidnapped, interrogated, tortured, defamed, exiled or assassinated.

A sector of the Roman Catholic Church had become 'the voice of the voiceless' and was consequently hit by government repression head on. One of the most outstanding martyrs in recent years was Monsignor Oscar Arnulfo Romero, archbishop of El Salvador,

assassinated while saying mass on 24 March 1980. He had pledged that if he had to sacrifice his life for the sake of the poor, he was willing 'to let my blood be a seed of freedom and the sign that hope will soon be a reality'.

During the two years before the Third General Conference of CELAM, there was considerable debate as to whether the Latin American bishops meeting in Puebla would confirm or discard the decisions taken in Medellín. The general secretary of CELAM, Monsignor Alfonso López Trujillo, a well-known conservative, headed up the campaign against liberation theology and the liberalization of the church. His

consultative document for Puebla on 'Present and Future Evangelization in Latin America', released in December 1977, set off a continent-wide debate not only among the clergy but also among thousands of grass-roots communities. As a result, the document was thoroughly revised under the leadership of the CELAM president, Cardinal Aloisio Lorscheider from Brazil.

The Puebla Conference was not nearly as original as the previous one. But under the influence of bishops such as Helder Camara and Paulo Evaristo Arns, from Brazil, Leonidas Proaño, from Ecuador, and Oscar Arnulfo Romero, from El Salvador, it reconfirmed Medellín's call to Christians to join in the struggle for justice. Furthermore, it openly condemned the national-security ideology, ratified the church's 'preferential option for the poor', and gave official approval to the grass-roots communities.

GRASS-ROOTS COMMUNITIES

Between Medellín and Puebla more than 200,000 small grass-roots communities had begun to function all over Latin America. It has been estimated that in **Brazil** alone there were 80,000 of them in 1979 – twice as many as in 1976 – and there are 150,000 at present.

The multiplication of these grass-roots communities is one of the most significant developments within the Roman Catholic Church today The bishops in Puebla saw in them a cause for joy and hope because

of the great potential they have as 'centres of evangelization and moving forces for liberation and development'. From a theological viewpoint, the phenomenon has been interpreted as 'a re-invention of the church' (Leonardo Boff). From a political viewpoint, it represents a significant step towards a more democratic system in which the poor affirm their dignity as persons and as citizens. From a sociological viewpoint, it provides a model for social change through the exercise of power from the bottom up.

There are several features which characterize these grass-roots communities:
● **The Bible is read in the context of poverty and oppression.**
● **There is a spirit of family solidarity and sharing, a critical understanding of the established order and co-operative action to bring about change.**
● **This helps people to perceive the practical**

Not all Latin American Catholicism is formal and ornate. Tens of thousands of grass-roots communities bring their understanding of the Bible to bear on the fierce social pressures that weigh on poorer people.

Continued on p.238

THE SUFFERING CHURCH
MORTIMER ARIAS

Jesus called his disciples to 'take up the cross and follow me'. The disciples were actively to *take up* and not merely *put up with* the cross of discipleship. Jesus saw that as the church fulfilled its mission in the world, suffering was inevitable. He told his followers: 'Watch out! You will be arrested and taken to court. You will be beaten...you will stand before rulers and kings for my sake to tell them the good news...Everyone will hate you because of me.'

Through Jesus' teaching to his disciples it is absolutely clear that his church was going to be a suffering church. We should not deceive ourselves: when the world speaks well of Christians, something is going wrong! A church which is not a suffering church in the fulfilment of its mission is not the church of Jesus Christ.

This is precisely the discovery and the experience of the church of Jesus Christ in Latin America today, which is in many areas a suffering church.

Heritage of suffering
The Protestant churches (also known as the Evangelical churches, in a positive and inclusive sense) have known suffering from their beginnings in Latin America a century ago. The presence of Protestant Christianity was resisted by the established Roman Catholic Church, which had enjoyed a practical monopoly and indisputable power for about four centuries. It was rejected as a 'foreign religion' and an intolerable invasion of a Christian land.

All the devices of law, custom, social pressure and the exercise of authority (legal and illegal) were used against the missionaries. In some countries the penal code included capital punishment for anyone publicly practising or propagating a religion other than Roman Catholicism. No citizen could marry legally, except through the Roman Catholic Church, and religious 'heretics' were not allowed to be buried in cemeteries regarded as holy ground.

Even when the laws and constitutions were liberalized, including religious freedom for all citizens, Evangelical Christians were still subjected to social pressure, cultural marginalization and public scorn, because of their different practices and styles of worship and life. In almost every country, churches were destroyed, Bibles burned and believers stoned – in some cases to the point of death.

Many churches from those times keep the names of some Protestant martyrs. This was a time when suffering was accepted as part of what it means to be a Christian, and as a mark of the true church.

Suffering with the poor
Today, Evangelicals generally enjoy religious freedom, a wide margin of acceptance, and a remarkable rhythm of growth. But many more Christians, from every confession (and especially from the Roman Catholic majority) have been experiencing again the meaning of the 'suffering church'. Many have started to speak of 'the church of the catacombs' or the 'church of the martyrs'.

In a documented French study, prepared for the Puebla Conference of Roman Catholic bishops, 1,500 priests, nuns, pastors and lay Christians were listed as having been through arrest, interrogation, prison, torture and exile. Many have been anonymously executed and disposed of, covered by the euphemistic label of 'missing persons' or 'disappeared'.

So why this new wave of persecution? These scrutinized, harassed, tortured and murdered Christians have been persecuted not because of their religious beliefs but because of their commitment to the poor and oppressed. One of the most fascinating chapters of Christian witness in Latin America in the twentieth century has been the defence of human rights in the name of the gospel of Jesus Christ. Christians have often been persecuted for their religious beliefs, but now they are suffering because of their love for others.

Of course, the military dictators who have been in power in several countries for the last two decades would justify their gross violations of human rights. Law and order, development and social stability, they say, must come first. But it is their ideology of national security that has become the main rod of persecution.

Christians and churches have now become the voice of the voiceless. They speak out for prisoners, the tortured and exiles, monitor 'missing persons' and assist political refugees and their families. They denounce injustices and unmask the concealed powers that shape the lives of the poor. They provide food, rehabilitation and pastoral support for the victims of the system. Not surprisingly, this has not been welcomed as a good service by 'national security' governments, who label such committed Christians as Communists and subversives. Their counter-insurgency strategies have sometimes reached the point of the massacre of whole populations, as in Guatemala.

Repressive governments have often been more afraid of Christians with their Bibles, raising their voices for the oppressed, than of any Communist rhetoric. The vast majority of martyrs – though not exclusively – have been committed Christians.

The tragedy of it all is that, as in several periods of church history, Christians have not been persecuted by a *secular* ideology, but by authorities who claim Christianity for themselves. Governments who act in the name of 'Christian Western civilization'; 'Christian' torturers who wear a cross around their necks, the same as those worn by the victims of their inhuman tortures...

Costly discipleship

Many good Christians stay in silence in the face of injustices or repression, and they even blame the suffering of Christians on their 'meddling in politics'. Many mistakes and wrong actions have taken place; Christians are not infallible. But one thing has to be recognized. Suffering Christians have not made themselves vulnerable simply for their own religious freedom or personal well-being – but for the freedom, dignity and life of others. In that sense – mistakes and all – they have taken seriously the cross of discipleship. As Dietrich Bonhoeffer would say, they have chosen costly discipleship, and not cheap grace.

In their suffering together with the suffering people of Latin America, Christians can say with Paul, 'I fulfill in my own self the passion of Christ... I carry in my body the wounds of Christ.' The suffering church completes the suffering of Christ, as his own body on earth. Paul said, 'It has been granted to you that for the sake of Christ you should not only believe in him, but also suffer for his sake.'

Christians who have felt the call to suffer for Christ and for his people in Latin America have no regrets. Like Archbishop Oscar Romero of El Salvador – murdered while saying mass – and the four missionary women from the United States – raped, tortured and assassinated by Salvadorean security forces – they know that there is no death without resurrection, and no love without lasting value.

Archbishop Oscar Romero was leader of Roman Catholics in El Salvador. Events in his country compelled him to speak out for social justice and political freedom. Then in 1980 he was shot dead by a right-wing death squad while celebrating mass. Praising Jesus for his sacrifice, he was called on to make his own.

Mexicans in Guadalupe join in a religious procession. Popular Christianity brings colour and a festive spirit into lives which are sometimes hard and monotonous.

See Doing Theology

implications of the Christian faith, and the poor become aware that it is possible to create new forms of political, social and economic organization.

● **Through the grass-roots communities pastoral work touches every aspect of life and places it under the influence of the gospel.**

The main concepts come from Pope Paul VI's Apostolic Exhortation *Evangelii Nuntiandi*. Evangelization is seen, not in a vacuum, but in the context of concrete realities, and that makes this approach

particularly relevant to the Latin American situation.

Recent events, however, have placed a question-mark over the future of the grass-roots communities. The 'Sacred Congregation for the Doctrines of the Faith', led by Cardinal Joseph Ratzinger in Rome, has questioned Leonardo Boff for what amounts to a masterful theological defence of these communities in his book, *Church: Gift and Power*, written in Portuguese. Moreover, Pope John Paul II has clearly expressed his objection to the concept of a 'popular church' that they represent. It remains to be seen whether Roman Catholic orthodoxy will be able to frustrate 'the new reformation' now taking place in Latin America.

In many ways, the Puebla Document provided a good basis for pastoral action in a situation of poverty and oppression. Its twenty-one sections gave guidelines to evangelize the poor, the elite, young people, the family, culture, popular religiosity, and so on. However, it also emphasized the Virgin Mary and Marian piety, and this was boosted by the pope's visit. This has proved a significant pointer. More traditional aspects of Roman Catholicism have been reinforced in the last few years.

Puebla's very limited reference to the question of Christian unity has been significant, too. Relations between Roman Catholics and Protestants continue to be one of the weakest aspects of the Christian witness in Latin America.

WHICH WAY THE PROTESTANTS?

The impoverishment of the masses which has taken place in the region in the last two decades has radically affected all the churches. As we have seen in the previous section, in the Roman Catholic Church the theology of liberation became the focus of debate. In the Protestant churches this theology has not had many adherents, but they

Bolivian Indians take part in a 'Calvario' ceremony. Many such practices link a superstitious Catholicism with a pagan folk religion in Latin America, not just among Indian people.

have not remained totally untouched by its concerns.

Social concerns began to be felt in the so-called 'historic churches', particularly during the fifties, when some of their younger leaders received the influence of European theological thinking through the World Student Christian Federation. The change which took place may be seen in the contrast between the Latin American Evangelical Conference (CELA) held in Buenos Aires in 1949, dealing with 'Protestant Christianity in Latin America', and the CELA held in Lima in 1961, on the theme 'Christ, the Hope for Latin America'. The Buenos Aires conference viewed Protestantism as an alternative to 'a formal and static' Roman Catholicism; the Lima conference, on the other

THE CARIBBEAN SCENE

Different Caribbean islands have quite distinct colonial histories, and so the pattern of their churches varies greatly.

In the Spanish-speaking and French-speaking islands, Roman Catholicism is usually strongest. In the **Dominican Republic**, for example, the Catholic church has been closely involved in the nation's history, and Catholicism is dominant. Charismatic Catholics are strong here. In **Puerto Rico**, however, although Roman Catholicism is the faith of the Hispanic population, there are also many who look to the United States as home, and Protestants have made progress here, especially Seventh-Day Adventists. In **Cuba** Roman Catholics lost many leaders after the 1959 revolution, and had disagreements with the state. There is less conflict now, but the church is much weaker than before. But Protestants, few in number before 1959, have grown in strength. French-speaking **Haiti** has many who try to combine Christianity with voodooism. Roman Catholics have suffered through state control of their church, and there are more Protestants here than in the Dominican Republic.

The English-speaking islands are more varied. In **Jamaica** the strongest Protestant groups are Pentecostal, but Baptists and Anglicans are also strong. Roman Catholics do well in poorer areas. The largest non-white indigenous church is Revival Zion. Many have found a substitute for orthodox Christianity in Rastafarianism. In **Trinidad** Anglicans and Roman Catholics are most numerous, and in **Barbados** it is the Anglicans.

In many West Indian islands Christians have to cope with poverty, and to find a faith that sustains their dignity.

hand, issued a call to evangelization in the context of social problems. Obviously, the churches represented at the two CELAs had moved from being concerned with their own preservation over against Roman Catholicism, and were now concerned for mission, which addressed the whole range of people's needs.

In the sixties two specialized groups related to the unity movement were formed: ISAL (Church and Society in Latin America) and MISUR (Urban Industrial Mission). These ecumenical groups, together with other student and youth movements, were affected by the crisis of the sixties and became radicalized in their views on social issues.

ISAL, identified by Orlando Costas as 'the most consistently radical Protestant ecumenical organization in Latin America', attracted a number of Protestant intellectuals disenchanted with the common social stance of their churches, which they saw as cultural enclaves within society. Under the leadership of a missionary mentor, Richard Shaull from Princetown Seminary (USA), they articulated a 'theology of liberation' which must be regarded as a decisive element in the formulation of liberation theology in Roman Catholic circles. Little by little ISAL became committed to structural change (along socialist lines) and alienated from the churches. The tension with the churches came to a head at the third CELA (at Buenos Aires in 1969), where a position paper

presented by ISAL culminated in a heated debate on the political responsibility of Christians which did not produce consensus.

With the emergence of national-security governments in the seventies, ISAL ceased to function as an organized movement. Some of the names that had given it prestige, such as José Míguez Bonino (Argentinian), Julio de Santa Ana (Uruguayan) and Rubem Alves (Brazilian), had by then become well-known in the theological world. Míguez Bonino is perhaps the most outstanding Latin American Protestant theologian today.

DISCOVERING THE POOR

Conservative Evangelicals and Pentecostals have generally been unable to respond to the challenge of poverty and oppression. A large number of them are committed to theological fundamentalism and adopt a right-wing stance on social, political and economic issues. In several countries they have even offered religious backing to dictatorial governments, such as that of Pinochet in Chile, in exchange for religious freedom. This has been called a 'legitimization of coercion'. It finds its basis in an understanding of atheistic Marxism as a common enemy of church and state which must be kept away at any cost.

However, an important number of conservative Evangelicals (Baptists, Brethren, Pentecostals and so on) have gone a different way. They have been involved in

'The kingdom of God does not fall from the sky. It is built with great effort and requires a permanent conversion and daily commitment. The poor have always been capable of sacrifice and giving their lives. Now in happiness and certainty we can work so that the future of our children will be completely new, as the Lord promised.'
Letter from a Nicaraguan pastoral centre

See Evangelicals at a Crossroads

a movement of theological renewal which began in the sixties and is mainly represented by the Latin American Theological Fraternity (FTL) and the Latin American Centre of Pastoral Studies. FTL was organized during the first Latin American Congress on Evangelism held in Bogotá, Colombia, in 1969. Since then it has become a significant option for Christians concerned for a faith which is both grounded in the Bible and relevant to a situation marked by exploitation and injustice. Well-known names such as Orlando Costas (Puerto Rican), Samuel Escobar (Peruvian), Daniel Schipani (an Argentinian living in Puerto Rico), Emilio A. Núñez (a Salvadorean living in Guatemala) and Rolando Gutierrez (a Nicaraguan living in Mexico) give a face to the FTL within and beyond the borders of Latin America.

Some FTL members had a decisive influence at the International Congress on World Evangelism which took place at Lausanne, Switzerland, in 1974. They insisted that evangelism and social responsibility must be kept together. This was echoed in the official recognition by the congress that 'Evangelism and socio-political involvement are both part of our Christian duty', and that 'We should share God's concern for justice and reconciliation throughout human society and for the liberation of men from every kind of oppression'.

The tensions due to the critical situation in Latin America are seriously affecting Evangelical churches. During the Consultation on World Evangelization held in Pattaya, Thailand, in 1980, which had been recently organized. These moves were hindered by the polarizations within and among churches, but they finally led to a meeting held at Oaztepec, Mexico, in September 1978, for the purpose of laying down the basis for the new council of churches. Four years later, in November 1982, the Latin American Council of Churches was definitively organized in an assembly which took place in Lima, Peru, with representatives from seventeen confessional groups and eighty-five national churches (including a good number of Pentecostal groups). The aims of the council were defined as evangelization, the unity of the church, and dialogue about mission and witness in the region.

Protestantism has by now become a movement rooted in Latin American soil. In various countries its rate of growth is higher than that of the population. It has inner vitality, and a significant sector has 'discovered' the poor and is seeking to respond to the challenges of the present critical situation in the continent. At the same time, however, it is seriously threatened by divisiveness and polarization along both theological and ideological lines. It lacks organizational cohesiveness and is often affected by activism, superficiality and anti-intellectualism. Also, the renewal of Roman Catholicism has

The church of St Francis of Assisi in the city of Salvador, Brazil. The Spanish and Portuguese colonial past of Latin America has left many buildings in the styles of Southern Europe.

outdated its strictly 'Protestant' role and posed before it in striking terms the question of where it stands in relation to society.

The Protestant churches are growing, then, in Latin America. But this does not mean their continuing effectiveness is guaranteed. The future of Protestantism depends on whether it can resolve its internal and external tensions and become an agent of the kingdom of God in the midst of the critical Latin American situation.

2.6 NEW-WORLD FAITH

Christians in North America

RICHARD J. MOUW

North American Christianity is a community of many moods today. Far more people attend churches than in western Europe. But there is no single set of emotions which Christians all over the United States and Canada are experiencing, nor is there a substantive unified 'quest' or project in which all are participating. If accurate generalizations are to be formulated they will have to be spelled out in terms of emerging patterns which can be discerned among the rich diversity of attitudes and activities which characterize the religious scene. And even here no generalization will be immune from criticism.

Suppose, for example, that we were to try to find a single 'mood' that characterizes North American Christianity at present. Is this a time, as some have suggested, of 'uncertainty' for Christians in the United States and Canada? Well, it surely is for some. Many groups and individuals do seem to be plagued by an unprecendented mood of uncertainty regarding spiritual matters. But at the same time there are others who seem to be energized by the discovery of new certainties, a discovery which leads them to display an obvious spirit of self-confidence about what they believe. Indeed, one can make a good case for the contention that North America has recently been witnessing new outbreaks of spiritual arrogance.

Are these days of 'ferment' in the North American churches? To some degree, yes. But there are also in some places unmistakeable signs of decay and stagnation. Is there a new turn toward 'inwardness' among Christians? To be sure – in some quarters. But elsewhere, among groups where 'inwardness' has long been held in high esteem, a new interest in 'outwardness' can be detected.

It does seem safe to suggest, however, that North American Christians are involved in the kinds of reflections in which they have always been engaged: about who they are, how they relate to other Christians, and how they are to pursue their involvement in the society in which they live. It is unlikely that there are any Christians who never think about

A French Canadian village on the St Lawrence river is clustered round its church. The many different European cultures that settled the United States and Canada brought a kaleidoscopic variety of Christian traditions into North American life.

these things. And many Christians today are, in reflecting upon these matters, rethinking their past patterns of thought and action. Of course, not all of them are rethinking the same things, and the manner in which they are conducting their rethinking differs greatly from case to case. But there can be no doubt that much new consideration is going on, across the theological spectrum.

LABELLING A KALEIDOSCOPE

Christians in the United States and Canada have always been conscious of the importance of the labels with which they describe their religious beliefs and loyalties. The history of Christianity in North America is intimately intertwined with the histories of immigrant groups. Immigrants brought their denominational identities with them to the New World; indeed, many came to North America precisely for the purpose of preserving those religious identities. For such folks, labels are not mere words; they are shorthand ways of telling important stories.

One kind of story which American religious labels tell is about traditional confessional differences in Western and Eastern Christianity. As many commentators have pointed out, one can learn about nearly every controversy in the history of the world-wide church by conducting a survey of North American denominational life. Thus, one set

A large choir leads the worship at a church in Indianapolis. Churches are often well attended in the United States, and many people take part in Sunday and weekday activities.

of religious labels has to do with the major divisions of Christendom: Roman Catholic, Eastern Orthodox and Protestant.

For many North Americans until very recently, 'I am a Roman Catholic' counted as a very adequate way of telling others about a person's religious loyalties. But not so for most Orthodox or Protestant Christians. Orthodoxy in North American is a divided community – although the bases for Orthodox disunity are not well-known outside the Orthodox churches.

Protestant disunity is much more visible. The Protestant labelling system in North America is so complex that the story cannot even begin to be told in a few words; it is doubtful that it can even be told adequately using many words. One source of Protestant disunity in North America lies in the patterns of Protestant disunity which prevail elsewhere. The fact that immigrants brought their denominational divisions with them meant that longstanding religious disagreements were introduced into the American Protestant scene at the outset.

The Protestant movement had always been a pluralistic one, with Lutheran and Reformed and Anabaptist parties appearing at the time of the Reformation, which also witnessed the Anglican break with Rome. Later Protestant splits in Europe were occasioned by the appearance of significant pietist movements: the Church of the Brethren in Germany, the Wesleyans in England, and various 'free

church' and 'house church' groups in the Scandinavian countries.

Each of these major Protestant movements was to make its mark on the church life of the New World. But many of them

subdivided within their original geographical settings, and these subdivisions were also exported. To take just one example, the Calvinistic churches: Scottish Calvinism had split into several different Presbyterian bodies, as had the Reformed community of the Netherlands. Immigrants from both countries brought their controversies with them, with the result that North America, which also managed to generate a few home-grown Calvinistic splinterings, came to harbour such a variety of Reformed and Presbyterian churches that even the most schismatically-minded European follower of John Calvin would have a difficult time sorting them out. And much the same story can be told of, for example, British Methodism and German and Scandinavian Lutheranism.

People from an old Amish community visit a market. This splinter group of Mennonites make few concessions to modern life and technology. They are part of the pattern of United States Christianity.

Worshippers at a Baptist church in Indianapolis. Some blacks join mainline churches, but many belong to congregations where the great majority are black.

See Evangelicals at a Crossroads; Renewal in the Holy Spirit

The American labelling-system, then, exhibits a bewildering display of geographical and doctrinal distinctives, with many labels pointing to disagreements which originated in a divided Europe, and others – for example, Restoration and Pentecostalism – pointing to American religious developments.

NEW PATTERNS

In the twentieth century a new labelling-system was introduced, one which did not replace these older labels but was superimposed on them. The new pattern had its visible beginnings shortly after the turn of the century, when the 'Fundamentalist-modernist' disputes were waged in some of the major denominations. These localized disputes broadened out, creating a situation which many have described as a two-party system in North American Protestantism.

The two parties are commonly referred to these days as **mainline** and **Evangelical**. These labels roam over the boundaries designated by the more traditional labels. The major denominations are considered to be officially mainline, although each has a significant group of members within its ranks who possess Evangelical sympathies. Evangelicalism, as some have suggested, is more a 'mosaic' than a party. Some denominations, both large and small, are properly called Evangelical. But for the most part the Evangelical identity is

sustained by means of a network of magazines, Bible conferences, institutions of higher education (including some of the largest seminaries in North America), youth associations and evangelistic organizations. Evangelicals have always made effective use of the radio waves in carrying on their ministries, but they have been especially successful in television programming in recent years, as pioneers in the establishment of 'the electronic church'.

The labels associated with this two-party notion have been applied in an over-simplifying manner, and have thus been used to reinforce some popular stereotypes. Mainline Protestants are often portrayed as 'secularizing' modernists, who jump from bandwagon to bandwagon with no controlling principles. Evangelicals, on the other hand, are regularly viewed as Bible-thumping obscurantists who are exclusively absorbed in preparation for the life hereafter.

These stereotypes are not totally divorced from reality. But they will not serve us as accurate portraits of the two camps. Certainly they are falsified in important respects by recent trends. For example, mainline groups promote Bible study and endorse programmes of evangelistic outreach, while Evangelicals engage in serious scholarship and launch programmes to combat racism. In the former connection, the writings of the Mennonite, John Howard Yoder, have been widely influential, while the Sojourners Community with its well-known magazine has played a vital role in pursuing justice and peace issues.

Tensions between Evangelicals and mainline Protestants have been less pronouced in Canada than they have been in the United States. For one thing, the Canadian churches did not experience the kind of wrenching battles between conservatives and liberals which caused such havoc in a number of United States denominations earlier in the century. Canadian Protestants maintain closer links with the churches of the British Isles than has been common south of the border, and consequently Canadians have been regularly exposed to more moderate types of Evangelical. Furthermore, Canadians have not developed the same kind of network of Evangelical institutions as their United States neighbours did, so that less reinforcement has been given to a sense of independent Evangelical identity in Canada.

But the sense of security in employing longstanding labels has been challenged, in both Canada and the United States, by two recent developments:
● Firstly, **very significant changes have occurred in Roman Catholicism during the decades following the Second Vatican Council**. Anti-Catholicism has long been a fact of Protestant consciousness in North America. Protestants with various denominational loyalties have been united in their distrust of, if not their outright hostility towards, the Roman Catholic Church. Mainline Protestants have been wary of Rome because of its traditionalism and dogmatism. Evangelicals, not intrinsically immune to traditionalism and dogmatism, have opposed the Roman church because its peculiar blend of tradition and dogma seemed clearly linked to unbiblical ideas about salvation, and even an overt spirit of superstition.

All this has changed as a result of the reforms stimulated by the Second Vatican Council. Roman Catholic worship seems much less sinister to Protestant ears when it is translated from Latin into English. And a social witness that draws on both the dignified themes of papal encyclicals and the quiet wisdom of traditional contemplative spirituality is attractive to many Protestants, both mainline and Evangelical.

DYING FOR JUSTICE

Jonathan Daniels was a young American Christian whose faith provoked him to join a civil rights protest in Selma, Alabama. He faced violent opposition from many whites, who called him 'white nigger'.

In August 1965 he took part in a peaceful demonstration, was arrested and held for several days before being released without charge. As he left the prison a white man came towards him hurling abuse and shot him dead; as he fell he managed to save the life of the black girl with him. The assassin was later tried but was acquitted.

Shortly before his death Daniels wrote: 'I lost fear in the black belt when I began to know in my bones and sinews that I had truly been baptized into Jesus' death and resurrection, and in the only sense that really mattered I am already dead and my life is hidden with Christ in God.'

Indeed, there has been a much-publicized Charismatic renewal in Roman Catholicism, causing many Roman Catholics to be deeply concerned with life in the Holy Spirit. And this has convinced many conservative Protestants that 'Evangelical Catholicism' is not a blatant contradiction in terms.

This development has had a strong psychological effect on many Protestants who had previously been unshakeably convinced that their favourite labelling-systems were based on hard-and-fast boundary lines. Having seen drastic changes within their own lifetimes in Protestant-Catholic relationships which they would have thought impossible a few decades ago, they will never again have quite the same confidence in

See Are Christians and Scientists Friends again?

THE EVOLUTION DEBATE CONTINUES
WALTER R. HEARN

After the notorious Scopes trial in Tennessee in 1925, popular debate in America over teaching evolution in public schools quietened down. Scientists busied themselves with refining Darwin's suggested mechanism for changes in biological populations over millions of years of geological time. Textbook publishers avoided trouble by putting less emphasis on evolution. Fundamentalists went on believing that the earth could be no older than a few thousand years because they still interpreted the biblical creation narratives in a literalistic way.

The majority of Christians probably retained some reservations about evolution, wondering whether it was inherently atheistic and therefore an enemy of Christian faith. In 1941 Evangelical scientists founded the American Scientific Affiliation to uphold the integrity of a scientific outlook, while witnessing to their faith in Christ and the Bible. Its publications distinguish between legitimate science on the one hand, and non-theistic or atheistic 'scientisms' like positivism and materialism on the other. In *The Christian View of Science and Scripture* (1954), Bernard Ramm argued that defence of Christian faith against

philosophical 'evolutionism' has never been helped by theological attacks on evolutionary science.

The truce over

In the past few decades the evolution debate has again erupted and again found its way into the courts. As interest in science and science education increased in the post-sputnik era, textbooks began to say more about evolution. Publication in 1961 of *The Genesis Flood* by John Whitcomb and Henry Morris seemed to spark off the formation of a number of Christian anti-evolution organizations, such as the Creation Research Society, the Bible-Science Association, the Creation Science Research Centre, and the Institute for Creation Research. 'Creation scientists' on the staff of this last organization in particular have engaged in formal debates over evolution with university scientists on campuses all over North America.

Most scientists and most Christians ignored 'scientific creationism' until anti-evolutionists entered the political arena, exerting pressure on state school boards (notably in California and Texas) and state legislatures

(notably in Arkansas and Louisiana). Their success in these states led to the trial *McLean vs. Arkansas*, where an act mandating 'balanced treatment of creation-science and evolution-science in public schools' was challenged in a United States District Court. On 5 January 1982, Judge William Overton ruled that Act 590 violated the First Amendment of the United States Constitution.

Finding creation-science not to be legitimate science but in reality, 'the literal Fundamentalists' view of Genesis', Judge Overton ruled that to mandate its teaching in public schools would constitute an illegal 'establishment of religion'. Even the most impressive evidence brought against certain aspects of evolution, he concluded, did not support 'a complex doctrine which includes a sudden creation from nothing, a world-wide flood, separate ancestry of man and apes, and a young earth'.

Early in 1984 the scientific creationists were hoping to win in Louisiana, partly because they had narrowed their definition of creation down to 'the sudden appearance of complex forms'.

classifying the varieties of Christian commitment.

● Secondly, **some Christians are increasingly insistent that we need a whole new way of sorting out Christian identities**. These protests against the older labels include feminists, blacks, Hispanic-Americans, and those who sympathize strongly with various Third World liberation movements. They argue that the old names reflect the concerns of those people who have controlled the theological agenda of the 'North Atlantic' Christian community – a community which considers the concerns of the poor and the oppressed to be marginal to the main thrust of theological reflection.

But now, many are arguing today, the felt needs of women

How did the Universe begin? Did God create it? And did life forms evolve, or did God create them as they are now? Evolution and creation are often seen as incompatible principles in the United States, and hotly disputed.

The Bible *and* science

Many Christians occupy a broad middle ground between what they consider to be the pseudo-science of creationism and the pseudo-religion of evolutionism. Determined to take seriously both the Bible and science, they acknowledge God's creative role throughout space and time. Some see that role as distinctive acts of progressive creation, others as guidance of evolutionary processes. Such middle ground is represented by Davis Young's *Christianity and the Age of the Earth* (1982) and *Is God a Creationist?* (1983), edited by Roland Frye. What annoys many about the extremists in the current debate was neatly summarized by John Wiester in his book, *The Genesis Connection*: 'Both sides are using science to teach religion.'

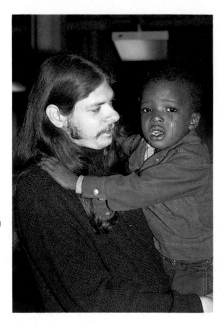

A daycare centre for poor children run by the Sojourners community in Washington D.C. Many Christian churches and communities are actively engaged in social care.

See Are Men and Women Equal? Churches Together

and racial minority groups and the poor nations of the southern hemisphere must no longer be marginal. They must become the central focus for understanding the meaning of the gospel. The issues which separate male from female, white from black, and oppressor from oppressed, are much more important than those which are debated by white male bishops or which occupy the attention of students in North American divinity schools. And so there is a growing insistence on cultural terms as the proper labels for Christian identity: black theology, feminist theology, liberation theology.

It is unlikely that this mode of labelling will ever be adopted exclusively by the majority of North American Christians – especially since it would require many of them to describe their theological perspective as 'white

male' or something equally unglamorous. But the very fact of these newer cultural 'causes' forces certain sensitivities on all North American denominations.

Many North American Christians are thinking about how such things as gender, race and class affect the way people think about God and his relationship to the world. They are being forced to reflect on how male, white, Western capitalist biases have shaped their understandings of the gospel. Few would agree with the most extreme defenders of 'cause' theologies, who seem to think that cultural and political and economic factors are the only matters which are important to theological reflection. It is not likely that there will be a widespread embrace of the thesis that, for example, Western theology has been pervasively and hopelessly 'sexist'. But there is good reason to expect that the concerns of the liberationists will find their permanent place, alongside other very important matters, on the agenda of theological discussion.

COMING TOGETHER

In all this sorting out of new patterns, many North American Christians are also exploring new modes of co-operation between Christian groups. This is happening differently in the different traditions:

● For **the Orthodox and the Roman Catholic**, concern for unity is a rather new experience. Prior to the Second Vatican Council, Roman Catholics had virtually no formal means for exploring relationships of Christian unity. This has changed considerably in recent years. Roman Catholics are involved in co-operative ventures of many sorts, although they maintain only 'observer' status at the National Council of Churches of Christ, the main ecumenical body in the United States. The Orthodox, however, have recently become official members of that body.

● **Mainline Protestants** actively promote unity. One important vehicle for such activities is a network of ecumenical agendas, of which the National Council is the main North American expression. More than this, mainline Protestants have also shown much enthusiasm for denominational mergers.

One of the earliest and most ambitious achievements in the Protestant quest for 'organic unity' is to be found in Canada. In 1925 **the United Church of Canada** came into being: a merger of Methodists, Presbyterians and Congregationalists. United Church congregations are to be found in virtually every village and hamlet of the Canadian provinces.

Significant mergers have occurred more recently in the United States, with the formation of **the United Methodists** (combining Methodists and United Brethren) and **the United Church of Christ** (bringing together Congregationalists and the Evangelical and Reformed denominations). A very comprehensive effort was officially initiated in 1962, with the formation of the Consultation on Church Union, which has brought together a broad range of denominations in the United States and Canada for discussion and planning with an eye toward the formation of a broadly inclusive Protestant denominational body.

However, many observers claim to detect a noticeable cooling in recent years of the Protestant ardour for organizational unity. Some claim that the kind of 'bilateral' efforts – of the sort that culminated in the recent reunion of the major Northern and Southern Presbyterian bodies in the United States – have drained energies away from more ambitious and broadly-conceived schemes. Some ecumenists seem to be acknowledging this by advocating more 'pluralistic' merger schemes than have been proposed in the past.

The Rev. Jesse Jackson addresses a meeting in Harlem, New York, during his presidential campaign in 1984. His success in consolidating the black vote owed much to his link with the churches.

● **Evangelical Christians, despite what is sometimes said, have done much to foster unity.** For one thing, they promoted practical co-operation among Christians from various denominations. The Billy Graham crusades are a good case in point. From the beginning of his ministry, Billy Graham has insisted on cultivating a broad base of support for his local evangelistic meetings. He has openly solicited the sponsorship of mainline as well as Evangelical churches, and recently has even begun to gain the co-operation of Roman Catholics and Orthodox. Indeed, a good case can be made out that two of the key ecumenical figures of modern times are Billy Graham and Pope John XXIII – neither of whom has had any official status in the so-called 'ecumenical movement'!

See The Unity Movement; Roman Catholics since the Council

Evangelicals have also promoted practical ecumenism in other ways. Most of the major Evangelical organizations such as the Gideons, Youth for Christ, Inter-Varsity Christian Fellowship, the Full Gospel Christian Businessmen's Fellowship, Wheaton College, Fuller Theological Seminary, are 'ecumenical' on any ordinary understanding of that term. Evangelicals have formed a variety of institutions and organizations in which Christians from different churches have worked together.

Evangelicals have been, in their own manner, activists for unity. But their ecumenism has been task-oriented. It has not been

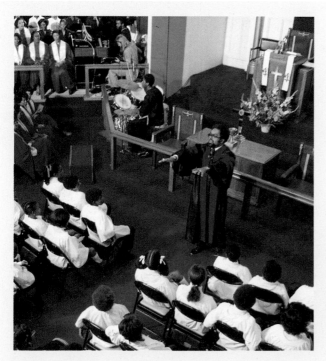

AMERICA'S BLACK CHURCHES

The black churches are among America's most vital centres of fellowship and exuberant worship, and their pastors are natural leaders of their communities.

Many such churches have little to say about injustice, but there is a movement of 'black theology' which affirms a central place for the black churches: 'without our church, we should have ceased to be as a people'. Just as their slave ancestors used the gospel to express their longing for freedom, so black Christians today should understand faith as the motive to fight racism and oppression. Jesus is the Black Messiah, in the sense that he identified with the enslaved and the powerless. Such black Christians feel close solidarity with the dominated and disenfranchised round the world.

very important to Evangelicals to think long and hard about what 'Christian unity' is all about. Rather, they have singled out certain tasks and set specific goals, and then banded together to fulfil them. Mainline Protestants, on the other hand, have consciously reflected on the nature of Christian unity; this has been for them an important topic for discussion and experiment. To be sure, they too have placed an important emphasis on practical co-operation. Indeed, mainline ecumenists have often promoted their vision of Christian unity with a 'doctrine divides but action unites' kind of emphasis. But it is nonetheless true that the mainline Protestants have been much more self-conscious in their interest in unity than have Evangelicals – and for that matter, more than the Orthodox and Roman Catholics.

RELATIONS WITH ROMAN CATHOLICS AND ORTHODOX

There are signs of significant changes in attitudes towards unity across the Christian spectrum. The National Council of Churches, like its international counterpart the World Council of Churches, has come under attack in recent years, from its own members as well as from more traditional critics, for what is perceived as a 'leftist' political-economic bias.

For mainline Protestants a turn toward more practical, and less structured, ecumenical activities can mean a major increase in ecumenical interests. Roman Catholics may be maintaining only an 'observer' status in formal ecumenical organizations, but on the practical level Roman Catholics seem to crop up everywhere. **Roman Catholic ecumenical involvement is happening on many fronts** – a diversity of activities which corresponds to an increasingly visible pluralism within the Roman church itself.

Roman Catholicism before the Second Vatican Council presented itself to the world as a rather monolithic community. Roman Catholic uniformity was very obvious in the area of theological reflection, where the Roman hierarchy maintained a careful supervision over public doctrinal discussion. To some degree, of course, the uniformity was more appearance than reality; North American Catholicism has always been a community offering many subtle nuances of emphasis in different situations.

But the nuances of the past were mere variations of a single theme compared to the fundamental diversity of present-day Roman Catholics. This pluralism does not lend itself to simple schemes of classification; in rough terms, however, it is possible to distinguish three major parties:

● The first party is **traditionalist** in its orientation. The far-reaching changes instituted in the Roman Catholic Church in the 1960s did not come without vocal opposition. The original traditionalists have been joined in recent years by

An American family share a thanksgiving dinner. Thanksgiving Day, which recalls the Pilgrim Fathers giving thanks for their first harvest on American shores, reminds Americans of their Christian roots.

some who, once supporters of change, have now come to doubt whether the innovations have been beneficial for the church. Traditionalist critics, of course, differ among themselves on specific items: not all, for example, would advocate a return to the Latin mass or a rigid anti-Protestant posture. But they share a general concern about what they perceive as the moral and doctrinal drift of contemporary Roman Catholicism.

● What the traditionalists think of as a rudderless drifting, the second group, **the progressive**

party, views as the coming-of-age of the Roman church. Progressives are enthusiastic supporters of the Second Vatican Council reforms, and they work for even more extensive alterations in doctrine and practice. Many would like to see changes in official teaching on abortion, birth control and the role of women in the church. Others advocate revising the way beliefs about the nature of the church and church authority are formulated.

Many progressive Roman Catholics are greatly influenced by Protestant thought. This is especially obvious in the area of biblical studies. Roman Catholic interest in the study of the Bible has intensified noticeably since the Second Vatican Council. Some observers insist that the changes in this area are so profound that they constitute a 'second Reformation' – one that this time has been contained within Roman Catholicism. However that may be, the theological mood in Roman Catholicism is such that it is sometimes difficult to distinguish the views of progressive Roman Catholics from those of Protestant liberals.

● A third group lacks the influence of the other two parties on the leadership level of Roman Catholic officialdom, but it has much strength among the grass-roots laity. These are **Roman Catholics who can properly be described as Evangelical**. This perspective has its most visible expression in the Roman Catholic Charismatic renewal, which promotes 'Pentecostal' emphases among Roman Catholics. The Evangelical Roman Catholics place a very central emphasis on the kind of personal experience of divine grace that is sustained by Bible study, spontaneous prayer, the 'sharing of testimonies' with like-minded Christians, and personal evangelism. Like the traditionalists, the Evangelicals promote a more conservative theological perspective than the progressives; but unlike the traditionalists they are open to very Protestant types of influences – and often actively seek out fellowship with Protestant Evangelicals. In organizations like, for example, the Society for Pentecostal Studies, Roman Catholic theologians work closely with scholars from the Pentecostal denominations.

The fact of Roman Catholic diversity, as suggested by these rough categories, greatly complicates the present state of Catholic-Protestant relations. Different Roman Catholic groups are moving in different directions ecumenically, seeking out persons and groups with similar concerns on the Protestant scene.

Even though **the Orthodox churches** have been quicker to move into official ecumenical dialogue than the Roman Catholics, they do not seem to be completely at ease there. The Orthodox communities are still struggling with questions about the degree to which they ought to 'Americanize' and 'Canadianize'. They are very much aware of the ways in which their theology and their understanding of the proper cultural role of the Christian community do not fit easily into North American patterns.

In various ways Orthodoxy finds it easier to pursue dialogue with Roman Catholics than with the Protestant churches – although Roman Catholic-Orthodox relations in North America are sometimes seriously strained by tensions in other parts of the world, especially eastern Europe. Co-operation between Orthodox Christians and Evangelical Protestants is on the increase; here too the situation is often complicated by Protestant efforts to evangelize in constituencies claimed by the Orthodox churches.

The most difficult relationships to cultivate seriously are those between the Orthodox community and liberal Protestants. The doctrinal looseness of mainline Protestantism – especially the North American variety, which is so closely linked to a thorough-going pragmatism – seems especially designed to offend Orthodox sensitivities. Liberal Protestants often resent, in turn, the deeply entrenched deference the Orthodox show to their patriarchs and the way they speak of 'the one true church'. The question of women's ordination has been an especially difficult issue in discussions between Orthodoxy and mainline Protestantism.

See The Orthodox Families

CHANGING EVANGELICALS

See Evangelicals at a Crossroads

As Evangelicals become further removed from the kinds of theological battles with modernism which were waged earlier in the century, there seems to be less resistance in principle to co-operation and dialogue with mainline Protestants. If Evangelicals continue to remain somewhat cool toward mainline Protestantism it is due not so much to outright hostility as to a wait-and-see attitude, based on the growing conviction that the aggressive liberalism of the past is no longer the cultural force that it once was. Indeed, with Evangelical churches and seminaries increasing in both numbers and respectability, Evangelicals are no longer the 'despised minority' they were in the past. As a result, they are having to learn to adjust their ecumenical attitudes to fit their new cultural acceptability.

One important stimulus for Evangelicals in recent years has been the growing awareness of the importance of cross-cultural dialogue among Christians. It might be possible, for example, for them to ignore Roman Catholics and mainline Protestants in the future. But it will not be possible for North American Evangelicals to ignore their fellow Evangelicals in the Third World.

Evangelical Christians have been enthusiastic supporters of 'foreign missions' – devoting more than their share of money and energy and personnel to

THE ELECTRONIC CHURCH

QUENTIN J. SCHULTZE

During the late 1970s, a handful of enthusiastic American Evangelicals took to the television screens to revive the nation spiritually and morally. By 1980 they stood at the helms of multi-million dollar, non-denominational 'ministries', which promoted conservative political causes and hawked dispensational theologies with the marketing skill of Madison Avenue.

While religious broadcasting was nothing new in North America, the techniques, scope and message of the 'electronic church' detonated debate throughout the United States and Canada. The popular press, as well as some Christian writers and spokespersons, charged electronic preachers such as Jerry Falwell, Pat Robertson, and James Robison with

using the Bible to propagate conservative ideologies and build personal empires.

Falwell responded by forming the Moral Majority, an independent fund-raising and political organization. His weekly television programme, *The Old-Time Gospel Hour*, although officially separate from the Moral Majority, hammered away in sermonic style at liberal trends in America. By the mid-1980s, Falwell – not to mention the other electronic preachers – had appeared on hundreds of broadcast and cable television stations.

In spite of the publicity given to Falwell and company during the 1980 presidential election, it appears in retrospect that the political influence of the electronic church was vastly

overstated:
■ Only a few million Americans claimed to be regular viewers of even the top-rated religious broadcasts. Although the Canadian audiences of these shows were not measured, they were probably small in comparison with those of her southern neighbour.
■ Most viewers were active members of local churches, many of which stood opposed theologically and politically to the messages of the electronic church.
■ The TV preachers never truly represented the mainstream of American Evangelicalism. The average viewer was over fifty years of age, female, and a resident of the South or the Midwest Bible belt.

To a large extent, then, debate about the electronic church was itself

such efforts. These missionary activities have been successful in ways that not all North American Evangelicals had anticipated. Their efforts have resulted in the establishment of large Evangelical church bodies in the Third World. Those churches have produced, in turn, talented leaders who are often very critical of many of the cultural attitudes and theological preoccupations of their fellow-Christians in North America.

The leaders of North American Evangelicalism have become aware in recent years – through many means, including such international Evangelical gatherings as the 1966 World Congress on Evangelism in Berlin and the 1974 Lausanne Congress on World Evangelization – that

their Evangelical 'converts' have much to teach the community who evangelized them. These sensitivities are gradually trickling down to the Evangelical rank-and-file in the United States and Canada. For many white middle-class Evangelicals, these

Eskimo people in northern Canada often have a hard time adapting to North American culture and morality, which have hit them especially hard through oil exploration in the Arctic.

a media event. The broadcasters never really represented a major source of power and authority in the church in general or Evangelicalism in particular.

The new performers

Since 1980, a variety of broadcasters with entertaining styles and upbeat messages have been challenging the older broadcasters for dominance of the air-waves. These 'health and wealth' preachers, such as Jim Bakker, Kenneth Copeland, and Jimmy Swaggart are flamboyant neo-Pentecostals whose spontaneous preaching and personal flair suit well the visually oriented medium of television.

Although the political ramifications of their dispensational theology is frequently very clear, they stress the personal experience of the faith and downplay social and political

activism. If members of the old school of electronic preachers were skilful rhetoricians, the new school is composed of adroit performers.

An anomaly among the health and wealth preachers is Robert Schuller, who in the early 1980s had the highest-rated religious show on American television. His weekly *Hour of Power* broadcasts were videotaped at the Crystal Cathedral, an impressive, 10,500-window, rhomboid prism with eighty motorized doors that opened to reveal a drive-in lot for worshippers in automobiles. Schuller's 'possibility thinking' instructed viewers to reject negative thoughts and to 'grab hold of God's dream for you'.

The major question that remains unanswered is how the cultures of the world will respond to the kaleidoscope of American-bred Christianity found on television. Old-style faith healers such as Oral

Roberts, political preachers such as Falwell, and neo-Pentecostals such as Swaggart are beaming their messages via satellite throughout the world. Perhaps the most fundamental effect will result not from the confusing mixture of messages, but rather from the medium itself. This may well lead to the growth of an entertainment-oriented Christianity that emphasizes visual images and personal experience.

relationships present the only unavoidable challenges that they encounter to their otherwise comfortable ways of thinking about God and the world.

'Ecumenical' literally means 'in the household'. Evangelicals, along with other Christians in North America, are being forced to rethink their past attitudes about the nature of the 'household of faith'. When North American Christians, along with their European counterparts, begin to grasp the significance of the fact that they are quickly moving toward minority-group status in the world-wide Christian family – in terms of both numerical strength and spiritual influence – they will have consciously entered into a new ecumenical age. The present signs are that such an age is quickly approaching.

CHRIST AND NORTH AMERICAN CULTURE

Christians in the United States and Canada are struggling with questions about how they are to relate to their surrounding culture. And they are rethinking some of their past attitudes and postures in this area. There is no simple way of sorting out the complex tensions which Christians are experiencing today as they think about these things and argue with each other about cultural involvement. There are many different proposals and moods in the air, and there are a number of different questions being asked about the relationship between Christ and culture.

Some Christians are struggling with the question of how Christian commitment relates to cultural involvement as such. This struggle has been most pronounced in the Evangelical community, where there has been a remarkable – and much remarked on – change of attitude in recent years.

Evangelical Christianity is one important contemporary example of inherited pietism. Pietist groups of the past, including earlier generations of Evangelicals, often had a much richer understanding of Christian discipleship than is usually associated today with the 'Pietist' label. This is true, for example, of seventeenth-century German Pietism, where a strong emphasis was placed on the need to promote social renewal and to serve the needs of the poor. This emphasis was also to be found among the Pietists associated with early Wesleyanism, in England and North America.

But for the past 100 years or so North American Evangelicals have gravitated toward a version of Pietism which shows little or no concern for the broad patterns of social life. They have pursued the sort of 'personal relationship with the Lord' which shuns 'world' involvements. This posture was reinforced by the growing popularity among Evangelicals, from the 1880s onward, of an apocalyptic brand of theology, according to which Christians can expect an increase in social unrest and degradation until the time of the 'rapture' when the faithful believers will be rescued from the present world

'Gradually the church became so entrenched in wealth and prestige that it began to dilute the strong demands of the gospel and to conform to the ways of the world. And ever since the church has been a weak and ineffectual trumpet making uncertain sounds. If the church of Jesus Christ is to regain once more its power, message and authentic ring, it must conform only to the standards of the gospel.' Martin Luther King Jr

so that the prophetic countdown for the 'end times' can begin.

This other-worldly sort of Pietism has gone hand-in-hand with an anti-intellectual attitude. Thus Evangelical Pietists have not only distanced themselves from what they have viewed as an unhealthy reliance on programmes of social reform, but they have also denigrated the kind of Christian commitment in which scholarship and doctrinal precision are highly valued.

During the past several decades there have been attempts to reform Pietistic Evangelicalism from within on these points. Some would-be reformers have promoted a careful, biblically-grounded intellectual life. Others have urged social concerns. The 'neo-Evangelical' movement, which began in the 1940s, emphasized the need for a scholarly Evangelicalism that went beyond the maintenance of Bible institutes and the promotion of Bible study in the churches; neo-Evangelical leaders called for their constituencies to support energetic programmes of scholarship and higher education, so that Bible-believing Christians could make their mark on contemporary intellectual life. Almost incidentally they also called for a social involvement that would promote responsibility for North American political and economic institutions and policies.

In the early 1970s a more persistent form of Evangelical social activism emerged. A loose coalition of Evangelicals – who earned the title 'the young

Evangelicals' – began to insist on a more critical posture toward North American cultural life. Many of these activists had been energized by the civil rights and anti-war movements of the 1960s. Having sensed a legitimate set of concerns embodied in these movements, they were unsettled by the ease with which many of

See Racism, Justice and Civil Rights

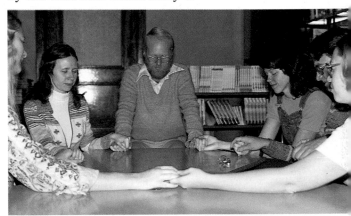

their fellow Evangelicals gave passive (and in some cases active) support to racial injustice at home and militaristic programmes abroad. These critics argued that the seemingly 'other-worldly' piety of previous Evangelical generations was in fact grounded in a tacit endorsement of the values of white middle-class Americanism. The youthful Evangelicals, and their older supporters, called for a biblically-directed 'radical discipleship' that would inevitably cut against the grain of 'the American Way of Life'.

Teachers at a school staffed by a Christian community in Detroit meet for prayer. But should prayers in state (public) schools formally involve the students? This is a fiercely contested question, touching the American philosophy of separating church and state.

MORAL MAJORITIES

But soon the American Way was to gain some very vocal Evangelical defenders. Much to almost everyone's surprise a new form of socially aggressive Fundamentalism has recently entered the public spotlight. This movement, led by the Moral Majority's Reverend Jerry Falwell and others, has been insisting that there is nothing intrinsically wrong with the American Way. Indeed, these Fundamentalist activists argue that the American value-system in its purest form constitutes the kind of 'righteousness that exalts a nation' – an American nation that lives up to its founding ideals, they contend, will be a God-fearing nation.

The way of national righteousness is being presently threatened, according to these Fundamentalist critics, not by an endorsement of traditional values by the middle class, but by the anti-Christian philosophy of 'secular humanism', which these activists see as gaining increasingly more leverage in public institutions, especially public educational institutions.

The leadership of the mainline churches has generally supported the kinds of social and political causes which Fundamentalists associate with 'secular humanism'. Liberal Protestants have worked out a mode of theological accommodation with evolutionary theory, for example, and they have endorsed many of the concerns of feminism and the so-called 'sexual revolution'. Significant tensions have begun to surface within the mainline churches over the issues of homosexual rights and the ordination of homosexual persons; organized opposition to

the 'leftist' bias of church leaders on many economic and political questions is also increasingly visible in the mainline denominations.

Evangelicalism and Fundamentalism as social movements are not so prominent in Canada as they are in the United States. For one thing, Canadians have not been attracted toward the sorts of 'God-and-country' themes which are central to the much-discussed 'civil religion' of the United States. For Canadians, the cultural agenda has been dominated by the struggles to develop a workable 'biculturalism' in which English-speaking and French-speaking people could operate with some sense of national unity. Nonetheless, some of the issues which have been debated in the mainline churches south of the border – feminism and homosexuality, for example – have also been matters of impassioned discussion in the Canadian churches.

CHRISTIAN CULTURAL IDENTITY

Not all Christians identify closely with the debates carried on by white Protestants, of both the mainline and Evangelical variety, over whose ideas shall have the position of influence in American culture. Black Christians, and other racial and minority groups, have often had to worry about the questions of basic cultural survival; they have not had the luxury of attempting to grab the cultural reigns. The civil rights movement of the 1950s and the martyrdom of Martin Luther King in 1968 raised public consciousness of racism, discrimination and the exploitation of blacks in America. The black churches combine a traditional Evangelical faith with a commitment to the fight for a better deal for blacks in American society.

Members of the Orthodox churches, too, regularly have difficulty taking sides in the arguments between traditionalist defenders of the 'holy-nation' idea and secularizing liberals. These arguments are, from the point of view of an Orthodox theology of culture, misconceived from the outset.

Strong cultural influence – the idea of Americanization – has also made its impact on North American Roman Catholics. Roman Catholic Quebec is a force to be reckoned with in assessing the patterns of Canadian power, and the large cities of the eastern United States have known the realities of Roman Catholic clout (the Boston Irish, for instance). Nonetheless, Roman Catholics have not always found it easy to identify wholeheartedly with the American cultural experience.

The rationale for 'the American experiment' was from the beginning heavily loaded with religious ideas. And neither of the two sources from which those ideas were drawn, Evangelical Puritanism and Enlightenment deism, was especially friendly toward Roman Catholicism. Long

THE NEW RIGHT

The Moral Majority movement, anxious about what it sees as pervasive secular humanism in public education, has established a network of Christian schools and also extended into the sphere of higher education. Strongly against abortion, family break-ups, violence on TV and homosexuality, the movement supported Ronald Reagan's right-wing policies in both his 1980 and 1984 presidential campaigns. Moral Majority is in favour of a strong military; it is fervently anti-communist, pro-Israel and wedded to the American Way. Its financial and numerical power-base has been built up partly through the nation-wide television ministry of some of its leaders.

A woman in New Orleans shares a picnic with a group of children. Many American Christians are deeply concerned over how to bring up their children. In particular, should they go to specifically Christian schools, or learn to work out their faith in a more mixed environment?

after anti-Catholicism ceased to be an official public ideology in North American life, it continued to lurk beneath the surface. Protestant America has always viewed Roman Catholicism with suspicion. For many Protestants, the authoritarian patterns of Catholicism, along with the aura of mystery until recently conveyed by the Catholic use of Latin as a vehicle for worship, has created the impression that sinister 'un-American' forces are at work in the Roman church.

The combination, in the early 1960s, of the election of a Roman Catholic president and the impact of the Second Vatican Council reforms dealt a serious blow to American anti-Catholicism. John F. Kennedy encountered much initial hostility because of his religious affiliation, but he was able to neutralize this factor by his own personal magnetism as a public figure – as well as by virtually promising the American people that he would not allow his Roman Catholicism to have any effect on his public career.

But neither the 'new' Roman Catholicism following the Second Vatican Council era nor the popular appeal of Kennedy-esque politicians has been able completely to put to rest the longstanding Protestant nervousness about Roman Catholicism as a cultural force. Many citizens of the United

States and Canada continue to suspect that there is an intrinsic tension, if not a fundamental incompatibility, between loyalty to Rome and a commitment to North American democratic ideals. These suspicions were openly aired during the 1984 national election campaign in the United States as prominent Roman Catholic politicians engaged in public debate with their bishops on the relationship between church teachings and public policy. It is unlikely that these controversies will disappear altogether in the near future. The discussion about how Roman Catholics and other Christians are to relate their faith to North American culture appears to be a permanent feature of the public dialogue.

BY WHAT STANDARD?

To rethink all these critical issues is not easy. Indeed, it is often a very painful process. It is not surprising, then, that in such times of re-examination Christian groups experience internal struggle and dissension.

It is a mistake to assume that all church controversies are grounded in theological disagreement. It is even a mistake to assume this when the debates are conducted in terms which are explicitly theological. Theological language is sometimes used to mask other motives and concerns. Very often the actual causes of controversy have much more to do with different personalities and conflicting styles of leadership than with genuine theological disagreements. Yet in the diverse debates that regularly stir up strong religious passions, it is often possible to discern a common topic of theological concern lurking not too far beneath the surface: the topic of **authority**.

The question of authority is certainly one of the factors which continues to separate the Eastern from the Western churches. The exercise of authority in the Orthodox churches in North America often strikes both Protestants and Roman Catholics as posing significant barriers to closer understanding and co-operation. The Orthodox, in turn, insist that when other Christians try to dismiss the styles and symbols of Orthodox authority as purely 'cultural' traps, they betray a deep-seated 'individualism' which does indeed constitute a significant threat to Christian unity.

See Authority

Perhaps the issues which presently divide Roman Catholics from Protestants are not as deep as those which divide the Orthodox from both – although some Christians on both sides of the divide would insist that the issues here are even deeper. It is clear, however, that there are many Roman Catholics who have come to adopt what is, for all practical purposes, a Protestant view of authority. On a practical level, many Protestants and Roman Catholics can work together with a strong sense of sharing a common outlook.

But the 'Protestantization' of significant portions of North American Catholicism does not really simplify the theological situation. Instead it often means that Roman Catholics are experiencing many of the same tensions which can be found within Protestantism in Canada and the United States.

And the Protestant situation is by no means a peaceful one. The Evangelicals continue to debate issues of biblical authority, not only with the Fundamentalists on their flank, but also from within, as many leaders in the new Evangelical coalition forged in the 1940s have recently waged a much-publicized 'battle for the Bible'.

See Does the Bible Speak Today?

A WORD FOR AMERICA

The questions about authority – whether addressed by Evangelical or liberal Protestants, or Roman Catholics, or Eastern Orthodox – may not always be discussed in the most helpful ways, but they are important questions which ought not too quickly to be laid to rest. North America is a continent which desperately needs the gospel. Not only are there millions of people in Canada and the United States who must be confronted with the claims of the gospel, but there are large and powerful institutions which need to be harnessed for the work of justice, peace and righteousness. These require a broad-ranging ministry on the part of Christians. For all their numerical strength, they will not be properly equipped for this task unless they have heard, and have been empowered to speak, a word from the Lord.

WOMEN AS MINISTERS

Women have had vital ministries in the church since New Testament days. But increasingly today the question is asked, should women be ordained to positions of leadership in the church's ministry, on equal footing with men? The Roman Catholics and the Orthodox still say a firm no. But many Protestant churches have practised it for some time, and others are deeply divided. Anglicans in the United States, for example, and Lutherans in Sweden have minorities strongly opposed to the policy of women's ordination which has come in.

Arguments used against it include that Jesus chose only male apostles, and that some of Paul's letters forbid women to teach. But others point out that some of the greatest missionaries are women, and that it seems wrong to bar from the full exercise of ministry anyone God has plainly gifted for it.

It is appropriate, then, that Christians continue to work out together how they can best hear a sure word from the Lord, and how they can effectively appropriate that message in their own lives – individual and communal – and propagate it in the larger society in which they live. These questions ought to be at the top of the agenda in discussions among Christians who are seeking to bring a message of redemption to North America.

United States society manages to be both highly religious and highly secular at the same time. This can make for great tensions and sometimes contradictory attitudes.

PART THREE
Faith, Thought and Action

3.1 THINKING THROUGH THE FAITH

The Gospel in Today's World

N.T. WRIGHT

The word 'gospel' literally means 'good news', and that is exactly how the earliest Christians thought of it. The Christian gospel is a message about certain world-changing events, and carries with it a summons to the world to take stock of itself as a result. There are many different ways of expressing this message. There have to be, for people today differ considerably from those of previous ages, and cultures differ too. We all need to hear the news in a way that we can understand. But the news itself is very simple.

NEWS ABOUT JESUS OF NAZARETH

He stands at the centre. Born to a Jewish mother around the year now called 4 BC, brought up in Galilee in northern Palestine, Jesus began to teach and preach around the age of thirty. Three features stand out in his ministry:

● **he repeatedly announced that God's reign was beginning;**
● **he demonstrated this as he healed all sorts of diseases;**
● **and he invited men, women and children of all sorts** – but especially those low down in society – **to follow him** and so to become part of the new work God was doing in the world.

Jesus incurred the displeasure of the Jewish authorities. After a trial on an apparently religious charge, he was put to death by the occupying Roman forces in the most brutal and unpleasant way known to the ancient world – crucifixion, a punishment normally reserved for outlaws or the organizers of armed revolt.

But everything we know about Jesus suggests that he was neither of those things. His aims were more far-reaching in their implications. He warned Israel that her constant and stubborn resistance was bound to bring down the wrath of Rome sooner or later. And he shocked his contemporaries by suggesting that when this event happened it should be seen as working out the wrath of God.

It is in this light that we can begin to make sense of the strange fact that Jesus appears not only to have foreseen his own death but to have invested it

Present-day secularity leaves many people's humanity unfulfilled. So increasing numbers of people are on a spiritual quest. What answers are there for them in the gospel of Jesus?

with a particular meaning and significance. He would die at the hands of the Romans: that is, he would drink the cup of the wrath of God – so that his people would not have to drink it. He would thus, by his death, complete what he had been acting out all his life whenever he welcomed sinners to eat with him or touched those who were unclean and brought them healing. **He would take their blame on himself and, astonishingly, exhaust and get rid of it. He would thereby create in and around himself a new family, a new people of God**. It is as though God's purposes for the world, having been focussed on the nation of Israel, were now to have that focus narrowed to one individual, Israel's representative. On his life

HAS FAITH A LANGUAGE?
ANTHONY C. THISELTON

All the world's major languages have received an influx of new words in recent years. Many of these are from the worlds of science and technology. Are these new words pushing out the language which was once thought appropriate to express religious ideas? Or can Christians still talk intelligibly about their faith? The problem of religious language is not chiefly a problem about individual words. Jesus did not use some uniquely religious stock of words to preach the gospel. He took ordinary words and put them to special uses.

Faith uses ordinary language

Jesus spoke of God and of other spiritual realities by using everyday language. He talked about farming, business deals, children's games, housekeeping, sweeping and cooking. But his hearers understood that these stories, told about everyday things, also pointed beyond themselves. They carried with them an extended meaning which concerned faith and response to God.

Analogies, symbols and metaphors are readily understood in everyday life to point beyond themselves. The principle is not peculiar to religion. Jesus preached the kingdom (the active reign of God as king) because there is an analogy between God's sovereignty and that of an ideal righteous king in the thought of ancient Israel. He invited trust in God as Father because another analogy exists between God's loving care and concern for his children and the very best kind of love shown by the very best of human fathers.

Analogies are never perfect. They remain, at best, pointers. So the language of faith usually includes warning signals about the need not to

and death hung the fate not of Israel only, but of the whole world.

The little band of Jesus' followers, who had been shattered by his death, were as surprised as anyone when the first reports came to them three days later that he had been seen alive. When the evidence of their senses had confirmed the reports, however, they realized that this event fulfilled and vindicated all that Jesus had been doing and saying. God had indeed established his kingdom through Jesus, and in doing so had given the answer to that fear of death which recurs in different ways in every age. He had made a way through death to a life beyond it, a way which all those who belonged to Jesus would now be able to travel.

press them. God is not simply Father; he is heavenly Father. Christ is not only light, vine, shepherd, bread; he is the light of the world, the true vine, the good shepherd, the bread of life. Often these warning signals are negative ones: a heavenly Father is a non-earthly Father. They are there to cancel out unwanted or unintended aspects of the analogy. Analogies which also become symbols appeal to the deeper levels of our personality than the purely intellectual. The bread of life answers to our deepest longings for nourishment, renewal and satisfaction. But bread and life remain ordinary words, put to a special use.

Faith uses language backed by action

Jesus Christ is not only God's Word, he is the word made flesh. God speaks through Christ in both word and deed. The gospel is lived as well as told. Jesus spoke with authority not only because he is this Word, but also because his own words had the consistent backing of his life. Words can be like paper currency. They are easy enough to produce. But they become valuable and effective only if they can be backed by the resources of action.

Jesus provided such backing. He did not simply tell the social and religious outcasts of the time that God loved them; he shared their table with them. He did not only speak about humility, he took water and an apron and performed the most menial of tasks. The crowning deed, in which the whole of his words and deeds are summed up, is his suffering and death by crucifixion and the event of the resurrection. Deeds need words, for without the word the deed might be misunderstood. Words need deeds, for without the deed the word might not be credible.

Today, and over the centuries, the credibility and power of the language of faith has been threatened less by the limitations of language than by the absence of its visible backing. We cannot talk credibly about God's forgiveness while our lives are crippled by guilt. We cannot speak authoritatively about God's mercy if we withhold it from others, or about the work of God's Spirit if we cannot be changed.

Faith uses shared language

If the language of faith uses ordinary words, Christians should not use the language of the cultural or religious ghetto. The language of faith should not be based on concerns and interests which belong solely to the believing community. For God is God of the world, and not only of the church. Besides, Jesus did not use language in this exclusive way.

Language is the main way in which human beings share their experiences and learn from the past. Because of speech and writing, no person need begin life without knowing the lessons learned from the collective past of human experience. For Christians this means entry through language into the varied experiences of people of faith in all times and places. And especially it opens up the whole world of faith mapped out in the Bible.

This in itself creates community. For the Christian reader experiences a sense of identity and solidarity with his or her fellow-believers in the pages of the Bible. He or she comes to think of the Bible as the family book. And if the outsider feels somehow that he or she is on the outside, this very experience can become one of invitation to enter and to enjoy the shared reality. Interpretation may be needed where once-ordinary words are no longer ordinary. But the language of faith does more than merely inform. It invites, it testifies, promises, warns, heals, and even creates understanding. It carries the hearer or reader beyond his or her own individual horizons, expanding them to embrace the shared gospel of Christ.

The news about Jesus, then, was and is that in him God's age-old purposes of salvation have been realized. And the cutting-edge of the message was, and is, that the news about Jesus is news about God himself.

NEWS ABOUT GOD

There were many different views about God, or the gods, in the ancient world. And there are as many today – not only among the major religions and the tribal religions of the world, but also in the popular folk religions of the West, and in the diverse cults and new-age movements we see around us. Against this background Christians claim that in Jesus the truth about God is revealed. And because human beings are very good at

GOSPEL AND CULTURE
CHARLES KRAFT

Culture is that set of guidelines, followed largely unconsciously and habitually in the living of life, which structure and pattern all that we think, speak and do. Gospel is that transforming good news from God which Jesus came into human culture to live and to proclaim. The gospel comes from God, so cannot be bound to a single culture. Yet both in Jesus' lifetime and today, the eternal, transcultural gospel has to be expressed in temporal, local cultural terms.

We all exist within culture much as fish exist in water. Totally immersed in it from soon after conception until death, human beings cannot live outside of culture or think except in cultural categories. So if God is to reach us at all, it has to be within the cultural 'water' in which we live.

God comes where we are

Ever since the days of Adam, God has been approaching people in ways that they can understand from within their own cultures. And he accepts their response to himself via forms appropriate to their own tradition.

In Jesus Christ, God became a human being within a particular human culture, conducting his ministry in the language and culture of those among whom he lived. The good news was both lived out and expressed in human cultural terms.

The original culture of the gospel was that of the Aramaic-speaking peoples of first-century Palestine. But the early Christians soon took it to other parts of the Greco-Roman Empire. In doing so, they adapted and translated the message into the cultural forms first of Greek-speaking Hebrews and then of Greek-speaking Gentiles. Nowadays we have a name for this process of adapting: we call it 'contextualization'.

Contextualization means the reformulation of the Christian message within another language and culture in such a way that essentially the same meanings are conveyed in the new culture as in the original one. The new culture's vocabulary is used, along with its organization and other cultural forms, to the extent that no substantial change in the message occurs. In this way the message comes home to the receivers intelligibly and relevantly: Christianity becomes genuinely theirs.

The early Christians followed Jesus' and Paul's example by adopting from the surrounding cultures words such as 'church', 'mystery', 'author and finisher of the faith', and rituals such as baptism and the Lord's Supper. Contemporary Christians today can therefore seek to use the cultural forms of the surrounding society in their life and worship.

The gospel, however, not only uses cultural forms, it also judges all of the human meanings and motivations channelled through them. When, therefore, a cultural form is used to convey a meaning that is opposed to the gospel, it must be rejected, unless with the passage of time the meaning changes.

Whose gospel is it?

One great danger is that as the gospel is taken from culture to culture, or passed from generation to generation, the group in power tends to impose its cultural forms on those who receive, as if the forms of the more powerful groups were endorsed by God. When this happens, the original meanings, far from being preserved, are automatically changed. The biblical approach was quite different. There we see older forms continually adjusted and replaced in order to

imagining God other than he really is, the truth about God is always surprising.

This truth came with different emphasis depending on the background of its hearers:
● Christianity gladly reaffirmed the basic belief of Judaism, that there was one God, the creator of the whole world. But whereas Judaism believed that the physical nation of Israel was the people of God, **Christianity affirmed that this people consisted of anyone at all who believed in Jesus and followed him**.
● **To non-Jews**, by contrast, Christianity presented a different sort of challenge: **it insisted that the creator God was the God of Israel who had now made himself known in Jesus** as the saviour of the whole world.

assure that the meanings would be correct. Those who stood against this reclothing of the gospel and tried to preserve the previous forms were regarded as heretics.

This was the problem lying behind the Council of Jerusalem recorded in the Acts of the Apostles. The early Jewish Christians took advantage of their position as those in charge of the gospel to insist that Gentiles, as a part of their faith-response to Christ, had to adopt Hebrew culture (including circumcision to signal their new cultural allegiance). As Paul pointed out, however, God did not obey this rule, since he gave his Holy Spirit to converted Gentiles on the basis of faith alone. Contemporary cross-cultural witnesses, though, have often sided against God's approach in this area by requiring converts to adopt large portions of the sending culture in order to be validated as truly Christian. This practice has regularly resulted in serious distortion of the message.

It is by no means easy, however, to know how much of the receiving culture can be put to use without adversely affecting the meaning of the gospel. Can God accept (even temporarily) practices such as polygamy and common-law marriage, as he seems to have in the Old Testament? Is it right to use indigenous terms for God within Christianity (as happens in the Bible), in spite of the fact that they seem inadequate to convey biblical meanings? Should local music and dancing be used in Christian worship? Is it right to require an ability to read as a precondition of church membership?

Many of the knottier problems are raised by the fact that the concepts of one culture never exactly correspond to the concepts of another. But experience has proved that it is seldom advisable to attempt to dodge such problems by simply borrowing terms and practices from the sending culture. That usually brings just that blurring of the gospel that those who advocate it are trying to avoid.

Far safer to imitate Paul the apostle. He made careful use of the cultural forms of the receiving culture, while at the same time developing a strong Christian community. By continually using those forms for Christian purposes, that community brought about changes in their meaning so that they became more adequate to serve the Christian cause.

Thus in recent times, 'Allah', 'Ndjambie' and many other indigenous terms for God have become for many Christians quite adequate to convey biblical meanings. 'Allah', of course, is the Arabic word for God, widely used by Muslims. 'Ndjambie' traditionally referred to a cosmic creator spider in the mythology of the Bulu, Kaka and neighbouring peoples of southern Cameroon.

In a similar way, non-Western churches throughout the world are transforming through the Christian message the meanings expressed in traditional forms of leadership, music and dance, drama, rituals, communication patterns, organizational structures and many other areas. In doing this they show that the gospel is able to take the best of human culture and transform it.

A North American Indian girl performs a dance depicting the Bible's creation story.

Pagan idolatry was confronted with the cross and resurrection as the full revelation of the one, true God. To Jew and Gentile alike, therefore, the news about Jesus came as a summons to see God, the world and themselves in a new way.

Without abandoning their Jewish monotheism, the earliest Christians realized that Jesus had accomplished a task which, according to the Jewish scriptures, was reserved for God himself. This meant that he was to be understood, *and therefore worshipped*, as himself fully divine.

To look at Jesus is therefore to see God and to realize what he is like. As Jesus welcomed sinners and outcasts, we see displayed the astonishing kindness and gentleness of God. As Jesus denounced hypocrisy and exploitation, we can recognize the justice of God. Jesus' death and resurrection show God at work, saving human beings from their own plight at his own expense. In short, the early Christians realized with delight and astonishment a truth which, though known to Judaism, had until now been grasped only dimly: that God is love.

NEWS ABOUT THE WORLD

The message about Jesus is good news for individual human beings, but it is not to be reduced to those terms alone. It is a message for and about the whole world. The gospel reaffirms, in the face of the horror and misery of evil, corruption and death, the truth that the world is God's world: he made it, he loves it and he is recreating it.

This is seen most clearly in the life of Jesus, who was able with a word to effect dramatic healing and even to control natural phenomena. He is the rightful sovereign of the world. This is what he meant when he repeatedly spoke of the kingdom of God: God is, in Jesus, restoring to the world his wise and loving rule.

It is not God's intention that the world should drift on for ever, sometimes better, sometimes worse. He plans to wind up history by sending Jesus once more, this time revealed for all to see as the Lord of the world. This belief gives depth to the Christian claim that Jesus is Lord and that in him God's purposes for his world are being realized. This claim offers an alternative to the sense of hopelessness so widespread today.

As a result, Christians have news for the world, which will be perceived as good or bad news according to who is listening. The world is God's world, and is neither the toy, the tool nor the ashtray of the human race. It belongs to a God of justice, who hates oppression and violence and will one day act to set his world to rights. He is the God of love: his authority, exercised through the power of love, stands in sharp contrast to the pattern of authority usually wielded by those who have power in this world. Whether or not people acknowledge him as Lord, he remains so none the less.

Because it is his world, people will become more fully and truly human insofar as their lives and their societies are ordered according to his design. Whenever and by whatever means human beings are given dignity and purpose, he is honoured.

God's people must not lose their grip on this good news about Jesus, God and the world. On the contrary, they must announce it and live according to it. But the gospel is not a mere impersonal programme. It is a message also of God's love and concern for individual people.

NEWS ABOUT PEOPLE

The news about Jesus not only reaffirms the Jewish belief that the world is God's world. It also re-emphasizes two other Old Testament beliefs:

● **Human beings are made in God's image**. The gospel has no place for modern cynicism about human nature. Being human is essentially a good thing. But, as everybody realizes, humanity is not what it should be. From the horrors of war to the pains of petty personal selfishness, evidence abounds that all is not well. The good news is that God, faced with this distortion of his intentions in making people, has not given up. He has devised a solution. He will still have a people worthy of himself – not by making a new race from scratch, but by making the old race new.

● With this as his object, God has fulfilled another ancient promise. He will not be a distant God, removed from the life and

GOSPEL TRUTH

In England in 1984 David Jenkins was appointed Bishop of Durham. In a TV interview he said he doubted whether the stories of Jesus' virgin birth and resurrection are literally true. The public debate that followed centred on his right to say this openly. But Clifford Longley, religious correspondent of *The Times*, London, redirected attention towards whether his 'theological reinterpretations' were in fact justified.

If the resurrection accounts are untrue, for example, 'it is dishonest to describe them as myth or allegory: the story is preposterous, and countless generations who have taken it as a more or less fair account of the events in question were utterly deceived...It must be a mark of the immense faith of modern theologians that they can believe in the essential truth of a religion whose earliest followers, and the writers of its foundation documents, were such liars.'

suffering of his people. As he lived among human beings in the person of Jesus of Nazareth, so now **he lives among and within his people in the person of his Spirit**. The Holy Spirit is the Spirit of Jesus, working within individuals and in the community of his people. He works to re-create them according to the perfect image of God. This work of God begins at an identifiable time for many people as they find themselves drawn to believe in Jesus and trust themselves to him. Whether or not this is so the process of re-creation is almost always long and painful. It involves the remaking of one's entire life: not automatically (God wants to re-create people, not puppets) but with one's own consent. The fatalism so

TRANSLATING THE BIBLE
PAUL ELLINGWORTH

The Bible is not only the world's long-term bestseller; it is also the most translated book. In 1983, out of an estimated 4,500 languages in the world, at least one book of the Bible had been translated into 1,785, the New Testament into 572, and the whole Bible into 283. At the same date, at least 764 translation projects were in progress, 549 of them in languages into which some part of the Bible was being translated for the first time. Most of these are in Africa, Asia and the Pacific.

Today, largely through the new science of linguistics, more is understood about how language works and how people communicate. Modern Bible translators have learnt a lot from this, but have also helped, in their world-wide work, to develop and test linguistic theories.

A fundamental principle of modern Bible translation is that meaning must have priority over grammatical form. To be faithful to the meaning, you often have to change the grammatical form of the original Hebrew or Greek. Take, for example, such words as 'repentance' or 'justification'. These are really about someone doing something, so it is best to translate them by verbs rather than by abstract nouns.

Finding out the meaning
What does the text of the Bible mean? Translators meet various problems in trying to find out:

■ **The text itself may not be certain**. Manuscripts often differ from one another. The evidence must be carefully assessed before translation can begin. Fortunately, we have several thousand New Testament manuscripts - much more evidence than for any other ancient document.

In the Old Testament the difficulties are greater, but new evidence such as that of the Dead Sea Scrolls has often tended to increase our confidence that the text that has been handed down to us accurately represents what was first written.

■ **We may not be sure what individual words mean**, especially very rare words - such as the one translated 'daily' in 'give us this day our daily bread'. There are many such words in the Old Testament. In cases of doubt, we need to collect all possible background knowledge, including evidence from related languages such as Arabic.

■ **The modern reader may not know facts which were common knowledge** at the time the biblical books were written. What were 'phylacteries', for instance, as mentioned by Matthew? The Good News Bible gives the answer in its translation - 'straps with verses on them which they wear on their forehead and arms'! But it may be better to add a footnote. And occasionally we have to admit we do not know.

In addition to all this, there are things in the Bible which may have no counterpart in the culture and experience of the people for whom the translation is being made. What does 'white as snow' mean to a tropical African? This is not very hard to overcome: the name for some other white object can be used. The problem is more serious with common and important items in the Bible, such as sheep or bread. Here, we may need to adapt and explain a foreign word.

All this can be summed up by saying that although Bible translation is more difficult and complicated now

than it used to be, modern translators have the resources which can make their translations more exact, more faithful to the meaning of the text, than ever before.

Who is the reader?
Translators have to decide, in consultation with publishers and others, for whom their translation is intended. This decision will affect at what level the translation is pitched. In small language communities the decision may be easy, since there are no great differences between one person's way of speaking and another's. But in large language communities, such as the English-speaking world, there are wide variations. In such situations priority is usually given to translations in common language, that is, translations which will be understood by almost all native speakers. Translations of parts of the Bible are also made for special groups, such as new readers and children.

Translating the Bible is part of a single, continuing process which began when the Bible was first written down. This process continues as translators try to find out exactly what the text meant, and ends as believers find out what it means today. Bible translators often use secular methods which can in principle be applied to any book, because the Bible was originally written in ordinary human language. But Christians believe that the Holy Spirit, who inspired the writing of the Bible, is also at work in the whole process of translation.

prevalent today is not justified. God can change us. Re-creation, though sometimes apparently slow, does happen.

God has designed this re-creation to happen within the family of his people. It is as Christians meet together – to worship and to read and be taught from the Bible, to encourage and exhort one another – that faith can be strengthened, hope nourished and love built. Often God will use one person as the means of speaking his message to someone else. Often he will use the central Christian action, the breaking of bread and drinking of wine in memory of Jesus, to bring home to individuals, in a deeply personal way, his love for them revealed in Jesus' death.

● At the heart of the news about people is a crucial fact. **When we entrust ourselves to Jesus as Lord, from that moment on we are welcomed and accepted by God**. This fact is known as 'justification by faith'. It makes new for each successive generation the welcome which

Jesus offered during his earthly life to people of whatever moral or racial background. Despite the widespread opinion to the contrary, we do not have to earn our acceptance with God. To know God, and be known by him, we do not need first to attain perfection of life, a high degree of mystical consciousness, a sophisticated level of theological understanding. Nor do we need to be born a member of a particular family or race. We merely need to entrust ourselves – past, present and future – to Jesus in an act of personal repentance, faith and commitment, and to become outwardly a member of his family by being baptized.

Human life is not without purpose or dignity: God intends it to have both. In Jesus and by his Spirit he offers the means for both to become realities. God loved the world so much that he gave his own Son, so that anyone who believes in him should not be lost, but should have true and eternal life.

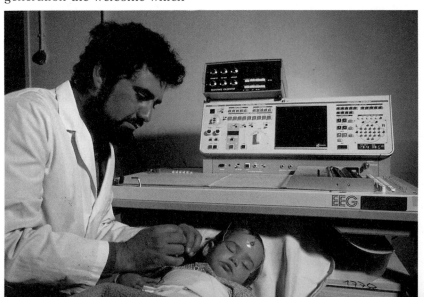

For good or ill, science penetrates most parts of our lives, and this researcher investigates a child's dreams. Against this background the mystery of the gospel can be hard to convey, because people are used only to things that can be quantified.

Theology Today
GEORGE CAREY

To the average person, current theology can often appear a complex and confusing mishmash of ideas and speculations. Much of it cannot be understood, and those parts that can still seem to be miles away from the straightforward message of the gospel. It must be freely admitted that this impression is largely true. Although the trends in theology all grow from the same root in Christ, their interpretation of the significance of the Christian message results in often contradictory conclusions.

What are the main issues in contemporary theology? Five broad areas, each of which contains diverse thinking, indicate the direction theology today is taking.

Theology must interpret Christian faith in a way that is comprehensible within a secular society. But how far should theologians themselves adopt secular perspectives?

SECULAR THEOLOGIANS
In a theological sense the word 'secular' means a way of looking at life without reference to God or spiritual values. Secular theologians are those who consider it their task to reinterpret Christianity in the light of current thought.

Although it would not be just to call Dietrich Bonhoeffer a secular theologian, there is little question that he helped to shape secular theology. His *Letters and Papers from Prison* reveal some attempts to grapple with the rejection of God in secularism. Cryptic statements from his letters have provided later thinkers with the language of secular theology: 'Man has come of age'; 'religionless Christianity'.

Bishop John Robinson drew inspiration from Bonhoeffer, although he also drew from Rudolph Bultmann, who rejected the supernatural, and Paul Tillich, who interpreted Christianity in terms of culture. Robinson's *Honest to God* (1961) drastically stripped Christianity to make it more appealing to modern people. God's transcendence was rejected – he is the 'ground of our being', and not 'out there'. Jesus as God incarnate was rejected – he was the 'Man for others' who allowed himself to be

pushed out of the world and on to the cross.

In the mid-1960s and early 1970s secular theology became associated with the 'death of God' theology. This trend stated that God as we know him is dead. We must accept the secular world as substitute for God. Harvey Cox, in his book *The Secular City*, saw the city as the place of God's abode; we are bidden consequently to reject all opposition between the human and divine, or sacred and secular.

The desire of secular theology to render Christianity intelligible to modern people is a good one, but quite clearly, secular theology has 'tossed the baby out with the bathwater'. It has emptied the faith of its meaning and, ironically, its relevance. Its optimism reflected a particular generation's confidence in human power to control the environment and create a new world. However, the optimism of the 1960s was followed by the pessimism of the 1970s, and as a result secular theologies faded in significance. This theological movement is an excellent illustration of the saying: 'He who marries the spirit of the age will soon be a widower.'

PROCESS THEOLOGY

This theological movement believes that just as the world is in constant change and flux, so is God himself. Alfred North Whitehead was its first architect, but later process theologians include Charles Hartshorne and Norman Pittenger. According to their understanding of the universe, we cannot talk of permanence: 'What is real is the transition of things, the passage of one to another.' The nature of being is that it is potential for every 'becoming'.

See The Secular Outlook of Today

THREE GERMAN THEOLOGIANS

For many years Germany has been a centre of radical thinking about Christian faith.

Jürgen Moltmann has written three influential books. *Theology of Hope* (1965) lays emphasis on Jesus' resurrection as the basis of hope for the future – not an otherworldly future but one in which God transforms the world into his kingdom. *The Crucified God* (1972) interprets the death of Jesus as showing God in his love identifying with godless, god-forsaken people, drawing close even to the most hopeless. In *The Church in the Power of the Spirit* (1975) Moltmann explores how these ideas indicate what the Christian mission should be – involved in people's struggle for liberation.

Wolfhart Pannenberg argues the case for Christian faith's credibility in a society where many no longer believe it. Using the methods of critical historical study, he defends the idea that God has revealed himself in history. Pannenberg believes that Jesus' resurrection is a fact that can be historically demonstrated. In his book *Jesus – God and Man* (1964) he claims that historical study can justify Christian faith in Jesus' divinity.

Hans Küng is the best-known Roman Catholic theologian. He has challenged belief in the infallibility both of the pope and of the Bible, and is now no longer authorized to teach as a Catholic theologian. In his book *On Being a Christian* (1974), he puts forward the thesis that only by being a Christian can people be truly human. He is keen to make use of the best in modern thinking, but equally prepared to expose secular ideas to pungent criticism where he finds them inadequate. Criticism should not be one way: humanism's record has not been conspicuously more successful than Christianity's.

Dr Karl Rahner was one of the most prolific Roman Catholic theologians. He has examined the effect on Christianity of a world in which the major religions must live side by side.

See Hope in a Despairing World; Liberation Theology

From this assumption, the bipolar nature of God is deduced – he has an eternal (potential) pole and a temporal (actual) pole. The first pole stands for God's oneness with all creation in what it can become. God is like a backstage director who organizes the cast ready for their appearance on the stage of the temporal world. The second pole means that God is involved in and responds to a changing world. He becomes part of the cast, on stage.

Although process theology is praiseworthy for its stress upon God as here-and-now, it represents a drastic revision of the Christian faith. It recasts God as one who is changing; Christ is seen as the final expression of God's involvement in the world in a symbolic sense only; sin and evil are seen as inevitable and indeed hopeful aspects of progress.

THEOLOGY OF HOPE

The theology of hope looks at faith from the future rather than from the past or present. Ironically, it was a Communist, Ernst Bloch, who helped to make this idea fashionable. Working from Marxist views of the future, Bloch measured the value of life not by what has gone before, but by what is to come. The past has no fixed or abiding value – what matters is the future 'breaking into' the present.

Jürgen Moltmann, who published *The Theology of Hope* (1965), acknowledges his debt to Bloch. According to Moltmann, God is the God who promises –

that is to say, he works towards future goals which are already breaking in upon our history. Thus the resurrection of Jesus is not merely a past event but the beginning of God's saving acts at the end of time. It is God's future, projected backwards into time, which gives history its meaning. The true nature of any event, including the resurrection, can only be made clear at the end of time. Moltmann believes that the church has an important role in the salvation of the world. It is the vanguard of a new humanity – a sign of hope.

Wolfhart Pannenberg is another prominent German thinker who takes up the concept of the future, although it is for him crystallized in history. All history is the stage on which God works and reveals himself. Pannenberg rigorously works this out with regard to the meaning of Jesus. Jesus gives mankind a glimpse of the new humanity to come in God. His resurrection is a foretaste of the future. As such, it stands outside history. For Pannenberg, historical research must be taken seriously as there can be no meaningful faith without knowledge. The theology of hope is not confined to Protestant theologians: J. Metz's incarnational view of history represents a Roman Catholic approach to the subject.

While such theologies of hope are stirring and visionary expressions of faith and proper reminders of the importance of the future, their common weakness is the loss of an assured present. Because there is not one unique and divinely controlled strand in history in which God's redemptive purposes are clearly revealed, there can be no absolute guarantees. As revelation is constantly unfolding itself in history, only the end is decisive. If a theology of hope, then, is to avoid drifting into pious optimism, it must be firmly based in history and in Christ who is 'the same yesterday, today and for ever'.

THEOLOGY OF LIBERATION

Although liberation theology originated in South America, we must be careful not to restrict its impact to that region. In essence it is a critical reflection on the world in which the church finds itself. It seeks to work out where the gospel is in the struggle against inequality, oppression and poverty. It sees theology as something active which changes structures and people, and not simply as a theoretical discipline. In this sense it is antagonistic towards European academic theology.

Liberation theology has been influenced by Marxism as well as by Moltmann's concept of hope. It has been justifiably described as 'riding on Marx's shoulders'. This does not mean a naive and uncritical acceptance of Marxism. The vast majority of liberation theologians work from a passionate commitment to Jesus Christ and his gospel.

Camillo Torres, who died in battle in 1966, was one of the

WHAT IS THEOLOGY FOR?

IS IT FOR STUDY?
Some theologians, particularly in Western universities, see their work primarily as an academic-discipline—to put texts under the microscope, to compare the Bible with other ancient writings, to take great care over the precise way Christian statements are expressed. The concern is for accuracy: to make sure everything is meaningful, self-consistent and supported by evidence.

IS IT FOR ACTION?
Particularly in the Third World, some theologians are impatient with study that stops short of practical involvement. The reason for studying the Bible, as they see it, is to see the ever-present poverty and oppression through God's eyes, and to find his way of deliverance.

first Roman Catholic priests to identify with the struggle against oppression, joining a revolutionary guerilla movement. His violent death ensured his place as the 'patron saint' of the movement. However, it is the Peruvian Roman Catholic, Gustavo Gutierrez, who is recognized as the spokesman for the movement. His book, *A Theology of Liberation* (1971), has given liberation theology its most coherent and comprehensive expression. A new way of doing theology is required, argues Gutierrez. Theology, rightly understood, does not require any kind of activity, but a specific participation on the side of the poor in the struggle between classes to bring about a more just society.

DOING THEOLOGY
ANDREW KIRK

The popular idea of theology is of a subject studied by those preparing for full-time Christian ministry. Yet during the fourth century ordinary Christians debated Christ's two natures in the marketplace. And today people living in shanty towns in the Third World are discovering that the Bible speaks to their situation. In each example, theology is done.

People will define theology according to their perspective. Someone teaching theology in a university will claim that theology is the disciplined study of ancient and modern texts. Someone answering an exam question may say it is an orderly study of belief in God. Liberation theologians in Latin America will say that it is a critical reflection on the church's activity in the light of God's Word. Poor slum-dwellers may see it as applying the gospel to their reality.

Ways of doing theology
The variety of descriptions does not imply confusion, for no one definition is adequate. Christians have always done theology in different ways. Its association with academic institutions is a recent development.

Doing theology means applying one's mind to the implications of Christian faith. Much of the Bible contains theological reflection. It records God's activity in the lives of individuals, communities and nations. It also interprets what God was doing. *Christ died* states a fact; *Christ died for the sins of the world* gives a special meaning to his death. *He was crucified* tells something more about the fact; *our old self was crucified with him* means that the crucifixion is relevant to people's personal lives.

The biblical authors explain the 'mighty acts of God'. Committed to the truth of what they say, they try to convince others that God is real and can be known. For 1,800 years theology was done within the believing community, and in a society that accepted the Christian view of life, theology was considered 'the queen of sciences'.

Nevertheless, theology has always been influenced from outside:
■ **Augustine's** *City of God* attempted to establish a proper relationship between church and state, following the state's official recognition of Christianity.
■ **Aquinas** allowed ancient Greek philosophers, newly rediscovered, to shape his theological reflection.
■ **Luther** reacted against the ethical achievements of human beings (humanism) being made the focal point of religion.

During the eighteenth century a profound shift occurred. Theological thinking in Protestant circles adopted a critical, historical approach to knowledge characteristic of other academic disciplines. It would not allow the church's faith to determine what results could be obtained from research. The critical approach has tended to conflict with orthodox faith, and in some cases has led to highly sceptical conclusions.

Removing theology from church control, however, has positive advantages as well. Church leaders may have vested interests in upholding certain beliefs and practices. Independence allows people to ask awkward questions, which can be healthy for the church. But modern theology's strength is also its greatest weakness. The academic fraternity, obsessed with freedom, tends to equate it with a rigorous critique of almost everything Christians have ever believed. Modern theologians have often fallen into the trap of treating their criticism as if it were an objective approach to faith and practice.

The pretended neutral approach to

The flavour and thought of liberation theologians can be caught in some of their striking ideas:

● Theology is not merely at the service of action, rather action itself is theology.

● The exodus is seen as the expression of the God who fights against political oppression.

● Traditional Christian theology has often been in bondage to cultural and social factors which have severely limited its revolutionary message.

● To confront and denounce political oppression is an act of love; to fight against injustice is to side with Jesus.

The ideas of liberation theology have been transported to other countries and cultures. A case in point is black theology. Martin Luther King's impressive

Christians learn about their belief for more important reasons than intellectual curiosity. They want such understanding to equip them to be agents of change in their society.

theology betrays weaknesses. Much reconstruction of the biblical text is based on speculation, rather than hard evidence. Scholars are used to dealing with ideas and may easily mistake conjectures for established facts. More importantly, the critical approach to theology has uncritically ignored the assumptions on which it is often based. Many of the 'assured results' of scholarship spring from a non-supernatural view of the universe. The wedge which Bultmann and others have driven between faith and history arises from their acceptance of certain aspects of existentialist philosophy.

Today it is recognized that every scholar reflects his cultural and intellectual context, and that knowledge is never free of bias. Doubt and scepticism, therefore, are as culturally conditioned as faith may be.

Theology's specific task

Those teaching theology are gradually realizing that beliefs already determine theological research and discussion. In the Third World this fact is recognized as a virtue because:

■ **The truth which theology discusses is not a theory but has practical implications** (theology as 'praxis'). The biblical text is not an interesting piece of information to be studied for its own sake; it confronts us with practical demands requiring a personal decision. Theology's purpose, therefore, is to help Christians to be transforming agents in society, not to arrive at theoretical conclusions about abstract principles.

■ **Theology must address itself to the main concerns of the context in which it is done**, such as political power, poverty, development, different ideological stances, the impact of other religions, human rights, popular customs, and many more. This approach is called 'contextualization'. The need to communicate the Bible's message across cultures will affect the theological task itself. Some believe that the Bible can only be applied to today's world by using the social

sciences as a bridge. Theology depends upon a whole range of research and observation to fulfil its task.

Theology has to become committed again to the gospel message of liberation in Christ. It will not dismiss the proven insights gained from serious biblical study, but then nor will it ignore the fact that much scholarship is distorted by cultural and historical biases. It cannot sit on the fence: **either it is working to transform human relationships and communities** in the direction of God's kingdom of justice and peace, **or it is an alienating force**, intent only on its own procedures and survival.

Theology is an activity for all God's people. It has been said of the grassroots communities in Brazil that 'the people's contribution to exegesis is made not through spectacles, but through their eyes. The eyes of the people are recapturing the sure vision with which Christians should read and interpret the Bible.'

The aim of theology, then, is not simply to explain texts, look at history or compare Christian belief with alternatives. It is an intellectual and pastoral discipline, the purpose of which is to serve the specific task of producing the results which Christ commanded.

Human technical ability achieves so much today, finding more and more ways to fuel and to control our industrial society, that there sometimes seems little space for God. Or do we need him in deeper ways than we realize?

Liberation theology has become for traditional Christianity its most profound challenge: indeed we might say, its accusing conscience. It has challenged the too-easy identification of the church with the rich, powerful and cultured. It has challenged the church's interpretation of the meaning of Jesus and his cross.

Nevertheless, liberation theology is not without weaknesses. It has not seen clearly enough some of the fallacies in Marxist thought. It has tended to shift genuinely spiritual issues into social and political areas. Parts of its exegesis of such passages as the exodus are dubious. But the positive contribution of liberation theology to modern theology and the witness of the church is undeniable, particularly in stimulating Christians to look critically at the middle-class image of God and Christ which has become an accepted part of inherited tradition.

ROMAN CATHOLIC WRITERS

One of the results of the Roman Catholic Second Vatican Council (1962-65) was to encourage biblical and doctrinal research. Before the council, Roman Catholic contributions to biblical research were not extensive, but now Roman Catholic scholars are prominent in all branches of biblical study.

Hans Küng, professor of theology at Tübingen, has had a prophetic role in challenging Roman Catholic assumptions

leadership of the voiceless black community acted as a catalyst for this theological sociological movement. James Cone, more than any other writer, has become the theologian of black theology. 'Blackness', states Cone, 'embraces all people who participate in the liberation of man from oppression.' Blackness is something to be proud of. 'I am black because God is black.'

concerning justification by faith, the infallibility of the pope, the church and unity. Because of his 'unorthodox' views and unwillingness to bring them into line with traditional Catholic teaching, Küng was removed from his position as a recognized Roman Catholic theologian, and now occupies a secular professorship.

Karl Rahner, the most prolific modern Roman Catholic theologian, mainly follows the general trend of Roman Catholic doctrine, although his bias is towards an existential approach. His insights and openness have made him acceptable to Protestant theologians and his contribution to modern theology is immense.

Edward Schillebeeckx, a Dutch theologian, has had an uneasy relationship with the Vatican, although he has not suffered Küng's fate. His two-volume work on Christ has led to charges that he denied the full deity of Christ – but this accusation is arguable. His contribution to the sacraments saw his rejection of the philosophy upon which the Roman Catholic doctrine of transubstantiation (in which the bread and wine become the actual body and blood of Christ) is based. Pleading for a new interpretation of the 'real presence' of Christ, he argues for 'transignification' instead. The substance of the bread is not changed; rather the meaning is changed. The bread is the focal point of the real presence of Christ among his people.

It is clear that diversity is the hallmark of modern theology, and it is pointless to look for clear agreement in philosophy or approach, apart from the common assumption that in Jesus, God has drawn near to us and that his gospel is relevant to our needs. He is the diamond and different facets are taken up by modern thinkers. Whether these interpretations are valid or not depends on their conformity with scripture. This must be the yardstick by which we judge the teachings of modern theology.

See America's Black Churches; Roman Catholics since the Council

Are Christians and Scientists Friends Again?

DOUGLAS C. SPANNER

There is still a strong suspicion today that science and conservative Christian faith are sworn enemies. There is even a feeling that churchmen and women who make friendly and encouraging noises in the direction of scientists are inevitably selling out their convictions. This popular view is frequently put forward in the media, and it underlies many attitudes taught in schools. But it is a view that is seriously out of step with modern scientific developments and the friendly relations enjoyed by scientists and Christians today.

The impression of antagonism between scientists and the church was greatly fuelled during the nineteenth century. Although there had been earlier problems (Galileo's house arrest by the Inquisition, for example), the two sides appeared to become polarized by the advent of geological science and by the writings of Charles Darwin.

'For the scientist who has lived by his faith in the power of reason, the story ends like a bad dream. He has scaled the mountain of ignorance; he is about to conquer the highest peak; as he pulls himself over the final rock, he is greeted by a band of theologians who have been sitting there for centuries.'
Robert Jastrow

See The Evolution Debate Continues

This led to one of the most colourful interactions ever between the church and scientists when Darwin expounded his theory of natural selection in *The Origin of Species* (1859). But contrary to popular belief, it is becoming clear to historians of science that there was much less opposition from orthodox Christians to Darwin's theory than there was from fellow-scientists. Within the church, Darwin's ideas on evolution were probably accepted most readily by those theologians who were most biblically conservative; it was the liberals who floundered. It also appears now that scientific aggressors like T.H. Huxley conceived their target as a certain type of clericalism rather than as the Christian faith. So the view of the debate over evolution as a battlefield on which the armies of faith and science fought is hardly true to history.

EVOLUTION AND CREATION

The controversy about whether biological evolution can be reconciled with the biblical doctrine of creation still goes on, and must be expected to do so. But alongside those who maintain that the two views are incompatible, there is an increasing body of

internationally-recognized scientists who are also biblically-minded Christians, and who take the opposite view. This is no new phenomenon, but its scale is significant.

Despite the enormous advances in biological knowledge (especially in molecular biology with the discovery of DNA and the genetic code), and the strenuous labours of the most eminent biological theoreticians, the question of whether natural selection is an adequate mechanism for evolution remains unsettled. This is felt especially by scientists (whether they are Christians or not) from disciplines other than evolutionary studies; the British astronomer Fred Hoyle is an example. He speaks scathingly of natural selection, though he

The Voyager II unmanned spacecraft sent back unique photos of Saturn, her ring and her moons. Recent thinking about the origin of the Universe talks of a Big Bang when it all began. This is more in accord with Christian teaching than some earlier theories.

SCIENTIFIC EDUCATION

Most scientists today see no conflict between religion and science. But the notion that there is such a conflict lingers on in many schools. And the media, which thrive on confrontation, often work to prolong the same idea.

Denis Alexander, until recently a medical researcher in Beirut, writes: 'Some Christians today still make the mistake of defending irrelevant positions in an authoritarian manner. Equally some scientists try to use their science as an authoritarian stick with which to berate religious beliefs. Thankfully there are now far more scientists who realize there are limits inherent in the kind of knowledge that science can give us. At the same time there are many Christians active in the scientific enterprise today who view their science as "thinking God's thought after him"'.

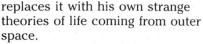

replaces it with his own strange theories of life coming from outer space.

Far from being a crippling blow to Christian belief, the theory of evolution has, in the event, stimulated Christians to enquire more deeply into what biblical creation really means. There is no doubt that the biblical doctrine of creation is very much alive. Associations of Christian research scientists have become quite influential, not only here, but also in connection with new issues – such as the impact both of computer studies on our understanding of the brain and personality, and of cosmological theories on our overall view of the human race and our place in the universe. The intellectual battle of our times on this front is being effectively advanced. But it must be understood that the battle is not against science, but against secularism, an outlook which aims specifically to deny God any place in human life.

THE NEW PHYSICS
Another respect in which the battle for biblical faith has been helped by scientific advance is provided by the new insights of physics. Classical physics used to regard the ideas of 'particles' and 'waves' as mutually exclusive ways of picturing the nature of light. Either one or the other might be correct, but it could not possibly be both. Physics has now accepted that it *is* both. Both are admitted as valid descriptions of light – and not only of light but of electrons and

other forms of matter as well. This extraordinary paradox permeates the new Quantum Physics through and through. It has never been completely resolved, and perhaps never will be.

This helps the Christian in two ways. Firstly, it suggests that apparently head-on encounters **within biblical thought** (such as the Bible's teaching on predestination and human responsibility) are not to be regarded as inconsistencies. There is a harmony underlying them that is too deep for present analysis. Secondly, it suggests that the same is true of apparent collisions **between science and faith** (such as scientific determinism and the effectiveness of prayer). Reality, physics suggests, may be, deep down, puzzlingly paradoxical.

Similarly, the approach taken by relativity physics can be helpful for Christians. It represents a relinquishing by fundamental science of any claim to be able to reach the absolute. That, of course, is a privilege the Bible assigns exclusively to faith.

Modern theories of cosmology (which deal with the origins and structure of the whole universe) have also reached some truly astonishing conclusions. These have given rise to what is known in scientific circles as the Anthropic Principle (from *anthropos*, Greek for 'man'). On the basis of the Big Bang theory of the origin of the universe, this

expresses the fact that it *appears* likely in the highest possible degree that the universe was designed at the outset so that human life could one day exist in it. The matter and energy content, the initial configuration, and the great physical constants were adjusted at point after point with extraordinary exactness for

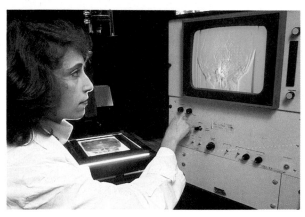

this to be possible. One theoretical physicist with no religious axe to grind, P.C.W. Davies, speaks repeatedly of 'extraordinary physical coincidences', 'cosmic co-operation of...a wildly improbable nature', 'a balancing act...of staggering precision' and of 'compelling evidence that something is "going on"'.

We must be careful not to claim that this is proof of the biblical doctrine of God the Creator. But it certainly holds out the hand of scientific friendship in an exceedingly encouraging way. All truth is, after all, God's truth.

Scientific research cannot answer religious questions. Much of the alleged conflict between religion and science has resulted from a misunderstanding of what science and faith really are.

Hope in a Despairing World

GEORGE BEASLEY-MURRAY

The twentieth
century has brought
so many wars and
disasters that
millions of lives
have been plunged
into despair.

For many people life is more shadowed by despair than illuminated by hope. Not everyone in the world is in despair, but anxiety is a feature of our time, and it eats away at the health of mind and body. The prospect of an annihilating war casts a dark shadow over the minds of multitudes. Tragically the young are often affected by this threat of Armageddon; if the future is so uncertain, what is the point of planning for it? And if our existence can be so brutally stamped on, what meaning is there in it?

Many have simply given up on the future. Geoffrey Dennis, in a previous generation, wrote a book entitled *The End of the World*. He examined all the ways in which it could happen: comet, fire, water, drought, cold, heat and cosmic crash (the nuclear bomb hadn't been invented when he wrote). He then asked *when* it could be. This year? Next year?

Sometime? Never? The one sure thing we can know, he said, is that the last is wrong: the end *must* come, and we are like rats in a trap, unable to escape.

Dennis expressed a universal fear when he admitted that this haunted him, and at times terrified him - but what is the point of being terrified? Life and the world itself are unreal. 'It is a dream. A dream of a dream, dream within dream for ever, with no reality behind it. Even the dream is an illusion. The joy and truth is zero, non-being, nihility. *There is no universe.*'

The difference between that outlook and Christian faith is that of night and day. And yet the Christian hope has to take notice of modern despair in order to rescue people from it. The Bible declares that this world, set in a vast universe, has come from God. He has revealed his purpose for it, and has acted decisively in history so that every person may have a part in it.

THE ROOTS OF CHRISTIAN HOPE

The Christian expectation of the future is rooted in the Old Testament and its accounts of people's experience of God. A constantly repeated theme is that as God had come to their aid in the past, it was sure that he would do so in the future. In this way the event of the exodus of Israel from Egypt became a symbol of future hope. God delivered the Israelite tribes from the clutch of a tyrant, set them free from slavery and brought them into a new land to live in freedom as his people. The later prophets looked for God to *come again* in the future and bring about another exodus, not only for the Jewish people but for all mankind.

In the same way the prophets pointed back to the times when God had delivered his people from their enemies, on what Jews called 'days of the Lord'. They then pointed forward to a final *Day of the Lord* in the future, when he would judge the nations and set right the earth's wrongs. As God showed himself as the Lord and King of his people, so the time would come when he would rule over the whole world and establish *the kingdom of God* in power, peace and universal righteousness. Christians today believe that these powerful ideas are not imprisoned in the times when they were first written, but that they are as relevant – if not more relevant – in the modern world of terror and despair.

The New Testament was written in the conviction that God's purpose for the world, expressed in the Old Testament, was realized in the coming of Jesus Christ. Jesus proclaimed that the kingdom of God was actively present in his work, and he appealed to everyone to submit themselves to God's life-giving rule and to experience his power. But he did not see the kingdom of God as simply for here and now. Instead, it was the first instalment of God's ultimate gift of life, when God's kingdom is revealed in power and glory at the end of time. For this he went to his cross, for this he was raised from the dead, and for this he is to appear in the glory and majesty of God; it is the same Lord who reigns as who died upon the cross.

Here is the heart of the Christian hope. It is bound up with the action of God in and through Christ. The action began in Jesus' life, death and

See Theology Today; Tomorrow's Church Today

'We reject as a proud, self-confident dream the idea that man can ever build a utopia on earth. Our Christian confidence is that God will perfect his kingdom and we look forward with eager anticipation to that day and to the new heaven and earth in which there will be justice and God will reign for ever.'
Lausanne Covenant, 1974

resurrection, it continues in the present, and it is to reach its climax in the future. It is one process, and each part of it points forward to the conclusion. It is not an automatic process that was set off long ago, but the work of the ever-living, ever-acting God.

The biblical picture of hope contains at least four key features:

● Belief in **the God of the Bible** must include belief in his will and power to complete his purpose when he first created the universe.

● God's purpose can and will be achieved through the activity of the Son of God. This is what it means to believe in **the Christ of the Bible**.

● The alienating power of sin is so powerful that only God's Son could reconcile a lost world to God. Jesus achieved this through his **death and resurrection**.

A child who has been saved from starvation through a feeding programme in Kenya. Relief work in the developing world is a battle to bring hope to the hopeless.

● The destructive effects of sin mean that only God's Son can renew the fallen creation for the Creator God. This will happen at **Jesus' final return**.

THE HOPE OF GOD'S 'YES'

The Christian hope stands out in sharp contrast against pagan hopes in 'the future' or in 'human progress'. It is first and foremost hope in God, who will work in the future but who is also with us in the present. So how does the Christian hope affect the world of here and now?

● Because the Christian hope is expressed in terms of the kingdom of God, **it spells hope for the individual and for the world**. The older, pagan hope, still current among many people today, is chiefly concerned with individual survival and a good life in the world beyond death. The biblical hope is not merely individual. It is concerned with the transformation of society and the individual discovering his or her place in that new social order. This theme runs through the whole Bible, but especially in its last book, the book of Revelation. There the final triumph of goodness is not only in the individual, the church, or the nations of the world, but in the entire universe.

This strengthens the motivation for Christian behaviour individually and socially. Paul appealed to the Christians in the heart of the pagan world, Rome: 'Do not conform yourselves to the standards of this world, but let

God transform you inwardly by a complete change of your mind.' That is a spur for those who long for 'a kingdom that cannot be shaken', and at the same time intend to make an impression on the society they live in. Precisely because Christian hope seeks *first* the kingdom of God, it seeks the welfare of this world.

● **The Christian hope is a good hope**. The church has often failed to make this clear. It has been so dominated by the thought of the last judgement that it has tended – and still tends – to inspire dread of the end instead of joy at its prospect. By contrast Karl Barth spoke of Christ's future coming as 'the miracle of the divine "Yes" '. The Bible stresses that beyond the end of time with God is hope and joy. Evil and pain are cast out; people are restored to the love and fellowship of God; an unruly universe is brought under God's good control. Christians can communicate this joy to a hopeless world and celebrate it in their worship.

● In contrast to contemporary pessimism, **the Christian hope inspires confidence about the future**. Roland de Pury, a French pastor incarcerated during World War II, stated, 'I was not able to stand firm except by remembering every day that the Gestapo was the hand of God – his left hand. The worst of

tyrants and the last of cowards will only end by accomplishing Christ's will.' This was written in the spirit of John, exiled on Patmos for his faith, who could even look on the last Antichrist as an instrument in God's hand for the achievement of his will.

This does not mean, however, that Christians turn a blind eye to suffering and oppression in order to dwell on the future hope. Christians take their own suffering – and the suffering of others – seriously. But while 'mourning with those who mourn', they look beyond the suffering of death to the new dawn of resurrection. It is this kind of hope, realistic about the world rather than escapist, that is needed by despairing people.

Is there hope beyond death? Many people, young as well as old, continue to believe that God gives an eternal hope, and belief in this 'eternal dimension' has a deep effect on the way we live our lives.

Does the Bible Speak Today?

GEORGE CAREY

Many millions of people in the world are convinced that the Bible speaks today – or, to be precise, that God speaks to them through it. The popularity of the Bible continues unabated, and it remains a world bestseller. The Bible, rather than forms of worship or doctrinal statements, hold Christians together, since all Christian churches and believers reckon it to be central to their faith. But this does not mean that all Christians are agreed about its interpretation or authority.

See Evangelicals at a Crossroads

An African woman reads her Bible: the Bible still has more influence on people's thinking world-wide than any other single book.

We may distinguish four approaches to the Bible, although of course, there are many who do not fit neatly into such categories:

● **'Fundamentalist'** is a term used for those who have an uncritical approach to the Bible. A Fundamentalist will be likely to treat all parts of the Bible alike, giving a verse from Leviticus the same value as a verse from the Gospel of John. He or she will be suspicious of literary and historical study of the Bible, and will probably not use its findings. The Fundamentalist will be insistent on the 'infallibility' of the Bible, claiming that it is 'inerrant'.

● **Conservative Evangelicals** work from the 'evangel' (gospel) at the heart of Scripture. The Bible is for them a collection of reliable, trustworthy books which testify to the crucified, risen Jesus. But conservative Evangelical scholars will readily acknowledge the importance of historical research, use the tools of critical study, and be aware of the need to distinguish between the different types of literature in the Bible. Many will speak of the Bible's 'infallibility' and 'inerrancy' but may refer such terms to the Bible's infallible and sure testimony to Jesus Christ and his salvation. Other conservatives, however, prefer to speak of the 'trustworthiness' of the Bible, drawing attention to its complete reliability as a guide to belief and action.

● **Liberals** may vary from a mild scepticism about the value of the Bible to a radical distrust. What is common to liberals is the view that historical criticism has made it impossible to treat the Bible as an infallible guide. Yet they are not keen to break the link between God and the Bible, and it is common for liberals to say that 'the Bible contains the word of God'. This has the advantage of dealing with different texts in different ways. But it has a crucial weakness. Who decides which parts of the Bible are the word of God and which are not?

● **Radicals** see the Bible as a

THE TWIN FOCUS

NO APPLICATION
Some people know the world of the Bible better than their own world. They have detailed knowledge of the societies of Bible times, but contemporary society they do not understand well, nor have they much sympathy with it. This means that they interpret Bible teaching mainly in terms of itself, for the fascination of being at home in this great book. But they do not apply it successfully to the needs of modern people.

MISAPPLICATION
Others are much more at home in today's world, but are careless about understanding and knowing the Bible. They only use the Bible to ratify the answers they find in other studies, such as sociology or psychology. This means their analysis of today's problems is not brought to the light of the Bible's teaching, and the God-dimension is often missed.

TRUE APPLICATION
Both the above approaches stop halfway to the goal of applying the Bible to present-day questions. The task of Bible interpretation requires us to study the Bible and to study our world—and to love both. Only so can real human needs be met with God's answers.

collection of ancient texts which cannot address us directly today. On this view, the culture of Bible times is so different from our own that it is impossible for the two to meet. The Bible may offer us suggestions about how the first Christians coped with problems of faith and conduct, say the radicals, but we ought to translate these into the 'myths' and culture of our own time, and not to regard the Bible itself as our 'normative' basis for faith and doctrine.

HISTORY AND FAITH

For the majority of Christians, the extreme positions do not offer viable bases for faith. Fundamentalism is weakened by its simplistic disregard of the original intention of Scripture, and by its tendency to neglect

AUTHORITY
TONY LANE

One of the problems facing the church in the modern world is a crisis of authority. All traditional authorities have been radically questioned and this has affected the church. The rise of modern science illustrates the change. In the Middle Ages 'science' was based primarily on authority. Appeal was made to the 'authorities' on the subject – great figures from the past such as Aristotle. The planets were held to move in circles because the circle is the perfect shape. But with the rise of modern science in the seventeenth century the emphasis lay on experiment, on looking to see for yourself. Modern science has progressed so far precisely because it has not been based on authorities and because, therefore, all theories have had to be tested and corrected by experiment.

This questioning of traditional authorities has spread to every discipline. One consequence has been a changed attitude towards the past. It is no longer held that 'nothing new can be true'. The teachings of the past are seen less as venerable tradition and more as old-fashioned and outmoded. In a world where everything changes with increasing rapidity all communities have been

forced to face this fact. The film *The Fiddler on the Roof* portrays the impact of this kind of change on a conservative Jewish community. In the modern world the elderly are increasingly seen not as the repositories of the venerable wisdom of the ancients but as old-fashioned and reactionary.

Traditional authorities, then, are widely questioned in the modern world. But this is not the whole picture. As the harmful effects of increasing technology become more

Authority of some kind is a social necessity. But attitudes have changed from a generally authoritarian approach to a more personal one.

apparent, there is growing a renewed respect for the ways of the past. It is widely recognized, for instance, that our grandparents ate more healthily than we do. Nor are all modern people opposed to authority. Authoritarian political parties of both left and right have flourished in this century. Authoritarian and reactionary

nearly 200 years of historical research. Biblical critics have certainly made some sweeping statements which have not stood up for long; their 'assured results' have not always proved very assured. But critical studies have been very valuable in many ways. They have often shown, for example, how the background of the times when particular Bible books were written affected the concerns of the writers, or how the Gospel writers used common material in a way that reflected what each of them saw as most important in Jesus' teaching. A blanket condemnation of all biblical criticism robs us of a lot of valuable insights. It can lead to a habit of trying to apply Bible teaching mindlessly, without asking the crucial questions along the way.

See Gospel and Culture; Has Faith a Language?

Islamic fundamentalism attracts many. Just as children prefer to live in an environment where there is a framework of firm discipline, so also many modern men and women look for a refuge from the burden of total autonomy.

Should Christians reject authority?

How does this affect the church? Traditionally Christianity has been based firmly on authority – the authority of the Bible as God's word, for Protestants; the authority of church and tradition for Roman Catholics and Orthodox. These authorities have come under heavy fire. The Bible has been attacked by historical critics and by many others. The pontiff (pope) is not popular when he pontificates.

In reaction to this, many Christians have opted for the liberal way, the *à la carte* approach to Christian truth. Liberals accept no infallible authorities. They treat the Bible with respect, but reject it where they find it unacceptable. All wish to retain some distinctively Christian beliefs, but in varying degrees. Some reject the virgin birth but continue to accept the resurrection. Some deny all miracles. Some deny that Jesus was the incarnate Son of God, but still see him as a special man.

The trouble is that it has not proved any easier to believe a few miracles than many, part of the Christian faith than the whole. If God could raise Jesus from the dead, he could just as easily cause him to be born of a virgin. People today look to religion for certainty and convictions, not for a liberal willingness to jettison beliefs in the name of modern thought. This can be seen in the fact that the churches which are growing are those which retain their loyalty to the Christian message, while seeking to relate that message to today.

What sort of authority?

Some distinguish between 'hard' or 'extrinsic' authority (claimed on the basis of status or office) and 'soft' or 'intrinsic' authority (the authority of experience or of a convincing argument). Many speak as if the latter type were enough. But both are needed. Without soft authority the church becomes harsh and authoritarian. Without hard authority the kingdom of God degenerates into an anarchistic society in which 'every man does what is right in his own eyes'. No secular state could survive without hard authority.

The two types come together in Jesus Christ. He has the extrinsic authority of being God's Son, to whom the Father has given all authority. Yet he came to earth not simply to demand human allegiance but to win it.

So also it should be with the church. Its message must be based on full acceptance of Jesus Christ's authority as God's unique Son, and on the authority of the Bible as the normative witness to Christ. Although the Christian message must of course be translated into contemporary terms, the Christian is not free to pick and choose which parts he will believe and obey.

But the authoritative Christian message is not nakedly authoritarian. Christians may not simply demand that people believe their message; they must also exemplify and demonstrate that message in their way of life and practical compassion for others. 'By this all men will know that you are my disciples, if you have love for one another,' said Jesus. We are not simply summoned in an authoritarian way to accept Christ, we are invited to 'taste and see that the Lord is good', to prove the truth of the Christian message in our own experience. Today, as always, the church needs to remain true to her authoritative message while demonstrating the truth of the message by her example.

Sometimes Bible reading must be fitted into a busy life wherever it can, as this doctor finds between ward rounds in a Third-World hospital.

There are a lot of Bibles around today. Braille Bibles will soon be available for speakers of Portuguese, Hindi and Tamil; 400 Bibles were recently presented to a prison in Surinam with an immediate response from one of the prisoners to find out more about the gospel; about four-fifths of the hotels in Macau have requested copies of the New Testament for their bedrooms. You can buy Bibles from a clothes shop in Rwanda and from vending machines in Tokyo.

The other extreme, radicalism, is also unacceptable to many Christians. Radicals deny that critical study necessarily leads to scepticism about the origins of Christianity. Indeed, many will claim that, rather than making Jesus more difficult to find and understand, historical research has made the New Testament period more accessible and the mystery of Jesus in his living, dying and rising more gripping. The mistake of radicalism is to separate Bible times completely from our own, abandoning the attempt to find the links between the world of the Bible and modern Christianity.

INTERPRETING THE BIBLE

It is now widely realized, then, that someone today cannot simply lift a passage out of the Bible and just apply it to his or her situation as if it were written for that person alone. Certainly God does use the Bible in a direct, personal way. But a faithful interpretation requires us to be aware that Scripture had an original purpose, a primary reference to its own age. When we apply it to our own times, we must remember the differences and make any adjustments necessary. This does not in any way diminish the Bible's value and importance, but it does demand that we explore the background of the text and seek to discover what it originally meant.

For instance, we need to ask what sort of writing it is – is it poetry, full of images and word-pictures, or prose? It helps to know to whom the passage was addressed and what prompted its writing. We must learn to look back sympathetically to the original situation. We also need to develop the skill to distinguish between a timeless truth and its cultural expression.

All this means that today we are involved in a twofold interpretative task. We must both look back to the primary purpose of the writer and also try to relate this to our situation today. For example, the book of Hosea gives us beautiful and timeless truths about God's unquenchable love for his people. Yet the form of the writing will seem very strange to the modern mind. We owe it to Hosea to interpret his prophecy in our terms, so that the strength as well as the wonder of God's love is not lost.

THE BIBLE'S AUTHORITY

All Christian churches are agreed that the Bible is authoritative. By this we mean that it is our final court of appeal, the highest of all tests, to which all Christian theology and actions must bow.

While this is agreed, the Bible varies in its significance among Christian traditions. For many Protestant churches the Bible is claimed to be the *sole* authority. Anglicanism, however, differs slightly in that it attributes to the Bible a unique authority but also gives authoritative status to the four general councils and its own Thirty-Nine Articles of Religion. For Roman Catholics the Bible is placed in a partnership with tradition as two forms of God's revelation in Christ. But since the

Second Vatican Council, Catholicism has given a clear 'normative' role to the Bible in the life of the church.

When we speak of the authority of the Bible, we are not talking about an intrinsic quality which belongs to a collection of old books because they are inspiring literature (although clearly they are that). We speak of an authority which belongs to God.

The authority of the Bible derives from the God who stands behind it and inspired its writers in a unique way. It also springs from the events which the Bible records. The Bible testifies to the deeds of God in history, of Jesus in his life and death, and of the Spirit in the church. As a reliable witness of these events, it conveys God's will for all who follow him. And so it is doing a great deal more than simply pointing back: it points to what God expects today from all who believe and obey, as well as indicating what is to come.

USING THE BIBLE TODAY

The Bible continues to flourish despite all attacks on it. It continues to feed the lives of millions of people, challenging unbelief, renewing faith and informing the life of the church. There has been little decline in its popularity or in its power to influence mankind. It is good to report that many churches place a great emphasis on Bible teaching, through house groups as well as through preaching. Organizations producing Bible-reading notes and group study aids influence the lives of millions through systematic Bible study. Through such aids, Christians are encouraged to

Constantly more people are discovering the attraction of the Bible, and are deeply concerned to get it and learn to read it for themselves.

include regular Bible reading in their discipline of prayer.

And yet in some ways Christian attitudes to the Bible have not changed for the better. It is now rare to find families reading the Bible together, and even among Bible-loving Christians knowledge of the Scripture is not as deep or as extensive as it once was. This constitutes a challenge to the churches to stop the slide. Without building on the foundations, Christians' lives could easily become superficial and unduly influenced by the attitudes of modern society.

3.2 PROCLAIMING THE FAITH

The Missionary Inheritance

KWAME BEDIAKO

The late twentieth century has seen a shift in Christianity's centre of gravity. The heartlands of the Christian faith have ceased to be the old Christendom of western Europe, and are now to be found in Latin America, in parts of Asia and Oceania, and in Africa. Even allowing for the massive influence of Christianity in North America, it is possible now to speak of a specifically 'Southern' phase of Christianity.

It is not only in numerical strength that the Christian communities of the southern continents are more dominant on a world scale; they are becoming important also in ordering the Christian agenda at the international level. These days Christians are becoming more aware that evil lies in world structures as well as in individuals; they appreciate more fully that belief in redemption has social and political implications. These new understandings are not unrelated to the fact that the vast majority of Christians live in the economically poorer and politically weaker nations of the South. In view of the inequities that exist between North and South, it is not hard to see how Southern Christians' conditions of life will make an impact on the conscience of the Christian church as a whole.

THE FRUITS OF CHRISTIAN MISSION

This alteration in the strength of the Christian presence on the different continents is one result of Western missionary endeavours – Catholic as well as Protestant. To that extent, the modern missionary movement has been a success story. It has led to a Christian church of universal proportions – truly embodying the book of Revelation's vision of that multitude which no man could number, from every race, tribe, nation and language. And it has also made it possible for the Christian faith to escape from a dangerous entanglement with the cultures of the peoples of the old Christendom just at a time when these latter are increasingly discarding Christian faith and embracing a generally secular and humanistic world-view.

This significant shift in the

See Christians North and South

The gospel today is good news for every part of the world. It is not the prerogative of some nations to take it to others. Christianity is now a world faith, and believers in every nation share in a joint responsibility to spread the gospel.

At a Christian meeting in Indonesia a Western missionary speaks in Mandarin Chinese and is translated into Hakka by a national Christian. The relationship between international and national Christianity has become quite complex in our day.

See Translating the Bible; African Independent Churches

centre of gravity of the Christian world can, therefore, be seen as a positive achievement for the Christian religion. It is equivalent to other similar shifts which have taken place in the course of two millennia during which the Christian faith has fanned out from being a minority sect within Judaism into its present status as a major world religion.

But the story is not all of success. In the corporate African and Asian minds, the Western missionary enterprise has become associated with the socio-political and cultural dominance of the West. This has been one of the more baneful aspects of the modern missionary movement. Latin America too, after long enduring Spanish and Portuguese political and cultural impact, has latterly come under the massive influence of North American interests.

Either way, the near-simultaneous entry of Christian missions and Western political and cultural imperialism upon these continents is quite unprecedented in Christian history. Since the dismantling of the European empires, the history of the churches of Africa, Asia and Latin America has been one of disengagement from 'imperialist' legacies of their various 'sending' churches and missionary agencies.

THE BIBLE NOT THE MISSIONARY

In the very success of the missionary enterprise were the seeds of the demise of Western missionary dominance in the now universal church. Not least among these ingredients has been the availability of the Bible in the languages of the new converts.

Unlike the parallel story of the evangelization of western and northern Europe, the history of the modern missionary movement has also been the history of Bible translation. The people of Europe accepted for almost 1,000 years an institutionalized, sacred and ecclesiastical language – Latin. But this element was strikingly absent from the modern Christian expansion into the southern continents. It was early recognized as a crucial factor in effectively communicating the faith that converts should have access to the original Christian sources. Even Roman Catholic missionary thinking, less keenly committed to the provision of vernacular Scriptures, came also to realize its importance.

Bible translation has been highly significant in modern mission, even where early attempts have since been improved on, because it has reaffirmed that the word of God can be translated and adapted to local cultures. The Bible is available to everyone everywhere on the same basis - where and as God has found them in their own cultural world. No new Christian convert, hearing or reading the New Testament for the first time in his or her language, could fail to identify with the crowd assembled in Jerusalem on the Day of Pentecost, who heard 'about the great things that God has done...*in our own language*'. Consequently, where the Bible was available in the local tongue missionary preaching was a less potent filter for the message than has often been assumed. It was the Bible more than the missionary who spoke.

An even more important effect of direct access to the Bible was that it could be used as an independent and authoritative yardstick to test, and sometimes to reject what missionaries taught and did. The Scriptures also guided some of the emergent Christian communities as they developed their own forms of Christianity. Studies on the rise of the so-called Independent Churches in Africa have often stressed the major role of the Bible in the converts' own language to help them discover some serious discrepancies between missionary practice and what an unmediated reading showed to be true biblical faith. The effect of the vernacular Bible in Africa has been compared with the impact of early English and German Bible translations in Europe in the century of the Protestant Reformation.

All this meant that, well before the passing of the European empires, the Western value-setting for the Christian faith was

Continued on p.308

A very poor Brazilian woman was learning to read and wanted to get a Bible. A Bible Society worker, Ewaldo Alves, offered her one and in payment she gave him an egg. It was all she had so Ewaldo agreed to accept it. She was delighted and holding the book, said, 'Now no one has more than I have, because I have a Bible!'

Some communicating of the gospel is still done between people of different races. But increasingly strong national churches throughout the world are responsible for their own evangelism.

THE CHURCH OF THE POOR

RAYMOND FUNG

There have been great moments in Christian history - moments when the church has known tremendous growth and become transformed in the process. In the days of Peter and Paul, when the Council of Jerusalem decided that the gospel could not be confined to the Jews, the door of the church was thrown open to the Gentiles. It was no longer necessary to follow the customs of Moses to be saved. The Christian church grew and became richer in its life and understanding as Gentile believers found their full place in it. Christianity ceased to be a Jewish cult.

Another moment of expansion came with the modern missionary movement of the nineteenth and twentieth centuries, when the churches of the West reached out to the South and the East. As national Christian communities were established, the door of the church began to be open to the peoples of Africa and Asia and other lands. Enriched once again by the infusion of different cultures, Christianity assumed a much more universal character; now it could justifiably lay claim to being a world faith, no longer merely European.

If we ask the question today, to whom will the door of the church be opened next? Who will be the ones, like the Gentiles in the first century or the Africans and Asians much later, who will embrace the Christian faith en masse, and in the process expand and transform the church? So many of the signs over the last fifteen years seem to be pointing to one conclusion: the poor. Peasants and labourers and workers in nearly all parts of the world are standing at the threshold. Already, in terms of numerical growth, churches in the Third World easily outpace their

counterparts in the West. In Europe and North America, the fastest-growing churches are congregations of minority peoples and new migrants, almost without exception belonging to the poorer sectors of the community. There is a decisive turn to Christianity among the masses of the earth's poor. The centre of missionary impulse is gradually shifting in this direction.

Admittedly, there is nothing new in the church's concern for poor people. The modern missionary movement of the nineteenth and early twentieth centuries was basically a movement

of the haves to the have-nots. Mission hospitals and schools were set up to serve the deprived and the underprivileged. The relief of suffering and misery has always been recognized as a prime form of Christian witness.

What is new is not a missionary awareness of the poor. What is new is the understanding of where the poor stand in the kingdom of God. It is to the poor of the earth that the gospel

Refugees in Phnom Penh, Kampuchea, take over a disused boat for their church.

was preached in the first place; it is the poor who are given the active role in the drama of proclaiming the coming kingdom. As it is, the poor are no longer seen as objects of the church's evangelization, no longer passive recipients of its charity and service, but allies - brothers and sisters to be fully invited to the community of faith, its life and its missionary task.

Of course this is to paint the picture with a very broad brush. There are all kinds of contradictions in a historical movement of such scale, many different dynamics, great diversity. But the most crucial discovery is that the poor, in both divine and human history, are intended to stand centre stage.

Looking with new eyes

Nowhere is this fresh discovery more evident than in Latin America. There, for centuries, history and religion have worked together to condition the poor into passively accepting permanent oppression and exploitation as the will of God. Profoundly religious people, they were taught a Christianity which was largely nominal, with a few Christian symbols - the Lord's Prayer, identification with the Virgin Mary and her Son's sufferings - superimposed on their life.

Then they began meeting in small groups among themselves. They began to read the Bible, often for the first time, with their neighbours. They began to relate their daily stories with the stories of the Bible, especially of Jesus. And they found in the newly-opened Bible that the God they worshipped was a personal God. They found out that God did not especially like to have them suffer as they were accustomed to.

Thus were born the basic Christian communities. Theirs are the stories of the church of the poor which is sweeping like wildfire through Latin America and changing the face of the

continent.

Similar movements, no less small in scale, are happening in Africa, where social change brings with it the break-up of the family and traditional communities, homelessness, hunger, civil strife, apartheid. But these human disasters have propelled the churches, both historical and independent, into a fresh examination of the Christian faith. As the poor read the Bible with their own eyes, they begin to see things that others who live in security and comfort do not see.

In China, during the last fifteen years, the church has experienced the cross and the resurrection. What has emerged is a much larger church, deeply rooted in rural homes, led by laymen and laywomen who live and work and share their faith among their fellow-peasants.

In other parts of Asia, the number of poor people who newly join the church has been considerable though far less spectacular. But a missionary movement based on solidarity with the poor has already taken hold. It understands its task as proclaiming the gospel among the poor, and in community with them. This is sending ripples through Asia's big urban slums, its industrial zones, as well as the villages of its mountains and plains.

A threat or an invitation?

When Christians genuinely choose solidarity with the poor, a threat is posed. Those whose interest depends on keeping the poor as objects of domestication and control are put on the defensive. The story of the church of the poor is therefore very much a story of martyrdom. There are no available statistics, but probably many more Christians, mainly from among the poor or those who stand with them, have died for their faith in the last fifteen years than ever before.

The emergence of the church of the poor is no less threatening to the

church. For Gentile believers fully to share in the Christian life, the power that Jewish Christians had over the early church needed to be broken. An equally full share for Asians and Africans required the same breaking of white Christians' power. The full participation of the earth's poor in the church today will require the breaking of the power of the middle class. Up to now it is they who have administered the church, determined its mission priorities and ethical agenda; they have set themselves up as sole authority on the making of Christian theology and the formulation of Christian beliefs. The church of the poor challenges all these claims.

But it is not a repudiation of what has gone before. When the early Christians welcomed the Gentiles, they did not thereby set aside the Jewish Christians. Neither has the challenge of autonomous Third-World churches involved rejecting white Christians. The challenge of the church of the poor is an invitation to the churches. It calls us all to recognize how bound we are by our own cultures. It asks us to fathom the depths of our faith, to find a true missionary obedience. Especially for churches in more affluent lands, it asks us to explore what it is to come to Christ in utter poverty.

already being discarded. With their own Bible, the single most important element of the missionary inheritance, the new churches possessed the apostolic heritage common to all Christians. Illiteracy often prevented many from benefitting fully from the Bible, but the pioneering work of Christian missions in the field of school education meant that substantial numbers of early converts were taught to read. By doing this, the modern missionary enterprise reaffirmed a characteristic of the earlier expansion of the Christian faith. In parts of Africa, new Christians were known simply as 'readers'.

SPIRITUAL PARTNERS

The gift of a translated Bible, and the consequences of that, constitute one of the more remarkable features of the modern southward expansion of Christianity. So it is not difficult to appreciate why the missionary inheritance in the world's new centres of Christian strength is often viewed much less negatively than might be expected. The material needs and the technological handicap of some of the new Christian communities may appear to perpetuate a certain dependence on Western (formerly missionary) resources. Yet there is little sense of being spiritually junior to the churches in Europe and North America.

On the contrary, the growth of a vigorous sense of Christian identity, coupled with an increasing awareness of spiritual and even missionary responsibility towards the now post-Christian West, has been one of the more striking developments in the churches of Latin America, Asia and Africa. Consequently, there is no sign that these churches want to be separated from the former 'sending' churches and 'go it alone'. An important African Independent church like the Kimbanguist Church of Zaire, with a membership of several million, considered it appropriate to join the World Council of Churches in 1969, bringing a unique contribution from its distinctive African experience.

The sky, however, should not be painted blue all over. In considerable areas of Christian life as found in the churches in Latin America, Asia and Africa there is much that bears the imprint of Westernization rather than the heritage of the apostles. European first-names continue to be widely given as 'Christian' names. Zaire provides the unique instance of a country where state policy on *authenticité* led to the abolition of all such 'Christian' names in a single legislation, in 1972; only indigenous African names have been allowed since. The Christian communities there have been none the worse for losing what were seen as badges of the West's cultural imperialism, and the Christian religion remains a massive reality in the country, which cannot be ignored.

The forms of worship practised in many of the Southern churches also continue to show that patterns developed in the

WHO SENDS, WHO RECEIVES?

❝ 'Go into all the world,' said Jesus to his disciples, 'and make disciples from all nations.' Through the centuries since, the Christian response to this commision has developed stage by stage. ❞

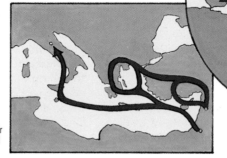

THE FIRST GREAT MISSIONARY was Paul the apostle. He travelled to all the main cities of the Roman Empire and set up churches in them. Later he revisited them, strengthened their faith and appointed elders to lead them.

IN MEDIEVAL TIMES missionaries went out from the Christian centres—such as Rome, Ireland, Byzantium—to bring other nations and tribes to the faith.

THE NINETEENTH AND EARLY TWENTIETH CENTURIES saw the great heyday of European and North American missionaries. Taking ship to other continents, then penetrating them by any possible means, they opened up whole regions to the light of Christianity. Inevitably their work could not always be kept distinct from the endeavours of trade and empire.

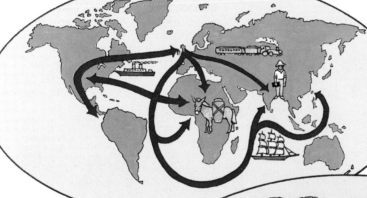

IN THIS GENERATION the fruits of the Western missionary movement can be seen. Christians travel from independent churches all over the world, using all known means of transport. Missionaries from young churches take the gospel to other Third-World nations, to other cultures within their own countries, and to Western countries—bringing fresh life where faith seems hard to find.

North were passed on as part of the essential core of Christian tradition. Yet, at least in principle, a positive cultural pluralism is accepted within the world Christian community, reflecting a rich and wide diversity of cultures. This needs to be so. It is essential to the quest for cultural and social relevance in the churches of Latin America, Asia and Africa that their expression of the one faith should be uniquely their own, not, as in the past, taken over from the North as part of the Christian tradition. Nowadays there is a welcome given to a plurality of 'theologies' within a unity of faith. This results in no small measure from the efforts of the theologians in the 'South'. The theology of liberation in

Christianity has been a faith for the have-nots of the world ever since New Testament days.

Latin America, and the various indigenous and political theologies of Asia and Africa, testify to a vitality of Christian reflection which is increasingly making its mark in the world Christian community as a whole.

HANDING OVER THE TORCH

It is probably inevitable that some evidence of the impact of the West in these churches will remain, and that it will be integrated into the new sense of Christian identity that is in process of being established. The persistence of European languages alongside indigenous languages is an obvious element in such an inheritance. But this need not prove to be a serious

handicap to the healthy development of the new Christian communities. It may well be that the multilingualism imposed on Christian thinking and learning in the new churches is what the universal Christian community itself could do with – the capacity to remain open to other cultural viewpoints without cutting loose from one's own cultural tradition.

When the International Missionary Council met in Whitby, Canada, in 1947, the only participant at that conference who could speak fluently in four European languages was an African! Since then, the World Council of Churches has institutionalized five European languages – English, French, German, Spanish and Russian – as its media of communication; while the recently-launched *Bulletin of African Theology* also has English and French but adds Portuguese. On the Roman Catholic side of the story, it is equally interesting that at the Second Vatican Council, African bishops wanted a vernacular liturgy for their congregations even though they themselves were fluent in Latin, unlike some of their colleagues from the North, particularly North America.

All this goes to show the complexity of the missionary inheritance in the churches of Latin America, Asia and Africa. Even more important, it indicates the extent to which the burden of responsibility for Christian scholarship and witness for the foreseeable future may have already been passed on to the new churches, as has consistently been the case in every successive shift in the centre of gravity of the Christian world. Although not many people may yet be aware of this, the fact itself is undeniable.

Some churches of the South will continue to be dependent on Western churches for some time to come, especially given the existing disparities in material and technological resources between North and South. Nevertheless, the watershed has been passed. There is every indication that the Christian communities in the southern continents, which issued from the Western missionary enterprise, have become a major part of the mainstream of modern Christian history. What happens in these churches is likely to determine the shape of the Christian religion in the coming century.

See Putting the Gospel in its Context

Telling the World

JOHN MORISON

Why is it that some Christians have such a strong desire to tell others about their faith? Indeed, the story of the development of the church can best be understood as a series of missionary movements. The Christian believes he has good news to share – a Third World definition of evangelism is 'one beggar telling another beggar where to find bread'. We believe that we have discovered in Jesus a way in which life can be transformed, and we want others to know it. Yet there is a great variety of ways to tell them, and it is not always easy to pick the best one.

The most comprehensive definition of evangelism is still that given by the Church of England Archbishops' Committee of 1918: 'To evangelize is so to present Christ Jesus in the power of the Holy Spirit, that men shall come to put their trust in God through him, to accept him as their Saviour and serve him as their King in the fellowship of his church.'

This definition clearly states that the purpose of evangelism is to make active members of the church of Christ. It follows our Lord's command to his disciples at the very end of his time with them, 'Go then to all peoples everywhere and make them my disciples.' The purpose of evangelism, in other words, is more than merely to proclaim the gospel irrespective of any response. We do not announce the Good News in a vacuum. We tell it to *people*, longing for them to repent, believe and follow Christ, and expecting that at least some of them will.

Of course we cannot determine the size of the response. That is God's business. But if we look at the parable of the sower, Jesus clearly expected results from the sowing of the word, whether thirtyfold, sixtyfold or a hundredfold. If there is no response, rather than saying, 'Well, that must be God's will', we need to question when and how we told the good news, and exactly what content we put into it. And we tend to get what we

The gospel is seldom grasped without someone to tell it. The words in which it is explained need careful choosing so as to be within the understanding of the hearers.

As well as enjoying the life of their home and neighbourhood, many people spend a large part of their time in a separate working environment. They need help to see a spiritual side to their work, so that their humanity is not divided. The witness of Christians in the workforce is a key factor.

aim for, so our understanding of the purpose of evangelism needs to focus on making disciples; that and nothing less.

GIVING EVANGELISM A CHANCE

Evangelism, to be effective, needs the back-up of a vibrant church life. Three aspects are particularly important:

● **The silent majority needs to be mobilized**. How often does this sort of exchange take place? Minister to lay leaders: 'I believe God is calling us to outreach in the neighbourhood.' Lay leaders: 'Yes, Pastor, you can count on us to back you with our prayers as you do your visitation.'

For centuries churches in the West have been able to pay full-time ministers. That in many ways is no bad thing, but with full-time paid clergy has come the feeling that only they are really equipped to minister. This attitude has spread so pervasively that if you say the word 'evangelist' most Western Christians immediately think of a powerful preacher who travels full-time round the country running missions. Yet research suggests that approximately 10 per cent of the ordinary Christians of any live congregation have the gift of an evangelist. They have a God-

AFRICAN EXUBERANCE

Africans do not seem to have the same problems as some others in sharing their faith. In a new African township a young black minister arrived to start a church. He had the gift of an evangelist and through house-to-house visitation he very quickly gathered round him a small group of newly-converted young married couples. First, he did not expend their energies on putting up a church building but used the local school. Second, he gave them basic teaching about Christianity and sent them out two by two to share their fresh experience of Jesus around the streets of the township. Many people were won by their joy and enthusiasm for Jesus and the church multiplied. Quite simply this happened because these young Christians were prepared to 'gossip the gospel'.

'The way in which a patient is welcomed to a clinic, the way he is examined, the way he is given his tablets, this is all part of evangelism...God has called us to a ministry of healing. When you expand "healing" to mean what the Bible means, it's not just giving pills, it's dealing with the whole human being.' Eddie Askew, of the Leprosy Mission

given ability to communicate the gospel effectively even to those whom they do not know. One secret of evangelism is to give such people the confidence to use their gift, and not leave it to the pastor.

We need 'witnesses' – people who will simply say how their lives have changed. And the most effective witnesses are those who have been recently converted. They have many friends who knew them before, with whom they can share their faith; their initial experience of Jesus is still fresh. What these new Christians need is not first-of-all a detailed, lengthy programming into the tradition and theology of the denomination; that turns them into consumers rather than salesmen. Rather they require

what Jesus gave his new disciples: a crash course in witnessing, then sending out in all their enthusiasm and inexperience to claim their friends for God. For the role of a witness, to which all Christians are called, is in essence simply to share with those you know the good news of what Jesus has done in your life. It is communicating personal experience.

● **We need to focus on life at least as much as words**. Western Christianity, like Western education, is word-orientated. Our basic mode of instruction is learning facts and churning them out again. Now faith is certainly based on historical gospel facts, but the early Christians were described as 'followers of the Way'. Christianity is not abstract theologizing, but transformed living. And it is this above all which convinces people.

Dr Peter Wagner has a helpful explanation of the various aspects of evangelism. It starts with **presence**: simply being with all kinds of people, caring for them, quietly living an authentic Christian life. Next there is **proclamation**, when the Christian starts to explain his faith, hopefully because someone has become intrigued enough by the Christian lifestyle to start asking questions. Thirdly there is **persuasion**, when the Christian encourages his friends to commit their lives to Jesus and to join his church. Each stage is authentic evangelism. The whole process ensures that the evangelist sensitively discovers the attitude and understanding of his friends and starts there.

Much current evangelism tends to focus too much on persuasion, without an adequate base of presence and proclamation. God, on the other hand, does things thoroughly. He sent us, not a set of instructions, but his Son.

● **Church life must be attractive and comprehensible to newcomers**. The church needs to feel like a warm, accepting family. A visiting pastor from South America was asked what most struck him about European churches. 'The services always start on time,' he said, 'even though the Spirit hasn't arrived yet.'

Do our traditions of worship leave enough space for the Spirit of God to breath life and warmth into our services? Those newly-born of the Spirit of Jesus need to sense him in the Christian community and worship. Only so are they likely to move from being short-term converts to long-term disciples.

THE SPIRIT BREATHES LIFE

Before his ascension, Jesus told his disciples: 'When the Holy Spirit comes upon you, you will be filled with power and you will be witnesses for me...'

I was once doing a preaching tour in northern Namibia with Bishop Kauluma. We had arrived at St Mary's Church on the battle-torn border with Angola. Hundreds of joyfully-singing Ovambos packed the large church. It was a confirmation and the bishop asked me to preach, though with the aid of an interpreter. As I spoke about the conversion of Zaccheus, I was

See Focus on Worship

Christian radio stations in many parts of the globe broadcast gospel programmes, music and documentaries in local languages into regions where thousands would not otherwise hear about Jesus Christ. The response is mainly by letter, and many write to say they have been helped and to ask for correspondence courses.

TRAINING THE WHOLE MINISTRY

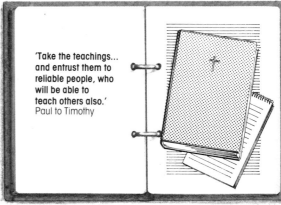

'Take the teachings...
and entrust them to
reliable people, who
will be able to
teach others also.'
Paul to Timothy

❝ A church will be effective in reaching its neighbourhood with the gospel to the extent that all its members are involved. So everyone must be trained to make the best use of the gifts God has given. ❞

FIRST TRAIN THE TRAINER...

Colleges, Bible schools, extension-training programmes are needed. Pastors and teachers must have a skilled understanding of the Bible, of Christian teaching through the ages, and of the particular needs of their own society. But their training is not geared to running a one-man show, with all the gifts concentrated in themselves. They are to train a team, to keep them looking to God and working from Christian principles.

not conscious of any interpretation going on, so at one were the interpreter and myself even though it was the first time we had met. There was a deep hush in the church; people were weeping. The Spirit of God took hold of the inadequate words of an evangelist and applied them effectively to the hearts of African tribesmen. And we all knew it, and we knew it was God's doing.

Throughout the developed world there seems to be a desire in the church for packaged solutions, a ten-week plan for the evangelization of the neighbourhood, for quick answers rather than searching questions. And we rule out the Spirit. God is a God of variety; he majors not in techniques but in people, for people are adaptable. Of course there are basic evangelistic principles, but flexibility is of the essence of evangelism.

Only a person who is open to the Spirit of God and willing to be flexible can have a lasting evangelistic ministry. Further, it is the Spirit who breathes life into the word and applies it effectively to the heart of the hearer. It is God's responsibility to germinate the seed; ours only to sow it and reap when the time is ripe.

HOW TO DO IT
Evangelism is a natural expression of spiritual life and vitality, both in the individual Christian and in the church. And

Opposite Millions of people still live in villages; they have not joined the exodus to the world's cities. Evangelism in villages requires an approach quite different from city evangelism. The rhythm and traditions of rural life must be understood and respected, and the Christian faith shown to relate to the life village people know.

'Jesus...called to himself the men he wanted... He chose twelve, whom he named apostles.'
Mark's Gospel

THEN EQUIP TEAM LEADERS...
Just as Jesus did, so church ministers should look for leaders within their church groups. Time given to them—building Christian character, praying together, helping them discover and use their gifts—is never misused.

'Jesus said, "There is a large harvest, but few workers... Pray to the owner of the harvest that he will send out workers to gather in his harvest."'
Luke's Gospel

WHO LEAD OTHERS IN SERVICE...
Close-knit groups of Christians, functioning under well-trained leaders, work best among their neighbours. Youth and children's work teams, social care teams, evangelistic teams, music groups—these can offer much more skilful service than can one minister acting in solitary grandeur. This is the New Testament way of fulfilling the mission of Jesus in the world.

just as individuals are diverse, so are the ways of sharing the good news:

● **Each situation is unique**. It is necessary to develop an approach which fits both the gifts of the evangelist and the context in which he is working. So the first step is to enter into genuine dialogue with people and learn to speak to their real needs. The Christian has to win the right to be heard, particularly in a non-Christian culture, where Christian presence and service must be the starting-point of any evangelism. Jesus spoke strongly about social justice, and in South America the church's involvement in championing the rights of the poor has drawn many to follow Jesus. In the same continent, the occurrence of healing miracles

within the Christian community has been an equally powerful validation of the gospel. As in the New Testament, so today, proclamation is by no means the only weapon in the evangelist's armoury.

● **True evangelism is person-centred**. Such evangelism is born in prayer and may initially be made through lifestyle. Sooner or later an opportunity will come to share experience or give an explanation of what it means to be a Christian. Most of us spend a good part of our lives with people – at home, at work, at play. These are natural places for evangelism. The Christian needs to develop a sensitivity to others and to God so that he or she can determine when it is appropriate to speak and when to wait.

Christians in Korea take part in a dawn prayer service. They know that the gospel will not continue to make progress in their country unless all attempts to preach it are backed by prayer. People come to faith through God's help, not just by human persuasion.

Personal evangelism can take place in a more organized fashion in a **visitation campaign**, when church members visit homes in their neighbourhood in order to share their faith and invite people to a special event. Jesus sent his followers out in pairs, and we should too.

● **Small groups are a most helpful setting for evangelism**. Of course the basic small group is **the family**. Christ-centred family life has a powerful impact on others. Sharing hospitality and a meal is a natural vehicle for the gospel. This principle has been fully grasped by the church in the Third World and from it has developed the idea of **basic communities** – small groups of Christians meeting in homes to share their life and care for the needs of each other in the locality. Many churches in the West run **home groups** where people meet for discussion or evangelistic Bible studies. **Holiday houseparties** are another way in which the relationship-building characteristic of small groups can be harnessed for the gospel.

The great advantage of both individual and small-group evangelism is that it provides plenty of opportunity for dialogue. We all find it much easier to share our questions in a small, informal context than in larger meetings. This kind of evangelism is also more effective in making contact with people who as yet are nowhere near ready to make a Christian commitment. It is much more flexible and less expensive than

A LIFE CHANGED

The only reason for 'telling the world' about Jesus is that faith in him changes people. Brian Greenaway was a hardened criminal, in England's Dartmoor Prison for grievous bodily harm. Someone gave him a Bible and he read Jesus' words about being 'the true vine'. He prayed to Jesus to change him.

'At that instant I began to feel all the pus and poison in me drain away through my feet. All the frustration and anger that had held me prisoner for most of my life just flowed away. At the same time it was as though a hole opened up in my head and God's love began pouring in. For the first time I was experiencing real love and it was God's pure love. In tears of joy I fell to my knees on the floor, thanking God for bringing us together. After that I slept a dreamless sleep – at peace with God.'

larger activities.

● **But large groups have a place**. They start at the level of the congregation, where the most usual expression is the **guest service**. Members of the congregation are invited to bring their friends to a lively service with a gospel message. Perhaps more useful is the method of **faith-sharing teams**. A group of ordinary Christians from one church spends a weekend in another congregation using every opportunity to share their faith simply. The cumulative effect of a great variety of testimonies has a powerful impact. This illustrates the principle that evangelistic effectiveness does not just depend on those with a special gift, but on the whole group together demonstrating the love

See The Church at Home

Afghanistan is a country where Christianity has made little headway. While such nations exist, Christians cannot imagine that their task is nearing completion.

and forgiveness of God.

The same style can be further developed in a **parish mission** of ten days or so, when an evangelist with a supporting team concentrates on an area. **Mission Audit** is a simple process in which a congregation looks at its internal life and the needs of the nieghbourhood. From this a strategy for evangelizing the area is developed.
● **Other methods are more broad-scale**. Sometimes churches join together in an area to provide **every household**

with a portion of the Bible. Throughout the world **television and radio** are extensively used to proclaim the gospel. This is mainly a 'seed-sowing' process. **Mass evangelism** is different and well-known through the work of evangelists such as Billy Graham who use a large tent or stadium. This style of evangelism depends very much on the support of the local churches, and recent statistics have shown that in the West it has its major impact on people already in contact with the church.

REACHING NEW PEOPLES
MIRIAM ADENEY

Since the mid-1960s, concern has been mounting among Christians concerned for world evangelism to identify 'unreached peoples': those among whom there is no significant, sustained witness to the gospel. The thinking is that to focus either simply on individuals or on artificially-constructed nations may not be the most effective way of breaking new ground for the gospel.

But how do you define a 'people'? What criteria mark out those who are 'unreached'? And is this a valid approach anyway?

A 'people' is basically a group with a common culture. The concept of a people is quite common in the Bible, where the word is *ethne*, giving our 'ethnic'. People from the same ethne can pray together in their mother tongue. But there is more to the idea than merely language: culture is involved too. Individuals identify with a culture in varying degrees. Therefore it is more useful to describe the core of an ethnic tradition than to define its boundaries, and to speak more of ethnic networks than ethnic groups. This gives credibility to the occasional focus on subculture 'people groups' – high-rise dwellers in Singapore, horseracing staff in North America – if viable primary networks exist.

Who are 'unreached'? Various questions need to be asked here. What percentage have heard the gospel? Is the Bible available? What proportion of the people are Christian? Do the Christians of this people evangelize their neighbours and nurture new churches?

An objection to this approach has been that it is sociological rather than theological. But the foundation is in fact deeply Christian, and rests on belief in the way God created human beings. God has made people in his image. As he is creative, so are we. With this God-given creativity we develop different cultures. The resulting kaleidoscope of patterns enriches God's world.

Practically the benefits are real and evident. Such basics as time, budgeting, electing church officers, can be handled so as to suit the particular culture. Evangelism flourishes. In a foreign country, an ethnic church – such as a fellowship of Iranians in the United States – can prepare students, businessmen and others to return to their home countries and communicate their faith in intelligible terms.

As evangelists try to reach new peoples, the most crucial practice is 'bonding'. The evangelist needs to stay close, not stand apart. He may use local housing, transport, possessions; he will learn the language among the people, not at some school. Bonding means recognizing that we do not take God to new people: he takes us, to back up and sharpen witness he has already given. Bonding means believing that as these people absorb Christ and his Spirit they will be able to make sound ethical decisions and to lead from a very early point. Bonding also means political empathy.

Focussing on unreached peoples makes people aware of the 'unreached' problem, and stimulates action to close the gap with the 'reached'. Many examples could be quoted:

■ After the fall of the Shah of Iran, concerned American Christians began to reach out to Iranians stranded in the United States. Today, the Fellowship of Iranian Christians helps Farsi-speaking congregations all across the continent.

■ In the southern Philippines in the last ten years, a wave of conversions to Christ has rippled through the Muslim Samals. These are illiterate fishermen whose migratory tendencies have been exacerbated by civil war in the region.

Through their roving, Christian witness has penetrated the Muslims of East Malaysia.

■ More specific groups, like the Christian Cowboys Association, or Prison Fellowships, effectively nurture people who would not respond to other kinds of outreach.

Books help to shape people's thinking, and Christian literature is an important aid to spreading the gospel.

● **Celebration evangelism is somewhat different**. Though preaching plays an important part, it focusses even more on the participants enjoying the presence of God. People's hearts are engaged through music and drama, not just as a preliminary to the proclaiming of the gospel but as an integral part. The team leading the celebration will often live as a community and the

MISSION TO THE CITIES
ROGER S. GREENWAY

This is the century in which the entire world has become urbanized. Half the human race already lives in cities and the percentage grows higher every day. In the 1980s alone, a million million people are expected to migrate from rural to metropolitan areas in the Third World. So the importance of Christian mission to the cities can hardly be overstated. Failure on the part of Christians to reach the great urban areas for Christ would be a failure of tragic proportions.

Signs of life
The world-wide Christian church has some significant strengths in cities. In Britain, Europe and North America, large and famous churches have existed in key cities for many years, and their influence is widely known. In recent decades, important black churches and ethnic congregations have emerged in the Third World, some with thousands of members and gifted leaders, and inevitably these churches are concentrated in cities.

In Seoul, South Korea, lighted crosses and church steeples seem to be everywhere. Seoul's Full Gospel Central Church, with more than 250,000 members, is the world's largest Protestant church. On

Sundays, 10,000 people crowd into the auditorium for each of the seven worship services, and thousands more watch by closed-circuit TV in adjacent rooms. In an Asian society, historically Buddhist, Korean Christians show the world what can be done in cities when the Spirit of God moves and God's people reach out with the gospel. The church's pastor, Dr Paul Yonggi Cho, attributes the phenomenal growth of his church to several 'basics': faith and prayer; the power of the Bible to change lives; energetic ministry to the sick, the needy, and the hurting people of the city; and to the development of 'home cells'. These are local groups which meet weekly throughout the city for Bible study, prayer, fellowship and evangelism.

Problems and challenges
However, the story of Seoul's churches seems to be the exception rather than the rule in the history of urban outreach. Traditionally, most Protestants have found it difficult to live and work as Christians in the city. In North America particularly, Protestantism has been largely rural, small-town and suburban. In recent years there has been a virtual stampede of white churches from the

cities and it has left behind empty church buildings, hurt feelings, and a diminished witness on the part of the major denominations. At the same time, waves of new immigrants, representing racial and cultural communities very different from the departing whites, have entered cities and transformed urban life. More than ever before, cities have become multicultural societies and they require mission work that reaches across cultural barriers, and that is specially adapted to meet the needs of urban people.

The sheer size of urban populations and the problems associated with large cities create emotional and practical barriers to Christian mission. Mexico City, for example, is now the largest metropolitan area in the world and grows at the rate of about 1 million people a year. The spiritual, social and emotional needs of the masses in such cities are so enormous that Christian workers tend to turn away in search of smaller, less bewildering places for ministry. This is especially the case for Christians who come from small communities. Not only do they find living in big cities difficult to adjust to, they also tend to interpret the urban environment as being inherently

whole approach is an expression of the life of commitment which they share together. It can speak powerfully to those who have had little previous contact with Christian things.

Whatever methods are used, however, it is the life that counts for most. When you have a witnessing Christian, a loving Christian family and a vitally worshipping church, evangelism happens naturally.

inhospitable to Christianity. Such reactions, unfortunately, are common among both foreign and national workers and they hinder the Christian mission in large cities.

Changing gear

Despite the difficulties, the shift to urban mission is well under way. As world population becomes increasingly urban, the strength of the church and its mission will have to take increasing account of the city. Church leaders everywhere are calling for conferences and seminars on the subject of urban mission. Courses on the subject of the church's ministry in and to cities are being offered in colleges and seminaries. Some major mission agencies are in the process of shifting the main thrust of their efforts to the cities. In some cases mission workers are being retrained to cope with urban realities.

Books on the subject of urban mission are increasing in number. A new journal called *Urban Mission* is tying together global efforts to reach cities with the gospel. Published in Philadelphia, *Urban Mission* blends scholarly research into urban issues with case-studies describing evangelical outreach world-wide, and reports on current events affecting urban outreach. The journal is a sign of what is happening as the main focus of Christian mission shifts to the city.

The burgeoning cities of the world confront the church, and the gospel itself, with history's most serious challenge. Those who win the cities will win the world. For people concerned with Christian mission, that can mean only one thing: these great urban concentrations, with all their influence, complexity and teeming millions of people, must receive our major attention.

There is no substitute in the end for personal evangelism. Jesus spread his message as he met people, individually or in small groups as much as in crowds. And Christians, like this city missioner in London dockland, are doing the same every day throughout the world.

Defending the Faith Today

GABRIEL FACKRE

From the beginning, Christians have made powerful claims with strong conviction. This has provoked criticism and attack. And so Christians have always had to put forward a 'defence of the faith'. As early as New Testament times, believers were urged to 'be prepared to make a defence to anyone who calls you to account for the hope that is in you...'. Paul did this in the synagogues and on the Areopagus in Athens, and many others since have done the same, in the spirit of Isaiah's words, 'Come let us argue it out.'

Defence of the faith has taken many forms over the centuries.

● Early exponents of the gospel had to reply to allegations of superstition and immorality. **They argued that Christian belief, which was more reasonable, encouraged higher moral standards** than did its critics and the surrounding culture. Justin Martyr was one of the earliest 'apologists' (from the Latin word *apologia*, meaning 'defence'). With him began a long tradition of Christian apologetics still very much alive, in which the value of the Christian faith is set forth by appealing to commonly-accepted standards of truth. People like this believe that although human beings are fallen they are still made in God's image - an image that although distorted is not destroyed. Therefore, human reason and conscience are still capable of grappling with the truth.

● Other kinds of Christian defence, however, are not as confident about human capacity to grasp the truth. They hold that sin has had disastrous effects on our reasoning processes. These proponents believe that dogmatics (the clear exposition of the faith) is the best apologetics. **They defend the faith by proclaiming the gospel** and clearing up misunderstandings about it. Unlike other apologists, they do not offer reasons for believing, because they are convinced that 'the Word will do it'.

Apologetics in almost every form assumes that Christianity has an intellectual content. It contains assertions about the way things are with God and the world, a faith *in which* to believe as well as a faith *with which* to believe. Views of faith which reduce it either to the trust of the heart or right conduct, eliminating 'belief' in the process, violate the wholeness of faith. Faith must include the love of God with the mind, as well as with the heart.

See The Gospel in Today's World; The Secular Outlook of Today

TODAY'S ATTACKS AND QUESTIONS

Today's Christian apologists, whether they argue out their faith or simply state it, confront an army of critics. In societies shaped by the eighteenth-century Enlightenment, with its trust in human wisdom and goodness, and its tendency to treat religion as an enemy of the mind and human progress, faith collides with all kinds of naturalisms, secularisms, humanisms and scientisms. These question God's existence and the Christian story of what God has done - from creation, through redemption in Christ, to the consummation of all things. To take just two examples:

● **Marxists** criticize Christianity by saying that it is preoccupied with the next life and its rewards, so keeping the oppressed from fighting for their rights in this life. They claim that religion serves to smokescreen the economic interests of the ruling classes.

● **A psychological attack** on the Christian faith also criticizes it as being an 'opiate of the people'. This attack says that belief in a realm and a hope beyond death is a self-serving compensation for frustrations experienced in this life. This prevents people from coming to terms with reality.

● In the encounter with **other world religions**, Christian defence today goes on within the context of a growing dialogue with other faiths. Christian witness here means openness to truth wherever it is found on the basis that God has revealed himself generally in creation. Yet at the same time it points to God's unique saving work in Jesus Christ and is prepared to argue out challenges to that claim.

● In a similar vein, Christians seek to learn from **movements of liberation, justice and peace**. But they are also prepared to challenge these when their ideologies call into question biblical teaching and classical Christian belief.

Where the Christian community meets either unyielding religious fanaticism or political zealotry, it can do no better than equip its own people with clarity and conviction about their own gospel, and fling that faith in the air joyfully.

Many different influences shape people's ideas – newspapers, television and radio not least. Often the opinions expressed are hostile to Christianity, or discount it. Christians are called to defend the faith – publicly, clearly and effectively.

THE AGGRESSIVE APPROACH

Some contemporary apologists, following ancient precedents, believe that intellectual attack is the best defence. Appealing to reasons which they hold are open to anyone who will look squarely at the facts, they argue that alternative or anti-Christian world-views are self-defeating.

Reinhold Niebuhr took this line in his famous book, *The Nature and Destiny of Man* (1941-43). He argued that the modern understanding of human nature either ignores the basic facts of life, or in the long run destroys society. A naturalist view, which reduces the self to body-chemistry, heredity, economic factors, psychological forces or social conditioning, denies the 'I' discernible to anyone capable of honest introspection. Niebuhr goes on to point out that naturalist philosophies have contributed to moral chaos by annihilating personal dignity.

On the other hand, idealist views of human nature, which reduce the self to mind or spirit, overlook our creaturely roots in nature and history. The result is that basic human needs are ignored, the individual gets lost in abstraction, and illusions about the future can grow up, cultivated by the naïve trust that human effort automatically takes us ever upward.

Because these views do not have the biblical understanding of the unity and depth of the self, and the reality of sin, Niebuhr argues that they succumb over time either to a destructive self-righteous fury or an enervating despair.

The apologetic writings of **Paul Tillich** and **Helmut Thielicke** also used attack as a means of defence. They took an attacking stance toward movements such as Fascism, Nazism, and Communism, declaring them to be anti-human. Tillich condemned them for turning race or class into a humanly destructive idol, while Thielicke argued that the end-point of the modern quest for independence from God and the gospel was not freedom but meaninglessness.

ATTACKING THE WEAK SPOTS

Another way of defending the faith is to challenge the rational consistency of alternative philosophies. One modern

Many people think distinctively Christian teaching is no longer needed in a world of many faiths. Against this background the uniqueness of Jesus must be spelt out, pungently but without confrontation.

apologist, **Carl Henry**, questions those who argue that all truth is relative. He asks how it is possible to state that all absolute claims to truth, such as those made by Christianity, are false because of their relativity to time and place, when that statement itself presupposes its own absolute truth. Such a philosophy either exempts itself from its own rule, or denies what it presupposes. To the logical positivists who declare nonsensical all statements that are not backed up by the evidence of the senses, he says: Your cardinal principle is a contradiction in terms for it is an assertion that itself has no empirical proof.

C.S.Lewis, a popular apologist who personally experimented with many modern options before coming to faith, believed that the alternatives to Christianity collapse before the data of sensory, moral and spiritual experience, and the laws of reason. While never a systematic apologist, his vernacular works, using a remarkable display of imagination and invention, defended the faith before a mass audience as few others have done.

A REASONABLE FAITH

Apologists are not simply in the business of demolishing their opponents. There is a strong positive side, showing that Christianity is a reasonable option for people who are willing to look at the facts and think clearly about them. Christianity is true to life - it illuminates human experience better than other perspectives.

Reinhold Niebuhr argues that an honest look into our own depths and a careful scrutiny of society backs up Christian realism about sin both in the self and society at large. Armed with the biblical recognition of fallen human nature, together with its affirmation of human dignity, we will be more morally responsible and effective - personally and socially - than either the utopians who ignore sin or the cynics who deny human dignity.

The European 'theologians of hope', such as **Jürgen Moltmann**, also portray the Christian faith as a way of making sense of life, pointing the way forward for individuals and societies. Believing in the resurrection of Jesus Christ and being confident that God will bring all things to a proper conclusion, the Christian is protected from despair when evil seems to have the upper hand in history.

This sense of purpose in history, coupled with commitment to the moral standards required by the coming of God's kingdom, far from being socially irresponsible, commits Christians to work out their faith in terms of justice and peace now.

LAYING CHRISTIAN FOUNDATIONS

One branch in the family of apologists attempts to clear the ground for the more distinctive Christian beliefs, by arguing for basic beliefs, such as the existence of God. In this way,

See Theology Today

their approach seeks to prepare people for the special revelation of Christ and the Bible.

Today this kind of defence attempts to recover or restate some of the age-old arguments for God's existence - based on the design and purpose of the universe, the need for an original cause to the world, a source for universal moral values, or the logical necessity for God's existence (the teleological, cosmological, moral and ontological arguments). Process theologians such as **Charles Hartshorne**, and the Roman Catholic apologist **Hans Küng**, have given new currency to these approaches.

FACING MODERN CHALLENGES

In the 1960s and the following decades, 'secular theologians' sought to adapt Christian faith to today's concerns - political, cultural, social and psychological. In their eagerness to *relate* faith to the contemporary scene - a legitimate concern - they often tended to *capitulate* to the assumptions and values of the day. as in the 'death of God', 'honest to God', and situation ethics phenomena.

A pendulum swing in a later decade gave religion higher visibility and brought with it the rise, in some cases, of fundamentalist movements, often with strong political agendas. While criticizing others for 'secular humanism', their own blending of religious teaching with right-wing political philosophy turned out to be the same kind of secularizing of the Christian faith, and thus a chameleon apologetic.

In the late twentieth century, liberation theologies - Third World, ethnic and feminist - have oriented faith to the justice issues of oppressed peoples. Moreover, in the wider encounter with world religions, pluralist theologies have emerged, attempting to relate the experience of other religions to Christian faith. These also walk the tightrope of seeking to connect the gospel to the challenges of a day of political ferment and religious pluralism. Ideology regularly imperils the rightful commitment to the struggle for justice and peace. And the loss of the Christian belief in the 'scandal of particularity' is the ever-present pitfall of legitimate efforts in dialogue with other religions.

PROCLAMATION AND PURIFICATION

Such eagerness to communicate in the language and logic of our own time and place seems sometimes to empty the Christian faith of its distinctiveness. Another kind of defence has made its voice heard in the twentieth century which certainly avoids such reduction. This was a voice that shunned rational argument and put proclamation in its place.

In Germany, in the years leading up to World War II, many Christians were shocked at the official church's acceptance of the blood and soil philosophy of Nazism. In 1934, at Barmen, the

Trainee Mormon missionaries outside a Mormon temple in Salt Lake City, Utah. A number of deviations from Christianity cause confusion in people's minds as they are aggressively promoted world-wide. This makes clear Christian teaching all the more vital.

Confessing Church defended the faith by dissociating it from entanglements with its surrounding culture. The Barmen Declaration was drafted by **Karl Barth**, and reflected his suspicion that natural theology and apologetics lead to the captivity of faith. The price the Confessing Church had to pay was high, as fierce persecution followed Christian resistance to Hitler.

Other apologists in this tradition are not prepared to go as far as Barth. Admittedly, they are not faced with the onslaught of a demonic political movement, but nor are they as pessimistic about apologetics. However, they do see their role in similar terms: challenging the way faith is modified to fit culture in secular, liberation and pluralist theologies, and among right-wing and left-wing Christians. They believe that before the faith can be proclaimed, it must be purified. Their stress is upon the supremacy of biblical teaching and the centrality of Jesus Christ over current ideologies.

THE RIGHT WORD AT THE RIGHT TIME

The defence of the faith is made today both by those who believe that a persuasive case can be made for it by reason, and also by those who hold that the proclamation of the purified gospel is its own best argument.

Those who use rational means for the most part gladly agree with the defenders-as-proclaimers that faith comes only by the inner testimony of the Holy Spirit to the good news. Yet the rational apologists also believe that the Spirit works through the disciplines of reason that seek to clear away the intellectual obstacles to the act of personal faith. And to that end the battle of the mind is joined.

Indeed, in matters of defending faith, 'there is a season, and a time for every matter under heaven,' as Ecclesiastes says. There is a time to reason and a time to testify. The church prays for the grace, in this day as in others, to speak the right word at the right time.

Stewards of Creation

PETER HARRIS

We humans have always changed the world we live in, but it is estimated that we have made greater changes since 1950 than in all the years of human history until that time. The changes we make become more drastic as each year passes. Christians have been no quicker than anyone else to appreciate the scale of the problems, and have usually continued to share in the often damaging lifestyles of their cultures. In fact, it has to be asked whether Christians are more part of the problem than the solution. So what are the main ways human activity has affected planet earth?

'The reality of the ecological crisis is becoming more visible with each passing day...and may impose general acceptance of what Christians have been proclaiming for many centuries – that man is the custodian and steward of the earth and not its outright owner.' Ian Blair

A TICKING BOMB

In the last 200 years, the human population has grown at an explosive rate. The first person to draw attention to the principles of human over-population was the English clergyman Thomas Malthus in 1798. His predictions of a great increase in world population have been largely borne out, but natural and man-made disasters have not limited growth as he thought. At the time he was writing, the world's population had just reached 1,000 million. But it only took until 1930 for that figure to double, and a further forty-five years for it to double again. Now the figure is around 4,700 million, with over a million more added every five days.

Why has there been this dramatic surge in human numbers? Improved medical care has greatly reduced infant mortality world-wide, although it remains high in many parts of the world. But even so, the greatest rates of growth are found in those countries where there is the greatest poverty. The number of children born to each woman in the world ranges from 1.9 in Europe and North America, to 6.5 in Africa and 4.4 in Latin America. Remarkable exceptions exist - such as China, which seems committed to negative population growth. But until social conditions improve, the world population explosion will continue until other and more terrible factors come into play with yet more force than today.

EXHAUSTING THE EARTH

Poverty and environmental

God has given us a beautiful world, rich in varied species of animals and plants. A careless use of the world's resources is obliterating many of them. Humanity needs to learn to share the world sensitively with the whole living creation.

damage go hand in hand. In India, the lack of wood for domestic fuel means that almost all the 2,000 million tons of manure produced by cattle, sheep and goats is burnt for fuel and the land becomes increasingly sterile. Overgrazing by animals has further reduced dry areas to desert, and a recent official report stated that 70 per cent of all the freshwater sources are now seriously polluted.

At the same time, resources for sustaining the world's people are diminishing rapidly. In 1980, The World Conservation Strategy estimated that if current rates of land degradation continue, nearly one-third of the world's arable land would be destroyed in the next twenty years. The same is true of the productive rain forests. If we continue to cut them down at the present rate, then by the end of this century one half of what remains will be lost.

And yet this demand for resources is by no means equally shared by the world's population. One Swiss, for example, uses the same quantity of resources as forty Somalis. And such inequalities are the rule rather than the exception.

DIRTYING THE EARTH
The impact of industry on the environment of the 1980s presents a grim picture. Much of the environmental concern of the 1960s and 1970s was directed to the problem of pollution as the effect of industrial emissions began to be realized, and toxic waste was detected in every part of the planet. But despite some

major advances, new problems are still emerging and the level of pollution continues to rise. The solutions to these problems are not easily reached, as the international arguments over acid rain show. Meanwhile, the rain continues to make many lakes and rivers sterile and to destroy vast areas of forest far from the sources of the damaging chemicals.

In the effort to maximize the yields of the earth, in agriculture and in fuel and minerals, technology has been applied in ever-widening ways. Nuclear technology in particular has been seen as both the great solution - 'electricity too cheap to meter'; and as the final evil - 'a fundamental threat to democracy'.

Wholesale interference with delicate ecological systems can have unforeseen consequences, and yet plans for projects such as the Soviet Union's massive river-reversal scheme go ahead regardless. The intensive farming practices of the United States, employed to produce greater and greater amounts of grain for world markets, are having a disastrous effect on the nation's soil. Although United States land provides 55 per cent of world exports in grain, about 4 per cent of its cultivated land will soon be worthless unless it is quickly taken out of production.

It can be seen therefore that questions of environment and ecology cannot be separated from political, economic, and of course, religious and ethical decisions. Sir Peter Scott, one of the most famous figures in the world-wide environmental movement, chose the prestigious tenth anniversary meeting of the original United Nations Stockholm Conference on the Human Environment to say that one man could advance the cause of the environment more than them all - the pope. However, the Roman Catholic Church still remains opposed to artificial means of birth control since the papal encyclical *Humanae Vitae* of 1968. The issues of population, the exploitation of the earth and pollution continue to generate heated controversy.

'CHRISTIAN ARROGANCE'

Are Christians part of the problem, or part of the answer? In a now-famous address in 1966, Lynn White Jnr claimed that the roots of the present eco-crisis lay in 'Christian arrogance'. Christians, he said, believe that nature only exists to serve mankind, and that mankind, as recorded in the Genesis account of creation, has a divine mandate to exploit nature.

Despite the fundamental misreading of the Bible (in Genesis 1:27-28) that his criticism implies, it has since become accepted among many secular ecologists that Christian thinking is responsible for environmental abuse. Noted Christian public figures have done little to reassure them, either by their apparent ignorance or, as with one prominent American politician who recently condemned conservation groups as 'shrills' and 'garbage-men', by outright hostility.

It is also true that for centuries many Christians have been guilty of following the heresy that divides the world into spiritual and material, in which the material is credited with very little importance. Yet this is far from the Bible's teaching. God's commitment to the earth is spelt out: 'I have set my rainbow in the clouds, and it will be a sign of the covenant between me and the earth. I will remember my covenant between me and you and all living creatures of every kind.' And as to man's killing of animals, in the same passage, God says, 'I will demand an accounting of every animal.' The prophet Isaiah makes it clear that the human destruction of the earth is the result of *breaking* God's laws, not keeping them: 'The earth is defiled by its people; they have disobeyed the laws, violated the statutes and broken the everlasting covenant - therefore a curse consumes the earth.'

In addition, the church in many parts of the world continues to be compromised by an affluent lifestyle that directly contributes to environmental catastrophe and human starvation elsewhere. Christians have (with a few notable exceptions) done little to challenge the lifestyle of the cultures they live in. In the struggle to survive, Christians in the poorer countries can hardly be criticized for perpetuating the ecological sins of their own culture. And yet, as was recognized recently in a leading article in the *New Scientist* magazine, what is needed in environmental issues is not so

HOW TO WRECK THE WORLD

❝ God gave humankind the role of manager over the natural world. This task includes the care of all life on the Earth, not just human life. It requires thought for future generations, not just our own. A selfish use of Earth's resources can do irreparable damage. ❞

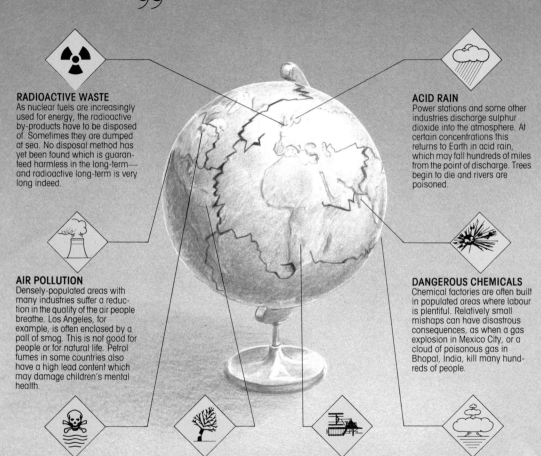

RADIOACTIVE WASTE
As nuclear fuels are increasingly used for energy, the radioactive by-products have to be disposed of. Sometimes they are dumped at sea. No disposal method has yet been found which is guaranteed harmless in the long-term—and radioactive long-term is very long indeed.

ACID RAIN
Power stations and some other industries discharge sulphur dioxide into the atmosphere. At certain concentrations this returns to Earth in acid rain, which may fall hundreds of miles from the point of discharge. Trees begin to die and rivers are poisoned.

AIR POLLUTION
Densely-populated areas with many industries suffer a reduction in the quality of the air people breathe. Los Angeles, for example, is often enclosed by a pall of smog. This is not good for people or for natural life. Petrol fumes in some countries also have a high lead content which may damage children's mental health.

DANGEROUS CHEMICALS
Chemical factories are often built in populated areas where labour is plentiful. Relatively small mishaps can have disastrous consequences, as when a gas explosion in Mexico City, or a cloud of poisonous gas in Bhopal, India, kill many hundreds of people.

WATER POLLUTION
Rivers, lakes and seas are sometimes poisoned by industrial waste, and sometimes polluted by oil spillage. Seabirds, fish and other marine life are gravely affected, and the balance of nature disturbed. The Great Lakes of USA/Canada and such enclosed seas as the Baltic and the Mediterranean are in particular danger.

DEFORESTATION
The urgent need for wood products, especially for the paper industry, tempts countries short of cash to allow excessive tree-felling. Great tracts of the Amazon forests, for example, are disappearing. It takes years to replace a tree. Deforestation has catastrophic effects on soil fertility, and on the rich natural life of the forests.

LAND DEGRADATION
The soil can be used for short-term gain in such a way as to impoverish its future fertility. This can happen through over-intensive farming and fertilization, as in the United States; or through burning manure and trees for domestic fuel, as in many poor countries.

NUCLEAR TESTING
In the early days of testing nuclear weapons (1950s and early 60s), remote areas such as Pacific islands and Australian deserts were badly affected by fall-out. Test-ban treaties have improved things, but what could be the results of extending conflict into space?

much new methods as a new spirituality. The Bible clearly teaches that humanity is responsible to God for the care of creation - both as part of creation and as a steward of it. This is the spirituality the world needs. Yet enquiries of the church world-wide elicit the same response - too little corporate involvement in this area at present.

Conservation must be a major concern for governments if it is to have any lasting effect. Yet it is not merely a political issue. The lifestyle of Christians and the concerns of the churches should reflect a far greater awareness of our ecological catastrophe than they presently do. As those who believe that the earth was created by a personal, loving God, Christians have a particular responsibility.

CHANGE MUST COME

There is evidence of change among Christians, although you may have to look hard to find it. Many Christian development projects, such as those of the relief organization Tear Fund, show concern for the environment. Other Christians work more directly with the environment, such as the forestry projects of the Mennonites in Haiti and Tanzania, and the A Rocha Field Study Centre in Portugal. As Christian concern grows, there is an urgent call for information and co-operation between the many individuals now involved.

Individual Christians have often been very influential, and maybe this will always be the pattern for Christian involvement, as some like Britain's Professor Sam Berry believe. His writings, and those of Professor Rowland Moss, have done much to inject Christian environmental thinking into society and into the church, and the number of Christian writers on ecology is growing. In the United States, writers such as Wes Granberg-Michaelson and Howard Snyder have shown Christians how much there is to be learned by adopting ecological principles.

For many Christians, the symptoms of environmental disorder such as famine and disease press more heavily than the causes. People matter more than things, it is argued. But a biblical ecology shows us that people and things cannot be so easily divided, and our preaching and living of the gospel must faithfully reflect all of God's intentions for the earth.

In the face of such mega-projects as the Soviet Union's river scheme, and the relentless stockpiling of arms (on which the world spends more in six hours than it has spent in ten years on the United Nations Environment Programme), many Christians feel completely powerless. Yet the gospel reminds us of the vital importance of individual choices, and calls us to honour God as individuals and as the people of God. In this area, possibly more than any other in this book, change must come.

'In the Bible the praise of God arises alike from nature and from man to blend together in a cosmic symphony.' Paulos Mar Gregorios

See Bread for the World; Spirituality Today

Bread for the World

JOHN MITCHELL

Millions of Christians in the rich countries of western Europe, North America and Australasia have become increasingly aware, through television and the experience of mass intercontinental air travel, of the gross disparities between the 'normal' material standard of living that they and their contemporaries now enjoy and the appalling poverty and starvation that is the normal way of life for so many who live in Africa, Asia and Latin America (a situation dramatically brought home by the television pictures in 1984 of the growing famine in Africa, particularly Ethiopia).

These 'rich Christians' have become convinced not only of this desperate material need in the Third World, but also of the Bible's teaching about wealth and poverty. They are becoming more aware of their responsibility to share their unparalleled affluence with the hundreds of millions of desperately poor people in God's world.

Throughout its 2,000-year history, the Christian church in all parts of the world has attempted to follow Jesus' practical example of caring both for people's spiritual and physical welfare. Over the centuries, Christians have been in the forefront of providing medical care, food and education – as well as spiritual help – to the poor and hungry in the communities where they live.

In the rich, industrialized countries of the world, few people now go to bed hungry or lacking basic medical care. The availability of health care and education (which are now provided free by the state in many countries), has developed well beyond the levels of

A Falasha girl carries water for her family in Ethiopia. Water is a vital resource, and when rains fail, as in many parts of Africa in recent years, the fragility of the structure sustaining human life is cruelly exposed.

previous centuries. However, life is very different in the countries of Africa, Asia and Latin America. These countries, which contain three-quarters of the earth's population, are often called the 'Third World'. They adopted this term to distinguish themselves from the capitalist world of North America and Western Europe and the communist world of the Soviet Union and Eastern Europe. Despite the tremendous advances of recent years, hundreds of millions in the Third World still suffer the agonies of starvation and die from diseases which have been all but wiped out in the richer countries of the world.

The Christian church in Third World countries is nearly always in the forefront of the struggle for economic and social development, and most of the churches' development work is done by Christian nationals from the country concerned. However, in the last forty years, there has been a growing move to imitate the early church's example of financial help between churches in different countries specifically to meet material need.

CHRISTIAN ACTION AGAINST HUNGER

Before World War II, the main way Christians in rich countries expressed their practical concern for the physical need of people in the Third World was through the missionary societies. Missionaries usually brought not only spiritual teaching but some practical care for the medical, educational and physical needs of the communities to which they went.

BASIS FOR DEVELOPMENT

George Hoffman, director of British relief agency TEAR Fund, spoke once of how issues of development are interwoven with spiritual issues:

'I can remember shortly after one of the upheavals in Bangladesh, the local Muslim leaders coming to the Christian missionaries and openly stating: "What our country needs is renewal. What our country needs is new men. Islam cannot give it to us. Can your Christ?" They recognized that to change man's condition without changing man's character, is to change nothing...It is no good trying to create new nations of men unless we can create men with a new nature, And I believe only Jesus Christ can do that.'

After the war, new Christian organizations began to grow up in nearly all the major industrialized countries. These were geared specifically to meeting the material needs of people in the Third World, though they have often channelled their help through the missionary societies and the national church in the particular country.
● **In Germany**, Bread for the World is the official relief and development agency of the German churches, and EZE and Misereor are supported by Protestant and Catholic churches respectively.
● **In France**, CIMADE was started during World War II and helped many of the victims of Nazi occupation. Today it works

A comment on the effects on the world's poorest of the international banking crises in 1984: 'Christians are called to proclaim, live for and work for the kingdom of God. For it is the kingdom that judges – and ultimately transforms – a society that makes it impossible to practice economics as though people mattered.' Charles Elliott

A Berber child in Morocco collects sticks to cook the family food. Whole areas are rapidly cleared of trees as populations expand, with devastating effect on the fertility of the soil.

among refugees and immigrants in France and it funds development projects in the Third World, usually through the World Council of Churches. For Roman Catholics, the Catholic Committee against Hunger and for Development (CCFD) is the main channel in France.
● **In the United Kingdom**, the efforts of the churches to help the millions of refugees in central

AID, TRADE AND DEVELOPMENT
JOHN MITCHELL

Over the last twenty years, there has been an increasing realization among many Christians in the world's rich, industrialized countries that they should not limit their concern for the world's poor to dealing only with the *symptoms* of poverty. Many Christians have come to believe that the *root causes* of poverty also need to be dealt with. Supporting the work of voluntary agencies working in the Third World is still obviously a vital part of a Christian's response to world poverty, but Christians also believe that God is a God of justice and that throughout the Bible he is concerned to ensure just structures in the world. They therefore see biblical reasons for working for what is often called a *New International Economic Order*.

Christians have therefore been trying to change the manifest injustices in the relationships between rich and poor countries that help to perpetuate poverty in the Third World. In doing this, they have not ignored the fact that policies *within* many Third World countries have also contributed to increased poverty and starvation. However, Christians in rich countries see their role as campaigning for the changes needed in their own country's policies

towards the Third World. The work of changing the internal policies of Third World countries themselves must be the task of Christians in those countries.

First steps
At first, Christians in the rich countries concentrated on the size and quality of their country's official aid programme. This was partly a natural progression from involvement with the aid given by voluntary agencies – but it also happened as Christians realized the relative size of government aid programmes. These range from ten to fifteen times the total voluntary giving in the United States and West Germany, to about twenty times in the United Kingdom and over 100 times voluntary giving in France.

This concern about government actions on aid was spurred on by the failure of all but a handful of rich industrialized countries to meet the agreed international target of giving 0.7 per cent of gross national product to the Third World. There was also a strong feeling that governments were using their aid programmes to achieve commercial and political objectives in

the Third World rather than to help the poor.

Following on from this, Christians also turned their attention to another key area of a government's policy – trade. For all but the very poorest countries, the price a country receives for its exports (often consisting mainly of just one or two primary commodities) is usually far more important than the level of aid.

More recently, Christians have also sought changes in government policy, not just in the areas of aid and trade, but in other areas such as international financial issues as well. These have included:
● **The policies of the International Monetary Fund** towards developing countries.
● The response of governments to **the mounting debt crisis of many Third World countries** – a crisis which is being aggravated by record international interest rates.
● The policies not only of governments, but also of **multinational companies and trades unions**. Their policies also have a profound effect on the poor in the Third World.

In all their campaigning in these areas, Christians are concerned with

Europe at the end of World War II led to the formation of the Inter-Church Aid and Refugee Service. This was the official development and relief agency of the British Council of Churches, and in 1964 it became Christian Aid. In 1962. the Catholic Agency for Overseas Development (CAFOD) was founded, and in 1969 the Evangelical Alliance Relief Fund (TEAR Fund) was launched, in response to growing concern among Evangelical Christians in Britain for the needs of the Third World.

● **In the United States**, although the Church World Service is the official relief and development agency of the National Council of Christian Churches, each of the main denominations also has its own relief and development agency,

the long-term economic and social development of a country, which goes well beyond the emergency application of aid. Such action seeks to support industrial and agricultural development, appropriate to the needs of the country concerned, using local resources as far as possible.

Campaigning for change

In many industrialized countries, this increasing level of concern and action among Christians about government policies that affect the Third World has been channelled through existing voluntary agencies and church organizations. But in the United States and the United Kingdom, separate organizations have grown up specifically to campaign on these issues.

● **World Development Movement** In the United Kingdom in 1969, a church-based sign-in on world poverty, urging the government to meet the UN target for official aid, attracted over a million signatures. From that upsurge in concern, the World Development Movement was born. It undertakes a work that British charities like Christian Aid and Tear Fund cannot carry out because of the restrictions placed on them under British charity law. Its aim is to link together individuals and local groups in the campaign for changes on the political issues of aid, trade and development.

The World Development Movement is not a Christian organization as such, but about 80 per cent of its finances come from churches and individual Christians, and a similarly high proportion of its members are linked to churches.

Among the movement's notable successes were the mass lobby of the British parliament in May 1981 on the Brandt Commission's first report, and a nationwide campaign in Britain of lobbying before the North-South summit of world leaders in Cancun, Mexico, that autumn. In autumn 1984, at a time when there was widespread concern about famines in Africa, the movement mobilized such extensive lobbying of members of parliament by their constituents that the British government was forced to withdraw its proposed cuts of at least £50 million in the aid programme.

● **Bread for the World** In the United States, Bread for the World was started up in 1973, as an explicitly Christian organization. It aims to mobilize Christians throughout the United States to lobby their members of Congress on hunger-related issues. Its many achievements include the 'Right to Food' resolutions passed in 1976, the setting up of the United States' emergency grain reserve of 4 million tonnes, passed in 1980, and legislation in 1982 directing that a greater percentage of United States aid should directly benefit people in absolute poverty.

unlike denominations in many European countries. The National Association of Evangelicals has a relief, development and refugee service called World Relief, but other agencies also draw support from American Evangelicals. The largest of these agencies is World Vision, which has specialized in child sponsorship. Over the years it has extended its fundraising efforts to other rich, industrialized countries, such as Canada, Australia and the United Kingdom.

● **In Canada**, the Canadian Council of Churches runs Inter-Church Aid as their practical expression of concern for the Third World.

● **In Australia**, the Australian Council of Churches runs World Christian Action.

REASONS FOR ACTION

Most of the Christian relief and development agencies in the rich countries, despite their differences in Christian experience and national culture, see their role in two ways: Firstly, to promote among Christians in their own country **a much greater understanding of conditions in the Third World** and why Christians should try to help.

Secondly, to provide **a practical means of expressing concern** through funding a combination of relief and development programmes. These are aimed either at relieving immediate distress caused by man-made or natural disasters, or longer-term development programmes to improve health services, food production and so on. In recent years, most of the agencies have tried to shift their resources away from relief to longer-term development needs. But a steady stream of disasters, many of them man-made, have often forced the agencies to divert scarce resources back to immediate relief needs.

NEW DIRECTIONS

The great strength of the churches' effort in development is the fact that there are national Christians on the spot in the areas of greatest need, who are therefore able to use help from other Christians effectively. But probably the most important change of all for the long-term future of Christian-supported development work in the Third World, has been the birth over the last twenty years of nationally-based Christian relief and development organizations

A supplementary feeding programme for children in the Maharashtra state of India.

THE POPULATION TIME BOMB

(figures in millions)

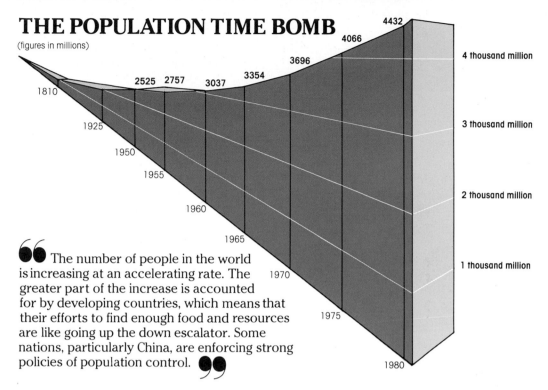

1810
1925
1950
1955
1960
1965
1970
1975
1980

2525 2757 3037 3354 3696 4066 4432

4 thousand million

3 thousand million

2 thousand million

1 thousand million

66 The number of people in the world is increasing at an accelerating rate. The greater part of the increase is accounted for by developing countries, which means that their efforts to find enough food and resources are like going up the down escalator. Some nations, particularly China, are enforcing strong policies of population control. 99

within the Third World.

In India, whose twenty-one states contain more people (750 million) than all the countries of Latin America and sub-Saharan Africa put together, the churches of North and South India work to promote economic and social development through an organization called Churches Auxiliary Social Action. In 1970 the Evangelical Fellowship of India started a Commission on Relief (EFICOR). This was initially intended as a response to help famine victims in north-east India, but it now supports development work throughout the subcontinent. In Africa, the All-Africa Council of Churches has concentrated its efforts on meeting one of Africa's most

serious problems, that of refugees.

Many of the major development agencies, whether based in the rich industrialized countries or in the Third World, find that their experience in development has increasingly led them to examine the underlying causes of world poverty and hunger. Christians are fast realizing that government policies on aid, trade and investment have a far more profound effect on the lives of the poor than the efforts of the development agencies ever will. This in turn has led both the agencies and some of the Christians who support them into increasing attempts to influence the actions of their governments.

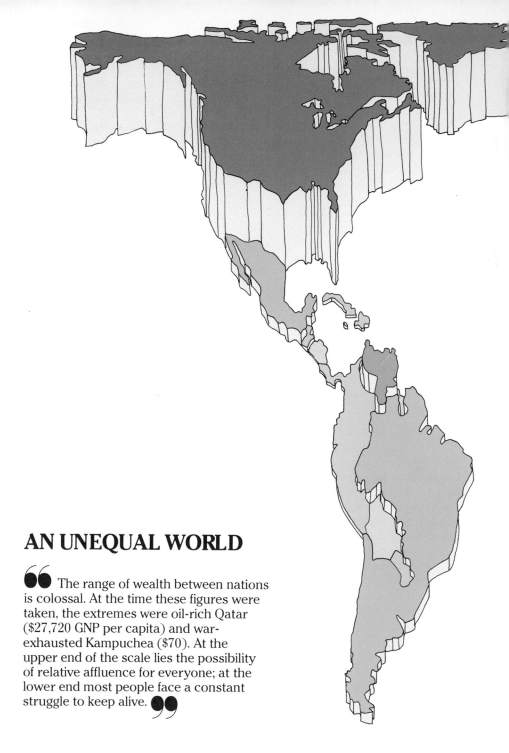

AN UNEQUAL WORLD

❝ The range of wealth between nations is colossal. At the time these figures were taken, the extremes were oil-rich Qatar ($27,720 GNP per capita) and war-exhausted Kampuchea ($70). At the upper end of the scale lies the possibility of relative affluence for everyone; at the lower end most people face a constant struggle to keep alive. ❞

Gross National Product
per head of population

Over $10,000

$6,000–$10,000

$4,000–$6,000

$2,000–$4,000

$1,000–$2,000

Less than $1,000

Figures are taken from Europa Yearbook, 1981

War and Peace in the Twentieth Century

ROGER WILLIAMSON

The optimism and belief in progress which characterized the prosperous Christianity of nineteenth-century Europe was shattered by World War I. Naturally enough, there was a strong pacifist reaction. But by the late 1930s, another major European war seemed inevitable. World War II marked the beginning of the nuclear age and the age of total war. The atom bomb was used twice, on Hiroshima and Nagasaki, with earth-shattering effects. Few leading Christians understood the significance of the new-born atomic era.

The Vietnam war made a generation think harder about whether war is ever justified.

Western policy after 1945 was dominated by Churchill's views of the Iron Curtain and the cold war. But beyond this perspective, profound changes were taking place in global relations and Christian thinking, through the movement for political independence in the Third World. The post-war period has been characterized by the search for a stable peace between East and West and the quest for justice between North and South.

EAST-WEST

East-West relations have been dominated by the unending race for newer and more powerful weapons, which the United Nations and other international organizations have been powerless to control. Twenty years ago, the 'eye-ball to eye-ball' confrontation of the Cuba missile crisis was a glimpse into the abyss. The world leaders saw potential destruction and drew back. In the last five years, there

has been a massive upsurge in concern about nuclear weapons. Christians have realized that the peace question is an urgent task; that a world of 50,000 nuclear weapons and massive poverty cannot be in conformity with God's will.

Particularly alarming is the prospect of a seemingly unavoidable new phase in the arms race, in which one side fears that the other may seek or even achieve a 'first-strike' capability. This would happen by developing highly accurate weaponry which would disable the enemy and allow no possibility of retaliation. This is the current Soviet fear, while the United States refuses to give up its technical lead because it fears the scale and determination of the Soviet armament programme. The arms control approach has not succeeded in achieving significant results and has certainly not led to disarmament. One real danger is that any smaller nation which wishes to regard itself as a major power will insist on its own nuclear weapons. Such a nation may not have as cautious a trigger finger as the superpowers.

It is now agreed almost universally among Christians that a nuclear war could not be a 'just war' because of the scale of destruction and the impossibility of ensuring civilian immunity from attack. Evangelical leaders like John Stott, Ronald Sider and Billy Graham have been driven by the logic of the just war criteria to be nuclear pacifists. Graham said at Auschwitz in 1978, 'The present insanity of the global arms race, if not contained, will lead to a conflagration so great that Auschwitz will seem like a minor rehearsal.'

The issue now is whether nuclear arms are legitimate and effective as a deterrent to nuclear war. Moral assessments of deterrence depend, at least in part, on how the threat to use nuclear weapons is evaluated. Some argue it is legitimate to threaten massive retaliation against the Soviet Union, since it is this threat which keeps the peace and prevents both nuclear and conventional war between the two major power blocks. In an imperfect world, all that can be done is to hold violence in check and to aim for relative justice, since we can never have perfect love within society. Utopian visions of laying down our defences are therefore immoral, as they are not a way to peace.

Others argue against

deterrence, regarding it as inherently unstable. They say that the potential for human error and the destabilizing effect of technological development can never make nuclear weapons a security against war. Another line of criticism is that it is wrong to threaten to do something which it is wrong actually to do.

Growing unease with the whole system of deterrence is reflected in the churches. The US Catholic bishops' statement (1983) and *The Church and the Bomb* (1982 - not completely accepted by the Anglican General Synod) are just two critiques. From

Wars of resistance have been a feature of the end of the colonial period and the first generation of independence. Whole populations have been effected by guerrilla activity, and women, like this Eritrean, have taken arms alongside men.

Eastern Europe, the Protestant churches of East Germany have condemned the 'spirit, logic and practice of deterrence', favouring the idea of Common Security: a realistic love for your enemy which sees that in the age of overkill there is only mutual security or mutual destruction.

In Western Europe, the Dutch Inter-church Peace Council calls for a world free of nuclear weapons, beginning with Holland. In West Germany and the United States, Christians form a large part of the peace movement. The Pacific Council of Churches has called for a nuclear-free Pacific. The World Council of Churches' Assembly at Vancouver in 1983 condemned completely the possession as well as the use of nuclear weapons.

Yet deterrence still has its weighty proponents, including the pope and the archbishops of Canterbury and York. The pope argues that deterrence may still be justified as an interim measure towards disarmament.

CAN CHRISTIANS MAKE WAR?

66 There have always been Christians who have refused to take up arms, finding it inconsistent with Jesus' way of love. Yet not all Christians are pacifists, and today several positions are held in good conscience by Christian people. 99

TOTAL PACIFISM
Jesus called people to live in the kingdom of God, which works on completely different principles from human kingdoms. The way of the kingdom, the way of love for enemies and of self-sacrifice, can never be reconciled with violence and achieving results by force. The Christian's response to evil is not to meet it with evil of his own, but to offer a living demonstration of the power of love. An example of this is non-violent resistance to civil oppression.

THE JUST WAR
Few Christians go along with naked militarism, or 'my country right or wrong'. But some believe it is possible for particular wars to be just, above all when there is no other means of resisting a greater evil. At such times it is wrong for Christians to opt out of their responsibilities as citizens, and let their neighbours do the fighting. A Christian must discriminate, refusing to fight if his country enters an unjust war but taking up arms when evil must be resisted. Similar arguments are used when the evil powers are those ruling one's own nation. Should a Christian join a resistance movement?

NUCLEAR PACIFISM
Some Christians hold that the age of nuclear weapons has brought a new dimension to this question. They deny that there can be a 'just war' in which such weapons are used, because the result would be so catastrophic that no other evil could compare with it. To use nuclear weapons is an attack, not just against an enemy, but against humanity as a whole and against God's creation. And if it is wrong to use these weapons, then it must also be wrong to seek to deter an aggressor by threatening to use them. Christians who think like this may not be total pacifists, and may support the strengthening of conventional defences.

What is sought now is a way forward to disarmament which gains widespread support from multilateralists and unilateralists alike. Possible areas where such agreement might be found are the campaign for a freeze on production, testing and deployment of nuclear weapons, and for increasing use of non-nuclear defence.

NORTH-SOUTH

But the concern for peace and justice does not only involve East-West superpower relationships. Since 1945, millions have died in 150 wars. At the World Council of Churches Assembly in 1983, the black South African theologian Allan Boesak expressed the 'concern of many Christians in the Third World that the issue of peace will not be separated from the issue of justice, making peace primarily a North Atlantic concern. This should not happen... One cannot use the issue of peace to escape from the unresolved issues of injustice, poverty, hunger and racism.'

In the 1960s, the Second Vatican Council marked a shift away from Europe and North America as the centre for theology and a new opening of the church to the world. Part of this openness was the liberation theology of Latin America, which argued that development was impossible while countries of the Third World were dependent on and dominated by the rich countries. Archbishop Helder Camara, a Brazilian, spoke of the 'spiral of violence'. The first violence was that of poverty, oppression and deprivation. The second violence was that of resistance, followed by government reaction, crushing any kind of resistance, non-violent or violent, whether by church, trades unions, students, opposition parties or anyone else.

One response from persecuted countries and communities has been to push to the fore great non-violent leaders like Archbishop Luwum of Uganda and Archbishop Romero of El Salvador. Martin Luther King, martyred in 1968, linked a non-violent protest for black civil rights to protests against the Vietnam War. Two of his former colleagues, Andrew Young and Jesse Jackson, have taken up his mantle.

In contrast, many black South Africans have pointed out that their exclusively non-violent techniques have had little effect in over fifty years, in spite of leaders like the Christian chief, Albert Luthuli and Bishop Desmond Tutu (both Nobel Peace Prize winners). Desmond Tutu still calls for 'reasonably peaceful change'. But others argue that if there can be just wars, as mainstream Western theologians have argued for 1,600 years, then there can be a just revolution. Many Christians in Namibia, for instance, say that their country is illegally occupied and that SWAPO is engaged in a defensive war to oust South African troops. They ask, what is wrong with armed resistance against apartheid, if Bonhoeffer's involvement in the plot against Hitler was right and if Christians

'I believe that the one who can completely protect me is my Lord, Jesus Christ. If I want to carry a gun I have to reject Christianity. This kind of thought to many Christians in the Middle East is simple nonsense, but we have to be able to give an example in this area that we are real Christians and we live by the love of our Lord and by his teachings.' Kamil Costandi, a Christian Palestinian Arab

See The Programme to Combat Racism

A full-scale nuclear war would mean the end of human life on the planet. Christians are in the forefront of those who call for a nuclear freeze.

were involved in the Dutch and French resistance?

The contribution of Christianity as a world religion should be of great importance to the development of peace and justice. But religion itself can become an obstacle to peace if it becomes an intolerant ideology - Northern Ireland, South Africa and the Middle East are three of the most religious areas in the world.

Our most urgent task is to beat our swords into ploughshares and to build *shalom* in our world, a peace based on right relationships, concern for the weakest and most vulnerable, and a true knowledge of God. As East German theologian, Gunter Krusche, has said, 'Many say, "You cannot rule the world with the Sermon on the Mount." Others say, "The world will not survive without it." '

The Changing Sexual Scene

LEWIS SMEDES

Experts tell us that 80 per cent of our sex life happens in the mind. We have no reason to disagree. It is also true, no doubt, that changes in sexual behaviour happen within the context of a culture's mind. That is, widespread changes in sexual attitudes are part of widespread changes in moral attitudes towards life in general. Changes in sexual morality can therefore be best understood within the broader changes in the moral ideas and perspectives of the modern world.

BRAVE NEW SEXUALITY

What are the obvious ways in which sexual behaviour has changed?

● **Pre-marital sex** For an unmarried person (especially a girl) to have sex before marriage used to be seen as a lapse, a fall, something that good people kept secret. Today, it is news if a poll of young women reveals that a good percentage do not feel pressurized by their contemporaries to have sex before marriage.

● **Extra-marital sex** In Western societies it was traditionally assumed that the adulterer (and again, especially the female adulterer) was a racy exception to prevailing sexual fidelity. Today, one out of five married partners – male and female – will sleep with someone else before they reach the age of forty.

● **Variant sex** Once, most people assumed that only kinky people had sex in any way other than eyeball to eyeball. Today, most people assume that any orifice can be used in sex and that we should do whatever we take it into our heads to do, as long as both parties like it, with unlimited experimentation in pleasure.

● **Homosexuality** Homosexuality was long considered a perversion to be kept hidden in a twilight zone of guilt and shame. Today, 'gay' is not only a label for a homosexual person, but is the name of a public movement for the acceptance of homosexuality as a normal and acceptable lifestyle. Taken out of the closet, homosexuality is now celebrated in some cities with an annual parade.

● **Public sex** Sex used to be confined to medical education, moral preaching, private jokes, or very discreet private conversation. Today, sex is the most visible aspect of private life, and the most powerful ingredient of advertising. Sex has been lifted from the private pillow-talk of married people into the public arena for everyone to hear and see.

SHIFTING SEXUAL VALUES

Sexual morality is a matter of values as well as behaviour. At least three changes have taken place in how people have come to feel about the value and purpose of their sexuality.

Sex is good. Many Western traditional values are rooted in our religious past; our feelings about the value of sex is no exception. There are elements in Christian theology and Greek thought that have led people in the past to feel that sex as we know it is an evil and not worthy of the human spirit. For Plato, the irrational passions associated with sex formed the biggest threat; if we were able to take part in sex with cool heads and quiet hearts, sex would not be evil. Augustine believed that sex practised in an unfallen world by unfallen persons would be rational, deliberate, and about as passionate as the relief of one's bladder. But sex as an expression of passion, hot sex, the way we know it and the way fallen people like it, is a symptom of decadence and moral rot. So, it was concluded, sex was sin.

It would be hard to find anyone today who agrees with Plato and Augustine on this point. Christians believe that sex – properly handled – is good, a gift of God and not a product of original sin. People who protest about the laxity of sexual morals today are not anti-sex, but oppose its perversion and its promiscuous practice outside

See Roman Catholics since the Council

marriage. Judging by the current cascade of Christian sexual literature, Christians today thank God for their sexuality, rather than feeling guilty about it.

Sex is good for its own sake. Sex for the modern person is, in a sense, like tennis or golf; you need no higher reason to justify your playing the game beyond the fact that you enjoy the sport. This is the modern mood, including that of the majority of Christians. Sex is still the normal way to produce babies, and having babies through sex is still the preferred way. But increasingly, most of us believe that we need not plan to – or even be willing to – have a baby in order to enjoy sex.

It makes the front page when the pope reaffirms the traditional Catholic view that sex without willingness to conceive a child is wrong. Anti-birth control declarations run counter to the prevailing attitude that sex can be beautiful and godly, even

when there is a specific intention not to let sex run its course in conception.

Sex is good when it brings people together. The higher purpose of sex is its power to enrich and deepen personal relationships. It can be a symbol of a union that already exists. It can be an experience of intimacy of body that enriches intimacy of spirit. In any case, the goodness of sex is measured by its success at making personal relationships deep and lasting.

For Christians, sex as a uniting experience for two people is still appropriate only for married people. For a large number of people, however, sex is good if it brings anyone closer together, married or not. Nor does that closeness together need to be permanent.

THE ROOTS OF CHANGE

Changes in sexual morality have not happened simply because

people have become less moral. People's lives have been shaped by profound shifts in the way they look at life as a whole, and at their own lives in particular. These changes in the way we see ourselves have created a moral vacuum in the West. What are the roots of this change in attitude?

First, there has been **a loss of a shared purpose for human life**. In societies influenced by Christian thinking, people believed that the purpose of human life was the glory of God and the perfection of human character. Naturally, our sexuality was meant to be dedicated to becoming truly human as God and our inner natures intended us to be. But the end for human life was social as well as personal. Here too, sex was subordinated to the purpose that God, the Creator, had in mind for human life. Sex fitted into the social picture by being the way in which families were created. Sex was for having children now, and to people God's kingdom in the future.

This sense of shared purpose was lost at the time of the Enlightenment. No longer members of a shared humanity with a shared nature, we have become individuals, a collection of sovereign personal atoms. People are not all created for one basic purpose; each person has to find his or her own purpose.

The loss of a single purpose for all people means that today, sexual morals are thought of only in terms of individual needs and individual preferences.

There has also been **a loss of**

Young people are growing up in a world with a very different sexual morality from previous generations. Christian teaching is often seen as anti-sex, when in fact it is pro-family.

ARE MEN AND WOMEN EQUAL?

LETHA DAWSON SCANZONI

In recent years throughout most parts of the world, increasing attention has been focussed upon the negative consequences of discrimination based on the sex of an individual. Traditionally, men and women have been treated differently from one another in laws and customs. They have been granted dissimilar rights and social status and have been expected to conform to different social roles regardless of personal interests and aptitudes. They have had unequal access to opportunities for education and employment, and have been assigned different responsibilities and privileges in politics, the family and religion.

This imbalance of power, privilege and prestige has generally favoured males, giving females a sense of lesser worth and second-class citizenship. Such an imbalance has been challenged many times down through history, but the movement for sexual equality today is gaining momentum as never before. Christians cannot ignore the issues and questions being raised by this rethinking of male and female roles, and the changes taking place in our time.

Some Christians express anxiety over these trends. They believe that the Bible teaches a fixed social order in which everything and everyone has its place. In this hierarchical order, males are dominant and females subordinate. Other Christians disagree, believing that this view is inconsistent with the basic thrust of Scripture, which regards women and men as equal in the sight of God.

Partners, not opponents

This basic emphasis on equality may be seen throughout the Bible:

■ **The equal standing of men and women** is taught in the first chapter of Genesis. There, both male and female are said to be created in God's image. They are given equal responsibilities both for the family and for the world beyond the home, being told to 'be fruitful and multiply' and 'to have dominion' without any distinction based upon sex. With sin's entrance into the world, that equal partnership was destroyed. God foresaw that the male would 'lord it over' the female as one tragic result of the fall.

■ Jesus made it clear that 'lording it over' others is not God's will and should not be characteristic of those who know, love, and serve God. In his life and teachings, **Jesus never trivialized women** but respected their full personhood and human dignity totally. He never indicated that women are only to be 'equal in God's sight' in some abstract, spiritual sense, and not in the day-to-day concerns of earthly life.

■ **Jesus entrusted women with the revelation of his Messiahship and his resurrection**. In his parable of the lost coin, Jesus compared God to a woman. In his reply to Martha, who criticized her sister Mary for discussing theology instead of helping prepare dinner, Jesus showed that he did not regard women in terms of stereotyped gender roles – a point also underscored in his reply to a woman who praised the womb that bore him and the breasts he had sucked as an infant. He refused to reduce women to their biological child-bearing function, and spoke instead of the need for all believers to follow him, regardless of gender.

Jesus' conversation with the woman who would not take no for an answer to her request for her daughter's healing, and his story about the widow who pressed for her rights before the judge indicate the admiration Jesus had for assertiveness in women.

■ **Jesus himself did not conform to traditional images of 'masculinity'**. He showed tenderness, shed tears, and took on a serving role, rather than glorying in the male privileges of a patriarchal culture.

■ **The coming of the Holy Spirit** at Pentecost meant that both God's 'menservants and maidservants' and 'sons and daughters' alike were empowered to speak God's message. Passages in the New Testament letters which speak of the Spirit's distribution of talents and gifts for service in the church do not make any restriction by sex. The fruit of the Spirit described in the letter to the Galatians consists of characteristics traditionally associated with the feminine role; yet that fruit is to be manifested in the life of all believers, whether female or male. In fact, Galatians 3:28 indicates that thinking in terms of male and female is inappropriate to the ideal of oneness in Christ, which does away with all divisive categories.

■ **The biblical principle of justice** calls for fair, equitable treatment of all people, and freedom from all that oppresses and exploits. Discrimination made on the basis of wealth, race or sex is therefore wrong.

■ **Loving our neighbour as ourselves** means that we will make sure that no person is held back from realizing her or his full human potential because of having been born a member of a particular sex. Males have been cheated by expectations that disregard their human need to express feelings, understand themselves and develop close, self-revealing relationships without fear of not appearing tough and in control. Females have been cheated by expectations that disregard their human need for achievement, strength, assertiveness and independence.

moral authority. In the absence of God, the only moral authority left today is the will of the individual, and the only person to whom I can speak with authority is myself. With no God, the Bible has become an interesting study in sexual history. Who is there to teach us what is good and bad about sexuality? No one. No one with any more authority than our own minds or feelings.

The only external authority today is the scientific expert, and experts tell us not what ought to be, but what is. In the sexual arena this means that sexual technicians, the people who have discovered the most promising erogenous zones of the human body, as well as the most effective erotic techniques, are the only real authorities.

The loss of moral authority in sex is just a part of a prevailing fear and distrust of all authority. Authority, the modern spirit feels, gets in the way of individual freedom; it threatens to kill our initiative for making up our own minds; it stifles creative adventure into experimental lifestyles. The so-called sexual revolution could not occur except in an age where moral authority has been shrunk to the opinion of the last person who talked loudly enough for you to hear.

With the loss of moral authority has come **the loss of morality itself**. If there is no human nature with a shared human end, then there is also no right way to behave that might emerge out of the sorts of creatures we are. What is left is taste: some of us like some

things and others of us like other things. Good or bad is not involved; all that matters is what turns anyone on. Or off.

Where there are no moral imperatives but only strong tastes, judgements about what is good or bad in sexual conduct are eroded. If you don't happen to like the homosexual lifestyle, enjoy your own thing; but do not judge homosexual people. If you are offended by such things as extra-marital flings, group sex, or pornography, cultivate your own feelings; but do not condemn others. For there is in life no dimension that really answers to what we traditionally mean by the moral dimension. There are only feelings about what you or other people do. This is the modern view; needless to say it is a view incompatible with the Christian perspective.

In the modern world, there has also been **a loss of a sense of mystery** in our approach to sex.

See Authority

Women rightly ask to be given equal opportunity with men to use their abilities at work.

Within Christian perception, there is more to life than meets the eye. Some things mean more than they seem. Sex is one of them; there is more to it than foreplay and orgasms. Christians believe that there is the symbolic meaning and the reality of a deep personal union to which we have given the name of marriage. For this reason, sex can be a symbol of the union between Jesus Christ and the church. This mystique has always been a buttress for traditional sexual morality; anything signifying so deep a spiritual reality must be kept in its proper place and for its proper purpose.

For all practical purposes, people today have lost the mystique of sex. If there is anything more than meets the eye, it is only the deeper personal experience that may or may not happen with sex. It has nothing to do with a spiritual realm that provides the moral context for sexual conduct. With no sense of the moral mystique of sex, modern people have a view of sex that asks only that sex be pleasurable and conducive to pleasing human relationships. Sex today is often in danger of being reduced to a set of feelings.

MODERN TIMES, MODERN SEX

The sexual expressions of modern life have their roots not only in a modern perspective on life in general, but also in modern technology, legislation and lifestyles. A number of facets of contemporary culture can help us understand the sexual atmosphere of our time:

● **Sex under the microscope** Human sexuality has become a rich field for psychological, sociological and neurological study. From Freud and Havelock Ellis to Masters and Johnson, sex has been set on the laboratory table and observers have watched what is going on.

Sociologists reassure us that our wild fantasies and kinky inclinations are not as off-beat as we feared, and it makes people feel good to know that lots of other people do crazy things. Psychologists help us understand how important happy sex is to our human fulfilment. And neurologists can teach us how to postpone or hasten our orgasmic ecstasy.

The scientific study of sex has

CHRISTIANS AND GAYS

Many men and women in the world are homosexual. This is usually not something they have chosen. And often they have to bear an additional burden of guilt, disgust and discrimination loaded on them by others – Christians not the least.

How should homosexuality be understood? Is it a sickness, a distortion of true sexuality for which a person needs counselling and loving care? Or is it a valid alternative sexuality – the way God creates some people and so to be accepted and affirmed? The gay Christian movements say the latter: Christians are just as free to have full homosexual sexual relationships as heterosexual ones. But Christians generally cannot square this with Bible teaching, and believe that, while deep friendships between homosexuals are evidently right and fulfilling, sexual relations are intended only between men and women within marriage.

made it all seem more natural and ordinary. And controllable. We are not alone in our sexual problems; we can do something about them. Nobody is destined to be a frustrated under-achiever in the game of sex. The important question for the modern secularist is not whether you obey moral rules about when and with whom you may have sex; the important question is whether you have learned the facts and mastered the techniques.

● **Legalized pornography** Society's unwillingness to put legal restraints on the sale of pornography has been a signal for the publication of sex in the media. There may be differences of opinion about the effects of pornography on any individual who looks at it, but everyone will agree that the open market for it has helped create a new sexual environment for us all.

The wonderful 'night language' of sex, the special words that were spoken only in passion by lovers in bed, has become the language of the street. The little sexy books that men once kept hidden in their office drawers are now tame antiquities in comparison with what anyone can see who has five dollars to get into a movie theatre. Nothing is reserved any more for the special times and special places. This intrusion into the intimacy of sex removes the wonderful possibility of discovery and mystery in human sexuality.

The legalizing of pornography has effectively vulgarized sex. And vulgarity eventually brings about boredom. It may be that

the legalization of pornography will be remembered most as society's most deadly move against sexual adventure and sexual joy.

● **Easy birth control** Even if morality allowed for pre- and extra-marital sex, prudence might have restrained it had it not been for effective birth control. People sleep easier after sleeping together when they know they do not have to be accountable for the natural consequences of a passionate encounter.

Technology and law have been partners in this new freedom from consequences. Technology has given us the pill and cleaner abortions while the law has permitted us to use them. We cannot say whether technology has changed our morality or whether it has only made the change in morality more convenient. But it is safe to say that the sexual revolution was made safer and easier by the gift

A crowded beach in Rio de Janeiro, Brazil. Many warn of a world population outstripping the earth's resources, unless birth control is universally accepted and used. But Roman Catholic official teaching remains opposed to birth control, as contrary to God's intention for the sexual act.

of science and the law.

● **Women's liberation** Women have been liberated from the antiquated male myth that women *endured* while males *enjoyed* sex. Once upon a time a woman might come to a counsellor to complain that her husband was a sexual beast who wanted sex too often; today she is more likely to come with the complaint that her husband is not tuned to her sexual needs and is unskilled as a competent lover. This does not mean that women did not enjoy sex before the female 'revolution'. It was just that men did not come to terms with the fact that women have as great a capacity for sexual pleasure as men have. But now they must. Men and women now meet on equal terms as searchers for happiness and joy in the sexual game.

Women in the West have also, to varying degrees, been liberated from confinement at home. They have come into the marketplace to compete with males at their own game. This means that more women are meeting more men, beyond the walls of their own living and bedrooms. Lunches, cocktail parties, committee meetings, quick passes at the coffee machine, all make it more possible for women to join the men's game of meeting people of the opposite sex and deciding whether or not to let the opportunities for deeper relationships develop into sexual affairs.

A SEXUAL COUNTER-CULTURE

No one can be precise about the cause-and-effect relationship between philosophical perspective and sexual morality. But we can be certain that the modern changes in sexual morality did not happen because people suddenly took a notion to throw off old restraints and become sexual fun lovers. The sexual changes have taken place in a setting that was created by profound changes in our religious and philosophical outlooks on the nature and purpose of human life.

What this means for people concerned to restore Christian values and standards is clear. We will not significantly change the sexual scene without changing prevailing opinions. We will not alter sexual behaviour unless we can persuade people to change their perspectives on the meaning of their lives as individuals and as members of a community of people. We will not change the sexual morality of our time by changing legal rules. We will change it only by changing the perspectives on life that in the end determine both the legal rules and the willingness of people to obey them.

Short of changing the perspective of the age, the Christian community may have to be content to establish a sexual counter-culture. The difference will be not just that Christians follow another set of rules, but that they see, interpret, and feel all of life in a way that gives the setting for a truly free, happy and meaningful sexuality.

Issues of Life and Death
REX GARDNER

In the twentieth century, medical research has advanced by leaps and bounds. Medical science is now coming within striking distance of solving such problems as infertility and congenital disease. But it has also raised a host of thorny issues. Nowhere is the controversy hotter than in the issues concerning the beginning and ending of human life - the issues, in fact, of life and death.

ABORTION

Abortion, without sanction of law, has been practised universally in all ages, and has carried a high price in infertility, disease and death. In the past two decades many countries have introduced legislation to permit abortion to be performed by qualified doctors in hospital. This has greatly reduced the danger to health of the procedure, but has resulted in an explosion in the numbers of abortions far beyond that intended. Christians have been divided in their reactions to this emotive issue.

● Some Christians have been in the movement to **press for the legalization of abortion**. They have taken this position out of sympathy for women, overburdened by the tyranny of unrestrained fertility, many of whom put themselves in danger through criminal abortion, or are driven to suicide by their predicament.

● Other Christians, including the Roman Catholic Church in its official pronouncements, **consider abortion to be totally forbidden**, although many make an exception when the mother's life is in danger. This absolutist position is based on the view that from the moment the mother's egg is fertilized there is a life already present, having 'a soul', or being 'a person', or exhibiting 'personhood'. In this view, abortion is therefore nothing but murder.

● Many Christians **take a middle view**. They cherish the value of embryonic and fetal life, but are aware that some 60 per cent of fertilized eggs abort spontaneously. They are also aware of the more insistent biblical command to show compassion to the mother, and to her existing family. In today's circumstances, they believe, it is sometimes impossible to do this without abortion.

British law is typical of that of most countries and can be used as an example of what legislation attempts to establish. It permits abortion if the continuation of the pregnancy were a greater risk because of:

● **the physical or mental health of the mother**;

● **the serious chance of an abnormal child**;

● **the suffering of the**

See Roman Catholics since the Council

mother's existing children.

Since in practice it is possible to include anyone under the 'mental health' clause, the law at present is not very influential. Many Christians, therefore, press for an amendment of the law to tighten up such loopholes. They also argue for improved social conditions which would make most such requests unnecessary. A number of Christian organizations now provide counselling and practical support for pregnant women who otherwise would be unable to cope. Some Christians have gone so far as to take unmarried pregnant girls into their own homes and care for them until after delivery.

But it is not only mothers-to-be who need help and support. Nurses or junior doctors who get unwillingly caught up in abortion cases find that their legal entitlement to opt out is often difficult to claim. Another difficult question being asked is; who takes the responsibility for deciding on an abortion? Does it lie solely with the mother (as is the current position in the United States), in which case the doctor may be seen merely as a technician? Or how far is the doctor responsible for taking the decision? This is one of the many questions that are fiercely debated among many of the flourishing Christian medical fellowships in different countries.

FETAL EXPERIMENTS

As with the issues of abortion, the area of fetal experimentation generates a great deal of controversy. Early investigation to identify the abnormal fetus is now widely practised in obstetrics, with the offer of abortion if one is found. Those who oppose abortion condemn this practice, but other Christians feel that it cannot be right to subject someone to the lifelong care of an abnormal child, with the inevitable strain on the marriage and the other children, if this can be avoided.

The possibility of discovering the fundamental causes of congenital fetal abnormalities has arisen through the in-vitro fertilization (IVF) programme. This programme has raised further ethical issues in its attempts to overcome infertility. Some cases of infertility are due to disease in the fallopian tubes which carry a woman's egg from her ovary to her womb. It is in these tubes that fertilization would normally occur. In the IVF technique, the egg (normally there is only one each month) is withdrawn from the ovary and fertilized by the husband's semen in a laboratory test-tube. If the fertilized egg grows well, it is placed in the mother's womb. Few Christians object to this, as it is merely a bypassing of a diseased organ.

Often, however, the egg does not attach itself to the womb and develop, but a better success rate can be obtained by giving the woman injections so that she produces several eggs at a time. Two or three of these eggs are then placed in the womb together. But this is where the problems start.

As a result of these injections, the mother may produce half a

Anti-abortion protesters in the United States hold a placard showing the perfectly-formed feet of an aborted fetus. Many Christians find themselves unable to accept abortion; it contradicts their belief in the unique value of each individual life.

the husband has no fertile semen, the same can be done with donated semen - Artificial Insemination by Donor (AID). There is wide approval among Christians for AIH, although some disagree with it because it requires semen produced by masturbation. But the technique of AID is the source of considerable disquiet. Under present law in some countries, the child produced by such a conception is illegitimate, although usually registered as that of the husband. Some have seen AID as adultery - an argument which is very difficult to sustain while others have welcomed it as providing a form of ante-natal adoption. However, most people agree that there will be emotional problems for the non-involved parent, and for the child, while the responsibility of the donor towards the child has not yet been fully explored.

Both the law and Christian opinion are in a state of flux. Many Christian gynaecologists, aware of the massive problems of infertility, of the non-availability of children for adoption, and also of the lifelong burden of the care of an abnormal child, support the IVF programme and early experiments. However, future developments should be watched with great care. Surrogate motherhood is now on offer - where a healthy woman 'leases' her womb for financial gain, to grow a pre-fertilized egg for another couple. The issues involved, not least the tearing-apart of the strong emotional bonding between womb-mother and child, are formidable. Few

dozen eggs, so that surplus eggs are left growing in the laboratory. These may be frozen, thawed, and used the next month - a technique that has resulted in the birth of a healthy child. But what happens if the spare eggs are not immediately needed? How long can they be kept? Would it be right to implant them into the woman if, in the meanwhile, her husband had died? If she does not need them, can they be placed in another woman's body - thinking of this as a sort of very early adoption? Or is it permissible to use them for research to discover and prevent the causes of congenital abnormalities in children?

Moreover, some women cannot produce eggs. Can, then, a spare egg be donated by another woman, fertilized in the laboratory test-tube with sperm from the patient's husband, and implanted into the patient? Is it moral to do this? Where male infertility is due to impotence, it is now common practice to obtain some of the husband's semen and inject it into his wife. This technique is known as Artificial Insemination by Husband (AIH). However, where

Pressure groups for euthanasia do not carry much credit in Christian hospices for the terminally ill, where people are helped to die painlessly and with dignity, fully understanding what is happening and able to talk about belief in the life beyond.

doctors, and fewer Christians, would approve this practice, even if the offer was made as an act of altruism and without charge.

EUTHANASIA

Although in many countries it is no longer a crime to commit suicide, it remains one for anyone to assist another to die. Attempts are periodically made to change the law with regard to long, slow, painful terminal illnesses. It has been suggested that in such situations a patient should be able to ask for death by a lethal dose of drugs.

Christians believe that our lives are given and taken away by God. This belief profoundly influences their approach to medical intervention to prevent birth or to hasten death.

Because a person's judgement may be impaired during pain, the pro-euthanasia lobby argue that it should be legal for anyone, while still healthy, to sign a document requesting such an easy death ('euthanasia') if the circumstances arise. Such a law would exonerate the person who administers the lethal dose.

Most Christians, and many others, are opposed to any euthanasia legislation. From their experience of the abortion laws they are aware that practice would rapidly become more widespread than intended, and that hospital staff would inevitably become unwillingly involved. Many people fear that the trust between patient and doctor would break down if there was suspicion that the doctor might be coming this time to administer the fatal dose.

There is also concern that euthanasia would soon become the practice for the congenitally malformed child. Once the voluntary aspect had been discarded, then other groups, such as the imbecile, would be at risk of liquidation.

Most advocates of euthanasia do not believe in any after-life. But Christian action in opposing euthanasia must in part spring from a belief that throughout life there is the opportunity to be reconciled to God. Christians are therefore opposed to any voluntary shortening of life. This does not mean that Christians would advocate using extraordinary medical techniques to prolong the process of dying, however great the price to be paid in pain and suffering.

Christians are in the forefront of the move to make death pain-free and dignified. There has been a long tradition of Christian medical care, and in recent years there has been an increase in the number of hospices founded and run by devoted Christians. These offer skilled medical, social and spiritual concern both for the dying and their families. While there are differences of emphasis, Christians are agreed that all life is God-given and to be cherished, as it was by Jesus, the great physician.

Racism, Justice and Civil Rights

CHRISTOPHER SUGDEN

A black person is unsafe on the streets of East London after dark. In South Africa, husbands and fathers have to live in camps outside major cities in order to get work. Their wives and children are left behind in separate black areas. In South India, a factory manager tells a Christian trainee manager: 'The workers are like dogs. Kick them and they will run away. Throw them a bone and they will come running back.'

● **Race and racism** Racism is a matter of establishing the identity of one's own group by pushing down another racial group. It is as old as the split between Jews and Samaritans in Jesus' time, as evil as the Nazi movement which triggered a world war, and as contemporary as the British National Front.

Racism feeds on insecurity. One racial group feels insecure about itself, so it asserts its identity by victimizing a group who are seen to be of less worth. The means used may be the forces of arms, theology or ideology. In India, caste discrimination is sanctioned by religion; in Germany, Nazism was sanctioned by 'proving' Aryan racial superiority; and in South Africa, apartheid is sanctioned by the Bible.

● **Violence and injustice** In the Philippines, Benigno Aquino, an opposition politician, was gunned down on his return to Manila airport on 21 August 1983. He joined the list of over 70,000 people world-wide believed to have been killed in the last ten years for political or military reasons. In Indonesia, a series of 'mysterious killings' has removed a number of wanted criminals without trial.

● **Civil rights** Another form of discrimination is to restrict the exercise of civil rights by certain sections of the population. The rights of religious believers are restricted in the Soviet Union. If a person has a responsible job or is undergoing higher education and is discovered to be a Christian, he or she will probably lose the position and find it very difficult to obtain more than even the most menial work. Their property may be attacked without the authorities intervening.

SOLID REASONS FOR PROTEST

Christians are certainly not the only people who have identified these injustices as targets for protest. But the reasons behind the different protests against injustice need to be examined.

● Some would urge that **injustice offends against the**

See Clouds over Southern Africa; Cradle of Faiths; Christians in Eastern Europe

brotherhood of man. But such brotherhood gives no standard of judgement beyond ourselves. People can always find 'rational' reasons for discrimination. Women are weaker, or blacks are less intelligent. The requirements of national security override personal rights to dissent or even to life. The monolithic ideology of the Soviet system cannot tolerate so competitive a view of life.

● Others appeal to **innate rights enjoyed by the very fact of being human**. But this argument is also inadequate. It can always be argued that some people are less than human, by virtue of their age or incapacity.

● Christians say that **we need a standard beyond ourselves**. They believe that this standard is that God loved people enough to

CROSSING THE DIVIDES

MICHAEL CASSIDY

The world has always been divided by distrust and even fear of those who are different from ourselves. In today's world, these divisions cause friction and violence between different groups. Perhaps more than ever before, Christians today are following Jesus in the way he healed the divisions and demolished the barriers that separated people. During his earthly life he constantly crossed divides of every sort and in so doing set in motion the most dynamic barrier-breaking movement the world has ever known. Paul put it succinctly: 'He has committed to us the ministry of reconciliation.'

But this did not come about cheaply or easily for Jesus – and neither does it for us. There was enormous cost involved, most especially for Jesus himself. Nailed to the cross, he made and offered himself as the bridge over every chasm. We do not have to be bridge-builders ourselves, because the bridge in Christ is already built. Christians simply have to be bridge-crossers. We cross every chasm on the Jesus bridge which is already there, recognizing that he has (past tense) broken down the wall of separation and hostility between peoples.

■ **Religious divides** When Jesus spoke to the Samaritan woman in John's Gospel, and when Peter went to the Gentile Cornelius in the Book of Acts, religious divides were crossed. Very early on the church discovered that the good news of Jesus was for all people, and not just one religious group.

Today this issue centres on modern denominational divides. One Sunday school child was heard to ask her friend, 'What's your abomination?' And to be sure, if we absolutize our denominations, that is just what they become!

One sign of Jesus at work in his church today is the fact that Christians of different traditions can now talk together and work alongside each other. In our work in Africa Enterprise (which seeks to reconcile Christians across many divisions) we always operate interdenominationally, whether in evangelistic missions or in conferences. In one conference in Zimbabwe with 500 people present we had fifty-two denominations represented. And it was fun!

■ **Social divides** In Jesus' day, men did not speak to women in public, let alone Samaritan ones. In doing as he did, Jesus shattered a social norm. In the same way, when Paul sent Onesimus the slave back to Philemon his master, 'no longer as a slave but as a beloved brother', he was forcing Philemon into something that was socially revolutionary.

In 1979 our Africa Enterprise team initiated a conference called SACLA (South African Christian Leadership Assembly). It drew 6,000 leaders on an inter-racial and interdenominational basis to Pretoria for ten days. Hundreds of blacks stayed in white Afrikaner homes, shattering South Africa's social norms. True witness must be born out of Christian community where all divides are crossed.

■ **Racial divides** It is perhaps not surprising that believers in Christ were first called Christians at Antioch, because it was there that the church first included Jews and Arabs, white and black, rich and poor, all mixed together.

In 1978 the Anglican bishop Festo Kivengere of Uganda was preaching with me in Cairo. Egyptians were amazed at the impossible combination: a black Ugandan and a white South African preaching together.

While in Israel in 1982, our team met an Arab pastor from Galilee who

create them, and, in Christ, to die for them. Each person is worth the love of God and the death of Christ. Therefore each person is to value himself or herself and others in recognition of the worth placed on them by God.

God has also called men and women together as his image to have authority over the earth and its resources. As God's collaborators in ruling over the created order, we are committed to a fair distribution of its resources. In this connection, it is interesting to note that the Law of Moses has specific provisions to prevent people from long-term poverty and oppression. It enshrined God's purpose that people should live together in freedom and equality.

This biblical view of human life is in contrast to the

See Bread for the World

has many Jews in his congregation. 'I love Jews more than they love themselves,' was his shining testimony of love which has crossed the racial divide.

■ **Economic and class divides** The Antioch fellowship also included a senior government official, Manaen from the court of Herod, plus rank and file citizens. That represented a crossing of the economic and class divide.

In a world where Marxist propaganda exploits the gap between poor and privileged, between management and labour, between upper and lower, it is good to see many Christian churches and communities not only embracing all classes but especially reaching out to the poor and oppressed. In this way, love and forgiveness rather than hatred and bitternes is generated.

In many parts of Africa and Latin America it is remarkable to see the extent to which many Christians are working on the frontiers of human need among the poor and oppressed. Charles Colson, former Watergate hatchet man for Richard Nixon, now has a ministry across the United States to prison inmates. He and his team have dramatically leaped the class divides to care for prisoners and to share themselves.

■ **Political divides** As with the early church, modern Christians who take their discipleship seriously will always jump political boundaries. Although obliged to be politically concerned and involved, they will never feel fully comfortable and fully settled in any one political group.

In the United States Senate and House of Representatives, Republicans and Democrats pray and read the Bible together. In the British House of Commons Conservative and Labour MPs who are Christians do the same. The same is true in many other countries. We cannot absolutize our political beliefs or camps. We must always cross the political divides.

Jesus is the world's greatest barrier-breaker. And his followers all over the world joyfully follow him over the walls and chasms of the twentieth century.

SOUL FORCE

Martin Luther King Jr made an immense impact on a generation's understanding of the power of non-violence. One speech summed up his philosophy:

'To our most bitter opponents we say, "We shall match your capacity to inflict suffering by our capacity to endure suffering. We shall meet your physical force with soul force. Do to us what you will and we shall still love you. We cannot in all good conscience obey your unjust laws, because non-cooperation with evil is as much a moral obligation as is co-operation with good. Throw us in jail, and we shall still love you. Send your hooded perpetrators of violence into our community at the midnight hour and beat us and leave us half- dead, and we shall still love you. But be assured that we will wear you down by our capacity to suffer"'.

individualistic view that the rights of the individual are paramount, a view that stems from a Greek philosophical understanding of man as a self-sufficient, usually male, independent individual. Individualism is strong on personal liberty, but weak on the responsibility that people have to one another as members of society. Western notions of human rights have tended to focus only on the rights of individuals to be treated equally before the law.

Such an individualistic approach is inadequate. The Two-Thirds World of Africa, Asia and Latin America, where the majority of the world's population live in poverty and oppression, stresses more the corporate dimension of the right to be human. This means having basic resources for human life: food, work and secure homes. Such corporate concern is always in danger of collapsing into 'improper collectivism', where power and authority are concentrated in one institution (often the state) which then makes the interests of the state the ultimate standard for the rest of life. A serious temptation for all totalitarian countries, whether of the East or West, this view gives a high priority to regimentation and order, but a very low priority to human freedom and responsibility.

In the protest against injustice, Christians must work towards the model for human society given in the Bible – the body of Christ, the church. In this striking image by the apostle Paul, every part of the body (whether a person or a group) has a gift to contribute or a role to play. Everyone has worth. These gifts are to be used not for selfish aggrandisement, but for the benefit of the whole community.

This applies to groups of people. Paul made it clear that both Jewish and Gentile Christians needed each other's contribution from their culture and their history in their joint membership of the body of Christ. If one part or group cannot play its role and contribute, then the whole group suffers.

JESUS AND JUSTICE
But how can such justice, such right and non-discriminatory

Soldiers of the Unita resistance group in Angola pause during a campaign. Is it ever right to oppose duly constituted authority by violence? If not, what can Christians do if they believe governments are evil or oppressive?

relationships, be established? The Bible points the way forward:

● **Breaking down the barriers** Paul argued that the division between Jews and Gentiles was an expression of the 'principalities and powers' of evil. He said that the good news of Jesus Christ established right relationships between these groups, because Jesus had defeated the power of evil. The sign of the overthrow of evil was the harmony between Jews and Gentiles, an assurance and expression of the ultimate harmony of everything that would come in Jesus Christ.

Because all people are accepted by God on the same basis, we learn to accept each other. Jesus is the one who establishes justice by crossing all the barriers which people erect against others with his welcome. Zacchaeus, the chief tax collector of Jericho, was shunned and discriminated against by the Pharisees. Jesus reached across the barriers of separation and invited himself to his house. He did the same with the Samaritans, lepers, the sick, women and children.

● **Discovering who we are** Jesus' death for human sin meant that each person could find his or her true identity. This would not be by claiming superiority over other people, but by accepting their status first as a sinner, and then as a forgiven sinner, a child of God in union with the Son of God and all other children of God in Christ. Paul's message was, 'Accept one another as Christ has accepted you.' When we belong to God's people, our culture and nationality, once a source of pride, have to take second place.

● **Taking sides with the poor**

The Bible has another pointer towards justice. Justice is established by positive discrimination in favour of the oppressed. When the Hebrew slaves were virtual prisoners in Pharaoh's Egypt, God did not ensure that Pharaoh's laws were impartially enacted, because laws which demanded the slaughter of male babies and cruel labour conditions were themselves unjust. Instead God delivered these slave people from Pharaoh's Egypt to demonstrate to the world that his justice works to raise up those who are disadvantaged. So the biblical idea of justice is not a blind even-handed operation of the law, but a positive discrimination in favour of the poor and oppressed.

Why should Christians be involved in establishing justice? Because the good news committed to them is God's way of establishing right relationships; because God is dishonoured when people, made in God's image, suffer the loss of their God-given rights to be human; because God's justice is shown in taking the side of the disadvantaged. Tragically, Christians have often been concerned only when issues of *religious* freedom are at stake. We have even been prepared to compromise with considerable

See Doing Theology

Police suppress a demonstration in Chile. When free speech is restricted and the media are censored, most Christians support the use of all available means to speak out for justice.

injustice as long as freedom to preach is allowed. Here our faith condemns our actions.

BEYOND EQUALITY
Christians have also, with more reason, been hesitant to affirm their rights over against others, as such demands seem linked to individual or corporate self-assertion for equality. But the Christian vision moves beyond equality to 'mutual subordination', that is, as Paul said, 'Submit yourselves to one another because of your reverence for Christ.' The opposite of the subjugation involved in the removal of human rights is not an independent, self-sufficient existence, nor the triumph of the masses in class war. It is servanthood, where each group and individual puts their resources at the disposal of the others.

To move beyond equality in this way, it is essential for those who have been subjugated to the level of animal existence to be restored to a level of equality so that mutual subordination is a

Most would agree that law enforcement is necessary to preserve freedom. But in many countries the police are drawn into political involvement. Christians need to follow the Old Testament prophets in demanding even-handed justice in society.

free and reciprocal process. This is why Christians face the challenge of opposing injustice – and overcoming their hesitancy in doing so. Their protest is not merely a protest *against*; it is a protest *for* the dignity God intends for all people.

Spirituality Today

JAMES M. HOUSTON

Spirituality is much talked about today. Retreat centres are spreading. Weekend programmes such as Spain's Cursillo movement are growing more popular, and many young people go to such ecumenical centres as Taizé in France. New books on spirituality are appearing, alongside reissues of devotional classics. The renewed concern for the 'spiritual' in Western society is also alerting Christians there to fresh perspectives on familiar themes.

This interest in spirituality is breaking down the differences between Christian traditions. Evangelical Christians, for example, are becoming more aware of the whole communion of saints throughout the Christian centuries. They also see the need for a spiritual life that spills over to the poor and downtrodden. Setting our minds on God's kingdom requires more than feeding our own souls.

See The Secular Outlook of Today

Since the Second Vatican Council, Roman Catholics have moved away from the heavy-baroque Latin mass to a more personal understanding of worship. Through the Charismatic movement, a personal response to the Holy Spirit has swept right to the heart of the Catholic Church. At the same time many Protestants are seeking spiritual guidance from Carmelites, Jesuits and other Catholic orders.

THE SEARCH FOR MEANING

Today even liberal and non-religious thinkers see the need of some spiritual recovery to guarantee a future for humanity. Technology can so easily exercise a dehumanizing pressure and modern life is complex and fragmented. Our very humanity requires spiritual safeguards.

But where are they to be found? Have all human beings an innate human and spiritual potential to be helped by God's grace? Or must we come empty to God's love and start afresh? It is an unresolved question among Christians.

We seem to be standing at a third major crossroads of reform in Christian history:

● The first, in reaction to Constantine's worldly imperial church, was **the rise of monasticism**.

● Then, at the Reformation, **God was seen to call not just the select few but every Christian to a holy life**.

● Are we now on the threshold of a third breakthrough, in **our spiritual hunger for a more authentic Christian life**?

This hunger takes many forms, both inside and outside the Christian church, so that it is hard to define its central core. But it springs essentially from the human quest for meaning. We live in an age when the behavioural sciences have so analyzed the self as to take away from it all mystery and religious significance. Psychology for some has become an inward-looking search for self-fulfilment. Closed in on itself, the self is left with a meaningless existence. And so we yearn for the spiritual, to listen to our inner selves before God. Even the threat of death, so strongly suppressed in this secular generation, has come alive again in many people's horror of concern. Of what use is a one-dimensional hope in face of that?

Modern discoveries about the brain show there is more to us than the practical and intellectual. The brain has a left hemisphere: linear, rational and analytical. But it has also a right hemisphere, little understood in a cerebral society, which is intuitive, imaginative and holistic. This side includes much of the feeling and spiritual part of our consciousness. None of us can operate from one hemisphere alone. So why do we assume that the rationalistic and active side of our existence is more important than the contemplative, quiet and feeling component? To develop our personal maturity we need both. Only so can we fulfil our quest for a fully meaningful life.

Neither do we have an option whether to be 'religious'. To be

religious is to be a person - accepting our joys and sorrows, our faiths and loves, our endeavours and hopes. We can no more opt out of religion than cut off our noonday shadow. But for what religion do we opt? Marxism, materialism, agnosticism can be made religious as much as Christianity, Islam or Hinduism. As A. N. Whitehead once said, 'Mathematics is what we do, but religion is who we are'.

CHRISTIAN SPIRITUALITY
Can we say, then, that spirituality is the spirit of all our religions? In one sense, yes: all mankind has a spiritual potential. Yet more is needed. Primitive religions make no distinction at

Only in relationship with God are we fully human. Christian spirituality is not an optional extra; it is at the centre of our lives.

all between sacred and secular, so have no sense of the spiritual. Only the more developed religions have the concept of spirituality, with individual choices and ascetic (self-denying) practices. Indeed the high degree of asceticism in the East today fascinates many from the West, for they see there a spiritual intensity they have not met in the Christian tradition.

Christian spirituality is not defined by ascetic self-denial. The Bible's faith that God created a good creation flies in the face of much Eastern contempt for the material world. It is a battle the church has always had to fight.

The spiritual life for Christians has to do with a God who is personal – the God of Abraham, Isaac and Jacob; the God and Father of Jesus Christ. This personal stress sits uneasily with professional academic theology's separation of mind and emotion; for all its technical skill, it is liable to quench the vitality of Christian spirituality.

Most distinctively, Christian spirituality is about a real personal experience of the risen Christ. The apostle Paul describes it as 'life in Christ'; the Gospel writers as 'following Jesus'; John as 'union in the love of God'. All are depicting a gradual transformation into the image and likeness of Jesus Christ. It is living out the presence and Spirit of Jesus within us. Some of its key elements are:

● **choosing new birth and daily repentance**;
● **knowing God's will and mind more deeply through Bible study**;
● **practising prayer as a disciplined yet natural way of life**;
● **understanding human nature and ourselves**;
● **accepting God's grace and love within us**;
● **hating evil**;
● **celebrating corporate worship**;
● **sharing Christian experience in compassion and community**.

All this is embodying within our own lives the reality of God's good news for a sick society and lonely people.

SPIRITUALITY IN CRISIS

Yet such a spirituality is under severe attack. Cultural, secular pressures threaten to strangle it, so that many Christian writers anticipate the demise of Christendom, with the nominal forms of what is superficially called 'Christian' eliminated.

There are many signs of this. Many Christians do not give evidence of their personal conviction by praying. In place of a sense of sin there is now a

Christians approach a God they know, because he has made himself known in Jesus. And so the Bible is crucial for Christian spirituality, helping us to encounter the real God, and to hear his words to us as well as speaking our words to him.

personal anxiety, which narrows our experience to being aware of ourselves instead of living before God. Just as asthmatics suffer shortness of breath, so do many Christians lack the vital breath of God, which comes from daily prayer and confession.

Our churches have no moral discipline, our leaders are mainly pragmatists, and we sink in a sea of relativism. The information society exaggerates the notional and neglects what is formative of our characters. With so much divorce, we think less of family life and tend to rely on the altar being in the church instead of primarily at home.

Much of this has happened because of formal Christianity's weaknesses. But the modern world puts heavy obstacles in the way of reformation:

● **Today's stress on technical competence puts human achievement at the centre, and cannot fathom where God fits in**. It reverses the Christian belief that God acts first and we walk with him.

● **The technocratic spirit is a rational, artificial, autonomous one**. It leaves no room for the Holy Spirit who comes to make us new.

● **Everything is valued in terms of money, time and possessions**. Focussing on success, modern people often ignore the side-effects of striving to 'succeed'.

● **The computer age tends to programme the whole of life**, leaving no sphere for unique individuals, the mystery of the person, or love beyond the sexual.

● **Life has become so specialized and professional that personal and moral responsibility have diminished**. Will American universities soon have degrees in friendship and doctorates in motherhood?

● **All this has provoked a 'revolt of the masses'**, a bland mass-mindedness that loses sight of personal authenticity. Such a complacency of the crowd dulls a people's spiritual life, inhibiting the moral creativity of personal convictions.

It is this plastic unreality of modern life which undermines the spiritual.

SPIRITUALITY OF THE FUTURE

Can we see the beginnings today of a reaction to what depersonalizes us? Is there now a new quest to express our genuine humanity?

The Christian faith declares that we cannot understand our own humanity unless we first begin to understand God. It sees the true norm for human destiny in the Man Christ Jesus.

Around this central declaration a number of spiritual traditions have grown up, each of which is alive today. (These are described elsewhere in this book.) But they all have to face the spirit of the age. Four features of this confrontation seem likely to dominate the spiritual scene in the coming years:

● **There will be less support in society for the Christian spirit**. Christians will need to do more than cling to orthodoxy.

See The Global Village

See All Things in Common; The Gospel in Today's World; Theology Today; Christians in Eastern Europe

They will have to find courage for individual decision against the social current, for conscience, for sacrifice, for the lonely way of refinding their personal direction. This may involve a new kind of martyrdom, forfeiting much to enrich the personhood of others within an increasingly alienated and self-seeking society.

● **Christians will have to find a social as well as personal spirituality**. Withdrawing into private mysticism is no following of God who 'loves the world'. To be salt and light in the world, we need to pray in full awareness of the world's needs, sensing the direction of God's justice in society, focussing less on Number One and more on Jesus' compassion for the crowds. Such a 'worldly holiness' means basic changes in attitudes and values. Church structures may need to adapt radically to contain such ministry to the poor and oppressed.

● **Such a spirituality of the future will demand deeper and more intimate forms of fellowship and community**. Instead of the destructive introspection of behavioural psychology, creative introversion will find ever more insights into the soul before God. This will call for deeper spiritual friendships, more ministries of spiritual direction. Personal closeness of spirit in the life of prayer and godliness may come into conflict with a superficial church life.

● **Theologians will need to communicate the faith in more living categories of experience**. Abstract concepts have little or no life for the spiritual needs of this generation. Many thus turn to psychiatrists rather than pastors. Since there is no cultural appeal to piety in our society, the Christian has to see his faith embodied by the touch of God's Spirit healing confused lives.

Whatever forms Christian spirituality may take in future, it will remain biblical. It is much more than the expression of the human spirit before God. Its resources lie in the whole Trinity: the Fatherhood of God counteracting the personal aridity of a technological society, the experience of the living Christ making spirituality a lived reality, the presence of the Holy Spirit within the believer.

These are the experiences that can transform even the weakness of a spirit cramped by the modern spiritual crisis into the strength of Christ's renewal.

Word and Deed

ANDREW KIRK

This last part of our handbook has been labouring at a massive task, to chronicle the faith, thought and action of Christians all over the world today. We have only been able to pick out key themes. Is there any way of bringing the whole picture into focus?

Difficult - and for one good reason. Today the church is an international community. Groups of Christians exist in every nation. So inevitably the way Christians think about, proclaim and live their faith varies according to place.

THINKING THROUGH THE FAITH

The issues facing Christians in the West, in Eastern Europe and in the Third World are different. Between the two wars the dominant theological figure in Europe was Karl Barth. Faced by many who believed that God's truth was found in personal experience, in human conscience or in historical events, he emphasized that above all God has revealed himself. God's word must come first. Jesus is the norm of all Christian truth. Barth influenced Hendrik Kraemer's thinking on the relationship between Christianity and other faiths. Kraemer maintained that faith in Jesus could not be compared to other religious systems, as they were attempts to manipulate God.

Pope Pius XII, in the encyclical *Divino Afflante Spiritu* (1943), encouraged modern biblical studies. The subsequent openness to other ideas paved the way for the Second Vatican Council (1962-65), during which the Roman Catholic Church looked afresh at many aspects of its life and mission.

After the war Protestant theology was dominated by philosophical movements. Bultmann gave Heidegger's existentialism a theological flavour. Harvey Cox and others sympathetically interpreted secular humanism. Jürgen Moltmann responded to the challenge of Marxist socialism and was part of the Christian-Marxist dialogue.

In Eastern Europe Christians have had to respond to a socialist society. Protestant thinkers, such as Hromadka and Lochmann, argued that Christian faith was not tied to the values of capitalism; Christians should be sympathetic to socialist ideals. Eastern Orthodox churches, since joining the World Council of Churches in 1961, have increasingly shaped the thinking of other Christians. They have a distinctive understanding of spiritual life and a strong insistence on the confession of God as Trinity, and these have deepened theological and pastoral reflection.

HOLY SPIRIT AT WORK

Helpers in Britain's Christian Aid week in May 1984 were invited to pray this prayer:

'Holy Spirit,
   You breathed life into paralyzed and
     frightened people,
   You smashed barriers of fear and
     misunderstanding,
   You opened up fresh visions,
   You formed and guided the infant church.
     We believe that you prompt every good
     work.
   Yours is the love and care shown to today's
     refugees and exiles;
   You are at work in those seeking peace in
     Lebanon and Nicaragua;
   You are at work where the hungry are
     being fed in the Horn of Africa;
   You are at work where people work for
     justice in the Philippines.
   So work in us we pray that as we plan and
     perform our tasks in Christian Aid week
     we may know ourselves to be doing your
     work.'

Christians in the Third World are increasingly aware of the need to do their own theological thinking. Many have therefore distanced themselves from Western theology. They are primarily concerned to reflect as Christians on their own reality. This means separating the gospel's universal message from cultural trappings inherited from the West. They are asking fresh questions of the Bible and finding its particular relevance for their own different cultural situations.

● In Africa many questions are raised as Christians seek to **rediscover their cultural roots**. What should they do about traditional marriage patterns, the respect due to ancestors? How can they find appropriate models of leadership? What should be the goals and means of their people's development? What pastoral concern can they show for rapidly growing churches? In southern Africa the question is of systematic racial discrimination.

● In Asia the most obvious concern is to relate the unique fact of Christ to **other religious traditions**. This has raised questions such as: What is evangelism? How does the church relate to the kingdom of God? How and when should baptism be administered? How far are non-Christian religious practices challenged by the gospel?

● In Latin America Christians have to bring their theological thinking to bear on the **desperate situation of poverty** for the majority and the strong repression used by political regimes to silence opposition and stop change.

No matter where they are, Christians have to clarify the relationship of faith in Jesus to popular religious beliefs and practices.

PROCLAIMING THE FAITH

In this generation a new era has dawned in Christian mission. There is now a world-wide church, and Christians from all nations are together in the task of making Jesus known.

Christian leaders gathered in Mexico City in 1963, recognized that 'the missionary frontier runs round the world; it is the unseen frontier which separates belief from unbelief'. If belief and unbelief are found in every nation, then all churches must together be involved in a mission which covers six continents. No longer can Christians in some nations pretend to direct the unfinished task of proclaiming Christ.

Some Western churches and agencies have been reluctant to hand over to younger churches complete responsibility for their life and witness. This has led certain Third World leaders to call for a moratorium on missionaries from the West. At the same time, they have asked for an exchange of evangelists and teachers across the Third World. The church's mission world-wide is thus becoming a complex pattern of people moving in all directions, including more and more from Third World to First.

The Christian missionary endeavour raises the vital question of partnership. How do different parts of Christ's body - the church - so learn to give and receive human and financial resources that the sharing is genuinely mutual? Certain attitudes to evangelism can sometimes block the path to full partnership.

The 'church growth' approach can have this effect. It stresses the need to plant churches in each culturally similar 'people group'. Once such a self-propagating church has taken root, it can start evangelizing its group. But this can result in Western agencies deciding the strategies and setting up the task-forces without full reference to the existing church in that nation.

The growth of 'para-church' agencies has caused tension in some Third World situations. Their recruitment of local leadership through financial incentives and their lack of local accountability have sometimes worked against evangelistic co-operation.

A more fundamental question concerns the gospel that is preached. The church's task is not simply to communicate the gospel in word. It should also embody it in concrete situations. If the overwhelming preoccupation is with increasing numbers, then concern for the Christian community's witness to the values of God's kingdom, so central to Jesus' ministry, diminishes.

Other Christians, therefore, without underplaying the work of leading people to new life in Christ, have sought to secure justice for the disadvantaged. The

See Which Way for a Continent? Cradle of Faiths; Good News for the Poor; The Missionary Inheritance; Reaching New Peoples

Christianity is now a world faith. People in all nations and circumstances follow Jesus. Has this fact really dawned yet, even on the church? Christians must learn to glory in belonging to this great, varied, international community.

church has to be part of the good news it proclaims. This is why, in situations of gross inequality, small groups of Christians have engaged in community development and the struggle for human rights. These 'base communities' are a new way of being the church.

Commending the faith adequately has always meant proper communication. One aspect of this concerns the use of mass-communication technology. Through television, radio and video-recording, Jesus is presented to increasingly large numbers of people. The communicating power of dance, drama and music is also proving an effective means of witness. But part of communication is also persuasion. By dialogue and

rational presentation people of whatever beliefs are being convinced that Jesus Christ is the way, the truth and the life for them and for all.

APPLYING THE FAITH

Christians are called to follow Jesus in his practical love for humanity. Sometimes they are slow to respond; sometimes they make mistakes. But still Christians are foremost in aiding the suffering and fighting injustice.

A remarkable number of aid and development projects are Christian-based. Aid aims to keep people alive and basically healthy in the face of natural disasters. But development provides permanent resources - wells, irrigation schemes, seed, fertilizers, technical skills - and helps promote industries and businesses based on local initiative and under local control.

These projects are little in comparison with the vast and growing need. And so Christians have also entered the debate about a new international economic order, which would make trading more equitable and provide low-cost funds for development. Because of ideological differences, Christians do not agree about the way forward. But an increasing number believe that world poverty is mainly due to unfair relationships between governments, international banking institutions and transnational corporations.

The World Council of Churches has initiated studies and consultations on this theme. They are concerned with securing a just, sustainable and participatory society:
● **just** in that economic and political power does not favour one group to the exclusion of others;
● **sustainable** in that the earth's non-renewable resources are carefully managed;
● **participatory** in that all members of the human community have a real say about their future.

Such a society must know how to use technology wisely, harnessing it for human ends, not for quick profit or destructive purposes. The church has debated the moral issues underlying technological methods, both good (as in the quest for improved strains of grain and rice) and questionable (as in experiments on human fetuses).

The escalating arms race between East and West is a major misuse of natural resources. Pouring capital and human skills into creating weapons of mass destruction appals the Christian conscience. Some Christians in the West defend nuclear weapons as necessary deterrents. The vast majority elsewhere, however, view both the expenditure involved and the danger of an irreversible conflict as intolerable. In recent years Christians from different churches have been seeking to explore together across national and ideological boundaries means of promoting lasting peace. One possibility would be an international Christian peace institute to investigate, monitor and help resolve conflict.

But Christians also want practically to tackle both the results and the springs of conflict:
● They are ministering to **refugees** who, fleeing from political upheaval or famine, are either in temporary camps across the border (Afghans in Pakistan, Kampucheans in Thailand), or permanently resident in other nations (Chileans after the coup in 1973).
● They are campaigning for **basic human rights** to be recognized and implemented. They want to see an end to torture and imprisonment without trial. They work for freedom of assembly, of the press and of travel. They resist both

See The Church at Home; Telling the World; Aid, Trade and Development; War and Peace; Racism, Justice and Civil Rights

'My own commitment is neither to liberalism nor to Marxism, but to a curious idea put about by a carpenter turned dissident in Palestine that the test of our humanity is to be found in how we treat our enemies.' Paul Oestreicher

And what of the next generation? Although the church now exists world-wide, Christians still face a challenging task to make Jesus known throughout the ever-increasing human family.

the growth of data banks for security purposes, and the curbs on labour unions.

● They are in the forefront of campaigns to **combat racism** and to promote multiracial societies. Many Christians have declared the policy of racially separate development (apartheid) in South Africa, for example, to be incompatible with Christian faith. The church has tried to reconcile conflicting groups in countries such as the Sudan, Uganda, Rwanda-Burundi, Namibia, Japan, Australia and India.

Most Christians in Nicaragua supported the overthrow in 1979 of a violent dictatorship; today many back a government concerned to promote the welfare of disadvantaged people. Yet in some places (notably Northern Ireland and the Lebanon) Christians are part of the unresolved conflict, though a minority are striving to bring antagonistic groups together.

In the Western world and in the communist bloc, the more affluent societies have their own casualties. Many people live aimless or degraded lives; inequalities in society persist. Christians are ministering to alcoholics, drug addicts, compulsive gamblers, victims of crime, discharged offenders, one-parent families, those under marital strain, people not adequately housed, fed or clothed and ethnic minority groups.

One final dimension to Christian activity is becoming increasingly important today. Because they are called to identify with society's outcasts, to denounce evil wherever they find it, and to oppose laws giving the state too wide a power, Christians must often suffer for their faith.

General Index

INDEX OF COUNTRIES